HUMAN RESOURCE DEVELOPMENT

HUMAN RESOURCE DEVELOPMENT
A CONCISE INTRODUCTION

Edited by

RONAN CARBERY and *CHRISTINE CROSS*

First published 2015 by
RED GLOBE PRESS

Red Globe Press in the UK is an imprint of Springer Nature Limited,
registered in England, company number 785998, of 4 Crinan Street,
London, N1 9XW.

Red Globe Press® is a registered trademark in the United States,
the United Kingdom, Europe and other countries.

ISBN 978–1–137–36009–0   ISBN 978–1–137–36010–6 (eBook)

This book is printed on paper suitable for recycling and made from fully
managed and sustained forest sources. Logging, pulping and manufacturing
processes are expected to conform to the environmental regulations
of the country of origin.

A catalogue record for this book is available from the British Library.

A catalog record for this book is available from the Library of Congress.

SHORT CONTENTS

CONTENTS

LIST OF FIGURES

LIST OF TABLES

CONTRIBUTOR BIOGRAPHIES

EDITORS

Dr Ronan Carbery is Senior Lecturer in Management in the School of Management and Marketing at the College of Business, University College Cork, Ireland. Ronan is co-editor of the *European Journal of Training and Development*. His research interests include career development, talent management and participation in HRD activities. He was awarded the University of Limerick Teaching Excellence award in 2013. He is co-editor of *Human Resource Management: A Concise Introduction* (2013).

Dr Christine Cross lectures in Organizational Behaviour and Human Resource Management at the Kemmy Business School, University of Limerick. Prior to joining UL she worked for a number of multinational organizations in both management and human resource management roles. This experience has led to a wide range of research, consultancy and publication interests covering areas such as the workforce experiences of immigrants; training and development in call centres; and investigating the glass ceiling. Christine is also a co-director of the Age in the Workplace Research Network (AWR-net), which is located at the Kemmy Business School. This network focuses on researching multiple issues associated with age in the workplace.

CONTRIBUTORS

Dr Claire Armstrong (B.Comm, PhD, MCIPD, FRAMI) is an associate lecturer in the Faculty of Business and Law at the Open University and an adjunct lecturer at the Kemmy Business School, University of Limerick. Prior to this, she held posts at DCU Business School, Limerick Institute of Technology and Shannon College of Hotel Management. She also held a visiting appointment at Aston University, UK. Claire's main areas of expertise are in organizational behaviour, HRM, research methods and health care management. She has published extensively on these topics in academic journals, including *Human Resource Management*, *The International Journal for Human Resources Management*, *The International Journal for Quality in Healthcare* and *Advances in Developing Human Resources*. She has also published several practice-oriented reports on topics such as high-performance work systems, training and development, and health care management. She is a reviewer for a number of HRM, organizational behaviour and health care management journals and is an associate editor for *Advances in Developing Human Resources*.

Dr Paul Donovan is Principal Researcher and Senior Lecturer at the School of Business at the National University of Ireland, Maynooth. He served a one-year period as Head of School and Director of Teaching and Learning immediately prior to this appointment. He was previously Head of Management Development and Registrar at the Irish Management Institute (IMI), specializing in Management Development.

Before joining IMI he worked as a general operations manager with Bord na Mona, the Irish Peat Development Authority. He was also Training and Development Manager of the Bord na Mona group. His private sector experience includes conducting major reviews of HRD capability with hundreds of clients, including IBM, and a comprehensive identification of training needs with Dell and trainer capability upgrades with Boston Scientific. He has designed and delivered extensive programmes in the public sector, most notably with the Department of Finance and Enterprise, the Department of Trade and Employment, and the Health Service Executive. He has written peer-reviewed articles on learning transfer and over ten books in training and general management, and writes a column for *HRD* magazine, the journal of the Irish Institute of Training and Development, of which he is a fellow. Paul holds a master's degree in organizational behaviour and another in technology and learning (both from Trinity College Dublin) and a doctorate from Leicester University.

Dr Linda Dowling-Hetherington has been with the School of Business at University College Dublin since 1996. She has many years experience in the management and development of part-time, distance learning and off-campus programmes, and has been the Director of the School's Centre for Distance Learning since its establishment in 2002. From UCD, she holds a Bachelor of Commerce (HRM), a Master of Business Studies (HRM) and a Certificate in Adult Education, along with a Doctor of Education (EdD) from the University of Bath. She has considerable teaching experience in the human resource management and human resource development areas on UCD programmes in Ireland, Hong Kong and Singapore. Her areas of research interest include human resource development, transnational education, student-centred approaches to the management of distance learning programmes, development of academic competencies, undergraduate research experiences, and the changing higher education landscape and its impact on faculty.

Dr Mary Fitzpatrick (BBS with Spanish, GDE (Business), MBS, MCIPD, SFSEDA, PhD) is the Regional Teaching and Learning Advocate in the Centre for Teaching and Learning and lectures in Academic Development, HRD and Organizational Behaviour at the University of Limerick. At a regional level, she successfully led an inter-institutional project on regional teaching enhancement within four higher educational institutions, establishing a wide range of professional development initiatives to this end. She completed her PhD in the area of learning and inter-organizational networks. Her research interests lie within learning and development, with a particular focus on the efficacy of professional development activities, the student experience in teaching and learning, and the role of learning and development at work. She is a chartered member of the CIPD and a senior fellow of SEDA. She has extensive HRD consultancy experience within both the private and the public sector.

Prof. Thomas N. Garavan is Professor of Leadership at Edinburgh Napier Business School. He was formerly Professor and Associate Dean in Postgraduate Studies and Executive Education, Kemmy Business School, University of Limerick. He teaches HRD, training and development, and leadership development. He is author of more than 100 academic articles, co-editor of *European Journal of Training and Development* and a member of the Board of Directors of the Academy of Human Resource Development.

Dr T.J. McCabe is Lecturer in HRM and Research Methods at the National College of Ireland. He leads a number of post-graduate and undergraduate modules, including Research Methods, Strategic Human Resource Management, Employee Relations and HRD. His research interests extend to trust and commitment among nursing professionals, and human resource management issues in the health sector. He has presented this work at national and international conferences, and co-chaired the HRM track for the 14th Annual Conference of the Irish Academy of Management. He has published papers in both academic and practitioner journals, and received the award for Best Paper, Healthcare and Public Sector Management Track, Irish Academy of Management in 2011.

Dr Martin McCracken is Senior Lecturer in Organizational Behaviour at the University of Ulster. He is the editor of *Education and Training* and is a member of the editorial advisory boards of a number of influential journals, such as *Employee Relations, Leadership and Organizational Development Journal* and *The European Journal of Training and Development*. He obtained a PhD from Edinburgh Napier University in 2002 and has been actively researching issues connected with human resource development/management, employability and organizational change. He has published his work in a number of leading academic journals, including *The International Journal of Human Resource Management, Human Resource Management Journal, Human Resource Development International* and the *European Management Journal*, and has played a key role in carrying out UK research projects commissioned by (among others): the Department for Education and Employment; Sector Skills Development Agency; and Leonardo Da Vinci Research Programme (EU).

Dr Clíodhna MacKenzie is a lecturer in the School of Management & Marketing at University College Cork. Prior to that she lectured at the University of Limerick. She holds a degree in business from the University of Limerick. She has previously worked for both US multinationals and global IT consulting firms. She has international experience in the IT and telecoms fields and has worked in the US, Singapore and Thailand, as well as many parts of Europe. Her academic research focuses on the 'dark side' of organizational behavior, such as organizational narcissism, leadership derailment, counterproductive work behaviour and organizational personality disorders (OPDs). Her research interests include risk-taking behaviour, corporate governance, ethics, corporate social responsibility, human resource management/development, and leadership and organization development. She is also a member of the University Forum for Human Resource Development (UFHRD) and the Irish Academy of Management.

Dr Jean McCarthy is a lecturer and researcher in the areas of Human Resource Management, Human Resource Development and Organizational Behaviour at the Kemmy Business School, University of Limerick. A graduate of the University of Limerick, and a former Fulbright Scholar at Colorado State University, her research interests include adult learning, high-performance work systems and the social psychology of work. Her research has attracted financial support from the Irish Research Council, the Alfred P. Sloan Foundation and the Fulbright Commission. She is also a Global Research Associate with the Sloan Center on Aging & Work at Boston College, and is founder and co-director of the Age in the Workplace Research Network (AWR-net), which is an international network of researchers seeking to address issues associated with age, generations and diversity at work. She has extensive experience in teaching and supervision at undergraduate, post-graduate and post-experience levels, as well as working with community-based and Youthreach education and training programmes.

Dr Sue Mulhall has worked in a variety of human resource management (HRM) and training/education positions and lectures in human resource development at the Dublin Institute of Technology (DIT), Ireland. She is a pracademic, combining theory and practice, particularly in the field of career management. Prior to joining DIT in 2012, she ran her own HRM learning, consulting and coaching business for over a decade and was previously a HRM professional for 13 years. Through her research and teaching, she offers fresh insights to the academic and practitioner communities resulting from her exposure to the dilemmas and challenges facing knowledge workers, managers and leaders in dynamic organizations in the contemporary workplace. Drawing on her depth and breadth of experience, She researched her international award-winning doctorate on career success, exploring how personal transitions impact on career experiences. Her findings have been published in international peer-reviewed journals and at conferences.

Dr Clare Rigg is based at the Institute of Technology Tralee, Ireland, where she leads an action learning-based MBA programme. Following an early career in economic development and urban regeneration in Birmingham, England, she developed an interest in collaborative working that was further fostered through encountering action learning as an approach to management development in 1990. She has researched and published widely on action learning, critical management learning and HRD, including the co-authored books *Action Learning, Leadership and Organizational Development in Public Services* (2006); *Critical Human Resource Development: Beyond Orthodoxy* (2007); and *Learning and Talent Development* (2011). She is co-editor of the journal *Action Learning: Research and Practice.*

TOUR OF THE BOOK

Learning outcomes

A set of learning outcomes are identified at the start of each chapter. After you have studied the chapter, completed the activities and answered the review questions, you should be able to achieve each of the stated objectives.

Key terms

Each chapter contains an on-page explanation of a number of important words, phrases and concepts that you need to know in order to understand HRD, its theoretical basis and its related areas.

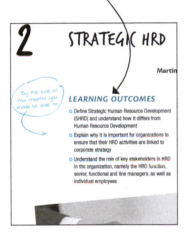

Making links

To allow you to see the interconnected nature of the topics in the field of HRD, areas that link to topics and concepts in other chapters are identified.

Consider this ...

This feature is designed to stimulate your thinking about a specific issue, idea or perspective related to the chapter topic.

HRD in the news

Each chapter contains an example of coverage of its main topic in the media. The aim here is to highlight how you can apply the constructs and concepts in the chapter to the management of people in the real world of the workplace. A set of questions accompanies each feature to assist with this application to a practical situation.

Building your skills

This feature asks you to place yourself in the position of a line manager and to think about what you would do in the situation that has been presented to you.

Chapter review questions

Each chapter has eight questions that can be used as class exercises or for self-testing and evaluating your knowledge and understanding of the chapter topic.

Active case study

These short case studies provide the opportunity for you to link the material covered in the chapter to a real-life situation. Questions are posed at the end of the case studies, which can be answered either in class or as part of an assignment.

Useful websites

An abundance of websites exist on topics related to HRD. At the end of each chapter we have identified those we believe you will find most useful in furthering your knowledge and understanding of the discipline.

Further reading

There are numerous HRD resources and other topics that are also covered in this textbook. The aim here is to highlight a few specific texts and journal articles we believe can assist you in developing your understanding and furthering your knowledge of the many areas introduced in this book.

SPOTLIGHT ON SKILLS: TEXT AND VIDEO FEATURE

This feature aims to encourage you to develop your skills in HRD by asking you to consider specific questions and activities. This gives you the opportunity to identify and diagnose problems and develop possible solutions or actions in relation to the chapter topic. Each of these features is accompanied by a link to video interviews with professionals on the book's companion website. The skills-related questions posed in the text feature are addressed by the practitioner in the video. To maximize this resource, you should first attempt to answer the questions in the book and then watch the video.

COMPANION WEBSITE

The book's companion website at **www.macmillan ihe.com/companion/carbery-hrd** offers a number of resources for both lecturers and students. Lecturers can access PowerPoint slides, a comprehensive testbank of mutiple choice questions and solutions to the Active Case Study questions.

SPOTLIGHT ON SKILLS

Working as an HRD manager, you have been asked to justify your expenditure on HRD programmes undertaken by the organization over the past 12 months. How can you demonstrate the value of HRD? Will you focus on the value to the organization, to employees, or both?

To help you answer the questions above, visit www. macmillanihe.com/companion/carbery-hrd and watch the video of Jemma Carty talking about the value of HRD.

CASE STUDY GRID

Chapter	Title	Industry	Focus
2	Developing Leaders for Competitive Advantage: The Case of JetBlue	Aviation, US	Development for strategic growth
3	Benefit or Cost?	Pharmaceutical, US	Budgeting for HRD
4	Improving Individual Learning at The Courtyard Hotel in Tokyo	Hospitality, Japan	Facilitating employee learning
5	After-Action Reviews in the US Army	Military, US	Capturing organizational learning
6	Organization Development in Netflix	Media, US	Developing organizational culture
7	The 'Free Hand' Approach to LNA	Manufacturing, UK	Identifying learning needs
8	Designing an Induction Programme at McBurger'n'Fries	Services, Ireland	Devising learning objectives and designing an induction programme
9	Training the Taxman!	Government	Delivering an HRD programme
10	Applying HRD Principles to the Cosmetics Industry: Case Study from Oriflame's Research and Development Subsidiary	Cosmetics, global	Evaluating HRD programmes
11	O'Brien's Homeware	Retail, Ireland	Developing a talent management strategy
12	Fosco Data Handling: The Leadership Challenges	Information and communications technology, UK	Identifying leadership development challenges
13	Enterprise Rent-a-Car Graduate Training and Development Programme	Car rental, global	Linking graduate training to business needs
14	The Ethical HR Value Chain	Information and communications technology, US	Developing an ethics awareness programme

MAPPING OF THE TEXT TO CIPD STANDARDS

The CIPD HR Profession Map captures what HR people do and deliver across every aspect and specialism of the profession, and it looks at the underpinning skills, behaviour and knowledge that they need to be most successful. The map identifies ten professional standards, and each standard comprises a range of performance behaviours that span four levels of competence. The standards we are most concerned with for this text are:

Standard 4: Organization Development
Standard 5: Resource and Talent Planning
Standard 6: Learning and Talent Development

We have mapped each chapter in the textbook to these three standards. For a detailed description of each standard, please see **http://www.cipd.co.uk/cipd-hr-profession/hr-profession-map/**.

CIPD Standard		Chapter(s)
4.1	OD strategy, planning and business case development	6
4.2	Organization capability assessment	2, 6
4.3	Culture assessment and development	2
4.4	Organization development intervention and execution	2, 6
4.5	Change communications	6
4.6	OD methodology	6
4.7	Project and programme management	6
4.8	Cultural differences	2, 5, 6
4.9	Culture change	5, 6, 14
4.10	Change management	3
4.11	Change communications	3
5.1	Workforce planning	1, 2
5.2	Resourcing	1, 2
5.3	Talent identification and succession	11
5.4	Assessment and selection	7
5.5	Induction	8
5.6	Exit	7, 13
5.7	Legal framework	14
5.8	Resourcing	1, 2
5.9	Recruitment	13
5.10	Talent and succession	11
5.11	Assessment	8, 9
5.12	Induction	8

CIPD Standard		Chapter(s)
6.1	Capability and skills assessment	1, 2, 7
6.2	Organization capability strategy, planning and business case development	1, 2, 3
6.3	Design L&D solutions	8
6.4	Deliver L&D solutions	9
6.5	Leadership development	12
6.6	Talent management	11
6.7	Capability assessment	2
6.8	Learning styles	4
6.9	Blended learning solutions	4, 8
6.10	Supplier management	8, 9
6.11	Facilitation	9
6.12	Diversity	1, 12
6.13	Measure and evaluate interventions	10

SKILLS DEVELOPMENT

PRESENTATION SKILLS

Regardless of the industry sector, or the size of the organization you work in, you will need to have the ability to present your ideas clearly and succinctly. This will often happen in a setting where you use a software programme such as PowerPoint to provide an overview of the context and key points. Increasingly, some job vacancies require you to make an oral presentation as part of the selection process. In order to present your ideas and arguments clearly, there are a number of stages involved in the making of an oral presentation. Some of the key issues involved are outlined here in order to assist you in developing this important skill, either through your coursework or after college.

Planning your presentation

Be clear about what your core message is and repeat this at different stages during the presentation in order to increase its impact. Is it to inform? To sell your idea? To defend a position? To present a new idea? Whatever the answer, keep asking yourself why in different ways. What is the objective I want to achieve? What will I accept as evidence that my presentation has succeeded? What do I want the audience to think or feel at the end of the presentation?

Analyse your audience. What are their expectations of your presentation? Do they expect to be informed? Persuaded? Have their existing ideas challenged? What do you they already know? The key to a successful presentation is to know what your audience expects and that you meet or exceed that expectation.

How much time do you have for your presentation? Be careful not to run over an allocated time slot. This will detract from your effectiveness.

What should you wear? This may seem a little strange to include here; however, confidence is an important element in an effective presentation. You need to be comfortable and appropriately dressed to project the 'right' message.

Handling nerves

Many people find this the most difficult part of making a presentation.

- Be well prepared and organized. Most people will feel nervous before a presentation. Knowing what you are going to say and being organized will reduce your level of nervousness. The first two minutes of any presentation are the most crucial. If you feel confident and clear about what you are going to say in the early stage of the presentation, this will help alleviate your nerves for the remainder of the presentation. Once you have passed the first two minutes and you mentally believe that the presentation is going well, this will allow the reminder of the presentation to run more smoothly.
- Don't read directly from your notes – use visual aids. This means that the words/pictures you use on the screen should act as your 'prompt'. Do not use hand-held notes as they will just act to provide a false sense of security. If you lose your place in the notes, or have learned what to say and then mix up your notes, your level of effectiveness in the eyes of the audience will be diminished.
- Rehearse in advance. Trial runs are an excellent method of preparation and allow you to establish how long your presentation will take. This also develops your self-confidence, which will work to reduce your nervousness.
- Pay attention to your 'mannerisms' and work to overcome them. Ask a friend/family member to highlight any repeated unconscious behaviours you might have, such as running your hands through your hair; shaking the change in your pocket; swaying from side to side; or speaking too fast. These are very distracting for the audience.
- Practise deep breathing before you get to the room/place where the presentation is to be made. This will help reduce the overall feeling of nervousness.
- Be in the room in plenty of time and check that the equipment and your presentation are working.
- Thinking positive means you are more likely to feel and behave positively.

Structuring your presentation

The golden rule is simple:
- Tell them what you are going to tell them (introduction).
- Tell them (main body).
- Tell them what you've told them (conclusion).

The introduction

- The introduction should comprise approximately 10 percent of your presentation. It should provide a map for the reader of what is going to come.
- Introduce the topic, and yourself (if necessary).
- Start with an attention-getting hook – make a bold claim, present a striking fact/statistic, ask a question, use a quotation. If you have a suitable quote, surprising information or a visual aid – use it to grab the audience's attention.

Body language

- Speak clearly and audibly throughout. Vary the tone of your voice, as this creates interest in your message.
- Face the audience, not the screen behind you or your laptop. Speak to the audience and make eye contact with people in the room. This demonstrates that you are paying attention to them and encourages them to pay attention to you.
- Don't speak too fast, as your message can get lost in translation.
- Show enthusiasm for the topic/issue/idea, as enthusiasm is contagious.
- Project your voice out towards the audience. Do not speak down to your shoes!
- Regard the presentation as an opportunity to shine.

The conclusion

- Remind the audience of what you set out to do at the start. That means stressing the key point of your presentation.
- Briefly repeat the main points you made.
- End on an interesting point, as this assists people in remembering your presentation.
- Thank the audience for listening and invite questions.

TIME MANAGEMENT SKILLS

People who effectively manage their time are the highest achievers in all walks of life, from business, to sport, to public service. Yet, they have only the same number of hours in a day as the rest of us. This is why time management is believed to be a critical skill for success. Many people spend their days in a frenzy of activity, but achieve very little because they are not concentrating on the right things. Mobile phones, laptops and e-mail mean we are virtually contactable 24 hours a day. People often feel unable to go on holiday without being able to be contacted. Technology has made us accessible no matter where we are, whether it's in the Outer Hebrides or on the Amazon. In the section below we provide some tips and techniques to help you become more effective at managing your most valuable resource – your time.

Your workspace

Where you work has a significant impact on your productivity and mental wellbeing! While some people are happy to work surrounded by paper, files, teacups etc., other people seem to be able to work at a clutter-free desk. In reality, the brain can only concentrate fully on one thing at a time. The more 'stuff' on your desk, the more tempted you will be to be distracted by it and to pick it up. This instantly causes a distraction. Cluttered desks are *not* conducive to clear thinking. You should:
- Clear your desk of *everything* not related to what you are working on now. Otherwise your attention is constantly being drawn to other issues/tasks.
- Resist the temptation to leave papers/a file/book on your desk.
- Always leave your desk tidy and empty when you are finished working at night.

Work efficiently

Handle each piece of paper/each e-mail only *once*. The principle behind handling paper/e-mails only once is that it forces you to make a decision about every piece of paper/e-mail you touch. Avoid reading something and then saying 'I'll deal with that later'. The rules are either:
- Do it straight away.
- Decide to postpone it until later and identify that it still needs to be done.
- When in doubt … throw it out or delete it!

Managing phone calls

The phone seems to have taken over our lives. We are now no longer able to go anywhere without a mobile phone. Patience has vanished with the advent of smartphones in particular. How much time do you spend on the phone at university or work? How much of that time is necessary? Talking on the phone can be very time-consuming and unproductive. If you spend 6 minutes an hour on the phone, that equates to 10 per cent of your day. Therefore:

- Set aside specific time slots for making phone calls.
- Turn your voicemail on to help manage your time.
- Then group all your outgoing calls together. This makes much more efficient use of your time rather than interrupting yourself every time you get a phone call.
- Change your voicemail message every day.

Managing your online communications

E-mail, Facebook, Twitter and other social media platforms have become the standard way of communicating at university and work. The biggest problem with this is that they consume large portions of your day, and yet help you achieve relatively little. e-mail inboxes can be overwhelming. E-mail is also the lazy option – especially when you want to avoid making a decision. To deal with these problems and at the same time manage your time better:

- Check your e-mail/Facebook/Twitter pages just two or three times a day – in the morning, at lunchtime and in the afternoon. If something is really urgent someone will contact you on your phone! Web apps such as SelfControl for Mac and Cold Turkey for Windows are free productivity programs that you can use to temporarily block yourself off from popular social media sites, addicting websites and games.
- Make a phone call to reply to an e-mail. We spend vast amounts of time composing and replying to e-mails when one phone call would have dealt with the issue much more quickly.
- Set up e-mail messages with auto-preview, as this will allow you to see whether the message needs to be opened and actioned straight away.
- Let people know when you don't want to be copied on e-mails.
- Use a subject message line each time you send an e-mail, even if it's a reply.
- Delete an e-mail once you have read and replied to it, or move it to a personal folder.

- Keep sent mails!
- Archive old e-mails regularly.

Persuasion and Influencing Skills: Learning how to influence and persuade people to do something they would otherwise not have done is an important life skill. Influencing is essentially getting your own way, unobtrusively. Managers do it most of the time. People are usually not aware that every human interaction involves a complex process of persuasion and influence. And, being unaware, they are usually the ones being persuaded to help others rather than the ones who are doing the persuading!

- Know what you want…! If you are not clear about what you want it will be difficult for you to persuade others around to your way of thinking.
- Look for points of mutual agreement and build on these.
- Build rapport and make a connection with the person you are trying to influence.
- Ask questions. The type of question is important. You need to use a mixture of questions to get the response you are looking for.
  ○ Find out what the other person is looking for out of the interaction: What do you want to get out of this discussion? What do you want to achieve from this discussion?
  ○ Probe to find out why they don't agree with you: What is the reason why you can't do that? What is stopping you from agreeing with me?
  ○ Ask hypothetical questions, as this allows you to gather information without the person actually committing to anything: What would happen if you agreed with me? What would happen if we went ahead and did it?
  ○ Find out what they need you to give them in order for them to agree with you: What do you need to get in order for us to agree? What do I need to give you to get you to agree?
  ○ Ask challenging questions to test the person's resolve/position. Search for specifics: Why you do not agree with this proposal? What specific reason do you have for not wanting to do this?

- Listen actively. This includes being able to paraphrase what the other person has said.
- Use positive body language and verbal language. This creates the right atmosphere and is more conducive to agreement.
  ○ Don't use 'flowery language'! Using too many adjectives and adverbs will lose the listener.

○ Use strong words, not weak words, when trying to persuade people. For example, which of these two sentences would persuade you? 'I think you might like this new product we have' or 'You're really going to like this new product we are offering.' 'Think' in this sentence is a weak word. Here is another example: 'I was wondering if you might want to go for a drink with me at the weekend?' A stronger question would be: 'Would you like to go for a drink this weekend?'

○ Focus on using the active voice, not the passive voice. Passive: an account was opened by Mr Smith. Active: Mr Smith opened an account.

● Stress the benefits to them of agreeing with you.
● Work towards a decision. Use all the techniques above to keep building towards their agreement.

PREFACE AND EDITORS' ACKNOWLEDGEMENTS

Having edited *Human Resource Management: A Concise Introduction* (2013) for Palgrave Macmillan, we suggested creating a series of books with the *Concise Introduction* subtitle. We decided to focus on human resource development (HRD) as the popularity of HRD has never been greater – at least 30 UK and Irish third-level institutes currently offer HRD courses, and in the US alone at least 281 colleges and universities offer degrees in HRD or related subjects.

While there are a number of excellent HRD textbooks available, there are few which deal with HRD at a basic introductory level, which can be taught in one semester in a UK, Irish, European or international context. Most textbooks contain much more material than is required for a one-semester introductory module. Our aim was to create a textbook that is accessible and easy to understand for students taking HRD/Learning and Development/Training and Development modules for the first time.

We have written this book in the same style as our earlier textbook *Human Resource Management: A Concise Introduction* and have presented the material in a way that highlights the practicality of the issues involved in HRD. There is a strong emphasis on skills and career development throughout each of the 14 chapters, with key features such as up-to-date news pieces (HRD in the News), Active Case Studies,

discussion activities (Consider This …), highlighted key terms with on-page definitions, and video interviews with experienced HR professionals (Spotlight on Skills). The book's companion website provides extra resources, including videos, multiple-choice questions and case study solutions.

We would like to acknowledge the help we received with writing this text. Ursula Gavin and Rachel Bridgewater at Palgrave provided tremendous assistance and support from the initial proposal stage to the design and layout of the final text. The anonymous reviewers of each of the chapters provided excellent feedback, for which we are very grateful. In addition to the contributors to the textbook, we would like to thank colleagues at the University of Limerick who provided us with support along the way – Patrick Gunnigle, Michelle Hammond, Noreen Heraty, Sarah MacCurtain, Juliette McMahon, Deirdre O'Shea, Michelle O'Sullivan, Jonathan Lavelle, Jill Pearson and Tom Turner.

We are grateful for the time the participants in the Spotlight on Skills video features so readily gave us and for their excellent insights into industry practice.

Finally, we would like to thank our families: Michelle and Julie Carbery; and Dave, Oisín and Luíseach Cross.

Ronan Carbery and Christine Cross
June 2014

FOREWORD

Over the past two and a half decades, the field of human resource development (HRD) has emerged as one of the most dynamic and multifaceted areas of business and management for both academics and practitioners. There is much debate over HRD's definition and remit and about the most appropriate methodological approaches to study and evaluate HRD interventions.

The ability for HRD academics and practitioners to respond to the ever-changing global economic and political environment will be critical for HRD's future evolution and sustainability. HRD experts must be able to operate across many different levels and engage with diverse stakeholders and, ever increasingly, across national boundaries. Not only do HRD experts need to be able to interpret and implement new policies and practices in response to rapidly changing global and technological environments; they must also be able to engage and contribute at strategic levels within organizations and must be able to demonstrate value for money for any and all HRD interventions undertaken.

In other words, students of HRD – many of whom will go on to become HRD practitioners – must be highly dextrous and able to work effectively and efficiently across multiple functions and cultures within organizations. Given these challenges, this textbook makes a significant and timely contribution to students of HRD, and will be pivotal in equipping future HRD academics and practitioners to transition challenges into opportunities. The book comprises contributions edited and written by scholars who specialize in HRD. Each scholar's chapter matches their particular area(s) of academic and practical expertise.

Not only does the book cover all the major areas of HRD in clearly written and engaging styles; it covers emerging areas of HRD, including strategic HRD, HRD in small and medium enterprises (SMEs), the interaction between leadership, talent management and HRD, graduate employability, and how HRD can contribute to corporate social responsibility (CSR) and business ethics.

Learners are exposed to the academic literature associated with each topic and also, critically and uniquely, the practical applications of the theory. This unique blend of theory and practice is greatly enhanced by the use of expanded case studies highlighting practices used in leading global organizations, and the website that accompanies the book features video interviews with leading HRD academics and practitioners. To ensure and solidify learning, each chapter also features review questions, additional readings and web links. Quizzes are also used widely throughout the book. I welcome and commend the book as an important and timely resource for HRD learners and one that will make a significant addition to the literature.

Maura Sheehan
Professor of International Management
JE Cairnes School of Business & Economics
NUI Galway

1 INTRODUCTION TO HRD

Ronan Carbery

By the end of this chapter you will be able to:

LEARNING OUTCOMES

- Define what HRD is
- Understand the evolution of HRD
- Recognize the context of HRD
- Identify the value of HRD for individuals and organizations
- Distinguish the differences between training, development, learning and education

- Recognize how UK, Irish, European and US approaches to HRD differ
- Relate to current issues in HRD, including the changing context of employment; knowledge work; ethics in business; management of diversity; globalization; and technology

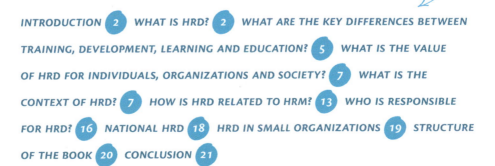

HRD: What's in a name?

This chapter discusses ...

INTRODUCTION

Here at the start of this book it is worth identifying that the term 'human resource development' is most often used to describe the activities involved in developing people. Therefore, if you are an employer, a manager or an employee, the issues dealt with in this book are going to be relevant to your working life. Human Resource Development (HRD) is essentially about facilitating learning that allows employees to fully develop and realize their potential in ways that benefit themselves, organizations and society.

In order to accomplish this aim, individuals, organizations and national agencies choose among a range of policies and practices that can assist in achieving this objective. By this we mean policies and practices such as how to identify what learning needs people have and what their learning styles are; how to design, deliver and evaluate learning activities; how to manage talented employees; who should pay for these activities; and what are the differing skill requirements of graduates, managers and leaders. These are just a few of the questions that face those charged with the management of employees, and each of these is dealt with in this book. The choice of policies or practices is, however, not as straightforward as it first seems. Do you think Google uses the same HRD policies and practices as your local supermarket, or the same ones you would use if you were starting up your own company? Why do you think there may be a difference? Here, in this chapter, we set out some of the issues involved in making these choices.

Given that the focus of this book is pitched at an introductory level to HRD, it would be impossible to provide a detailed description of every single issue involved in the choices we are talking about. Instead, we concentrate on identifying some of the key concepts and encourage you to read more about these in order to further your understanding of them. Here, in this first chapter, we will look at the term 'HRD', where it originated and the evolution of the term over the last 60 years. This leads us to consider the difference between competing terms such as training, development, education and learning. The value of HRD for individuals, organizations and society will also be addressed.

It is important to understand the context of HRD, and we consider how the changing context of employment and labour markets, knowledge work, ethics in business, management of diversity, and technology impact upon HRD. The difference between HRD strategies at a national level is important to understand and we will look at how approaches to HRD differ in different countries.

Most of you reading this book will probably have studied, or are currently studying, Human Resource Management (HRM), so we will look at the relationship between HRD and HRM and consider both the differences and the similarities between the two concepts. We then outline who is (or should be) responsible for HRD.

We identify the key differences between HRD in small and large organizations and the variations in HRD activities between the two. Finally, we look at how the book is structured and outline the content of the remainder of the chapters. At the end of this chapter you should be able to understand why HRD is such an important area of study for you as a future manager.

WHAT IS HRD?

The term 'human resource development' was first used by Harbison and Myers (1964) in the context of human capital theory. Both were economists, and believed that HRD was important for national development. Schultz's (1961) human capital theory suggested that organizations receive economic value from their employees' knowledge, skills, competencies and experience and that human capital can be increased by training and education. Attempts to define HRD were subsequently dominated by academics from the US, with the majority focused on the link between HRD and organizational performance. Over time, definitions expanded to incorporate organization development ▶ Chapter 5 and society (McLean and McLean, 2001). Irish, UK and European definitions have focused more on the link between HRD and the individual, taking the perspective that learning lies in the hands of the individual, and that this is the main outcome of HRD activities (McGuire et al., 2005). Any improvements in organizational performance are a result of this learning. Fifty years after the first mention of HRD, academics have not been able to agree on an exact meaning of the term. If you search academic journals and books, at least 20–30 different definitions of HRD exist. They can broadly be divided into individual, organizational, societal and multi-level definitions. Table 1.1 presents a selection of some of these definitions.

Hamlin and Stewart (2011) analysed these definitions and identified four core purposes of HRD:
- Improving individual or group effectiveness and performance
- Improving organizational effectiveness and performance
- Developing knowledge, skills and competencies
- Enhancing human potential and personal growth

Table 1.1 Definitions of HRD

Level of analysis	Authors	Definitions
Individual	Craig (1976)	HRD focuses on the central goal of developing human potential in every aspect of lifelong learning.
	Meggisson et al. (1993)	HRD is an integrated and holistic approach to changing work-related behaviour using a range of learning techniques.
	Nyhan (2002)	HRD refers to educational training and development activities related to working life. It relates to development and learning activities for those who are at work and have completed their basic professional or vocational education and training.
Organizational	Harbison and Myers (1964)	HRD is the process of increasing the knowledge, the skills and the capacities of all the people in a society. In economic terms, it could be described as the accumulation of human capital and its effective investment in the development of an economy. In political terms, human resource development prepares people for adult participation in political processes, particularly as citizens in a democracy. From the social and cultural points of view, the development of human resources helps people to lead fuller and richer lives, less bound by tradition. In short, the processes of human resource development unlock the door to modernization.
	Nadler (1970)	HRD is a series of organized activities conducted within a specific time and designed to produce behavioural change.
	Bergenhenegouwen (1990)	HRD can be described as training members of an organization in such a way that they have the knowledge and skills needed within the context of the (changing) objectives of the organization.
	Garavan (1991)	HRD is the strategic management of training, development and management/ professional education intervention, so as to achieve the objectives of the organization while at the same time ensuring the full utilization of the knowledge in detail and skills of the individual employees.
	McCracken and Wallace (2000)	HRD is the creation of a learning culture, within which a range of training, development and learning strategies both respond to corporate strategy and also help to shape and influence it.
	Gourlay (2000)	HRD focuses on theory and practice related to training, development and learning within organizations, both for individuals and in the context of business strategy and organizational competence formation.
Societal	Stead and Lee (1996)	HRD is a holistic societal process of learning drawing upon a range of disciplines.
	Horwitz et al. (1996)	HRD is concerned with the processes whereby the citizens of a nation acquire the knowledge and skills necessary to perform both specific occupational tasks and other social, cultural, intellectual and political roles in a society.
Multi-focus	McLean and McLean (2001)	HRD is any process or activity that, either initially or over the long term, has the potential to develop adults' work-based knowledge, expertise, productivity and satisfaction, whether for personal or group/team gain, or for the benefit of an organizational community, a nation or, ultimately, the whole of humanity.
	Hamlin and Stewart (2011)	HRD encompasses planned activities, processes and/or interventions designed to have impact upon and enhance organizational and individual learning, to develop human potential, to improve or maximize effectiveness and performance at either the individual, group/team and/or organizational level, and/or to bring about effective, beneficial personal or organizational behaviour change and improvement within, across and/or beyond the boundaries (or borders) of private sector (for profit), public sector/ governmental or third/voluntary sector (not-for-profit) organizations, entities or any other type of personal-based, work-based, community-based, society-based, culture-based, political-based or nation-based host system.

Figure 1.1 Trend analysis of term usage in books: 1950–2008

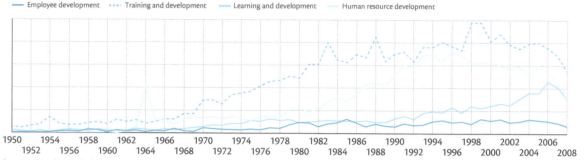

Source: Google Books http://books.google.com/ngrams

It is arguable as to whether this multitude of definitions has harmed or helped the field of HRD. Lee (2001) even refused to offer a definition of HRD because of the wide variety of ways in which it is practised and interpreted around the world. Garavan *et al.* (2007) suggest that HRD was 'segmented, incomplete, lacking comprehensiveness and coherence', but others, most notably Mankin (2001), suggest that the lack of agreement makes HRD distinctive.

A number of professional bodies and groups have sought to increase the visibility and credibility of HRD, including the Academy of Human Resource Development (AHRD), the University Forum for HRD (UFHRD), the American Society for Training and Development (ASTD), the Chartered Institute of Personnel and Development (CIPD) and the International Federation of Training and Development (IFTDO) (see **Useful Websites** at the end of the chapter for links to these bodies). A number of academic journals have also contributed to the maturity of the field, most notably *Human Resource Development Quarterly*, *Human Resource Development Review*, *Human Resource Development International*, *Advances in Developing Human Resources*, and *European Journal of Training and Development*. Members of both AHRD and UFHRD are primarily US and European academics, which has led to criticisms that there is a gap between what academics are talking about and what organizations are actually doing. CIPD is a UK and Irish association for HR professionals with over 120,000 members, and it is worth noting that they use the term 'learning and talent development' rather than HRD.

It is unlikely that you will work (or have worked) in an organization that has an HRD department or encounter anyone outside of academia with 'HRD' in their job title. The term HRD is rarely used in organizational settings (Sambrook and Stewart, 2002), with most organizations labelling HRD activities 'learning and development',

'training and development' or 'employee development'. While not 100 per cent scientific, Google NGram and Google Trends are useful tools that allow us to look at usage of these different terms over time. Figure 1.1 presents a trend analysis of the usage of the four terms measured using Google Books between 1950 and 2008. We can see that, as usage of training and development falls off pre 2000 usage of learning and development increases significantly. The usage of HRD has risen steadily since the 1980s but decreases just as usage of learning and development reaches its peak in 2006.

Google Trends allow us to see what people are searching for on the web, and Figure 1.2 presents a comparison of the four terms between 2005 and 2013. We can see that 'training and development' is the most popular search term, but that the frequency of searches for it has fallen in recent years. Searches for 'human resource development' and 'learning and development' are relatively consistent, but it is worth noting that there has been a significant decline in searches for 'human resource development' since 2005. Looking at these results from a regional perspective, it shows that 'learning and development' is searched for most in the UK, while 'human resource development' is searched for most in the US and Asia.

Even though this book is entitled *Human Resource Development: A Concise Introduction*, it is possible that the module you are using it for has a different title. At the time of writing, five Irish third-level institutes offer HRD modules, one offers a 'Leadership Development' module and another offers an 'Employee Development' module. Out of a sample of 20 UK universities, seven offered modules with HRD in the title, seven offered modules with variations of 'Learning and Development' in the title, and other modules used titles such as 'Employee Development and Workplace Learning' and 'Resourcing, Learning and Talent Management'. In the US alone, at least 281 colleges and universities offer degrees in HRD

Figure 1.2 Trend analysis of web searches: 2005–2013

— Employee development ···· Training and development — Learning and development — Human resource development

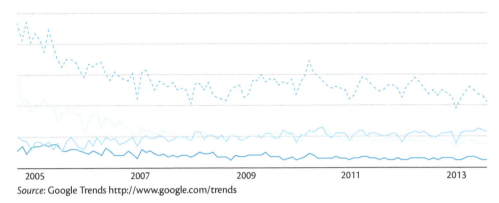

Source: Google Trends http://www.google.com/trends

or related subjects (Roberts, 2011). Institutions often have three or four HRD-type modules on programmes, but use different labels to differentiate them on course offerings, e.g. 'Human Resource Development', 'Learning and Talent Development' and 'Strategic Learning, Training and Development' could all be offered at undergraduate and post-graduate levels.

Regardless of the title of the module you are using this book for or what organizations call it, there are a number of activities that encapsulate the nature of HRD. Wilson (2012) suggests they include:

- Training and development
- Education and training
- Technical training
- Personal development
- Career development
- Leadership development
- Management development
- Performance improvement
- Coaching
- Talent management

WHAT ARE THE KEY DIFFERENCES BETWEEN TRAINING, DEVELOPMENT, LEARNING AND EDUCATION?

To understand the basic ideas underpinning HRD, we need to first consider what it means when we talk about training, development, learning and education.

competencies competence is the practical application of knowledge, skills, attitudes, motivation, values, beliefs, cognitive style and personality that enables an individual to work effectively and autonomously in a clearly defined context

training the process of acquiring knowledge, skills and attitudes required to perform an organizational role effectively

While these concepts have many elements in common, there are a number of important distinctions that illustrate their differences. To do so, we need to look at some common terms that are used in the terminology to differentiate each, namely competencies and competence.

Competencies are often compared with knowledge, skills and abilities (KSAs). Knowledge is defined as specific information components of a task, job or role that the learner should acquire. Skill refers to dimensions of performance that the learner should be able to demonstrate. Attitudes refer to beliefs and values that the learner should espouse and put into practice and sustain. Competencies, however, are different in that, while they both indicate an ability to perform in a role, competencies are broader than KSAs. Competencies are normally worded in a way which identifies specific behavioural aspects of the role. They are often developed by organizations to represent a set of factors that help in achieving success at an organizational level, rather than specifically just in one role. An individual competency is described by the particular skills, knowledge and individual characteristics required for its purpose.

Training is generally defined as a planned and systematic effort to modify or develop knowledge, skills and abilities through learning experiences, to achieve effective performance in an activity or a range of activities (Manpower Services Commission, 1981).

It is preparing you for the requirements of a specific job, usually your present job, and is very narrow in focus, requiring a short time to acquire and immediate application. Training needs are generally determined by organizations to bring about an instant improvement in job performance, and training tends to take place in the workplace.

In contrast, Baum (1995) characterizes development as a process that can take place at any time and is not constrained by formal parameters or at specified points within an individual's life. While training is for a specific job, development is concerned with the growth of the person and is not related to a specific job or even a future job. It is not confined to the classroom or workplace situation, nor is it a situational term restricted to planned or formalized group sessions. Development is a broad concept that is future-orientated and is concerned with the growth and enhancement of the individual. Whereas training needs are determined by organizations, developmental activities can be determined by either the individual or the organization. As we will see later in the chapter, however, the onus on taking responsibility for development has shifted to the individual.

Education may be defined as a process or a series of activities which aims at enabling an individual to assimilate and develop knowledge, skills, values and understanding that are not simply related to a narrow field of activity, but which allow a broad range of problems to be defined, analysed and solved. Education is generally associated with schools, universities and colleges, with education needs being determined at state level in the case of schools. It may be understood in informal or formal terms (Garavan et al., 1995) and is completed in a much longer timeframe than training, for example.

Mankin (2009) summarizes the differences between the three terms as follows: 'training focuses on work; education focuses on the whole person; development is often a mix of the two' (p. 36). Table 1.2 lists some of the distinctions between training, development and education.

The majority of definitions of training, development and education include the word 'learning'. Learning involves the acquisition of new knowledge and how this changes the individual in some way or another (Mankin, 2009). It is a relatively permanent change of knowledge, attitude or behaviour that occurs as a result of formal education or training, or as a result of informal experiences, e.g. how you think about something or how you behave. Acknowledging that learning is not a static concept, the term lifelong learning recognizes that learning is not confined to childhood or the classroom but takes place throughout life and in a range of situations. The Irish Department of Education and Science (2000) defined lifelong learning as the 'ongoing, voluntary, and self-motivated pursuit of knowledge for either personal or professional reasons'. In essence, education, training and development, and learning are interlinked and interdependent, rather than separate and distinct from one another.

---

development an ongoing acquisition of skills and knowledge aimed at long-term career growth rather than immediate performance

education any experience that has an effect on the way we think, feel or act

learning the act of acquiring knowledge or skill

Table 1.2 Differences between training, development and education

Comparison factor	Training	Development	Education	
			Informal	Formal
Focus of activity	KSA and job performance	Individual potential, future role in work	Personal development	Structured development
Clarity of objectives	Specified clearly	General terms	Unique to individual	General terms
Timescale	Short-term	Long-term	Lifelong	Specified period
Nature of learning process	Structured/ mechanistic	Instructional/organic	Structured/ mechanistic	Instructional/organic
Payback to organization	Almost immediately	Medium–long-term	No direct payback	Long-term at most

CONSIDER THIS ...

When studying for your exams, how do you go about learning new material? Our brains create fresh pathways whenever we experience something new. Repeat the activity and the pathway will be reinforced. London taxi drivers are required to memorize a map of the capital comprising over 25,000 streets and thousands of landmarks. Recent research found that they have larger hippocampi (part of the brain that plays a major role in memory) than the city's bus drivers, who are responsible for learning only a few routes.

WHAT IS THE VALUE OF HRD FOR INDIVIDUALS, ORGANIZATIONS AND SOCIETY?

Consider the cost of your current course of study – what is its value to you? A three-year undergraduate degree in the UK costs in the region of £50,000, in Ireland €15,000, and in the US average tuition in public and private institutions is over $18,000 per year (National Center for Education Statistics, 2012). US organizations alone spend more than $71 billion annually on HRD activities (O'Leonard, 2013). In 2012, the UK government spent £56.27 billion on education, while US federal, state and local sources spent $1.15 trillion on education in 2012 (Department of Education, 2013). Given the vast sums spent by individuals, organizations and governments, what is the value of these activities? Aguinis and Kraiger (2009) examined the benefits of training and development at three levels and suggest that they include:

For individuals:
- To fulfil potential and develop a sense of identity
- To meet the demands of change
- To change behaviours and enhance other behaviours
- To enhance self-worth/self-esteem and self-efficacy
- To enhance employability and expertise
- To remain employable
- To facilitate learning and change
- To increase earning potential and secure a better job

For organizations:
- To facilitate organizational learning, the achievement of strategy and organizational change

- To enhance organizational performance, increase competitiveness and profitability
- To reinforce and manage the culture of the organization
- To encourage and facilitate compliance with external regulatory requirements
- To align individual behaviour with that required by the organization
- To facilitate the dissemination, diffusion and sharing of knowledge
- To facilitate the motivation and retention of employees
- To attract employees to the organization and be an employer of choice
- To manage the psychological contract
- To manage talented employees
- To allow organizations to adapt to change

For society:
- To contribute to the economic growth of a nation through the development of human capital
- To enhance the culture of a country
- To build communities and make society more cohesive
- To enhance the well being of people in society

While these benefits are encouraging, we need to consider the context in which HRD takes place to assess how realistic they are in the current economic climate.

BUILDING YOUR SKILLS

An employee approaches you asking if they can have time off to pursue a night-time degree course in a nearby university. They also ask if the organization will pay the fees. Should organizations finance or part-finance learning and development programmes such as MBAs for their employees? An employee could conceivably obtain their qualification and leave the organization shortly afterwards, so what is the return for the organization?

WHAT IS THE CONTEXT OF HRD?

There are a number of contextual factors that impact upon the design, delivery and extent of HRD activities undertaken by organizations and individuals. We will consider a range of these in turn.

Economic factors

Economic uncertainty and instability in global markets since the global financial crisis (GFC) of 2007/2008 has had significant implications for HRD. In 2008 and 2009, spending on HRD activities by US organizations fell by 11 per cent each year (O'Leonard, 2013). Organizations demand greater productivity and performance with fewer workers. Changes to the organizational structure such as downsizing and delayering bring significant demands for employees. They are expected to be able to respond rapidly to changing conditions, to ensure that customer expectations are met. While 20th-century organizations were characterized by hierarchical organizational structures with numerous layers of bureaucracy, 21st-century organizations are flatter and resemble a network that links partners, employees, external contractors, suppliers and customers in various relationships.

Based on 2011 patterns, the OECD expects that 15–29-year-olds in the UK will spend 2.3 years on average either unemployed or outside the labour force (slightly higher than the EU average of 2.2 years). The proportion of 15–19-year-olds in the UK not in education, employment or training (NEETs) has remained relatively constant between 2008 and 2011 – at 10 per cent, this is still a considerable proportion of young people, however. In 2013, the rate of unemployment in the EU zone reached an all-time high of 12.2 per cent, but youth unemployment (those aged 15–24) is far, far higher. 2013 figures for youth unemployment in Italy show a figure of 41 per cent, Spain 56 per cent and Greece 62.5 per cent (Eurostat, 2013a). These are not uneducated youths; 40 per cent of these unemployed Spanish youths are college educated, while the corresponding figure for unemployed Greek youths is 30 per cent. Ninety-five per cent of net job losses during the GFC were in middle-class occupations such as office workers or machine operators (Jaimovich and Siu, 2012). Thirty per cent of employees in Europe are not classified as 'regular' workers (Eurostat, 2013b) and new jobs created since the GFC are mostly low-paid and insecure (contract and temporary positions in services). The challenges involved in up-skilling or reskilling these individuals are a major public policy concern.

Employees in the US and Europe who survived the GFC have been left disillusioned and disengaged (PwC, 2012). The younger generation has been hit particularly hard as they see their opportunities dwindle and their career path blocked by older workers who cannot afford to retire. Low levels of employee engagement tend to result in a higher turnover of employees, less effort put in on the job and lower productivity. Cappelli and Keller (2013) found that organizations that spent less time training employees were more likely to use non-standard workers, such as agency or temporary workers. By not even giving job-specific training opportunities to these employees, organizations assign the workers simpler tasks, which gives them little chance to enhance or develop their skills on the job. The Matthew Effect is derived from a passage in the New Testament (Matthew 25: 29) and states: 'For unto every one that hath shall be given, and he shall have abundance: but from him that hath not shall be taken away even that which he hath' and has had a significant effect on learning (McCracken and Winterton, 2006). There is evidence that those who have previously been engaged in learning are significantly more likely to be current participants than those who have not (McGiveney, 1999). Managers and related professionals tend to enjoy a higher level of participation in learning activities at work than their subordinates. If organizations are unwilling to invest in training for employees whom they perceive as having little value to the business, this risks an ever-widening gap between those who receive training and those who do not, but are perhaps most in need of it. The onus is, then, on individuals to seek out opportunities and for national agencies to prioritize activities that focus on upgrading skills, especially among those groups of workers with low levels of qualifications or skills.

When organizations choose to invest in HRD activities, they tend to focus on two groups of employees: first, those whose skills are considered valuable or essential to achieve an organization's strategic goals or objectives; and, second, workers who have longer-term relationships with their employers. Lepak and Snell (1999) developed a human resources (HR) architecture that examines how organizations allocate their HR. They argue that the competencies and contributions desired by an organization from its employees drive its choice of HRD policies and practices, including learning and development and career management. They suggest that the decision by organizations to invest in HRD activities is based on the relative value and uniqueness of each individual. Employees are valuable to the extent that their competencies contribute to the amount a customer is willing to pay for products or services produced by the organization, while they are considered unique if their skills are useful to the employer but are not widely available in the external labour market. Lepak and Snell posit that, if employees have both high value and high uniqueness, organizations will attempt to keep them committed and engaged by providing more opportunities for participation in HRD activities.

Recognizing that cutting training expenditures is counterproductive, as training is a foundation for the development of core competencies and an underlying source of competitive advantage, expenditure on HRD activities has increased since 2009, rising by 2 per cent in 2010 for US organizations, 10 per cent in 2011 and another 12 per cent in 2012 (O'Leonard, 2013). This positive investment in HRD indicates that organizations are, indeed, focusing on reskilling their workforces. As the pace of innovation continues to accelerate and companies look to expand their operations globally, employees need to acquire more specialized skills (O'Leonard, 2013). These employees must also adapt to a workplace that is becoming more transient, mobile and self-serving. These changes to the global workforce are challenging our traditional assumptions regarding how we develop and deliver learning, as well as our assumptions about the role of HRD. We will look at a number of these challenges and consider how modern organizations are embracing these changes by rethinking how they operate to link their business needs with their HRD activities.

While a lot of studies of work and employment consider the employment relationship from the perspective of 'regular' full-time employees, recent years have seen a dramatic shift in how we view the way people work. Full and part-time employees work for the organization that employs them and uses their services, with the organization controlling how work is done. The distinction between full and part-time is based on the number of hours worked, with part-time workers generally working fewer than 35 hours per week. Benefits are typically less, as are career prospects, in part due to the reduced number of opportunities for participation in HRD activities offered to part-time employees. Over 30 per cent of workers in Europe (Eurostat, 2013a) and over 20 per cent of workers in the US (Cappelli and Keller, 2013) fall outside the regular categorization of employment. Instead of distinguishing between just full-time and part-time workers, Cappelli and Keller (2013) identify ten different types of working arrangements that organizations can use. These include relatively common arrangements such as temporary employees (employed on a short-term basis to complement the workforce, e.g. seasonal employees) and on-call employees (employees who do not have a regular schedule for work and are called into work only when needed, although they can be scheduled to work for several days or weeks in a row).

Workers are coming from an increasingly fragmented supply of labour, however. This includes:

- Professional Employer Organizations (PEOs) are administrative organizations that engage in a contractual relationship with their client organizations. PEOs do not provide labour to worksites; instead, an organization transfers their current workforce to a third-party agency. The workers stay put, often doing the same tasks with similar terms and conditions of employment, but legal responsibility for the employees is transferred to the PEO (Cappelli and Keller, 2013). The PEO industry had a growth rate of 386 per cent between 1992 and 2002, and was estimated to employ two to three million Americans as of 2009 (Lombardi and Ono, 2008). There are over 700 PEOs in the US but significantly fewer in Europe, possibly due to important differences in health insurance, pensions and taxes.
- Leased employees are employed by an agency, working alongside regular employees for the organization that controls the work to be carried out, but the leasing agency retains control over recruitment and selection, compensation and termination.
- Independent contractors work for themselves and are not employees of an organization; they are employed to carry out specific work by an organization, but how the work is done is up to the independent contractor. This type of work is generally done on a project basis.
- Vendor on premises is an arrangement whereby an organization contracts with a vendor to perform work. Those who perform the work are either employed by or are engaged as independent contractors by the vendor. The vendor controls how work is done and it is the vendor who is responsible for payment of wages, recruitment and selection, and termination.
- Agency temporary workers, whereby an agency provides workers to an organization for short-term assignments. Workers return to the agency once the work is completed.

Bonet *et al.* (2013) use the term 'labour market intermediaries' (LMIs) to describe these groups that stand between the individual worker and the organization that needs work done, and expand it to include social media sites, executive search firms and online job boards. To put this in context, China's job51.com claims to have resumes for 63 million individuals (51job.com, 2013), while LinkedIn has 238 million members in over 200 countries, and two million companies worldwide have LinkedIn pages (LinkedIn, 2013), where the vast majority of activity is either individuals looking for new jobs or employers seeking out candidates for job vacancies.

Whereas the traditional employment relationship is generally thought of as a two-way process between the individual and the organization, the use of LMIs creates 'triangular relationships that complicate the workplace' (Bonet *et al.*, 2013: 346). Cascio (2007: 6) identifies the five main activities of the HR function in an organization as being staffing, retention, development, adjustment and managing change. The introduction of third parties into these main functions blurs the boundaries as to where responsibility lies. For example, how committed will individuals be to an organization if their contract is with an agency? Who is responsible for training and development of employees – the agency or the organization? What opportunities for career advancement exist in frequent but short-term bouts of employment with different organizations? Bonet *et al.* (2013) highlight that these new work arrangements are likely to diminish the incentives of firms to invest in workers (p. 370). Benner *et al.* (2007) looked at instances where LMIs did provide training and found little evidence that it helped workers get ready for specific jobs or build successful careers, partly because the LMI often had limited knowledge about what skills were necessary in the client organization. Another important implication from an HRD perspective is that LMI workers are likely to make the jobs of an organization's 'normal' employees more demanding because they typically have less firm-specific knowledge, receive little training and orientation from the client, and therefore need more help and time from regular employees, which is rarely compensated (Broschak and Davis-Blake, 2006).

Technology

Most of you reading this book will probably be taking an HRD module in a traditional classroom setting where you physically attend lectures for two to three hours per week and do additional reading and assignments in your own time outside the university or college. This is the customary module for training and development in organizations too – in 2007, over 80 per cent of training and development in Irish organizations was delivered in a classroom-based setting (Garavan *et al.*, 2007). Technological advancements have transformed the landscape of how we now view HRD. The percentage of the world's population with internet access has doubled between 2006 and 2013, with more than 40 per cent of people able to use the internet. The proliferation of broadband and fibre optic communication services has enabled us to consume vast amounts of media, while the growth in cloud computing services such as BambooHR, Dropbox and Office 365 gives both individuals and organizations access to a wide variety of sophisticated services online. Included in these services is the opportunity for online learning (or e-learning).

E-learning is a broad category of learning methods that use digital technologies to enable, distribute and enhance learning (Fee, 2009). These technologies offer a variety of different opportunities to learners and arguably enhance the quality of education and learning (Ladyshewsky and Taplin, 2013). In the early 2000s, e-learning generally referred to a person accessing company intranets or web-based and CD/DVD-based modules at their computer, and initial proponents argued that e-learning would revolutionize the way in which training and development was delivered and that it would fundamentally alter the work of HRD specialists (Sloman, 2001; Dobbs and Smith, 2002). The poor design and lack of interaction with early e-learning technologies was characterized by high drop-out rates (McLaren, 2004) and negative learning experiences (Song *et al.*, 2004), with negative attitudes in smaller organizations where it is less frequently resourced, supported and recognized (Garavan *et al.*, 2010).

With the advent of Web 2.0 technologies that encourage collaboration, interaction and sharing of knowledge between users, some of the early revolutionary claims surrounding e-learning have begun to be realized. According to O'Leonard (2013), 'technology has made it possible for workers to collaborate in ways that were almost unimaginable a decade ago' (p. 13). Social media and networking platforms include virtual learning environments, webinars and other forms of networked e-learning; social media such as Twitter, LinkedIn and Facebook; and the integration of smartphone technology into the learning environment and the use of connected apps. The number of US organizations using wikis for learning purposes increased from 7 per cent in 2007 to 24 per cent in 2012, while the use of **communities of practice (CoPs)** increased from 11 per cent to 33 per cent over the same period (O'Leonard, 2013). Over a quarter of organizations now use social media sites such as Facebook and Twitter for learning and development purposes.

ASTD (2012) estimate that approximately 37 per cent of the overall expenditure in US organizations

communities of practice (CoPs) a group of individuals who share a common interest in a topic, and who deepen their knowledge of it through ongoing interaction and relationship building in their group

is on **e-learning**. According to O'Leonard (2013), US organizations spent an average of $13,675 per employee on social learning tools and services in 2012, a 39 per cent increase over 2011 expenditure. Large organizations spent more than $46,000 per employee on average in 2012, nearly three times what they were spending in 2010. ASTD (2012) also note the increasing popularity of mobile delivery of training on smartphones and tablets.

While initial attempts at e-learning were focused on providing formal training or development courses to the end user without significant interaction or involvement on their part, organizations are now focused on delivering learning content that is available to their employees regardless of time or location, and they use technology to make sure the learning function is always on with social networks, specific resources and online courses instantly available to support employees within their jobs. Social learning tools allow a more blended style of delivery in which, for example, formal courses are combined with e-learning activities such as online discussion forums and web-based activities. More successful organizations create 'employee networks, connecting novices to experts through expertise directories, and sharing knowledge through CoPs. In this way, social learning, combined with formal programmes, experiential learning, and ongoing support and reinforcement, is facilitating a shift from blended training programmes to continuous learning environments' (p. 13). Sitzmann (2011) carried out an analysis of studies looking at the effectiveness of e-learning and found that people who participated in e-learning activities had 11 per cent higher knowledge of facts, 14 per cent higher knowledge of skills, and 9 per cent higher retention levels than those who received alternative instruction methods. In addition, their confidence that they have learned the information taught and can perform training-related tasks was 20 per cent higher.

In 2013, the MIT Center for Business predicted that, technology-wise, the next ten years would be even more disruptive than the previous ten. One area that has implications for HRD is the proliferation of massive open online courses (MOOCs). MOOCs have already had a major impact on the education sector. A MOOC is a college or university course just like the one you are currently taking, except that it is designed for thousands of students, can be taken by anyone with an internet connection, and all content assessment is delivered online. The key attraction of MOOCs is that the vast majority of them are currently offered for free. EdX, founded in May 2012 by Harvard University (where individual MOOCs

e-learning a broad term that includes computer-based training, technology-based learning and web-based learning activities

have over 30,000 students enrolled) and MIT, pledged $60 million of its own money for MOOC development, and is now a consortium of 28 institutions. FutureLearn, headed by the Open University, which pioneered distance learning in the 1970s, is a consortium of British, Irish and Australian universities, which began offering MOOCs in 2013. Students are expected to keep pace with the content and their assessment receives regular evaluation from groups of tutors; just like a regular course, at the end, they either pass or fail. While the goal of these offerings is primarily to democratize education and allow as many people as possible to participate in courses that appeal to them, given the costs involved in setting up MOOCs, institutions have looked at various ways to recoup some of their investments. Another MOOC provider, Coursera, charges for the provision of certificates for those who complete its courses and want proof, perhaps for a future employer. Udacity, a competing MOOC provider, works with organizations to train current and future employees. It has links to several firms, including Google, and recently formed a partnership with AT&T, along with Georgia Tech, to offer a master's degree in computer science. One possible outcome of this technology is that larger organizations are afforded the possibility to centralize their HRD activities, so that an employee in Dublin can participate in the same training course as an employee in San Francisco, or organizations could have a single induction course delivered for their new employees worldwide in a MOOC format instead of having each geographic location delivering separate programmes. It also leaves the possibility of large organizations licensing their own training courses to smaller enterprises that may not have the resources to develop their own. What smaller-sized organization wouldn't want access to IBM's or General Electric's selection of training programmes, for example?

CONSIDER THIS ...

Would you prefer your education to be carried out online or in a classroom? Proponents of MOOCs hype the advantages in terms of widening access to education, but one aspect that is overlooked is the social side of education. Many of your friends probably date from your time spent in school or college, and these social networks tend to be long-lasting. How will these networks be developed online?

Another aspect of HRD facilitated by technology is the increase in virtual organizations. Virtual organizations are composed of a number of individuals, departments or organizations, each of which has a range of capabilities and resources at their disposal (Norman *et al.*, 2004). These organizations are created in order to share resources and services along with the possibility of exploiting a perceived gap in the market. One example of this is Wikimedia Foundation, which has many thousands of members globally. The main aspect of Wikimedia's work is Wikipedia. Another example is Dell Computers, who rely on a vast array of partners to supply various aspects of the parts necessary to manufacture their products. Most of the components in a Dell computer are made by other companies while Dell focuses on its strengths – marketing, customer support and integration of these components into the final computer products. The delivery of HRD activities in virtual organizations is complicated somewhat by the geographic dispersion of employees and tends to be done via intranets. Bennett (2009) suggests that virtual HRD involves 'a media-rich and culturally relevant Web environment that strategically improves expertise, performance, innovation, and community building through formal and informal learning'. Cloud computing services described earlier have facilitated the growth in the virtual HRD services.

SPOTLIGHT ON SKILLS

Working as an HRD manager, you have been asked to justify your expenditure on HRD programmes undertaken by the organization over the past 12 months. How can you demonstrate the value of HRD? Will you focus on the value to the organization, to employees, or both?

To help you answer the questions above, visit www. macmillanihe.com/companion/carbery-hrd and watch the video of Jemma Carty talking about the value of HRD.

Globalization

Globalization is understood as growth in the integration of national economies and is driven by powerful economic factors including market cost and competitive factors. Examples of market factors include the growth of common customer preferences, largely created by successful global branding. In terms of cost, globalization is said to offer the advantages of economies of scale and standardization such as cost advantages in advertising, material sourcing and economies of scale due to larger market potential. It has reduced the requirement for manual work and fostered new kinds of skills such as those found in customer service work and call centres. Countries, companies and employees are now interconnected more than ever before, with global labour markets driving both organizational and worker mobility. Competition for employees does not only come from a competitor in the same region or city, but also from the employer on the other side of the world. The challenge for organizations is how best to become an employer of choice.

Since the early 2000s, there has been a lot of discussion regarding how countries and organizations can move towards a 'Smart Economy' or 'Knowledge Economy'. This basically involves an up-skilling of workers, greater employee involvement and greater innovation, not only in products and processes but also in how work is organized. The term 'knowledge worker' was proposed by Drucker (1989) to describe individuals who carry knowledge as a powerful resource that they, rather than the organization, own. Organizations must learn quickly, drawing on information from many external as well as internal sources, in order to be able to repeatedly improve and innovate. Sustained competitive advantage depends on the rapid generation and application of 'dynamic capabilities', defined as the firm's ability to integrate, build and reconfigure uniquely valuable competencies (Eisenhardt and Santos, 2002). Venkatraman and Subramaniam (2002) argue that the key resources that drive value creation are knowledge and expertise. Managing knowledge employees requires the HRD function to produce and promote processes and initiatives to support the acquisition of subject matter expertise, learning to identify and deal with new problems, cultivating reflective skills, acquiring communication and social skills, supporting self-regulation of motivation, affinities and emotions, promoting peace and stability, and stimulating creative turmoil (Kessels,

2001). This means that those responsible for HRD need to act as facilitators of learning and promote a culture of learning throughout organizations rather than focus primarily on job-specific training.

Corporate social responsibility (CSR) and business ethics

A multitude of corporate scandals in the last 10–15 years and collapse of financial institutions during the GFC have led to calls for greater links between HRD, CSR and business ethics. In particular, the economic and social impact resulting from the GFC has called into question the role of HRD in many failed financial institutions (MacKenzie *et al.*, 2014). Capitalistic ideologies have taken a lot of the blame for these failures, and, while capitalism appears beyond the scope of responsibility for the HRD profession, cultures, rewards, leadership development and employee performance are important parts of the role that HRD plays in developing organizations and their human capital to sustain results and achieve competitive advantage (Bierema, 2009). We will look at the relationship between HRD, CSR and ethics in Chapter 14.

Management of diversity

The diversity of the leadership pool in organizations has become a major issue. Under-represented group members of all types (gays and lesbians, people with disabilities, and those who are obese, in addition to women, lower socioeconomic status individuals, and 'non-White', ethnically diverse employees) are typically provided with fewer HRD opportunities than other groups of employees. It has long been recognized that gender and racial inequality is a problem (Ayman and Korabik, 2010) for many organizations when it comes to their leadership populations. Women and people of colour are significantly under-represented in senior management positions. Eagly and Chin (2010) argue that discrimination remains commonplace in organizations, primarily in more subtle, covert and unintentional forms, suggesting that the majority of managerial roles have become infused with masculinity. This has the effect of excluding particular groups from leadership roles, including women and minority groups based on race, ethnicity and sexual orientation. Individuals from these categories have fewer networking, mentoring and leadership development opportunities (Ardichvili and Manderscheid, 2008).

Females have generally performed better in education than men, without necessarily receiving the same career opportunities as men. Now, however, single childless females under the age of 30 are earning more than men of the same age in the US. With the majority of those in third-level education also being female, this gap is going to widen further. For family-related reasons, women tend to cede this advantage over time as they put their career on hold, to have children, for example. This presents two issues from an HRD perspective. First, women find it particularly difficult to return to work at the same level due to a perceived suspicion that either their skills are outdated or they no longer have the required commitment deemed necessary for the job. Second, if women are, paradoxically, better educated and trained for work, how can men be enabled to pick up the slack when women reduce their commitment to work?

HOW IS HRD RELATED TO HRM?

Those of you taking a module or course in HRD will probably have already taken a HRM module as part of your studies. Wilson (2012) highlights that most university courses at both post-graduate and undergraduate levels incorporate HRD within broader HRM disciplines, giving the impression that HRD is a subsidiary to HRM. This can often confuse matters as to the distinctiveness of HRD.

The confusion exists in organizations too. Mankin (2009) highlights that HRD roles in organizations were traditionally included within the HRM department, where the individuals involved often had very little background or training in HRD due to the ambiguous nature of HRD. The key role of the HRM function is to enable the organization to achieve its strategic objectives and to positively impact organizational effectiveness by dealing effectively with all aspects of the employment relationship. Ideally, HRD should be seen as a partner to HRM rather than subservient to it, under the broader title of human resources.

As the organizational chart in Figure 1.3 highlights, the human resources function is involved in enabling growth, productivity and profitability, through the creation of complementary HRM and HRD strategies, in line with the overall business strategy. These strategies are plans that address and solve fundamental strategic issues related to the management of human resources in an organization. HRM and HRD strategies are used to create a set of complementary policies designed to achieve the organization's strategic goals. These policies are then

Figure 1.3 Organizational chart

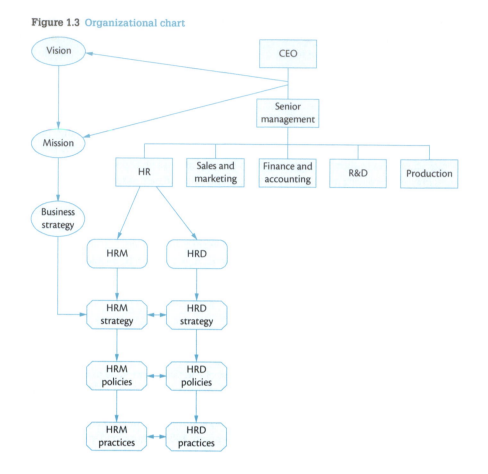

translated into specific HRM and HRD practices, again aimed at meeting the strategic goals.

The chart highlights that HRD should have a strategic role ▶ Chapter 2. HRD practitioners are responsible for learning and development, talent management and career development, among other strategic roles;

therefore, it can be argued that identifying human capital (Ulrich and Brockbank, 2005) goes beyond developing talented individuals already within the organization to helping the HRM function identify, select, recruit, manage, motivate and retain those people considered necessary to achieve organizational goals and objectives.

People Analytics at Google

In 2013, for the fourth consecutive year, Forbes named Google the best company in the world to work for. The likes of Facebook and Apple did not even make the list. The reasons for Google being considered so great to work for are legendary, and it is almost a cliché of ever increasing luxuries – from 100,000 hours of subsidized massages per year to paying 50 per cent of an employee's salary after their death to their spouse or domestic partner for ten years. Increasingly, however, more attention is being paid to how they develop their staff.

Google call their HR department 'People Operations', and in recent years they have applied the same data-gathering and analysis techniques that they apply to web searches and consumer behaviour to managing and developing employees. In 2009, Google recognized that they had a problem with their managers; most of Google's employees hated them, most notably their prized engineering team! Among engineering teams,

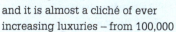

there is often the perception that management is a necessary evil. Google's engineering employees reported that management stifled their creativity and were overly concerned with bureaucracy. The People Operations team were tasked with initiating a project (which became known as Project Oxygen) to see whether managers mattered.

Unlike gathering information on your browsing history to target you with ads that you might like, gathering information on human interactions and behaviours is much more challenging and subjective. The team gathered over 100,000 observations from approximately 100 variables on managers in Google, looking at data gathered from performance reviews, feedback surveys and interviews.

When the findings revealed that managers were a fundamental part of the organization and that good managers increased both job satisfaction and employee retention within their teams and the organization as a whole, the focus of the project shifted to determine how Google could develop better managers. Eight behaviours for great managers were identified. There was nothing particularly earth-shattering about the behaviours identified – they include 'be a good coach', 'empower the team and do not micro-manage', 'help with career development', 'express interest/ concern for members' success and personal well-being' and 'use your technical skills to advise'. Google

traditionally had a *laissez-faire* approach to management, taking the view that employees should be left alone to do their work, and if they had a technical problem they would approach a manager. However, when the project team ranked the eight behaviours, they found that technical skills received the lowest ranking. What Google's engineers valued most was a manager who acted as a coach and mentor, asking questions to stimulate thinking rather than prescribing answers, and who showed an interest in the employee's life.

Once Google had their list of eight behaviours, they started teaching it in training programmes, as well as in coaching and performance review sessions with individual employees. Performance reviews in Google are carried out every three months on a 360-degree basis, i.e. an employee's performance is reviewed by both their subordinates and their managers. One of the most challenging aspects of facilitating the development of effective managers was getting managers to commit to receiving performance reviews from people who reported to them. The project team spent several months developing tactics to make Project Oxygen more appealing to Google's senior management. Tactics were established from the bottom of the corporate structure, encouraging junior employees to make their voices heard. Top-level managers were asked to make their own manager scores public to

encourage mid-level management to take part. Those managers who received low ratings were given one-to-one coaching for periods of up to six months by dedicated in-house coaches to focus on improving the behaviours on which employees scored them low.

The simplicity of the behaviours belies how successful the project has been – Google cite an improvement in performance for three-quarters of their worst-performing managers as a result of the initiative. Unlike management books or articles providing guidance on how to be a better manager or leader, Google developed a framework that was unique to their own organizational context and gathered data on what worked in Google, rather than what worked in other organizations.

Sources

Garvin, David A., Alison Berkley Wagonfeld, and Liz Kind. 'Google's Project Oxygen: Do Managers Matter?' Harvard Business School Case 313–110, April 2013.

http://hbr.org/search/313110

Google's Quest to Build a Better Boss

http://www.nytimes.com/2011/03/13/business/13hire.html

Questions

1 What role did HRD play in making Google's managers more effective?
2 If these behaviours are so straightforward, why isn't everyone a great boss?
3 How could other organizations go about devising their own essential managerial behaviours?

Table 1.3 Main activities of the human resources function

Organization level	Employee resourcing	Inducting, developing and retaining employees	Managing the employment relationship	Exiting employees	Employee and organization welfare
Strategy formulation and development	Human resource planning	Induction	Managing disciplinary issues	Managing poor performers	Health and safety
	Recruitment	Performance management	Grievance handling	Dismissal	Employee wellbeing
	Selection	Motivating employees	Managing redundancy	Employee turnover	Counselling
	Providing contracts	Managing rewards	Negotiation	Employment legislation	Organization climate
	Managing expatriation	Learning and development	Managing employee relations		Corporate social responsibility and ethics
		Career development	Providing fair and equal treatment of employees		Employee assistance programmes
		Talent management	Managing diversity		
			Conflict resolution		

In *Human Resource Management: A Concise Introduction* (2013) we looked at the main activities of the HRM function (see Table 1.3). By highlighting the distinct areas that fall under HRD in pale blue, and the overlapping areas of responsibility in dark blue, we can see how both areas are partners in the overall human resources function.

BUILDING YOUR SKILLS

It is estimated that the average cost of replacing an employee who leaves an organization is between 10 and 30 per cent of their yearly salary (due to productivity losses, the costs of hiring and training a new employee, slower productivity until the new employee gets up to speed in their new job). In Analog Devices in Limerick, Ireland, the cost of hiring one new engineer is approximately €80,000. Investing in employees' training and development can be a powerful retention tool. If training and development is expensive, it pales in comparison to the cost of replacing an employee!

What arguments would you make to persuade a senior manager of an organization of the benefits to be gained from investing in HRD activities?

WHO IS RESPONSIBLE FOR HRD?

Responsibility for HRD is a fraught area for individuals, organizations and society. Should governments subsidize third-level education? Should benefits be withheld from those who are unemployed unless they undergo some form of training and development? Should organizations finance or part-finance programmes such as degree programmes or MBAs for their employees? Or should individuals bear the cost of these development activities themselves?

Changes in organizations as a result of globalization and advancements in technology discussed earlier have led to a revised notion of the traditional career contract, resulting in less commitment and willingness to retain individuals on the part of employers. An individual retiring at the age of 65 in 2014 is likely to have, on average, changed employers over 11 times over the course of their life (Bureau of Labor Statistics, 2012). For those of you entering the workforce for the first time in the near future, the picture is very different. Those born between 1977 and 1997 expect to change jobs every two to three years (Future Workplace, 2012). This lack of job security thus places the onus on individuals to take control of their future employability. Job security is being replaced with security based on the individual's value in the marketplace. Organizations are now adopting greater flexibility in terms of business risks to employees through the introduction of share ownership, profit sharing and profit-related pay schemes and differentiating between core and peripheral employees. Employees are simultaneously seeking individualized opportunities that fit their career and work–family relationships and therefore expect greater flexibility on the part of their employer to provide opportunities for the achievement of these goals.

In order to consider responsibility for HRD and how this impacts on people's careers, we must consider the nature of the psychological contract. **Psychological contracts** are the individual belief systems held by employees and employers regarding their mutual obligations to each other (Rousseau, 1995). Employment relationships are subjectively interpreted and experienced by individuals and their employers. How each understands their obligations to and agreements with the other constitutes the psychological contract. The content of the psychological contract is twofold (Rousseau, 1995). First, it is transactional, where the focus is on specific monetary exchanges which are short-term in focus and include working longer hours and accepting new job roles and responsibilities in exchange for increased pay and training and development benefits (Herriot and Pemberton, 1997). Second, it is relational, with the focus being on loyalty and discretionary behaviour in exchange for job security, financial rewards, and training and development opportunities. If the psychological contract is relational, individuals tend to identify with the organization, promoting support for the organization's efforts to improve performance (Rousseau and Tijoriwala, 1999). It should be noted that transactional and relational psychological contracts are not mutually exclusive; all contracts contain elements of both, but the contract may lean more towards one or the other.

Transactional psychological contracts have given rise to 'i-deals' (Rousseau, 2005) – idiosyncratic deals that individuals negotiate with their employer regarding terms that mutually benefit both parties. They are voluntary, personalized agreements of a non-standardized nature that vary in scope from a

psychological contracts the unwritten rules and expectations that exist between the employee and employer

single feature to the entire employment relationship. For example, an employee studying part-time for a degree programme may have to work fewer weekends than other employees, but otherwise share the same job duties, pay scales etc. The market power of individuals and/or the value the employer places on them enable employees to engage in individualized bargaining. When the work offered is neither highly standardized nor easily monitored or where it is scarce, individuals are in a position to exert considerable bargaining power. This level of power allows the individual to decide when, how and for whom to be productive.

The emphasis on the need for people to take responsibility for their own learning is the premise of what is known as lifelong learning. In the early part of the 2000s, the EU claimed that lifelong learning was necessary for individuals to adapt to more knowledge-based work and defined lifelong learning as an 'all purposeful learning activity, undertaken on an on-going basis, with the aim of improving knowledge, skill and competence' (European Commission, 2000). While broader in scope than workplace learning, in the context of the employment relationship lifelong learning can be viewed as an approach for helping people adapt to change in the workplace and for enhancing employability in the wider labour marker (Rainbird, 2000). From an organizational perspective, investment in lifelong learning has been found to have positive effects on individuals' psychological contracts and, significantly, transferring what they learn on HRD programmes to the workplace (Pate *et al.*, 2000). Advocates of lifelong learning claim that it plays an important role in enhancing economic competitiveness, but there is a risk in the European approach to lifelong learning, in that, by making individuals responsible for their own learning, it may polarize the workforce into learners and non-learners. Keep (2000) points out that, as most employer-provided training is usually job specific and aimed towards those in certain occupations, an inequitable distribution of wider HRD opportunities defeats the concept of both lifelong learning and employability, which in turn leaves those most in need of training and development with the fewest opportunities for broader, transferable learning activities. For the majority of workers, the workplace represents the sole location to develop and/or learn their vocational practice (Billet, 2004). Keep (1997) highlights that, even though there are good reasons for policy makers to place greater emphasis on individuals' responsibility for learning, structural and societal barriers are in existence for many learners. Habitually, the least skilled and least qualified are more likely to be unemployed than those with higher educational qualifications. In a system where there are neither individual rights of access to training nor an obligation on employers to invest in training, the aforementioned emphasis on the learner could be expected to reinforce patterns of inequality in access. This leads us to look at how HRD is practised at a national level.

NATIONAL HRD

National HRD (NHRD) is a broad term and approaches HRD from the perspective of governments and society. It combines all activities related to human development to create greater efficiency, effectiveness, competitiveness, satisfaction, productivity, knowledge and wellbeing of its citizens. It includes education, health, safety, training, economic development, culture, science and technology. Gibb (2011) identifies three elements of NHRD: large-scale public HRD programmes that focus on addressing disadvantaged groups of a population; private HRD programmes that are highly fragmented and driven by specific organizational objectives; and partnership HRD programmes that combine private and public bodies.

McLean (2004) outlines a number of reasons why it is important to look at HRD from a national perspective. For example, for a number of countries, human resources are their primary resource. For countries without significant natural resources, they need look at how their human resources can meet the needs of their people. Japan and Korea have succeeded because of the emphasis placed on developing human resources in the absence of access to abundant natural resources. Human resources are also important for national and local stability. Countries that do not have sustainable development policies, combined with high unemployment rates leading to high levels of poverty, reflect a lack of stability at a national level. Developing human resources is one approach to addressing these conditions. NHRD policies may also help in increasing productivity by facilitating the development of individuals' capacity to produce high-quality goods and services. Third, if the cycles of welfare, poverty,

violence, unemployment, illiteracy and socially undesirable employment are to be broken, integrated and coordinated mechanisms for people to develop need to be provided. In addition, HRD has the potential to improve individuals' quality of life at work.

NHRD policies driven by governments generally range from engagement in education from childhood onwards to retraining mature individuals. These policies are usually developed in conjunction with other agencies in order to develop a skilled and knowledgeable workforce. An important part of this is vocational education and training (VET), defined by Cedefop (2008) as 'education and training which aims to equip people with knowledge, know-how, skills and/or competences required in particular occupations or more broadly on the labour market' (p. 202). VET focuses on two distinct areas – initial VET (IVET) and continuous VET (CVET) (Cedefop, 2008). IVET refers to general or vocational education and training carried out in the initial education system, usually before entering working life. Some training undertaken after entry into working life may be considered as initial training (e.g. retraining). Initial education and training can be carried out at any level in general or vocational education (full-time school-based or alternate training) pathways or apprenticeship. Apprenticeships are very much part of the industrial cultural landscape of countries such as Germany, Austria, Switzerland and Denmark, whereas the likes of France, Spain and Italy tend to follow more school-based vocational education approaches (Nyhan, 2009). CVET addresses education or training that comes in after entry into working life and looks at helping people improve or update their knowledge and/or skills; acquire new skills for a career move or retraining; or continue their personal or professional development (Cedefop, 2008).

Governments tend to promote VET as a tool for improving competitiveness, growth rates and job prospects, and promoting social inclusion. At the Lisbon Council in 2000 the EU institutions, Member States and social partners made a commitment to devise policies to modernize their education and training systems to make them the best in the world by 2010. With this date having long passed and mixed progress made on the overly aspirational goal, there is a danger that NHRD and VET policies will become sidelined as countries continue to deal with the fallout from the GFC.

The huge breadth and variation in NHRD and VET policies from one country to the next makes a detailed comparison beyond the scope of this book (for those of you who want more information see Wilson (2012) for an excellent overview), but Cho and McLean (2004) proposed five NHRD categories that separated developed, developing and transitional economies based on the extent to which the role of national HRD strategy was centralized or decentralized. The first, a centralized NHRD model, is where there is a top-down, state-driven approach to education, the government plays a critical role in the development of HRD policy, and HRD addresses social and moral needs. This approach persists in China, Poland and Mexico, for example. The second, a transitional NHRD approach as seen in India, Singapore and Brazil, is where governments, employers and unions take a tripartite approach to HRD policy. HRD policy is designed to meet economic and social needs. Third, a government-initiated approach towards standardization sees uniformity of aspects of HRD as a main element. National frameworks are established with a network of smaller agencies tasked with delivering policies and the private sector is pressured to comply. This approach is characteristic of the UK, Ireland, Australia and South Africa. The US and Canada are examples of the fourth type, a decentralized or free-market NHRD model, where education and training is for the private sector and the government supports individual and private sector initiatives. The fifth model is the small-nation approach to NHRD, where there is cooperation between regions via the establishment of regional intergovernmental bodies. Nations in the Pacific Islands cooperate together, while St Lucia cooperates with other small countries in the Caribbean to gain the benefit of sharing resources.

Another important consideration is the current issue regarding increasing the mandatory retirement age for workers. For example, in Ireland, along with numerous advanced countries, the ratio of people aged 66 and over to working-age population is set to rise dramatically, with financial pressure on fewer workers and taxpayers to provide for more pensions. The official retirement age dates back to the late 1880s and the then German Chancellor, Otto von Bismarck, who, when faced with a challenge by rival socialist parties, proposed that states had a duty of care to older workers. He duly set a retirement age of 70, even though the average life expectancy of Germans was just over 60 years at the time! In 1916, Germany lowered the retirement age to 65, with most countries following suit, and in 1935, the US also set 65 as the retirement age (even though the average life expectancy of a US citizen in 1935 was 60 for a male and 64 for a female).

In 2013, life expectancy at birth is over 80 years in the majority of developed countries. With the increase in life expectancy, retirement at 65 makes much less sense when people can look forward to another 20 or so years of life. Increasing the retirement age has been suggested as a possible solution, but this requires significant investment on the part of both employers and employees. Recent legislation in the UK will also increase the state retirement age – to 67 between 2026 and 2028, followed by future increases linked to life expectancy. This is likely to see many of you now in education not retiring until you are in your 70s. Ireland has also enacted legislation that will see the retirement age increased to 68 by 2040. However, many organizations tend to discriminate against older workers in terms of access to training and development opportunities. For countries where the retirement age is raised, individuals themselves need to prepare for longer working lives and ensure that they remain employable by updating their knowledge and skills.

HRD IN SMALL ORGANIZATIONS

HRD in small to medium enterprises (SMEs) tends to be very different from that of larger organizations. A lot of the treatment of HRD neglects to look at SMEs and focuses on large organizations. In the European Union, over 23 million SMEs provide around 75 million jobs and represent 99 per cent of all enterprises (European Commission, 2013). In 2003, the EU defined a SME as one that employs fewer than 250 employees (European Commission, 2003). As part of this definition, a micro company has fewer than 10 employees, a small company has fewer than 50 employees, and a medium-sized company has fewer than 250.

Kitching (2008) highlights that SMEs have fewer dedicated training departments and budgets, while Hoque and Bacon (2008) found inferior levels of training provision and quality, and less participation in government training schemes (Matlay, 2004). HRD in SMEs is also hindered due to financial resources (Castany, 2010) resulting in a shortage of management skills and provision of training. Many SMEs often do not recognise the value of HRD. SME strategy tends to be indicative of the personality of the owner-manager, and Barnes (2002) found that the intentions of owner-managers are generally not expressed in formal policies or plans. This unstructured approach to planning and strategy implementation is a significant barrier to

HRD. HRD in SMEs tends to follow the same pattern as that experienced by its owner-manager (Nolan, 2002). Professionally trained and qualified owner-managers often place more value on HRD, whereas those who learned through the process of apprenticeship consider the informal approach to be the optimum one (Matlay, 1999). Those who created their companies themselves with little formal schooling or education may take the view that 'if it's good enough for me, it's good enough for my staff' when it comes to training and development.

The types of HRD practices that exist in SMEs tend to be informal in nature (Kitching and Blackburn, 2002). These are an important part of work routines in SMEs, helping employees develop skills, but are often not perceived as being 'proper training'. Examples of these informal practices include trial and error (Birdthistle, 2006); using one employee who trains in a new skill and passes the skill on or cascades it 'down' to colleagues (Rigg and Trehan, 2002); rotation of employees between jobs to enable multi-skilling (Scott and Cockrill, 1997); assigning a particular employee who can provide advice to others (Kitching, 2008); and the use of informal talks where more skilled employees provide instruction, advice and knowledge to other staff members (Raffo *et al.*, 2000).

Each of the chapters in this book will consider how HRD in smaller organizations differs from larger organizations under each of the remaining 13 topics.

STRUCTURE OF THE BOOK

The remainder of the book is structured into three parts. Section 1 (*Fundamentals of HRD*) first looks at Strategic HRD, and outlines why HRD should be a strategic business activity. Managing the HRD Function discusses the roles and responsibilities of the HRD function in organizations; Individual-Level Learning considers how we learn and looks at the different types of learning; Organizational Learning examines learning in organizations and whether organizations themselves can learn; and Organization Development then looks at ways in which HRD can facilitate changes needed in organizations to help them achieve particular goals and objectives.

Section 2 (*Process of HRD*) is made up of four chapters, each addressing an important stage in the cyclical manner in which HRD activities unfold. First, Identifying Learning Needs outlines why and

Figure 1.4 Process of HRD cycle

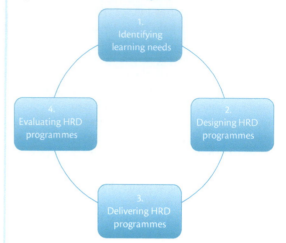

how training needs are identified before any HRD activity; Designing HRD Programmes looks at the second stage in the process and tackles the design of HRD programmes and activities; Delivering HRD Programmes then assesses the most effective ways HRD activities can be provided; finally, Evaluating HRD Programmes considers the importance of evaluating whether or not the activities were effective, and, if not, why not. The model presented in Figure 1.4 illustrates the process of the HRD cycle and will be revisited in each of these chapters.

The third part of the book, Section 3 (*Contemporary Challenges*), comprises four chapters that consider topics that are particularly relevant in a contemporary climate. Managing Talented Employees looks at the role HRD plays in identifying and managing talented employees; Leadership Development reflects on the importance of leadership and management development and how it differs from other types of HRD activities; Graduate Employability focuses on developing graduates' employability and asks what role HRD plays in facilitating graduate employability; and the final chapter, Ethics, Corporate Social Responsibility, Sustainability and HRD, examines the relationship between these topics and asks whether CSR and Business Ethics should be an important consideration for HRD, and whether HRD can facilitate an ethical culture in organizations.

One aspect of HRD that is not covered in this book is career development. However, there is a chapter devoted to this in our earlier text, *Human Resource Management: A Concise Introduction* (2013).

Please see Figure 1.5 for the layout of the book.

Figure 1.5 Layout of book

Human Resource Development: A Concise Introduction

Fundamentals of HRD
2. Strategic HRD
3. Managing the HRD function
4. Individual-level learning
5. Organizational learning
6. Organization development

Contemporary challenges
11. Managing talented employees
12. Leadership development
13. Graduate employability
14. Ethics, corporate social responsibility, sustainability and HRD

Process of HRD
7. Identifying learning needs
8. Designing HRD programmes
9. Delivering HRD programmes
10. Evaluating HRD programmes

CONCLUSION

In this chapter we have seen that the term 'HRD' has increasingly replaced 'training' as the description of choice for the development of people in most organizations. By considering the major characteristics of HRD and looking at who is responsible for HRD, we see where the HRD function should fit into the organization's structure. The context in which HRD takes place is in a particular state of upheaval, and this will have major implications over the next decade or so.

The next chapter considers the link between business strategy and HRD so that we can understand how HRD adds value to an organization and see the link between HRD and organizational performance and the extent to which HRD can shape the strategic objectives of the business.

 CHAPTER REVIEW QUESTIONS

1 What do you understand by the term 'HRD'?
2 How do the terms 'training', 'development', 'learning' and 'education' differ?
3 What is the benefit of HRD for individuals and for organizations?
4 What do you see as the most important contextual factors that impact upon HRD?
5 Describe your own country's approach to HRD.
6 How does HRD differ from HRM?
7 Who should be responsible for HRD?
8 What accounts for the difference in approaches to HRD between SMEs and larger organizations?

FURTHER READING

Gibb, S. (2011) *Human Resource Development: Foundations, Processes, Context* (3rd ed.), Basingstoke: Palgrave Macmillan.

Gold, J., Holden, R., Iles, P., Stewart, J. and Beardwell, J. (2013) *Human Resource Development: Theory and Practice* (2nd ed.), Basingstoke: Palgrave Macmillan.

Hamlin, B. and Stewart, J. (2011) What is HRD? A Definitional Review and Synthesis of the HRD Domain, *Journal of European Industrial Training*, 35(3), 199–220.

Kitching, J. and Blackburn, R. (2002) *The Nature of Training and Motivation to Train in Small Firms*, DfES, London, Research Report RR330.

McGuire, D. and Jorgensen, K. M. (2010) *Human Resource Development: Theory and Practice*, London: Sage.

Wilson (2012) *International Human Resource Development: Learning, Education and Training for Individuals and Organisations* (3rd ed.), London: Kogan Page.

(WWW) USEFUL WEBSITES

CIPD: http://www.cipd.co.uk/
The Chartered Institute of Personnel and Development website is an excellent starting point for anyone interested in HRD. CIPD is based in the UK and Ireland and is the world's largest chartered HR and development professional body.

AHRD: http://ahrd.org/
The Academy of Human Resource Development is a global organization made up of a scholarly community of academics and reflective practitioners. The Academy studies human resource development theories, processes and practices and disseminates information about HRD through four affiliated peer-reviewed journals.

UFHRD: www.ufhrd.co.uk
The University Forum for Human Resource Development is a non-profit-making partnership that seeks to create, develop and inform leading-edge HRD theories and practices through an international network of universities, individuals and organizations promoting cooperative research initiatives.

ASTD: http://www.astd.org/
The American Society for Training and Development is a US-based association, founded in 1943, for workplace learning and performance professionals. ASTD focus on linking learning and performance to individual and organizational results, and provide a number of different resources including publication of research reports, analysis of training and development trends, benchmarking, online information, and book publishing.

Harvard Business Review: **http://hbr.org/ video/2761856636001/how-google-proved-management-matters**
In this video, watch how Google communicated the value of HR and management to a group of engineers.

BIBLIOGRAPHY

Aguinis, H. and Kraiger, K. (2009) Benefits of Training and Development for Individuals and Teams, Organisations, and Society, *The Annual Journal of Psychology*, 60, 451–474.

Ardichvili, A. and Manderscheid, S. (2008) Emerging Practices in Leadership Development: An Introduction, *Advances in Developing Human Resources*, 10(5), 619–631.

ASTD (2012) *State of the Industry Report*, Alexandria, VA: ASTD.

Ayman, R. and Korabik, K. (2010) Leadership: Why Gender and Culture Matter, *American Psychologist*, 65, 157–170.

Barnes, D. (2002) The Manufacturing Strategy Formation Process in Small and Medium-Sized Enterprises. *Journal of Small Business and Enterprise Development*, 9, 130–149.

Baum, T. (1995) *Managing Human Resources in the European Tourism and Hospitality Industry: A Strategic Approach*, London: Chapman and Hall.

Benner, C., Leete, L. and Pastor, M. (2007) *Staircases or Treadmills? Labor Market Intermediaries and Economic Opportunity in a Changing Economy*, New York: Russell Sage Foundation.

Bennett, E. (2009) Virtual HRD: The Intersection of Knowledge Management, Culture, and Intranets, *Advances in Developing Human Resources*, 11(3), 362–374.

Bergenhenegouwen, G. J. (1990) The Management and Effectiveness of Corporate Training Programmes, *British Journal of Educational Technology*, 21(3), 196–202.

Bierema, L. L. (2009) Critiquing Human Resource Development's Dominant Masculine Rationality and Evaluating Its Impact, *Human Resource Development Review*, 8(1), 68–96.

Birdthistle, N. (2006) Training and Learning Strategies of Family Businesses: An Irish Case, *Journal of European Industrial Training*, 30(7), 550–568.

Billet, S. (2004) Learning Through Work, In H. Rainbird, A. Fuller and A. Munro (Eds) *Workplace Learning in Context*, New York: Routledge, (109–125).

Bonet, R., Cappelli, P. and Hamori, M. (2013) Labor Market Intermediaries and the New Paradigm for Human Resources, *The Academy of Management Annals*, 7(1), 341–392.

Broschak, J. P. and Davis-Blake, A. (2006). Mixing Standard Work and Nonstandard Deals: The Consequences of Heterogeneity in Employment Arrangements, *Academy of Management Journal*, 49(2), 371–393.

Bureau of Labor Statistics (2012) *Number of Jobs Held, Labor Market Activity, and Earnings Growth among the Youngest Baby Boomers: Results from a Longitudinal Survey*, accessed 7 August at http://www.bls.gov/news.release/pdf/nlsoy.pdf

Cappelli, P. and Keller, J. R. (2013) A Study of the Extent and Potential Causes of Alternative Employment Arrangements, *Industrial and Labor Relations Review*, 6(4), 874–890.

Carbery, R. and Cross, C. (2013) *Human Resource Management: A Concise Introduction*, Basingstoke: Palgrave Macmillan.

Cascio, W. F. (2007) *Managing Human Resources: Productivity, Quality of Work Life, Profits*, New York: McGraw-Hill.

Castany, L. (2010) The Role of Size in Firms' Training: Evidence from Spain, *International Journal of Manpower*, 31(5), 563–584.

Cedefop (2008) *Terminology of European Education and Training Policy. A Selection of 100 Key Terms*, Luxembourg: Office for Official Publications of the European Communities.

Cho, E. and McLean, G. N. (2004). What we Discovered about NHRD and What It Means for HRD, *Advances in Developing Human Resources*, 6(3), 382–393.

Craig, R. (1976) *Training and Development Handbook*, New York: McGraw-Hill.

Dobbs, B. and Smith, B. (2002) Current Outcomes and Developments in e-Learning, *Industrial and Commercial Training*, 34(2), 44.

Drucker, P. F. (1989) *The New Realities*, Oxford: Heinemann.

Eagly, A. H. and Chin, J. L. (2010) Diversity and Leadership in a Changing World, *American Psychologist*, 65(3), 216–224.

Eisenhardt, K. M. and Santos, F. M. (2002) Knowledge-Based View: A New Theory of Strategy? In A. Pettigrew, H. Thomas and R. Whittington (Eds) *Handbook of Strategy and Management*, London: Sage (139–164).

European Commission (2000) *A Memorandum on Lifelong Learning*, Brussels: Commission of the European Communities.

European Commission (2003) Commission Recommendation 2003/361/EC, *Official Journal of the European Union*, 124, 36. 20 May 2003.

European Commission (2013) *The New SME Definition: User Guide and Model Declaration*, Brussels: Enterprise and Industry Publications.

Eurostat (2013a) *Youth Unemployment Trends*, accessed 7 August 2013 at http://epp.eurostat.ec.europa.eu/statistics_explained/index.php/Unemployment_statistics#Youth_unemployment_trends

Eurostat (2013b) *Employment Activities Statistics*, accessed 7 August 2013 at http://epp.eurostat.ec.europa.eu/statistics_explained/index.php/Employment_activities_statistics_-_NACE_Rev._2

Fee, K. (2009) *Delivering eLearning: A Complete Strategy for Design, Application and Assessment*, London and Philadelphia: Kogan Page.

Future Workplace (2012) *Multiple Generations @ Work: Findings from a Global Survey of Employees and Managers*, accessed 7 August at http://futureworkplace.com/the-2020-workplace/

Garavan, T. (1991) Strategic Human Resource Development, *Journal of European Industrial Training*, 15(1), 17–30.

Garavan, T. N., O'Donnell, D., McGuire, D. and Watson, S. (2007) Exploring Perspectives on Human Resource Development: An Introduction, *Advances in Developing Human Resources*, 9(1), 3–10.

Garavan, T. N., Costine, P. and Heraty, N. (1995) The Emergence of Strategic HRD, *Journal of European Industrial Training*, 19(10), 4–10.

Garavan, T. N., Carbery, R., O'Malley, G. and O'Donnell, D. (2010) Understanding Participation in e-Learning in Organizations: A Large-Scale Empirical Study of Employees, *International Journal of Training and Development*, 14(3), 155–168.

Gibb, S. (2011) *Human Resource Development: Foundations, Processes, Context* (3rd ed.), Basingstoke: Palgrave Macmillan.

Google Books http://books.google.com/ngrams, accessed on 25 August 2013.

Google Trends http://www.google.com/trends

Gourlay, S. (2000) *Knowledge Management and HRD*, First Conference on HRD Research and Practice across Europe, Kingston University, 15 January, 90–104.

Hamlin, B. and Stewart, J. (2011) What is HRD? A Definitional Review and Synthesis of the HRD Domain, *Journal of European Industrial Training*, 35(3), 199–220.

Harbison, F. H. and Myers, C. A. (1964) *Education, Manpower and Economic Growth: Strategies of Human Resource Development*, New York: McGraw-Hill.

Herriot, P. and Pemberton, C. (1997) Facilitating New Deals, *Human Resource Management Journal*, 7(1), 45–56.

Hoque, K. and Bacon, N. (2008) Investors in People and Training in the British SME Sector, *Human Relations*, 61(4), 451–482.

Horwitz, F., Bowmaker-Falconer, A., Searll, P. (1996) Human Resource Development and Managing Diversity in South Africa, *International Journal of Manpower*, 17(4/5), 134–150.

51job (2013) accessed 1 July 2013 at http://www.51job.com

Irish Department of Education and Science (2000) *Learning for Life: White Paper on Adult Education*, Dublin: Stationery Office.

Jaimovich, N. and Siu, H. (2012) *The Trend is the Cycle: Job Polarization and Jobless Recoveries*, NBER Working Paper No. w18334, Available at SSRN: http://ssrn.com/abstract=2136004

Keep, E. (1997) There Is No Such Thing as Society …: Some Problems with an Individual Approach to Creating a Learning Society, *Journal of Education Policy*, 12(6), 457–471.

Keep, E. (2000) Learning Organisations, Lifelong Learning and the Mystery of the Vanishing Employers, *Economic Outlook*, July, 18–26.

Kessels, J. W. M. (2001) Learning in Organizations: A Corporate Curriculum for the Knowledge Economy, *Futures*, 33, 479–506.

Kitching, J. (2008) Rethinking UK Small Employers' Skills Policies and the Role of Workplace Learning, *International Journal of Training and Development*, 12(2), 100–120.

Kitching, J. and Blackburn, R. (2002) *The Nature of Training and Motivation to Train in Small Firms*, London: DfES, Research Report RR330.

Ladyshewsky, R. K. and Taplin, R. (2013) Factors Influencing Mode of Study Preferences in Post-Graduate Business Students, *The International Journal of Management Education*, 11, 34–43.

Lee, M. (2001) A Refusal to Define HRD, *Human Resource Development International*, 4(3), 327–341.

Lepak, D. P. and Snell, S. A. (1999) The Human Resource Architecture: Toward a Theory of Human Capital Allocation and Development, *Academy of Management Review*, 24(1), 31–48.

LinkedIn (2013) About LinkedIn, Retrieved 1 July 2013, from http://press.linkedin.com/about

Lombardi, B. and Ono, Y. (2008) Professional Employer Organizations: What Are They, Who Uses Them, and Why Should We Care? *Economic Perspectives*, 4Q, 2–14.

MacKenzie, C. Garavan, T. N. and Carbery, R. (2014) The Global Financial and Economic Crisis: Did HRD Play a Role?, *Advances in Developing Human Resources*, 16 (1), 34–53.

Mankin, D. P. (2001) A model for Human Resource Development, *Human Resource Development International*, 4(1), 65–85.

Mankin, D. (2009) *Human Resource Development*, Oxford: Oxford University Press.

Manpower Services Commission (1981) *Glossary of Training Terms*, London: HMSO.

Matlay, H. (1999) Vocational Education and Training in Small Businesses: Setting a Research Agenda for the 21st Century, *Education and Training*, 42(4/5), 200–201.

Matlay, H. (2004) Contemporary Training Initiatives in Britain: A Small Business Perspective, *Journal of Small Business and Enterprise Development*, 11(4), 504–513.

McCracken, M., and Wallace, M. (2000) Towards a Redefinition of Strategic HRD, *Journal of European Industrial Training*, 24(5), 281–290.

McCracken, M. and Winterton, J. (2006) What about the Managers? Contradictions between Lifelong Learning and Management Development, *International Journal of Training and Development*, 10(1), 55–66.

McGiveney, V. (1999) *Excluding Men: Men Who Are Missing from Education and Training*, Leicester: NIACE.

McGuire, D., Cross, C., O'Donnell, D. (2005) Why Humanistic Approaches in HRD Won't Work, *Human Resource Development Quarterly*, 16(1), 131–137.

McLaren, C. (2004) A Comparison of Student Resistance and Performance on On-line and Classroom Business Statistics Experiences, *Decision Sciences Journal of Innovation Education*, 2(1), 1–10.

McLean, G. N. (2004) National Human Resource Development: What in the World Is It?, *Advances in Developing Human Resources*, 6(3), 270–275.

McLean, G. N. and McLean, L. (2001), If We Can't Define HRD in One Country, How Can We Define It in an International Context?, *Human Resource Development International*, 4(3), 313–326.

Meggisson, D., Joy-Matthews, J. and Banfield, P. (1993) *Human Resource Development*, London: Kogan Page.

Nadler, L. (1970) *Developing Human Resources*, Houston, TX: Gulf.

National Center for Education Statistics (2012) *Tuition Costs of Colleges and Universities*, accessed 7 August at http://nces.ed.gov/fastfacts/display.asp?id=76

Nolan, C. (2002) Human Resource Development in the Irish Hotel Industry: The Case of the Small Firm, *Journal of European Industrial Training*, 26(2/3/4), 88–99.

Norman, T. J., Preece, A., Chalmers, S., Jennings, N. R., Luck, M., Dang, V. D., Nguyen, T. D., Deora, V., Shao, J., Gray, W. A. and Fiddian, N. J. (2004) Agent-Based Formation of Virtual Organisations, *Knowledge-Based Systems*, 17(2–4), 103–111.

Nyhan, B. (2002) Knowledge Development, Research and Collaborative Learning, In B. Nyhan (Ed.) *Taking Steps towards the Knowledge Society: Reflections on the Process of Knowledge Development*, Luxembourg: Office for Official Publications of the European Communities (Cedefop Reference Series; 35).

Nyhan, B. (2009) Creating the Social Foundations for Apprenticeship in Ireland, *Journal of European Industrial Training*, 33(5), 457–469.

O'Leonard, K. (2013) *The Corporate Learning Factbook 2013: Benchmarks, Trends and Analysis of the US Training Market*, New York, NY: Deloitte Development LLC.

Pate, J., Martin, G., Beaumont, P. and McGoldrick, J. (2000) Company-Based Lifelong Learning: What's the Pay-off for Employers?, *Journal of European Industrial Training*, 24(2), 149–157.

PwC (2012) *Key Trends in Human Capital Development 2012*, Saratoga: PwC.

Raffo, C., O'Connor, J., Lovatt, A. and Banks, M. (2000) Attitudes to Formal Business Training and Learning amongst Entrepreneurs in the Cultural Industries: Situated Business Learning through 'Doing with Others', *Journal of Education and Work*, 13(2), 215–230.

Rainbird, H. (2000) Skilling the Unskilled: Access to Work-Based Learning and the Lifelong Learning Agenda, *Journal of Education and Work*, 13(2), 183–197.

Rigg, C. and Trehan, K. (2002) Do They or Don't They? A Comparison of Traditional and Discourse Perspectives of HRD in SMEs, *Education and Training*, 44(8/9), 388–397.

Roberts, P. B. (2011) *Human Resource Development Directory of Academic Programs in the United States*, Tyler, TX: The University of Texas at Tyler.

Rousseau, D. M. (1995) *Psychological Contracts in Organizations: Understanding Written and Unwritten Agreements*, Newbury Park, CA: Sage.

Rousseau, D. M. (2005) *I-deals: Idiosyncratic Deal Employees Bargain for Themselves*, Armonk, NY: M. E. Sharpe.

Rousseau, D. M. and Tijoriwala, S. A. (1999) What's a Good Reason to Change? Motivated Reasoning and Social Accounts in Organizational Change, *Journal of Applied Psychology*, 84, 514–528.

Sambrook, S. and Stewart, J. (2002) Reflections and Discussion, In S. Tjepkema, J. Stewart, S. Sambrook, M. Mulder, H. Horst and J. Scheerens (Eds) *HRD and Learning Organisations in Europe*, London: Routledge (178–187).

Schultz, T. W. (1961) Investment in Human Capital, *American Economic Review*, 51(March), 1–17.

Scott, P. and Cockrill, A. (1997) Multi-Skilling in Small and Medium-Sized Engineering Firms: Evidence from Wales and Germany, *International Journal of Human Resource Management*, 8(6), 807–824.

Sitzmann, T. (2011) A Meta-Analytic Examination of the Instructional Effectiveness of Computer-Based Simulation Games, *Personnel Psychology*, 64(2), 489–528.

Sloman, M. (2001) *The eLearning Revolution: From Propositions to Action*, London: CIPD.

Song, L., Singleton, E., Hill, J. R. and Koh, M. H. (2004) Improving On-Line Learning: Student Perceptions of Useful and Challenging Characteristics, *The Internet and Higher Education*, 7(1), 59–70.

Stead, V. and Lee, M. (1996) Inter-Cultural Perspectives on HRD, In J. Stewart and J. McGoldrick (Eds) *HRD Perspectives, Strategies and Practices*. London: Pitman (120–138).

Ulrich, D. and Brockbank, W. (2005) Role Call, *People Management*, 11(12), 24–28.

US Department of Education (2013) *The Federal Role in Education*, accessed 7 August 2013 at http://www2.ed.gov/about/overview/fed/role.html

Venkatraman, N. and Subramaniam, M. (2002) Theorizing the Future of Strategy: Questions for Shaping Strategy Research in the Knowledge Economy, In A. Pettigrew, H. Thomas and R. Whittington (Eds) *Handbook of Strategy and Management*. London: Sage (461–474).

Wilson, J. (2012) *International Human Resource Development: Learning, Education and Training for Individuals and Organisations* (3rd ed.), London: Kogan Page.

PART

1

FUNDAMENTALS OF HRD

**Human Resource Development:
A Concise Introduction**

Fundamentals of HRD
2. Strategic HRD
3. Managing the HRD function
4. Individual-level learning
5. Organizational learning
6. Organization development

Contemporary challenges
11. Managing talented employees
12. Leadership development
13. Graduate employability
14. Ethics, corporate social
    responsibility, sustainability and HRD

Process of HRD
7. Identifying learning needs
8. Designing HRD programmes
9. Delivering HRD programmes
10. Evaluating HRD programmes

The first section of the book, *Fundamentals of HRD*, begins with an overview of strategic HRD in Chapter 2 and outlines why HRD should be a strategic business activity. This is a particularly important consideration as, all too often, many organizations do not treat HRD as a strategic pursuit. If the benefits of HRD are to be realized and HRD is to be viewed as important in helping organizations achieve strategic goals and objectives, HRD needs to be integrated within the organization at a strategic level.

Chapter 3 looks at how HRD function can be managed in organizations. This chapter is closely linked to strategic HRD and looks at how strategic goals and objectives can be implemented by those responsible for HRD in organizations. This chapter discusses the roles and responsibilities of the HRD function in organizations and looks at the role that the HRD practitioner plays in organizations.

Chapter 4 considers how we learn and looks at different types of learning. Given the variety and range of ways in which individuals learn, it is unlikely that a 'one size fits all approach' to learning is suitable for many workplaces. Before HRD activities can be designed or delivered, it is important to understand how learning is affected by human and dispositional factors and identify the barriers to effective learning.

Having considered how individuals learn, Chapter 5 then examines learning in organizations and considers how organizations themselves can learn. We can recognize how individuals learn, but how can organizations? Can the sum of knowledge that employees in an organization possess be captured somehow? It is important to understand the challenges of organizational learning, and how organizational learning can be supported.

Chapter 6 then looks at ways in which HRD can facilitate changes needed in organizations to help them achieve particular goals and objectives. This process is known as organization development and looks at ways in which knowledge can be applied to improve performance through planned learning and change. Ways in which HRD can contribute to planned change are examined and potential barriers to change addressed.

2

STRATEGIC HRD

Martin McCracken and Thomas N. Garavan

By the end of this chapter you should be able to:

LEARNING OUTCOMES

- Define Strategic Human Resource Development (SHRD) and understand how it differs from Human Resource Development

- Explain why it is important for organizations to ensure that their HRD activities are linked to corporate strategy

- Understand the role of key stakeholders in HRD in the organization, namely the HRD function, senior, functional and line managers, as well as individual employees

- Explain how an organization can develop a learning culture to support SHRD

- Explain how learning and development specialists can perform a strategic role within an organization

- Understand that there are key differences between small and medium enterprises (SMEs) and large organizations regarding SHRD

Strategic HRD – Partnership in action

This chapter discusses ...

INTRODUCTION

Following on from our introduction to HRD in Chapter 1, this chapter looks at the related concept of SHRD and ultimately how an organization can create a human resource development philosophy. Organizations have become more aware of the need to seriously invest in their human resources as they experience constant change in many aspects of their businesses. Not surprisingly, the importance of education, training and development in private and public sector organizations has come to the forefront, with commentators noting that without appropriately directed continuous learning strategies at both the organizational level and individual level organizations will rapidly fall behind their competitors. At the heart of this is a realization of the need to train and develop employees and to ensure that there is a clear link between their training and development or HRD activities and the organization's overall strategy. Ultimately, the training and development which employees undertake must contribute to the present needs of the organization, but, increasingly, they should help build an organization which can look to the future. Therefore, SHRD is all about planning for the future needs of the business and understanding that investment in HRD activities will allow the organization to continue to innovate, grow and prosper in an increasingly competitive and global environment.

Although it is now accepted that HRD is vital for an organization's survival, like much HRM activity it has been shown that training and development is frequently considered as less important when placed alongside some of the other business functions (Werner and DeSimone, 2006) Indeed, even within the Human Resource functional area, HRD can be sometimes viewed as a 'poor relation', and, when times are financially tough for organizations and cuts are required, employee development activities are often scaled back ▶Chapter 1.

A key aim in this chapter is to illustrate that, when integrated properly with resourcing and retention, SHRD is of vital importance for organizations. In the first section an overview of key terms in the SHRD area is presented, then in the second section the key differences between the most important concepts relating to SHRD are illustrated. After this, some of the most important definitions for SHRD are presented in order to help you appreciate what is actually involved in the concept. The next section considers two key theoretical models of SHRD which help to illustrate the fundamental basis for understanding what SHRD actually involves. In subsequent sections the responsibilities of the key organizational stakeholders, such as senior managers, departmental and line managers and, ultimately, individual employees, to allow SHRD to flourish and make a real contribution are discussed. In addition, we briefly look at the difference in approaches to SHRD activities in SMEs versus larger organizations. Towards the end of the chapter we spend some time thinking about why HRD does not happen in a strategic way and note some of the implications for organizations when HRD is not a strategic activity.

human resource development philosophy focuses on the underpinning values and principles that drive the design, implementation and evaluation of HRD in organizations

organizational level HRD strategies focus on the development of a firm's resource-based capabilities including its capacity to learn and change

individual level HRD strategies focus on the development of skills and behaviours that are required to meet business goals

SHRD focuses on enabling an organization to both implement and develop new strategies that enhance the competitiveness of employees to perform current and future tasks in organizations

DEFINING HRD AND STRATEGIC HRD

The concept of SHRD has been heavily explored in the HRD literature (see, for example, Garavan, 1991; Holden and Livian, 1993; Rainbird, 1995; Stewart and McGoldrick, 1996; Harrison, 1997; McCracken and Wallace, 2000a and 2000b; Tseng and McLean, 2008), with authors arguing that, if a more strategic approach to HRD activities is taken, enhanced organizational performance can be obtained in the future. Initial conceptions of HRD focused on training that helped individuals perform jobs effectively; however, recent conceptualizations of HRD have gone beyond a narrow concentration on training to include strategies and practices that focus on enhancing individual, teamwork process and organizational system performance. ▶Chapter 1

This extension in meaning can help explain the emergence of the concept of SHRD. SHRD emerged out of recognition that HRD should include a strong connection to business strategy, focus on team learning and place more emphasis on internal consultancy, organizational learning, knowledge management and the development of the intellectual capital of an organization. Before we get into detail regarding the key features of SHRD, it is important to have a clear definition of the concept.

At the outset it should be acknowledged that actually defining such a complex term is not easy, with authors such as Blake (1995: 22) noting: 'The field of human resource development defies definition and boundaries. It's difficult to put into a box'. However, when we delve more deeply into the area we can begin to appreciate that the pioneering work of several authors, most notably Garavan (1991), provides a clearer understanding of SHRD, in terms of academic theory as well as the practical application of the concept in organizations today. One of the key problems, which has led to considerable confusion regarding the concept, is that the term 'HRD' is used in many different contexts and concerns a range of differing activities (Garavan *et al.*, 1995). With this in mind, it is perhaps not surprising that a multitude of definitions have emerged, but for the purposes of this chapter we will look at three:

> *Strategic HRD involves introducing, eliminating, modifying, directing and guiding processes in such a way that all individuals and teams are equipped with the skills, knowledge and competencies they require to undertake current and future tasks required by an organization.* (Walton, 1999)
> *Strategic HRD is development that arises from a clear vision about people's abilities and potential and operates within the overall strategic framework of the business.* (Harrison, 2000)
> *Strategic HRD is a coherent, vertically aligned and horizontally integrated set of learning and development activities which contribute to the achievement of strategic objectives.* (Garavan, 2007)

These definitions are similar in language and direction to those offered by other authors such as Beer and Spector (1985: 225), who have used words such as 'proactive, system-wide intervention, linked to strategic planning and cultural change' in their definition to illustrate that, as a practice, SHRD 'contrasts with the traditional view of training and development as consisting of reactive, piecemeal interventions in response to specific problems'. Meanwhile, authors such as Harrison (1997: xv) argue that SHRD is concerned with being 'responsive to the business

learning culture focuses on encouraging employees to demonstrate positive discretionary learning behaviours and actively seek to acquire knowledge skills and attitudes that promote and align with the objectives of the organization

needs of an organization', while others argue that, when a more strategic approach towards HRD is taken, the result is what is described as a '**learning culture**' (Tseng and McLean, 2008), where all employees' true potential can be realized.

Ultimately, all the above definitions emphasize that SHRD adopts a broad and long-term view about how strategies, policies and practices can support the achievement of organizational goals and strategies. It is a business-led activity, and how it formulates its strategies is related to the content and intention of business strategies. The essential features of SHRD can be articulated as follows:

- **Relationship with Business Strategy:** SHRD makes a significant contribution to the successful achievement of business objectives through the enhancement of human resource capability. It operates from the premise that the quality of an organization's human resources represents a major source of competitive advantage.
- **Development of Individual and Organizational Human Capital:** SHRD is focused on developing both individual and organizational human capital. It tries to ensure that employees have the skills to meet present and future strategic needs. However, at an organizational level, when a strategic approach to developing human resources is taken, the employees of the organization can become the rare resources, difficult to imitate and substitute, which enable the organization to truly differentiate itself from competitors.
- **Development of a Climate of Learning:** SHRD helps to create an environment in which employees are encouraged to learn and develop. Increasingly, employees are expected to be concerned with their employability both within and outside the organization, and SHRD helps to create the conditions where employees are proactive, self-directed and self-managing in relation to their development.
- **Vertical and Horizontal Integration of SHRD Strategies, Policies and Practices:** SHRD policies and strategies should be vertically integrated with business strategies and horizontally integrated with other HRD practices and HRM strategies ▶ Chapter 1. Vertical integration ensures effective alignment, whereas horizontal integration helps to ensure synergistic performance outcomes.
- **Involvement of Multiple Actors:** SHRD is not solely the responsibility of human resource or learning and development specialists. It requires that the HRD agenda is driven by top management, supported and implemented by line managers, and individual employees craft their learning and development to allow them to fulfil their true potential.

An aspect which is clearly agreed upon in all of the definitions shown above is that SHRD is clearly in evidence when there is a long-term focus upon planning and implementing HRD activities.

As you can appreciate, SHRD clearly stresses that if an organization is to truly have a strategic approach to its HRD activities it has to do more than simply align training and development to corporate strategy, but, in fact, must elevate these to a higher level.

CONSIDER THIS...

Organizations use a variety of terms to describe the work that SHRD professionals undertake. Some use the term 'learning and development specialist', others the term 'organizational development specialist', and others describe the SHRD specialist as a 'learning solutions specialist'. Why do organizations use so many different titles? What would you suggest?

THEORETICAL MODELS OF SHRD

This part of the chapter explores two of the most influential theoretical models of SHRD. In 1991 Garavan (1991) produced a model which illustrated that, for SHRD to truly take hold, nine key characteristics need to be in place in relation to a number of fundamental factors. These nine factors are shown in the second column in Table 2.1 and include such issues as senior management support, role of line management in HRD and how evaluation is carried out. As can be seen from the table, Garavan's original nine characteristics of SHRD include such fundamentals as ensuring that training and development is integrated with organizational missions and goals and that environmental scanning in terms of training and development takes place in the organization.

However, since Garavan's original model was created several authors have attempted to enhance and elaborate upon his SHRD elements. Most notably, based upon empirical research with a number of large UK-based organizations, McCracken and Wallace (2000a) produced an enhanced list of key SHRD characteristics (see Table 2.1). These nine characteristics are discussed in more detail in the following paragraphs.

1 Organizational missions and goals

Garavan (1991) suggested that at the most fundamental level SHRD needs to be integrated into business planning, and that those involved in developing the workforce should illustrate how HRD activities can contribute to the corporate goals and mission of the organization. Clearly, this fit or integration is vital, but McCracken and Wallace (2000a) contend that a more proactive role should be

Table 2.1 Key SHRD characteristics – Garavan (1991) versus McCracken and Wallace (2000a)

SHRD factor	Garavan (1991)	McCracken and Wallace (2000a)
Organizational missions and goals	1. Integration with organizational missions and goals	1. Shaping organizational missions and goals
Role of senior management	2. Top management support	2. Top management leadership
Understanding the external environment	3. Environmental scanning	3. Environmental scanning by senior management
HRD strategy and policy development	4. HRD plans and policies	4. HRD strategies, plans and policies
Role of line management	5. Line manager commitment and involvement	5. Strategic partnerships with line managers
Complementary HRM activities	6. Existence of complementary HRM activities	6. Strategic partnerships with HRM
The role of the trainer	7. Expanded trainer role	7. Trainers as organizational change consultants
Culture issues	8. Recognition of culture	8. Ability to influence culture
Evaluation of HRD activities	9. Emphasis on evaluation	9. Emphasis on cost-effective evaluation

at the heart of SHRD. SHRD needs to be elevated from supporting and implementing strategy towards a more proactive role, where SHRD helps to shape, influence and formulate corporate strategy. Thus, the characteristic originally proposed by Garavan is enhanced to reflect a more proactive role for SHRD. Integration with missions and goals suggests that HRD activities are merely implemented, but truly strategic HRD should also shape and influence organizational mission and goals. In more recent work from Garavan (2007) the implications for practice of linking HRD strategy to the overall corporate strategy are highlighted. He clearly notes that, by linking HRD strategy to the overall corporate strategy, when any change in the corporate strategy is implemented then HRD strategy also has to be realigned.

2 The role of senior management

Garavan (1991) suggested that the support and active participation of top management are vital for the development of SHRD. Indeed, others (Lee, 1996 and Harrison, 1997) have gone further in suggesting that this support needs to be visible in their operational roles *and* their own personal development. With this in mind, to be truly strategic in nature, McCracken and Wallace (2000a) propose that, as a key SHRD characteristic, top management *support* should become top management *leadership*. In other words, HRD of all members of the organization should be led, rather than simply supported, by senior managers. Torraco and Swanson (1995) and Noel and Dennehy (1991) propose that, to earn such support, HRD professionals must demonstrate their strategic capability by helping strategic planners to acquire the conceptual, analytical and interpersonal skills they require to perform their jobs. Again, Garavan (2007) notes that, for HRD specialists, there is a need

to understand contextual issues and provide the kind of information that can lead to effective senior management decision making in relation to learning and development.

3 Understanding the external environment

Continuous knowledge of the external environment, in terms of opportunities and threats for the business and for HRD specifically, is vital for SHRD to develop and is clearly seen as a cornerstone of SHRD by authors such as Garavan (1991) and Higgs (1989). Developing this further in their model of SHRD, McCracken and Wallace (2000a) contend that other senior managers, and not just HRD professionals, should be involved in collecting and analysing such vitally important information. Who conducts the SWOT (Strengths, Weaknesses, Opportunities and Threats) and PESTLE (Political, Economic, Sociological, Technological, Legal, Environmental) analysis, and whether it is done specifically in HRD terms, is critical. Truly strategic HRD is where senior management automatically consider the HRD implications of any changes in the external environment, rather than seeing this as the job of the HRD professionals. In this way, HRD becomes fully integrated into the organization and into the strategic planning process. It is not enough for environmental planning simply to take place; though this is critical, it must be done in HRD terms and by senior management.

4 HRD strategy and policy development

Garavan (1991) also states that, for HRD to be strategic in focus, it must formulate plans and policies which flow from, and are integrated with, business plans and policies.

planned strategy focuses on the role that HRD plays in helping to achieve already formulated strategies

emergent strategy focuses on the contribution of HRD to the development of strategy and the inclusion of development issues in the formulation of business strategies

In other words, SHRD professionals must be able to illustrate how they can make both planned strategy and emergent strategy contributions. The SHRD model put forward by Garavan suggests that the monitoring of environmental trends can give HRD professionals the opportunity to influence, rather than simply react to, business planning. McCracken and Wallace (2000a) go further by advising that, while the need for HRD policies and plans is clearly important, if HRD is to be truly elevated there needs to be a more strategic

BUILDING YOUR SKILLS

SHRD practices are often the first to be cut during periods of economic downturn. What arguments would you make to senior decision makers to continue to invest in SHRD practices during times of economic difficulty?

emphasis in organizations, and hence they propose that it is vital that there are also HRD strategies in place, as distinct from policies and plans. They further note that strategy is all about the present and future direction of the organization, from a broad perspective, whereas policy can be seen as the specific route to be followed and the tasks to be undertaken in order to achieve the strategy. Training plans represent the next level down and usually consist of the details of priority training interventions from the point of view of who, how, when and where. In his later work Garavan (2007: 14) sums up: 'all major strategic plans are weighted in terms of human skills available to implement them and specify alternative ways to obtain these skills'. Ultimately, if such a scenario can come to fruition then a clear link can be drawn from strategy to the actual skills and competency development activities that employees are offered on the ground.

BUILDING YOUR SKILLS

You are working in the HR department of a relatively small organization in the construction sector (50 employees with various construction trade expertise). Your manager has been asked to the Senior Management meeting to present a discussion paper on what are the key external challenges for the organization in terms of skills for the organization's employees in the future and what they need to think about in devising a coherent SHRD plan in the future. Your manager has turned to you for help in preparing this discussion paper.

To help you with this task, visit http://www.cskills.org/nsacademy/ and watch the video which illustrates the role of the National Skills Academy for Construction in relation to skills development for employers in the construction sector.

5 The role of line managers

The enthusiastic involvement of line and functional managers is considered by Garavan (1991) to be critical for SHRD to take hold in an organization. It is pointed out that there is a need for clear role clarification for HRD and that HRD staff also need to be clear about the kind of support they expect and desire from their line

manager colleagues. Lee (1996) and Harrison (1997) stress the need for shared ownership of HRD activities, where line managers and HRD staff work in partnership regarding HRD issues. However, it is likely that in reality the role of line managers in HRD is underdeveloped for a variety of complex attitudinal and cultural reasons (see, for example, Garavan, 1987; Leicester, 1989; Harrison, 1992; Sinclair and Collins, 1992). It may even be the case that training specialists exclude line managers because of concerns over the threat that their own role may be diminished in value and they may ultimately be replaced (Grace and Straub, 1991). Certainly, embedding training into the line manager's role would appear to be no easy task, but more and more organizations are devolving HRD responsibility to the line (see Bond and McCracken, 2005).

Such integration is clearly crucial to the development of SHRD. Therefore, in the model proposed by McCracken and Wallace (2000a) it is contended that something more than line management commitment is needed for SHRD to flourish. These authors propose that it is also vital that collaborative and strategic partnerships between HRD professionals and line managers are developed and maintained. The importance of developing and maintaining such partnerships is echoed by others, and with this in mind Peterson (2008) provides a framework which, at its very heart, proposes that the central role of SHRD professionals is to forge strategic relationships and create alliances with top management, line, HRM and employees.

CONSIDER THIS...

Why do you think line managers may be reluctant to take responsibility for SHRD activities? What would you suggest that would help line managers to perform SHRD activities more effectively?

6 Complementary HRM activities

Garavan (1991) argues that HRD must view itself as part of a wider package of HRM strategies, and therefore it is important that HRD activities are integrated into the full suite of HRM activities. However, there are doubts about whether, in reality, such coherency and consistency exists in many organizations. For McCracken and Wallace

(2000a), ensuring that strategic partnerships between HRM and HRD professionals are fostered is an essential requirement if SHRD is to truly happen in organizations. The integration of HRM and HRD activities within the organization is vital because there are so many areas where the two influence and are influenced by each other. Without such integration, McCracken and Wallace contend that there is little hope of either HRM or HRD influencing the development and implementation of corporate strategy. In relation to all of the major HRM areas of responsibility, from recruitment and selection to performance management and provision of organizational welfare services, HRD can play an active role, in terms of training and developing HR professionals to be more effective in their jobs.

7 The role of the trainer

Garavan (1991) suggests that a strategic HRD function requires those who are actually delivering the training to be more innovative and consultancy focused rather than simply providers or managers of training material and events. It is believed that only when trainers obtain such an elevated role will they be able to meet the strategic needs of the organization instead of focusing solely upon the individual. Other authors (Talbot, 1993) also suggest that trainers need to ensure that they are performing their roles in adaptive (adapting the skills and knowledge of staff to fit existing systems), adoptive (getting staff to adopt new values or attitudes) or innovative ways in order for them to truly add value to the organization. It is felt that the latter role is about informing and influencing organizational change processes, and, with this in mind, McCracken and Wallace (2000a) assert that, through playing an 'Organizational Change Consultant' role as defined by Philips and Shaw (1989), HRD professionals can more fully illustrate their strategic contribution. In this sense, to play a truly strategic role, HRD staff need to be leaders of change as well as facilitators (Laird et al., 2003). They need to be proactive rather than simply reactive and to see themselves in a central rather than a peripheral role. In their model, therefore, McCracken and Wallace extend Garavan's (1991) original view that HRD specialists need to develop and expand their role, and place a heavier emphasis upon them playing more of an organizational change role. They also advocate that for this change consultant role to truly take hold there is the need for a common understanding across the organization about just what it is HRD staff do in their jobs. In addition, trainers also

need to be made more fully aware of the expectations and perceptions of the rest of the organization regarding their role ▸Chapter 2.

With this in mind, Peterson (2008: 90) provides a useful discussion relating to the skill and competency needs of HRD professionals, and notes that to be truly effective they need to raise their understanding of key business issues and develop their acumen by 'seeking out opportunities to become conversant with leaders of key functions throughout the organization on whom responsibility for competitiveness rests'. If trainers and the HRD function can do this, they should soon be able to identify what it is that makes the organization competitive and ultimately design better HRD solutions.

8 The importance of organizational culture

Garavan (1991) stresses that HRD professionals must be acutely aware of corporate culture and understand the need for a match between culture and strategy in the organization. McCracken and Wallace emphasize that culture should be seen as the most important variable when deciding how HRD should be delivered and evaluated. With this in mind, they claimed that, to truly achieve SHRD, HRD professionals need to understand how they can influence and change culture rather than simply maintain it ▸Chapter 5.

Many authors have noted that organizational culture is a complex concept and notoriously difficult to pin down and clarify (Ogbonna and Harris, 2002). The influence that SHRD might have in changing corporate culture is, therefore, unclear and possibly even more difficult to isolate. However, this is an issue which has been addressed by authors who have investigated the learning organization concept (see, for example, Garratt, 1990; Senge, 1990; West, 1994; Pedler et al., 1997). In more recent writing on the subject, Peterson (2008) argues that a key 'goal for HRD is to engage in practices that lead to a high-performance work system and culture'. It has been shown by others (Holbeche, 1998) that in order to produce such a culture HRD professionals need to design competency frameworks and effective reward systems and ultimately ensure that there are development structures in place that are attractive to talented employees.

In essence, it is believed that learning is the most important way of transmitting and changing an organization's culture, and therefore, given the increasingly turbulent environment that all organizations now operate in, ensuring that learning of all employees can flourish is of vital importance. With this in mind, the existence of a learning culture would seem to be crucial for any organization seeking to elevate HRD to strategic levels. Therefore, in the model proposed by McCracken and Wallace (2000a), it is asserted that, for SHRD to be truly present, there needs to be a recognition of the capacity of HRD in developing and enhancing organization culture. This vitally important issue is explored in more detail in the following section.

> **performance-based HRD** focuses on programmes that meet the personal and organizational needs of employees and serve to enhance performance

SPOTLIGHT ON SKILLS

You have been asked for advice by a friend who has just taken on an important senior role within the SHRD function of a large multinational. Your friend is concerned about how the first six months in the role should be planned out. She has told you that she 'wants to make an impact as quickly as possible and demonstrate that SHRD practices can add value'. To help your friend, think about the advice you would give regarding the following:

1 What activities should your friend focus on during the first month in the role?

2 Whom should your friend talk to as a matter of priority and what questions should she ask?

3 What policy documents should your friend read within the organization to understand the priorities and focus on the organization?

4 How should your friend evaluate her first six months in the role? What will be the metrics of success?

To help you answer the questions above, visit www.macmillanihe.com/companion/carbery-hrd and watch the video of Suzanne McElligott talking about SHRD.

9 Evaluation of HRD activities

In Garavan's (1991) model the issue of evaluation is stressed as the important final element in ensuring that SHRD becomes an integral aspect in organizations. Garavan (1991) suggested that, in order to be strategic, the HRD function must evaluate all activities associated with training and development. However, McCracken and Wallace (2000a) add another dimension here by proposing that to truly understand the value of HRD activities there needs to be a specific focus on cost effectiveness. They underline that, unless such investment calculations are made, there is the potential for a culture to be perpetuated in which HRD is seen as a luxury rather than an essential investment in the long-term future of the organization ▶ Chapter 10. In other words, these authors are arguing that there is a need to develop what might be termed performance-based HRD. Again, Peterson (2008) discusses the need for proper evaluation when he notes that HRD needs to develop a system of accountability in relation to any HRD activities offered. He makes the very important point that evaluation needs to be long term oriented and focuses on how value has been created as a result of development activities offered by the organization.

CREATING A SHRD CULTURE: PRACTICAL STEPS WHICH FACILITATE SHRD

Although the above commentary is useful for illustrating the key properties and issues surrounding SHRD, it is important at this point to understand the key factors that organizations need to consider to allow SHRD to truly flourish. In this section a number of practical steps that organizations can take to develop a SHRD culture and climate are proposed.

1 **Top Management Commitment:** A learning culture can be developed in an organization only when the top management and executive are committed and deeply involved. The learning culture has to be top down and is best cascaded when 'Learning Culture' is stated as one of the organization's Key Performance Indicators (KPI) or Annual Objectives. Learning should be embedded in the work culture and the people must live and breathe learning culture, with senior management being seen to encourage macro-management and empowerment to their employees.

2 Aligning Learning Culture to Business Needs: The SHRD specialists should ensure that their strategies are aimed at learning. Management must make the employees feel that learning is aligned to business strategies. SHRD professionals should regularly talk with the line managers or section heads about the issues and problems they are facing and enable the employees to find solutions through the learning process.

3 Setting Clear Objectives: There should be a clear and firm idea of the goals and objectives to be achieved. As stated above, 'Learning Culture' should be a corporate goal and stated at the highest level of objectives in order that it is cascaded down to the organization's employees and becomes a part of every employee's personal, annual goals. The strategic nature of the job must be reflected through plans. The best plans are developed not in isolation but through joint involvement of colleagues, clients and other stakeholders in business.

4 Personalizing Learning: Organizations should promote the idea that learning is work and work is learning. The learning content must be appropriate and timely for every employee. The learning content and outcome and objective must be customized to each employee. The learning needs can be identified through performance appraisals or competency-based assessments (or centres). Employees should be made to analyse their learning needs vis-à-vis their performance to achieve the organizational objectives. Employees can be encouraged to work in teams and share information, learning and knowledge through a team learning process. Peer group networks must be encouraged so that employees learn from others in teams.

5 Create the Right Environment for Learning: In order to build a learning culture we must cultivate active learners by creating a learner-centric environment. Employees must be provided with necessary tools and the relevant content to become self-learners. Refining one's approach to learning must continually develop learning culture. It is possible to refine the learning approach after getting feedback from employees.

6 Developing a Contract for Learning: In developing a learning culture, employees are expected to play a role in their career development. The ownership and accountability for learning should be with the employees. The contract of employment shall be clear about what the company is prepared to offer and what the company expects from the employee towards continuous learning. But the learning contracts may not be appropriate in all situations. The main objective of a learning contract is to create a clear learning strategy and communicate the same to employees. The learning contract, through communicating the clear-cut strategy to employees, must get their tacit commitment for the learning process to achieve the goals of the organization.

7 Removing Barriers in Learning: A key issue in self-managed learning is that the learners may not tolerate any obstacle. The obstacles, if any, should be removed and work life must become hassle free for learners. The learning courses must be intuitive to use and must be available in one place and easily accessible. As the learning is important, cost must not be a hurdle in implementing a learning culture.

8 Building Learning Culture: This can be achieved through the use of coaching and mentoring. Care and attention must be paid to the wider culture of the organization and the management style.

 **CONSIDER THIS ...**

Many of the most innovative organizations in the world have emerged from the Scandinavian region, with companies such as Spotify, Skype, Electrolux and Ikea now household names. One reason why these organizations have become so successful is their commitment to innovate and enhance their products and services. But how do such organizations achieve this while others from other regions appear to have stumbled in recent times? A key reason for their success appears to be linked to the Nordic principle of encouraging collaboration through learning together. A familiar proverb in Sweden is 'En god affär är när båda parter vinner', which translates into English as 'A good deal is when both parties win.' This ability to create a good deal for all parties is the cornerstone of developing a learning culture where everyone receives tangible benefits and can fully develop to their true potential. In organizations this means that employees from all levels of the hierarchy and functional areas can come together and achieve results that benefit all organizational stakeholders.

Take some time to explore the websites of the above organizations (and other Scandinavian companies) Are there any factors which are common to these organizations?

9 **Encourage an Experimental Mindset:** Employees must be encouraged to experiment with new ideas and to take calculated risks. Organizations should encourage employees to take advantage of changes taking place in business. In fact, they must be able to foresee changes and be prepared to make changes. Employees must be encouraged to try new things at their workplace and within the context of the organization. Employees who are innovative, creative and experimental must then be rewarded.

10 **Listen to Feedback:** Management should listen to and consider the feedback from the learners about the effectiveness of the learning process practised in the organization. It is better to have an online assessment tool and conduct surveys to find out the employees' views on the learning process and build an improvement plan. Table 2.2 provides an example of a self-audit that an organization can use to assess its learning culture.

Table 2.2 A learning culture self-audit

Pro-learning culture	1 – 5	Anti-learning culture	1 – 5
People at all levels ask questions and share stories about successes, failures and what they have learned.		Managers share information on a need-to-know basis. People keep secrets and don't describe how events really happened.	
Everyone creates, keeps and propagates stories of individuals who have improved their own processes.		Everyone believes they know what to do, and they proceed on this assumption.	
People take at least some time to reflect on what has happened and what may happen.		Little time or attention is given to understanding lessons learned from projects.	
People are treated as complex individuals.		People are treated like objects or resources without attention to their individuality.	
Managers encourage continuous experimentation.		Employees proceed with work only when they feel certain of the outcome.	
People are hired and promoted on the basis of their capacity for learning and adapting to new situations.		People are hired and promoted on the basis of their technical expertise as demonstrated by credentials.	
Performance reviews include and pay attention to what people have learned.		Performance reviews focus almost exclusively on what people have done.	
Senior managers participate in training programmes designed for new or high-potential employees.		Senior managers appear only to 'kick off' management training programmes.	
Senior managers are willing to explore their underlying values, assumptions, beliefs and expectations.		Senior managers are defensive and unwilling to explore their underlying values, assumptions, beliefs and expectations.	
Conversations in management meetings constantly explore the values, assumptions, beliefs and expectations underlying proposals and problems.		Conversations tend to move quickly to blaming and scapegoat with little attention to the process that led to a problem or how to avoid it in the future.	
Customer feedback is solicited, actively examined and included in the next operational or planning cycle.		Customer feedback is not solicited and is often ignored when it comes in over the transom.	
Managers presume that energy comes in large part from learning and growing.		Managers presume that energy comes from 'corporate success', meaning profits and senior management bonuses.	
Managers think about their learning quotient, that is, their interest in and capacity for learning new things, and the learning quotient of their employees.		Managers think that they know all they need to know and that their employees do not have the capacity to learn much.	
Total for pro-learning culture		**Total for anti-learning culture**	

The Future of the British Army?

In November 2013 it was announced that the British Army was to embark upon a major restructuring exercise, which would allow it to be able to operate effectively and efficiently in a global arena in the future. The most important SHRD implication of the proposed changes centred around the skills and competency requirement arising from increasing the size and expertise of the Army Reserve (soldiers who are employed by the army on a part-time basis and still have regular civilian jobs) to 30,000 soldiers while simultaneously reducing the size of the regular full-time army (by around 20,000 soldiers). The rationale given for the restructuring was that as the international security environment changes there will be less need for large numbers of regular soldiers or 'boots on the ground' as innovations in military technology continue to change how war and security situations are managed. Ultimately, these innovations would also impact on skills and competency requirements for soldiers at all levels in the army. Speaking on BBC Radio about the restructuring, the UK Defence Secretary noted that the changes were designed to reverse the decline of the Army Reserve, which had been 'run down, ignored, underfunded and marginalized' in recent times and that the changes would allow a more skilled and 'agile' armed forces fit for the 21st century.

Sources

BBC News (2013) 'Army Reserve Rebellion in Prospect among Tory MPs', BBC News Politics, www.bbc.co.uk/news/uk-politics-25012907

Questions

1 What effect do you think the changes will have on the culture of the British Army?
2 What are the implications of this restructuring exercise for HRD professionals and those who are tasked with developing skills and training soldiers in the British Army?

PRACTICALITIES FOR THE HRD SPECIALIST: PERFORMING TO A STRATEGIC LEVEL

HRD specialists frequently struggle to perform strategic roles in organizations. Research undertaken by Deloitte (2011) has identified the characteristics of learning and development specialists who are effectively performing strategic roles. In a useful contribution to the debate, they make a distinction between what they describe as 'lagging' versus 'leading' learning and development specialists. Table 2.3 outlines the differences between the types of specialists.

These important differences between a lagging and a leading HRD specialist highlight that, to operate effectively as a leading specialist, there must be a strong focus on strategic issues that contribute to business growth and competitiveness. The specialist must also have the skill to take a big picture perspective regarding organizational strategic priorities and goals and must project personal impact and credibility to have an influence with key decision makers. In addition, such a scenario requires that HRD specialists are considered vital to the success of the business. To enhance their chances of being considered vital, HRD professionals must continuously link their targets to key areas of business results.

Table 2.3 Lagging and leading HRD specialists

Lagging	Leading
• Retain a large proportion of their operational duties	• Spend their time primarily on strategic tasks that contribute to key business priorities
• Struggle with making an impact in the business	• Clearly measure and articulate the value they bring to the organization
• Find it difficult to balance business and HRD agendas	• Effectively deliver against aligned SHRD and business agendas
• Lack clearly defined responsibilities or handoffs with other HRD/HRM areas	• Have a clear and transparent role to play in SHRD service delivery
• Require further support with developing critical business skills or SHRD skills	• Are considered top talent within the organization

Table 2.4 shows some of the activities that an HRD specialist who performs in a leading role can perform to demonstrate that SHRD adds value. However, the shift to a strategic role requires a significant change in the mindset of the HRD function. Learning and development specialists can, however, implement a number of actions to move from a lagging to a leading SHRD specialist. These actions will need to focus on: (1) the identification of capability gaps; (2) enhanced role clarity; and (3) the development of performance metrics that demonstrate the business impact of SHRD.

Addressing Capability Gaps: SHRD specialists typically experience capability gaps in three areas: they are too focused on transactional-type SHRD work (e.g. monitoring who attends training or ensuring that a 'happy sheet' evaluation form is completed post activity); they have few opportunities to develop strategic skills because they are not given the opportunity to do so; and there is a lack of support from senior decision makers and those senior within the HR function to enable SHRD specialists to develop strategic capability skills. Capability gaps can be addressed in a number of ways, such as the following:

- Identify the critical skills necessary to make a contribution at a strategic level **within an organization**.

- Use multi-source feedback, including self-assessment, to analyse existing competencies.
- Take proactive steps to develop competencies, including coaching from senior managers.
- Move to a business unit and work there for a period of time to develop business and strategic skills.

Scoping the Strategic Role: SHRD specialists frequently do not clearly tell organizational stakeholders what they will contribute and the types of contributions they will make to an organization. As a result, senior decision makers have a lack of clarity concerning what they themselves can contribute, or they operate on the basis of previous experience or prevailing stereotypes within the organization. These issues can be addressed through a focus on the following:

- Conduct an analysis of the transactional activities currently performed and identify how they can be removed or moved to a shared services centre.
- Clearly define and communicate role delivery capabilities to senior management.
- Develop a clearly defined service delivery model with the identification of duties and responsibilities.

Table 2.4 The activities of HRD specialists

Business outcomes	SHRD specialist strategic priorities	Example of target
Sustained revenue growth	• Implement talent development strategies to enable entry into new markets • Focus development initiatives on critical talent groups • Refocus the SHRD function to support high-growth business units • Help the business to manage organizational change and restructuring effectively	Percentage of staff operating in new markets developed (10%)
Profit growth and cost reduction	• Contribute to implementation of the change process associated with cost reduction • Focus on reducing the operating costs associated with SHRD • Develop the skills of line managers to manage change effectively	Cost reduction for SHRD of 10%
Work smarter, enhance flexibility, speed and adaptability	• Emphasize flexibility and adaptability in the design and delivery of learning strategies • Contribute to the development of a culture that emphasizes speed, flexibility and adaptability • Develop the organization's talent pool to perform effectively	Increased speed of entry to new markets (20%)
Customer loyalty and retention	• Enhance the skills of customer-facing staff • Develop values around customer service and customer focus • Be responsive to the requirements of internal customers in delivery of SHRD strategies	Enhanced customer retention by 5%
Strategy execution capability	• Develop leadership talent and be ready for succession gaps • Build execution capability into leadership development programmes • Enhance the capacity of employees to be resilient	Enhanced performance of leadership talent pool by 10%

- Clarify relationships with the HR function and other delivery units within the organization, such as centres of expertise.

Define the Business Impact of the Role: The SHRD function is often accused of focusing on 'low hanging fruit', or it engages in activities that do not impact the bottom line. This arises because frequently the function has a poor awareness of business priorities or the critical tasks that need to be performed. There is also a focus on inputs and processes rather than outputs, and consequently the metrics used to measure the SHRD contribution focus on efficiency rather than effectiveness. The SHRD specialist can take a number of actions to enhance this dimension – business impact – such as:

- Define clearly the brand of the SHRD function and the personal brand of the SHRD specialist.
- Prioritize business critical tasks and engage with business stakeholders to help define and prioritize how these tasks should be executed.
- Define business metrics that speak to the business agenda. Communicate successes to organizational stakeholders and show how value is achieved.

STRATEGIC HRD IN SMES

It is important to note that, while many of the issues covered in this chapter, designed to outline what an organization needs to do to ensure that it has a fully strategic approach to HRD, are important regardless of organizational size, some consideration needs to be given to issues connected to this important issue. At the outset it should be understood that, as Westhead and Storey (1996: 18) assert, 'the small firm is not a scaled down' version of a large firm and that as a result small and medium enterprises (SMEs) will face particular issues when designing and implementing HRD strategy (Lyons and Mattare, 2011; Shepherd et al., 2011). Hill and Stewart (2000: 105) outline the central problem for such organizations when they argue that 'SMEs frequently do not have the HRD expertise, infrastructure and general resources which larger organizations frequently enjoy.' However, for those who have investigated the issue of firm size, the most important difference between large and small firms can be summed up in the word 'uncertainty'. Hill and Stewart (2000) make the important distinction which shows that it is ultimately 'external' uncertainty,

as opposed to 'internal' uncertainty, that is the most salient issue for small firms.

In terms of internal uncertainty, as we have seen throughout this chapter, one of the main challenges for larger organizations when developing a strategic approach to HRD is to ensure that organizational stakeholders, including senior leaders, line and departmental managers as well as employees and the HRD function, are 'on message' and deliver consistent HRD plans, policies and strategies. In larger organizations, as a result of the many layers that decisions have to be filtered through, there is the possibility for increased 'internal' uncertainty. For example, line managers may interpret decisions incorrectly or fail to act on instructions in the way that senior leaders in the organization had intended. Hill and Stewart (2000) argue that in smaller organizations there is less opportunity for internal uncertainty to be in evidence, as senior managers, who are in closer proximity to all employees, are in a better position to personally communicate decisions. As a result, smaller organizations may obtain more consistency among stakeholders in terms of HRD strategy and the implementation of HRD practices. Relatedly, in smaller firms there may be increased opportunities for senior managers to obtain more detailed and rich feedback on ideas, which may allow them to more quickly assess the potential success of any particular strategy or course of action. Such a scenario can also allow smaller organizations to be more agile and oriented towards teamworking and collaboration, and, as Storey (1994) concluded in his research, SMEs may be more innovative and better able to exploit niche markets and positions than their larger counterparts.

However, as well as these potential benefits for smaller organizations, there are also constraints and associated drawbacks linked to size. Perhaps the most important of these is the lack of both financial resources and expertise, which may mean that in reality SMEs are not able to offer longer-term-oriented HRD opportunities to employees. Similarly, SMEs often have to contend with challenges associated with their precarious market position: they are frequently reliant on a few large clients, which may erode their bargaining power and resource base even further. Unsurprisingly, when researchers have investigated the type and amount of HRD activities offered by SMEs they have found an emphasis on more tactical and short-term training and development. For example, Lyons and Mattare (2011: 15) noted that in many cases 'orientation for new employees, in-house, on-the-job, experientially-grounded supervised training and skills training for one's immediate job role' are normally the most that SMEs can offer their employees.

Hill and Stewart (2000) argue that two crucial factors will determine HRD provision in SMEs. First, they note that the owner-manager must have a positive attitude and be favourably disposed towards HRD activities, and also needs to be motivated to promote these among employees. Second, and perhaps more importantly when we consider the scarce resources which SMEs may have at their disposal, Hill and Stewart assert that it is vital that HRD activities are perceived to positively impact upon organizational performance and in particular enhance financial returns and the bottom line. This latter point is particularly important because, as was observed above, all too often organisations (both large and small) are unable to determine whether the training that they provide is cost effective and worthwhile. Closely related to the issue of cost effectiveness is the often-cited perceived problem of 'poaching', where SMEs may fear that if employees are trained to a certain standard they may leave to join competitors. In their case study research into HRD issues among SMEs in the UK, Hill and Stewart (2000: 107) noted how this problem was uppermost in the mind of the personnel manager of a small organization specializing in telecommunications equipment installation, who voiced concern that when employees were trained they would 'want more money or find another job'.

It is clear that there are particular problems associated with implementing SHRD in SME and micro-organizations. These are further elaborated upon by Garavan *et al.* (2004), who investigated HRD in micro- and small firms in Ireland and found that issues connected to firm size, owner-manager perceptions, HRM and the strategic orientation of the firm were significant factors in determining the HRD landscape in smaller organizations. Ultimately their findings confirm that, much more so than their larger counterparts, HRD in SMEs tends to be based upon individualized employment relationships and a focus on cost, short-termism and bottom line considerations.

WHAT HAPPENS WHEN HRD IS NOT A STRATEGIC ACTIVITY?

As a way of concluding this chapter, it is important to understand what happens in organizations when HRD is not a strategic activity. Each week in the business sections of the press we hear of organizations reducing profit forecasts, laying off employees, or at worst being placed into administration. When we take a closer look at reasons why this happens, many of the problems appear to be connected to their failure to plan for the future and remain relevant to their customers and other stakeholders. As we have seen throughout this chapter, HRD has a vitally important role in ensuring that any organization has a coherent strategy with highly trained and committed employees at all levels. For example, the case of former retail giant Woolworths is well documented. Woolworths was one of the UK's best-known high street retail chains, trading since 1909 in the UK, but in 2009 it went into administration, resulting in 30,000 job losses (Hall, 2009). Much of the problem for organizations like Woolworths and other victims of the recent global slowdown was their failure to adapt to changing environmental circumstances and formulate a strategy that allowed them to compete in an ever more diverse and competitive marketplace. In Woolworths' case, one of the major problems was their failure to stay in touch with their customers and deliver what they were looking for (quality, choice and value) in the right location. For example, it was once famously remarked that, while Woolworths in theory were able to offer 40 different types of pencil case, the chances were, because of a poor 'on the shelf availability index' of just 73 per cent, in reality customers would have been unlikely to have anything like this choice. Additionally, because of their physical location, in city and town centres rather than the more convenient out-of-town shopping malls, customers drifted away from Woolworths towards their large supermarket competitors such as Tesco and Asda.

Throughout this chapter we have seen that, in essence, for an organization to truly have a strategic approach to HRD it needs to have a holistic long-term view of where the organization is going and how it might possibly get there. However, it is crucially important that all the key stakeholders in the organization, from senior-level directors, through line and functional managers, right down to team leaders and front-line employees, 'buy into' an HRD strategy which will deliver the right kind of training to the right people at the right time. This means that they understand what type of HRD is important at each level, why it is important and, critically, how long it will take for the fruits of training activities to become apparent.

Returning to the case of Woolworths, at all levels in the organization there were deficiencies which illustrated that a strategic approach to HRD was not taken. At the most senior levels, vital elements of any leadership or management development programme which develop skills in senior leaders to scan the environment in order to understand consumer tastes and market developments and make effective decisions were not realized. For example, at the time of their demise Woolworths had a portfolio of 807 stores, the vast majority of which were located in expensive city centre locations where footfall was declining. This lack of strategic awareness fundamentally contributed to the decline of the organization, but also, at upper middle management levels, not having the skills to effectively feed back vital performance information was a serious problem. Meanwhile, at store management level, not having employees trained in efficient stock control or procurement procedures resulted in many advertised products not appearing on shelves, which frustrated customers. Ultimately, many of the problems faced by Woolworths might have been addressed if a more coherent approach to HRD had been taken, which could have contributed to the organization's overall strategy of offering a good range of low-cost quality products in locations that were convenient to shoppers.

In essence, if an organization does not have a strategic approach to HRD then all the aspects that were discussed in this chapter are absent and HRD activities become isolated and fragmented and are not supported by stakeholders or perceived to add value. In many cases employees returning from training events never get a chance to fully implement the training they receive. In short, as a result of a lack of holistic strategic buy-in from key stakeholders throughout the training process, training gaps are never properly diagnosed, participation in training is not supported and therefore skills are never fully transferred to the work environment. Ultimately a vicious cycle is created whereby, as a result of a poorly devised HRD strategy, training and development activities are perceived to be ineffective because the skills they purport to develop are never utilized, and thus stakeholders feel that HRD is a waste of resources.

Developing Leaders for Competitive Advantage: The Case of JetBlue

The development of leaders to contribute to the strategic growth of an organization is recognized as a major challenge. JetBlue, which over a period of 13 years has grown from eight to 193 aircraft, took to the skies in 2000 using a novel concept – bringing humanity back to air travel. Based at New York's Kennedy International Airport, JetBlue, a non-union airline, distinguished itself from other low-fare carriers by offering seat-back entertainment systems with live television, comfortable seats and blue corn chips. The company quickly grew to about $1.9 billion in annual revenue in 2012 and became increasingly popular with travellers. It soon realized that its massive growth had created a major leadership gap within the organization. It had a lot of inexperienced supervisors and middle-level managers, and the JetBlue Speakup Survey revealed that both managers and employees perceived that leaders within the organization were not effective and lacked the skills to manage people.

JetBlue senior executives, including CEO David Neeleman and president Dave Barger, realized that this leadership gap needed to be addressed and designed a new leadership development programme. The executive team recognized that leadership development should be closely integrated with the corporate culture and that leadership should be developed at all levels: supervisors, managers, directors and vice presidents. In order to systematically identify development needs, JetBlue used the Myers-Briggs Type Indicator to help in the needs identification process. Following the needs identification process, both the CEO and the president articulated a vision that contained five leadership principles:

1 Treat your people right.
2 Do the right thing.
3 Communicate with your team.
4 Encourage initiative and innovation.
5 Inspire greatness in others.

The Learning and Development (L&D) Group were tasked with developing an intensive, individually focused development solution that incorporated those leadership principles. The L&D Group developed a curriculum of leadership programmes called the Principles of Leadership (POL) series. This series consisted of three elements: Principles of Leadership Foundations; Principles of Leadership in Action; and a Lecture Series on Leadership. The Principles of Leadership Foundations programme introduced leaders to how JetBlue envisions leadership and focused on developing critical leadership skills such as self-awareness, relationship building, interpersonal communication and gaining commitment. A strong emphasis was placed on how the leader's behaviour impacted both the corporate culture and business performance. Participants were exposed to a number of skill-building exercises, using a 'progressive guidance' model which helps leaders to learn how to deal with problem behaviours and develop appropriate action plans. Participants received extensive feedback from each other. The Foundations Programme also included a 'teach back' feature whereby participants teach the material they have just learned. JetBlue executives took part in the programme. They led panel discussions, allowing participants to ask any questions about leadership in JetBlue. They spent approximately 90 minutes with participants, dealing with questions and providing insights.

Once participants had completed the Principles of Leadership Foundations Programme, the second programme was customized and personalized to the needs of each participant. The Principles of Leadership in Action Programme focused on building effective and actionable skills to make participants more effective leaders. It placed a strong emphasis on leaders working with their teams to enhance performance. The L&D Group played a major role in delivering the Principles of Leadership in Action Programme, including providing skilled facilitators and coaches. Participants received detailed feedback and support, one-to-one coaching sessions, 360-degree feedback, group feedback and videotaped activities. Participants were required to create a detailed action plan to support ongoing development. Participants were exposed during the Action Programme to the principles of introspection and the importance of self-reflection, self-understanding and recognition and understanding of others' differences.

JetBlue is strongly committed to the development of its people. According to CEO David Neeleman: *"You have to remain focused on your people. That's the key to great service. I want our crewmembers to feel that they're important and that we're on a mission together to put humanity back into air travel.*

That's where a strong culture comes in. Hopefully, it makes them feel this is the best job they've ever had. If they like coming to work, that gets passed on to the customer. It all starts with hiring though. We're highly selective – we want crewmembers who like people, not just 'certain people'." (Bailey and Cawood, S, 2006)

Questions

1 Consider the advantages of having the senior executives actively involved in the development programme.
2 How would you describe the role of the Learning and Development Group? Were they supporting or enabling strategy?
3 What changes would you make to the core programmes to give them more of an organizational learning focus?
4 Given the dynamic competitive environment in which JetBlue operates, what additional activities would you suggest could be introduced to support the development of leaders?
5 How would you measure the impact of the programmes?

SUMMARY

In this chapter we emphasized the importance for organizations of having a strategic approach to HRD. By analysing the major characteristics of SHRD and examining the dimensions of an effective learning strategy, it is possible to demonstrate 'why' and 'how' SHRD can fit into an organization's strategy. A central notion of SHRD is that there is a link between business strategy and the types of learning strategies that are implemented in an organization. SHRD has typically played a supporting role to the implementation of business strategy; however, SHRD advocates that it must perform a shaping role and influence the strategic objectives that the business sets. The chapter concluded with a discussion of the skills and role behaviours of SHRD specialists to perform this shaping function effectively.

CHAPTER REVIEW QUESTIONS

1 Please provide a definition of SHRD and explain how it differs from HRD.
2 Why is it important for HRD activities to be linked to corporate strategy?
3 Who are the key stakeholders in HRD in the organization?
4 What are the practical challenges for SHRD specialists in implementing SHRD?
5 Why is learning culture important to explaining the effectiveness of SHRD?
6 Describe three barriers to the development of a learning culture in organizations.
7 What are the key skills requirements of SHRD specialists?
8 What are the key differences between SMEs and large organizations regarding SHRD?

 **FURTHER READING**

Garavan, T. N. (2007) A Strategic Perspective on Human Resource Development, *Advances in Developing Human Resources*, 9(1), 11–30.

McCracken, M. and Wallace, M. (2000) Exploring Strategic Maturity in HRD – Rhetoric, Aspiration or Reality? *Journal of European Industrial Training*, 24(8), 425–467.

McCracken, M. and Wallace, M. (2000) Towards a Redefinition of Strategic HRD, *Journal of European Industrial Training*, 24(5), 281–290.

Peterson, S. L. (2008) Creating and Sustaining a Strategic Partnership: A Model for Human Resource Development, *Journal of Leadership Studies*, 2(2), 83–97.

Tseng, C. and McLean, G. N. (2008) Strategic HRD Practices as Key Factors in Organizational Learning, *Journal of European Industrial Training*, 32(6), 418–432.

 **USEFUL WEBSITES**

http://www.ila-net.org/

The International Leadership Association (ILA) website offers excellent resources, sourced from a global network of members who practise, study and teach leadership and SHRD. By engaging with the resources on offer, students should be able to develop and advance their leadership knowledge and be better able to understand the role of leaders in developing SHRD.

https://www.shrm.org/Pages/default.aspx

The Society for Human Resource Management (SHRM) is the world's largest HR membership organization devoted to human resource management. Representing more than 275,000 members in over 160 countries, the Society is the leading provider of resources to serve the needs of HR professionals and advance the professional practice of human resource management/development.

BIBLIOGRAPHY

Bailey, R. and Cawood, S. (2006) *Destination Profit*, Davies-Black Publishing: Boston.

Beer, M. and Spector, B. (1985) Corporate Wide Transformations in Human Resource Management, In R. E. Walton and P. R. Lawrence (Eds) *Human Resource Management. Trends and Challenges*, Boston, MA: Harvard University School Press (219–253).

Blake, R. R. (1995) Memories of HRD, *Training and Development*, 49(30), 22–29.

Bond, S. and McCracken, M. (2005) The Importance of Training in Operationalising HR Policy, *Journal of European Industrial Training*, 29(2/3), 246–260.

Deloitte (2011) *Business Driven HR: Unlock the Value of HR Business Partners*, London: Deloitte.

Garavan, T. N. (1987) Promoting Natural Learning Activities within the Organisation, *Journal of European Industrial Training*, 11(7), 17–30.

Garavan, T. N. (1991) Strategic Human Resource Development, *Journal of European Industrial Training*, 15(1), 17–30.

Garavan, T. N. (2007) A Strategic Perspective on Human Resource Development, *Advances in Developing Human Resources*, 9(1), 11–30.

Garavan, T. N., Costine, P. and Heraty, N. (1995) The Emergence of Strategic Human Resource Development, *Journal of European Industrial Training*, 19(10), 4–10.

Garavan, T., McCarthy, A., McMahon, J. and Gubbins, C. (2004) Management Development In Micro and Small Firms in Ireland: Linking Management Development Practices to Firm Size, Strategic Type, HRM Orientation and Owner Manager Espoused Values, In J. Stewart and G. Beaver (Eds) *Human Resource Development in Small Organisations: Research and Practice*, London: Routledge (285–311).

Garratt, R, (1990) *Creating a Learning Organisation: A Guide to Leadership, Learning and Development*, Cambridge: Director Books/Institute of Directors.

Grace, P. and Straub, C. (1991) Managers as Training Assets, *Training and Development*, June, 49–54.

Hall, J. (2009) Woolworths: The Failed Struggle to Save a Retail Giant, *The Telegraph*, 14 November.

Harrison, R. (1992) *Employee Development*, London: Institute of Personnel Management.

Harrison, R. (1997) *Employee Development* (2nd ed.), London: Institute of Personnel and Development.

Harrison, R. (2000) *Employee Development* (2nd ed.), CIPD: London.

Higgs, M. (1989) A Strategic Approach to Training and Development, *Training and Development*, November, 11–14.

Hill, R. and Stewart, J. (2000) Human Resource Development in Small Organizations, *Journal of European Industrial Training*, 24(2/3/4), 105–117.

Holbeche, L. (1998) *Motivating People in Lean Organisations*, London: Routledge.

Holden, L. and Livian, Y. (1993) Does Strategic Training Policy Exist? Some Evidence from Ten European Countries, In A. Hegewisch and C. Brewster (Eds) *European Developments in Human Resource Management*, London: Kogan Page (101–116).

Laird, D., Naquin, S. and Holton, E. (2003) *Approaches to Training and Development* (3rd ed.), Cambridge, MA: Perseus.

Lee, R. (1996) What Makes Training Pay?, *Issues in People Management 11*, London: Institute of Personnel and Development.

Leicester, C. (1989) The Key Role of the Line Manager in Employee Development, *Personnel Management*, March, 53–57.

Lyons, P. and Mattare, M. (2011) How Can Very Small SMEs Make the Time for Training and Development: Skill Charting as an Example of Taking a Scenistic Approach, *Development and Learning in Organizations*, 25(4), 15–19.

McCracken, M. and Wallace, M. (2000a) Towards a Redefinition of Strategic HRD, *Journal of European Industrial Training*, 24(5), 281–290.

McCracken, M. and Wallace, M. (2000b) Exploring Strategic Maturity in HRD – Rhetoric, Aspiration or Reality? *Journal of European Industrial Training*, 24(8), 425–467.

Noel, J. L. and Dennehy, R. F. (1991) Making HRD a Force in Strategic Organisational Change, *Industrial and Commercial Training*, 23(2), 17–19.

Ogbonna, E. and Harris, L. C. (2002) Managing Organisational Culture: Insights from the Hospitality Industry, *Human Resource Management Journal*, 12(1), 33–53.

Pedler, M., Burgoyne, J. and Boydell, T. (1997) *The Learning Company – A Strategy for Sustainable Development* (2nd ed.), Cambridge: McGraw Hill.

Peterson, S. L. (2008) Creating and Sustaining a Strategic Partnership: A Model for Human Resource Development, *Journal of Leadership Studies*, 2(2), 83–97.

Philips, K. and Shaw, P. (1989) *A Consultancy Approach for Trainers*, Hants: Gower.

Rainbird , H. (1995) The Changing Role of the Training Function; A Test for the Integration of Human Resource and Business Strategies, *Human Resource Management Journal*, 5(1), 72–90.

Senge, P. (1990) *The Fifth Discipline – The Art and Practice of The Learning Organisation*, Boston: Doubleday.

Shepherd, C. D., Gordon, G. L., Ridnour, R. E., Weilbaker, D. C. and Lambert, B. (2011) Sales Manager Training Practices in Small and Large Firms, *American Journal of Business*, 26(2), 92–117.

Sinclair, J. and Collins, D. (1992), Viewpoint: Training and Development's Worst Enemies – You and Management, *Journal of European Industrial Training*, 16(5), 21–25.

Stewart, J. and McGoldrick, J. (1996) *Human Resource Development: Perspectives, Strategies and Practices*, London: Pitman.

Storey, D. J. (1994) *Understanding the Small Business Sector*, Routledge: London.

Talbot, C. (1993) Strategic Change Management and Training: Adaptive, Adoptive and Innovative Roles, *Journal of European Industrial Training*, 17(5), 26–32.

Torraco, R. J. and Swanson, R. A. (1995) The Strategic roles of Human Resource Development, *Human Resource Planning*, 18(4), 10–22.

Tseng, C. and McLean, G. N. (2008) Strategic HRD Practices as Key Factors in Organizational Learning, *Journal of European Industrial Training*, 32(6), 418–432.

Walton, J. (1999) *Strategic Human Resource Development*, London: Financial Times Press.

Werner, R. L. and DeSimone, J. M. (2006) *Human Resource Development* (4th ed.), California: Southwestern.

West, P. (1994) The Learning Organisation: Losing the Luggage in Transit?, *Journal of European Industrial Training*, 18(11), 30–38.

Westhead, P. and Storey, D. J. (1996) Management Training and Small Firm Performance: Why is the Link so Weak?, *International Small Business Journal*, 14(4), 13–24.

3 MANAGING THE HRD FUNCTION

Ronan Carbery

By the end of this chapter you will be able to:

LEARNING OUTCOMES

- Understand the role of the HRD function
- Discuss the responsibilities of the HRD function
- Explain the role of the HRD practitioner in the organization
- Outline how budgets for the HRD function can be utilized
- Describe how HRD policies and practices can be communicated
- Consider how the role of the HRD function differs in SMEs

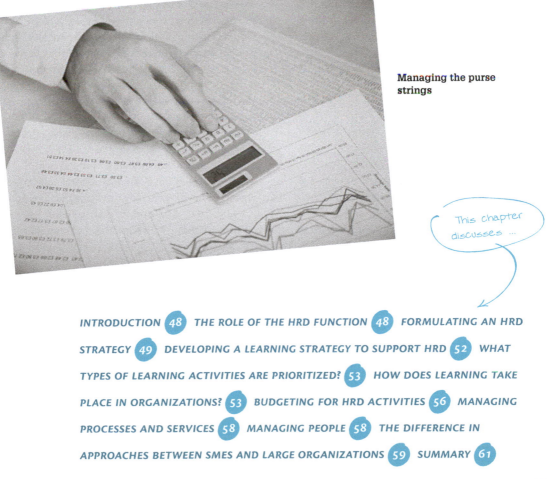

Managing the purse strings

This chapter discusses ...

INTRODUCTION

We discussed in Chapter 1 how HRD should be seen as a partner to HRM rather than subservient to it, under the broader title of human resources ▶ Chapter 1. HRD practitioners are responsible for learning and development, talent management and career development, among other strategic roles, and the HRD function should ideally complement the HRM function in identifying, selecting, recruiting, managing, motivating and retaining employees considered necessary to achieve organizational goals and objectives. Figure 1.3 portrayed the HRD function as a partner to HRM, but it may be the case in some organizations that the HRD function will be situated within the overall HRM department. Indeed, some organizations, especially SMEs, may not have any form of HR department at all. The availability of cloud computing services and technological advancements discussed in Chapter 1 allows organizations to manage both HRD and HRM services remotely as virtual services, while other organizations are taking the option of outsourcing their HRD functions. Regardless of the approach taken, whoever is ultimately responsible for managing the HRD function needs to recognize the requirements of the task. We will first look at the role of the HRD function.

THE ROLE OF THE HRD FUNCTION

HR departments generally employ people with responsibility for specialized areas within the overall HR function. A number of HR activities, once the sole remit of the HR function, are often **devolved** to **line managers** in order to allow the HR function to engage in faster decision making and free up time to focus on strategic activities ▶ Chapter 2. It is the line manager who works most closely with the employee. The types of activities normally devolved to line managers include employee selection, discipline and performance management. From an HRD perspective, the line manager is also in an ideal position to identify performance gaps and learning needs, and through the performance management process they can offer opportunities to participate in HRD activities ▶ Chapter 7.

devolved refers to the process of moving decision making downwards, from HR to line managers

line managers managers who have employees directly reporting to them and who have a higher level of responsibility than those employees

The HRD function needs to provide support and guidance to line managers in these activities; this also allows the HRD function to move towards aligning the HRD agenda with the strategic goals of the organization. Adopting a partnership approach between HRD and the line manager is important to achieving successful outcomes for both the employee and the organization. This approach requires that line managers are equipped with the appropriate skills, knowledge and attitudes to effectively manage and develop their staff. It should be noted, however, that this approach can create tensions between line managers and HRD practitioners, as line managers often believe they are already busy enough with the technical aspects of their role. Line managers are increasingly given responsibility for induction activities, challenging work assignments, job rotation, the implementation of multi-skilling programmes, and coaching, mentoring and guidance activities. Line managers express doubt concerning their skills to deal with learning and development issues. They frequently feel exposed due to inexperience or lack of knowledge or capability (Garavan *et al.*, 2008). Line managers are often accused of lacking time to focus on HRD issues and have not necessarily bought in to the idea that they should be part of a leader-led training and development strategy. Research on the devolution of HRD to the line suggests that HRD specialists are sometimes reluctant to devolve, due primarily to concerns about losing control and power and having to focus on issues that are more strategic in nature.

It is the overall vision, values and managerial ideology of the owner, chairman or CEO, however, that have the critical influence on the way in which HRD operates in an organization. In a larger organization, it is generally the managing director or senior management team who create the environment for the operation of HRD policies and processes. The status, role and profile of the overall HR function are influenced by the strength of the belief of senior management in the added value that HRD can contribute to the organization. For example, Richard Branson, founder of the Virgin Group, adopts a developmental approach to HRD and believes in continuously thinking about how to retain employees over the long term. One of the ways he does this is to promote from within whenever possible by creating a culture of opportunity so that learning is not restricted to set training periods, but happens in all areas of the organization on an ongoing basis. He cites the example of David Mackay, the chief pilot of Virgin Galactic, which provides suborbital spaceflights to space tourists, who was once captain of a Virgin Atlantic long-haul airplane, and spent four years training for his new role as an astronaut after 11,000 hours flying airplanes.

Contrary to what you might expect, the HRD function is not the place where learning actually takes place. Rather, the role of the HRD function is to facilitate and enable learning. This can be done by working with key stakeholders in the organization structure whose support is needed for HRD initiatives to succeed, by recognizing whom the HRD function should form business partnerships with, and those who could act as advocates of learning in the workplace, e.g. union learning representatives or influential team members.

The numbers of staff working in HRD functions tend to be low. In 2012, the size of an HRD team relative to the overall workforce in organizations continued to shrink for the fourth year in a row (O'Leonard, 2013). US organizations employed approximately four HRD staff for every 1,000 employees in 2012, down from a high of seven in 2008. This is possibly due to e-learning activities, as well as the move to informal and collaborative learning, in which co-workers and subject matter experts take on responsibilities once held solely by HRD staff. Shrinking staff-to-employee ratios are one way in which the role of the HRD function is changing. With fewer staff, more budgetary pressures and a demand to demonstrate value, HRD functions need to build skills in performance consulting, gain expertise in new technologies, including social and mobile platforms, and work to cultivate strong learning cultures within their organizations (Erasmus and Loedolff, 2012).

FORMULATING AN HRD STRATEGY

As highlighted in Chapter 2, the process of formulating an HRD strategy is a long-term one. Mayo (2004) suggests that it is a rational and staged process and HRD strategy should seek to be both proactive and reactive. Important proactive drivers of HRD strategy include the business goals and objectives, organizational change processes, and the organization's HRM philosophy and strategies. Reactive drivers of HRD strategy include operational issues, responding to external changes in customer or supplier expectations, and sudden changes

in business strategy. An effective HRD strategy will include a number of important components:

- Articulate a set of beliefs and values about learning in the organization.
- Propose a set of coherent HRD practices that reflect values and philosophy.
- Select learning strategies that support short-term operational goals as well as medium to long-term objectives.

In formulating HRD strategy it is important that the HRD function adopts a pragmatic and continuous approach that involves engagement with stakeholders. Anderson (2007) proposes five important actions necessary to formulate an HRD strategy:

- Participation by HRD practitioners in business planning processes.
- Dialogue with organizational stakeholders so that they take account of organizational HRD priorities.
- Develop and communicate a strong business case for investment in HRD activities that fall outside the formal business plan.
- Ensure the cost-effective use of HRD resources and continually focus on organizational priorities.
- Evaluate the strategic-level contribution that HRD processes make to the organization.

HRD strategies must be sufficiently flexible to account for changes in individual and organizational priorities and must be able to cope with emergent opportunities and challenges. Table 3.1 outlines the staged approach to HRD strategy formulation.

The formulation of an HRD strategy is a collaborative effort involving multiple stakeholders who are committed to its implementation. One example of an HRD strategy comes from the British Columbia Public Service in Canada, who employ 30,000 employees in 280 communities. Their strategy has four goals:

Goal One: Creating a Culture of Learning
This is achieved by building and sustaining an environment that inspires and supports employees to pursue learning through diverse formats, methods and streams. It attempts to create a personalized, inclusive approach to learning that is championed by executives and supervisors at every level. This is accomplished by:

(a) Strong support from senior management
(b) Supervisors who empower their staff and promote learning
(c) Recognition that some of our most significant learning comes from careful risk taking and failure

Table 3.1 Staged approach to HRD strategy formulation

Step	Actions
Take responsibility for HRD strategy development	• Create an HRD strategy development group • Involve key stakeholders such as line managers, HRM specialists and employees
Clarify the organizational mission and strategy	• Read formal strategy documents to gain insights into current strategic priorities • Gather and interpret information from key individuals in the organization
Conduct an internal and external stakeholder analysis	• Specify the key performance issues from the perspective of each stakeholder • Identify how each stakeholder contributes to HRD and their expectations of HRD • Analyse the key barriers and enablers to strategic alignment and the emergence of a learning culture and climate
Specify the strategic challenges and opportunities facing the organization	• Clearly differentiate strategic from operational effectiveness issues • Clearly identify issues that have HRD implications • Be careful to clearly differentiate those issues that have HRD implications and those that do not
Generate strategic alternatives for HRD and gain commitment from stakeholders	• Prioritize HRD goals that add value to the strategic imperatives of the organization • Focus on issues that can achieve quick wins as well as long-term successes • Focus on issues where there are clear HRD applications • Identify benefits for individuals as well as the organization
Agree a strategic HRD strategy and plan	• Specify clear HRD goals to be achieved within a specified timeframe • Clearly specify the resources required to achieve the goals • Allocate accountabilities and responsibilities to achieve HRD goals

Source: Adapted from Mayo (2004) and Harrison (2009)

(d) Employees being personally motivated to learn in all types of settings – formal and informal
(e) Ongoing and strategic investment in resources, training and tools
(f) Opportunities for employees to take what they have learned and apply it
(g) A continuous feedback cycle with ongoing adjustment and coaching when needed

Goal Two: Embracing Innovative Technologies and Tools to Prepare for the Future
This is focused on creating better awareness of and providing increased access to online learning, e-learning, podcasts and short software application courses. This is accomplished by:
(a) Accelerating knowledge transfer through two-way generational mentorship whereby younger employees mentor others to build their confidence in the use of new technologies and, in doing so, allow others to share their knowledge and experience with those new to the public service
(b) Establishing a virtual learning site that can be personalized by each employee and that will provide easy access to all their learning tools

Goal Three: Responding Flexibly to Learning Needs
Recognizing the need to respond quickly to emerging needs, the Public Service identifies that people have different learning styles and preferences. To account for this, the organization:
(a) Maximizes regional offerings and support through a combination of in-person, online, e-learning and virtual collaboration tools
(b) Invests in instructional approaches and formats that will better accommodate different learning styles, preferences and other diverse cultural and generational needs

Goal Four: Valuing Diversity and Advancing Inclusiveness through Learning
In order to ensure that the HRD strategy facilitates inclusiveness, the organization:
(a) Markets the benefits of diversity and increases awareness of diversity issues and inclusive practices with the aim of promoting and building a more diverse public sector
(b) Embeds the principles of diversity into all learning curricula

In 2010, Google launched GoogleEDU, the company's learning and leadership-development programme. GoogleEDU aims to formalize learning at the company in a relatively new way, relying on data analytics and other measures to ensure it is teaching employees what they need to know to keep profits humming. In 2011 approximately a third of Google's 33,100 global workforce participated in the in-house programme. According to Karen May, Google's vice president of leadership and talent, 'What's important is that it aligns with our overall business strategy.' For more information see www.google.com/edu/.

In 2009, McDonalds were awarded Best Learning and Development Strategy by CIPD in the annual HR Excellence Awards. McDonald's has an HRD strategy for each employee group: 'crew members'; restaurant management teams and franchisees; and office staff and middle managers. Training of crew members happens on the restaurant floor and in other settings. Proof of its success is the fact that 94 per cent of McDonald's business managers began their careers flipping burgers. For restaurant management teams and franchisees, the focus has been on flexible and field-based training. Other initiatives include a service leadership programme and an extended hours workshop. The former, designed to improve staff confidence, raised McDonald's mystery diner score by 2.5 per cent. The latter was developed to help managers prepare for a change to trading hours in certain restaurants. For office staff and middle managers the emphasis has been on providing more opportunities for personal and team development. As a result of these initiatives, employee turnover in UK branches of McDonalds has fallen from 80 per cent in 2004 to under half that today, and staff engagement has increased dramatically. The average length of time a crew member stays with the organization has increased from 18 months to 2½ years, while the average tenure among restaurant managers is 15 years.

HRD policies are an outcome of an HRD strategy. A policy is generally something that gives guidance on the way things should be done. In other words, the HRD policy should provide clear guidance on what needs to be done to develop specific behaviour and performance standards, by whom and why. Stewart *et al.* (2013) suggest a number of headings that can be used to structure an HRD policy statement:

1 Purpose and objectives – the specific aims of the policy in relation to the overall aims and objectives of the organization
2 Priorities – how the organization will make decisions on what HRD activities should be prioritized
3 Role and responsibilities – the specific responsibilities of various groups should be detailed, e.g. senior managers, line managers, the HRD function and individual employees
4 Cost allocation – how HRD activities will be funded
5 Application of policy to various categories of employees – will all employees be given equal access to all HRD activities or will certain categories of employees have differing activities?
6 Application of policy to various categories of HRD activities – what methods will be used, e.g. educational programmes and/or internal programmes
7 Place of and access to HRD records – where records will be stored and how they can be accessed

Interestingly, one organization that has taken a less structured approach to HRD policy formulation and implementation is Netflix (McCord, 2014), who are based in California, US. A sample of general HR policies includes: all salaried employees in Netflix are not given a specific amount of holidays per year; instead, they are allowed to take whatever time off they feel is appropriate. Their expense policy is five words long: 'Act in Netflix's best interests', while their most blunt policy is 'adequate performance gets a generous severance package'. In addition, they stopped carrying out formal performance reviews and adopted informal 360-degree reviews where employees are asked to identify things that their colleagues should stop, start or continue. From an HRD perspective, their strategy is to make clear to managers that their top priority is building great teams. Leaders should create the company culture, and the HR function should think like innovative businesspeople.

CONSIDER THIS...

The HRD function in Symantec, a US-based software maker, considered the strategic role it played in the organization and realized that it needed to fix how it was perceived by restructuring its HRD function to better align with business goals. In Symantec's former model, HR employees each supported individual business units, with the result being a fragmented approach to HR. The organization underwent a restructuring in which the overall HR function was split into two groups. First, HR Direct, an operational HR function, supported employees' e-mail and phone enquiries that were not easily answered by the internal HR website. It also worked on project-related activities on behalf of business partners and global products. Second, a strategic HR function was established with senior HR employees who focus on HRD activities, including assessing and retaining top talent and integrating organizations that Symantec acquires. By documenting the nature of HR Direct's enquiries – the topics people are asking about and how often similar questions arise – it has enabled the HR function to improve their HRD offerings and the quality of information available online.

DEVELOPING A LEARNING STRATEGY TO SUPPORT HRD

Articulating an effective learning strategy is central to managing the HRD function, as it serves as a supporter and enabler of business strategy. Learning strategies provide a clear statement about what employees need to learn, but they also provide a clear articulation of why learning is central to business strategy and how that strategy will be realized in an organization. It is important to have an explicit statement of learning strategy because this helps to communicate expectations as well as the capabilities of the HRD function to be strategic. There are a number of issues that need to be considered in this context, and the following subsections outline how these issues should be addressed. These are: (1) The dimensions of a learning strategy; (2) Achieving business alignment; (3) Deciding on how best to deliver

learning; (4) Where does responsibility for learning reside?; (5) Assessing the fit of the learning strategy; (6) Assessing the impact of the learning strategy on the organization's performance. Figure 3.1 illustrates that the dimensions of a learning strategy that enables the HRD function to both support and enable strategy address a number of fundamental questions concerning why, what, how, where, who and the so what of learning. The remainder of this section addresses these questions.

Why does learning matter in the context of organizations and individuals?

When organizations seek to address why learning matters, they invariably answer this question in terms of its alignment to organizational goals and its environment. However, it is also important to consider how learning meets the needs of employees. As we discussed in Chapter 1, the justifications of why learning matters typically include the following:

● It is a necessary precondition to enable the organization to achieve its business goals.
● It enhances the performance of individuals. This justification can often be viewed as remedial or gap-focused.
● It enhances succession management and the organization's talent pipeline. This justification may focus on a select group of employees, but may in some cases be concerned with developing the potential of the entire workforce.
● It helps the organization to address major change initiatives, especially transformational change.
● It facilitates the development of a strong corporate culture and/or is used to support a set of organizational values.
● It helps the organization to utilize its knowledge capital and enable both sharing and seeking of knowledge.
● It is necessary in order to meet regulatory procedures or requirements set down by industry regulatory bodies.

This is an interesting list of justifications and is typically what you will find in many organizational policy documents. However, the needs of individuals are frequently lost in this wider strategic justification. The reasons for this are complex; however, it reflects the predominance of strategic imperatives and the organizational agenda.

Figure 3.1 Dimensions of learning strategy

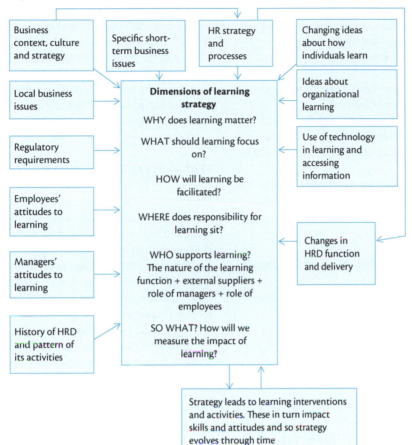

WHAT TYPES OF LEARNING ACTIVITIES ARE PRIORITIZED?

The answer to this question invariably revolves around the strategic goals of the organization and the extent to which the HRD function is concerned with alignment ▶ Chapter 2. However, a number of areas appear to be given universal priority across businesses. These include:

- **Leadership Development:** Managers and leaders are viewed as a key talent group and are vitally important to HRD in terms of the role of leaders in modelling learning behaviours throughout the organization.
- **Generic Competencies:** Many organizations prioritize learning activities that focus on the development of generic competencies. Competency frameworks typically focus on generic skills, such as interpersonal skills,

relationship-building skills and change management skills. These frameworks are used to both prioritize and organize learning strategies.

- **Technical Learning:** Organizations devote a considerable amount of time and resources to technical learning activities. Technical training activities typically encompass technology training, functional, professional and job-specific training, and product knowledge training.

HOW DOES LEARNING TAKE PLACE IN ORGANIZATIONS?

The third component of learning strategy addresses the question of the blend of learning strategies that is used to achieve the strategic intention of HRD function. The previous section outlined some of those strategies; however, five important trends are evident in organizational practice. These are:

- An increased emphasis on experiential or informal learning and the value of learning by doing
- The emergence of the centrality of reflection as part of the learning process
- The importance of developmental relationships and social capital as a means of learning
- Increased recognition of the value of informal and incidental learning and the realization that formal, bureaucratic learning strategies may not necessarily be the most effective
- The use of electronic learning management systems to identify learning opportunities and to monitor what learning employees undertake

Where does responsibility for learning reside?

The locus of responsibility for HRD and its associated learning activities will differ depending upon the organizational context and whether it is a SME, a multinational global headquarters, a subsidiary of a MNC or a public sector organization. There is evidence of a move to shared service models for more transactional learning activities ▶ Chapter 2, an increased use of developed or decentralized responsibility to line managers, greater use of centres of expertise and strategic business partner models. A unifying theme running through these various models is the notion that responsibility for learning is shared among senior managers, line managers, employees, and HR and HRD specialists. Organizations typically express how these roles are performed in policy documents.

Who delivers the learning strategy?

There is no typical or standardized HRD function; rather, there is considerable variation in how HRD is organized and resourced. Figure 3.2 captures some of the complexities in how HRD is organized. In some organizations, HRD is located within the HR function; in others, it may be a separate function that focuses on all aspects of learning. As a separate function, it may only focus on management and generic skills, with technical training activities located within business units. Examples of more innovative approaches include outsourcing, strategic partnerships with customers, suppliers and training agencies, and business partner roles.

Figure 3.2 Managing and resourcing HRD in organizations

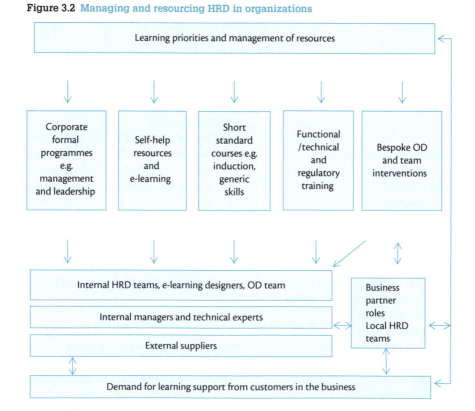

How can the HRD function measure the impact of HRD activities?

Organizations use a variety of metrics in their measurement efforts. Efficiency metrics are useful for benchmarking against other organizations. Comparing these metrics against industry standards allows HRD functions to identify potential problem areas and make improvements. Other metrics, such as adoption, utility, alignment, attainment and performance, are also important in addressing and improving the HRD function. HRD as an organizational activity is always open to the threat that in difficult times it is often first to be cut or scaled back. HRD specialists can take some of the blame for this, simply because they do not take sufficient steps to measure the impact of HRD. It must, however, be acknowledged that there are a number of significant obstacles to demonstrating that learning activities make an impact on the business. First, the demonstration of a causal link between investment in learning strategies and business results is complex, and, some would argue, impossible. The concept of return on investment (ROI) has remained elusive and there is an absence of robust measurement methods. Practice within organizations suggests that a variety of metrics are used, albeit not very coherently. Chapter 10 looks at this topic in more detail, but here are a few examples of metrics that can be used:

return on investment (ROI) the benefits gained from spending money on HRD activities

- Where there is a clear strategic plan for learning activity, were these activities carried out to the volumes planned, on time and within budget? This is a **basic measure** of 'did we do what we said we would?' It can extend beyond courses to other activities – the number of project assignments found or developmental job moves made, for example.
- **Customer satisfaction** with learning activities is measured either immediately, or some time after, events and through staff surveys. The Prudential's simple rating scale for customer satisfaction with each learning event seems an attractive option. People in its learning delivery team and its customers rate each event as unacceptable, bronze, silver or gold. Each category has detailed criteria which must be met to achieve each of the different levels.
- **Customer responsiveness** – time from enquiry to delivery of a bespoke intervention, for example.
- **Take up** of activities or use of resources – use of e-learning materials, for example.

- **Pass rate** for training, which represents a 'licence to practise' in regulated environments.
- **Behavioural change** as a result of learning, where this is possible to measure before and after – through 360-degree feedback for leadership skills, or sample surveys after appraising training etc.
- Employee **attitude surveys**, especially as a means of tracking how employees regard the quality of management and leadership over time, including whether leaders role model the espoused values. Employees can also give a perspective on other softer metrics – the degree of support for learning, the extent to which employees share know-how, how mistakes are dealt with etc. – although attributing shifts in these to learning interventions is problematic.
- Succession and **talent pool cover** and the ability to resource leadership positions, as in an acquisition, for example, are ways to measure the quality of the leadership talent pool.
- More rigorous **evaluations of specific interventions** from multiple stakeholders.
- **Business measures** in focused areas of training – manufacturing quality, numbers of accidents at work, customer complaints, speed to market etc.
- More **general HR metrics** – attraction and retention, for example – but these are harder to attribute to learning activity.

Coordinating the HRD function

Defining roles is one of the most frequently highlighted challenges in ensuring that the HRD function has a key role to play in organizational effectiveness. A particular aspect of this positioning concerns whether the HRD specialist is part of the top team and located at an appropriate level within the organization. Understanding how establishments with the strongest performance on HRD have succeeded in getting the HRD specialist to be a strategic partner highlights a number of important features:

○ **Business Environment Dynamism:** Establishments with a stronger and more high-profile training and development specialist are more often found in industries and competitive niches characterized by rapid change than in those where business models and social norms are more stable.

- **Integration of HRD:** The degree to which understanding and management of the impact of HRD activities are integrated into business operations, and, more importantly, in the strategic decision-making process, emerges as an important factor in strategic partnering.
- **Competencies of the HRD Specialist:** Training and development specialists who possess a broad knowledge of business objectives, organizational development and business consultancy skills are more likely to be part of the senior team and to work more closely with the line.

High levels of alignment of HRD tend to go hand-in-hand with integration of learning and development practices within organizations. It is, however, very difficult to say whether integration leads to better alignment or whether alignment supports an integrated approach. Organizations that excel in their approach to HRD do so by integrating learning into both their everyday business processes and strategic decision-making processes. This suggests that organizations need to invest in HRD processes aimed at influencing operational and strategic processes to ensure continuous learning. The ability to make this happen rests on the shoulders of corporate leaders, line managers and HRD specialists. It requires that establishments invest resources and ensure sufficient internal power to influence the evolution of an integrated approach to learning, training and development.

It is particularly important for the HRD function to assess whether and how the organization's competitors manage their people (Clardy, 2008). This depends on the organization's concerns regarding how skilled its competitor's employees are. This is dependent on the overall HR function's policies and practices dealing with manpower planning, staffing, compensation, performance evaluation, and training and development, in addition to the general administrative and supervisory systems and procedures used in the context of the organization's culture ▶ Chapter 6. The HR function is well placed to carry out competitive intelligence (Kahaner, 1996) on these issues in several ways: by recruiting employees who work for competitors and debriefing them after hiring; by learning about competitor HR practices through professional contacts and associations; by analysis of documents, ads and reports; or by formal benchmarking studies. Using this gathered information, the HRD function can report on competitor HRD practices with recommendations for how they can be addressed, nullified or replicated.

SPOTLIGHT ON SKILLS

Your CEO is unconvinced of the value of the HRD function and has asked you to consider restructuring the function or eliminating it completely and letting each individual department handle their HRD responsibilities themselves. How do you respond? How can you can convince the CEO that an HRD function is vital from a strategic point of view?

To help you answer the questions above, visit www.macmillanihe.com/companion/carbery-hrd and watch the video of Declan Deegan talking about the HRD function.

BUDGETING FOR HRD ACTIVITIES

Research suggests that organizations cannot succeed without devoting resources to employee development (O'Leonard, 2013). Following double-digit HRD budget cuts during the recession, 2010 saw the beginnings of a turnaround. In 2011, US organizations' HRD budgets rose 9.5 per cent, and in 2012 companies committed even more resources, with budgets increasing 12 per cent. The largest budgetary gains came in the technology and manufacturing industries, both with 20 per cent increases in HRD expenditure spending. The picture is mixed in the EU, where a 2009 study found that 29 per cent of private and public sector employers did not know the total cost of the training they provided, while 62 per cent did not know how many people were attending courses (Lovell, 2009). Where there is a scarcity of skilled talent in the labour market, organizations cannot solve their skills shortages from the outside. Instead, they must commit to developing their internal talent to build the right skills to foster a competitive advantage.

Since 2010, the trend has been towards more outsourcing of HRD services. In 2012, US companies spent 16 per cent of their HRD budgets on external learning services, up from 12 per cent in 2009 (O'Leonard, 2013). This movement could be driven in part by the additional funds in HRD budgets and by the reduction in size of the HRD function. With more money to spend and fewer HRD staff members, organizations are relying more on external providers by purchasing off-the-shelf content and spending less on customized development activities. The largest portion of the outsourced spending (30 per cent) goes to external instructors, followed by external classes and certifications (27 per cent). Organizations are turning to less costly and more time-efficient learning solutions. The trends impacting HRD organizations have implications for these third-party providers. It is important for the HRD function to decide what products and services to purchase and what tasks they themselves will perform.

Decisions regarding the size of the HRD budget are mostly made at either senior management level or board level (Garavan *et al.*, 2008). The role of the HRD function in influencing the HRD budget in decision making has significantly decreased in scope since the global financial crisis in 2007/2008. But in larger organizations, decisions are still largely a centralized process. HRD budgets often focus primarily on direct costs, with indirect costs rarely factored in. Direct costs include course fees and books and material costs. Indirect costs include opportunity costs, such as the salaries of those who are involved in HRD activities.

The HRD function is often treated as a cost centre within organizations. A cost centre is a department within an organization that does not directly add to profit, but which still costs an organization money to

---

A recent CIPD report found that, in the UK, the average spending on HRD activities per employee in the public sector was £116, compared with £320 in the private sector. With tight budgetary constraints, getting value for money is vital for HRD functions in public sector organizations, and increasingly they are taking advantage of managed learning services (MLSs) to do so. These are third-party providers who act as a broker between the organization and external training providers and negotiate discounts with external suppliers, part of which are passed on to the client. Some MLS providers claim they can get discounts of up to 70 per cent off brochure prices on IT training suppliers, with discounts on management training courses ranging from 10 per cent to 20 per cent off listed prices.

MLSs also offer training administration, which can include invoicing and assessing the effectiveness of the training, or else act as the complete HRD function. These arrangements tend to be long-term deals. One MLS provider, Capita Learning, has long-term outsourcing deals with Southampton City Council and Swindon Borough Council, and they estimate that the savings will be approximately 15 per cent of the training cost per year.

Another example, Service Birmingham, a joint venture between Birmingham and Capita to improve working practices through technology, was previously in the position of being able to frontload £2 million of spending on HRD back in 2006, but now has to make efficiencies to maintain HRD in light of a revised budget of £290,000 per year. The head of HRD in Service Birmingham suggests that e-learning has been invaluable in keeping costs down without sacrificing HRD activities.

'E-learning allows us to reach far greater numbers. But it's important it's not used in isolation and that it's constantly assessed so that we can follow-up with traditional classroom training for those that need extra support.'

Sources

How one training pot can cut costs http://www.theguardian.com/public-sector-training/managed-learning-services

How are the cuts affecting training? http://www.theguardian.com/public-leaders-network/2012/jan/23/how-cuts-affecting-training

Service Birmingham Public-Private Joint Venturing http://www.service-birmingham.co.uk/case-studies-container/public-private-joint-venturing.aspx

Questions

1 What do you think accounts for the significant difference between public sector and private sector expenditure on HRD activities?
2 What are the drawbacks of using managed learning services?

operate. Cost centres are generally treated differently within an organization. Because a cost centre does not produce a profit directly from its activities, managers of cost centres are responsible for keeping their costs in line or below budget. Service centres, on the other hand, are an organizational unit which provides a specific service or product. An increasing number of large establishments consider the HRD function to be a service department (Garavan *et al.*, 2008). This is a positive trend for HRD, as it indicates that the importance of HRD and its impact in organizations is perhaps gaining respect.

MANAGING PROCESSES AND SERVICES

Organizations with an advanced HRD function tend to invest resources a bit differently, spending less on off-the-shelf content and more on developing their own customized content and delivery services. These organizations also invest more in assessment services, which help the organization to target the HRD activities to develop skills where needed. In general, most organizations start with generic or standardized content and then recognize the need for a more customized learning approach as the organization matures. In addition, best-practice organizations dedicate more internal staffing resources to develop interactive learning content and maximize these efforts by reusing and repurposing content across the organization. While the cost is higher than developing generic content, the investment pays off in improved employee performance and organizational capabilities (O'Leonard, 2013).

The question of whether to develop employees through recruitment and training or to recruit highly skilled employees from the external labour market is increasingly being answered with the advice to recruit from outside. Having traditionally been developed and performed in-house, single HR services or significant parts of the responsibilities performed by HR have gradually been outsourced to other organizations and companies (Ulrich *et al.*, 2008). This change applies not only to larger companies and public organizations but also to SMEs (Cardon and Stevens, 2004). An increasing number of organizations turn to different employment agencies, recruitment firms and temporary work agencies, but also to new third-party organizations called labour market intermediaries (LMIs) and Professional Employer Organizations (PEOs), which provide a

variety of HR services, including the delivery of HRD activities ▶ Chapter 1.

The reason organizations outsource their HRD activities is to save on the costs associated with training, assuming that someone else will carry out the training to ensure the delivery of key skills. Skill loss can have damaging effects on competitiveness, however (Kock *et al.*, 2012). Also, it allows organizations to benefit from the advantage of specialized HRD providers who may have expertise in the areas required that may not be available within the organization. Using third-party providers gives organizations a degree of greater flexibility by using temporary subcontractors to cover fluctuating demands for labour depending on productivity demands (Cooke *et al.*, 2005). This flexibility also brings other advantages of saving direct costs, such as reducing headcount and overtime working, and indirect costs, including recruitment and induction costs, and saving on absenteeism costs (Kock *et al.*, 2012).

BUILDING YOUR SKILLS

Working in an HRD function in a large banking institution in London with responsibility for coordinating HRD activities for the whole European region, you realize that technological advancements give you the opportunity to alter how training sessions are scheduled. Usually your HRD activities are held in London. You have asked your line managers to identify opportunities for development during performance discussions, and that information is sent to your branch. Based on the data received, you will determine the most cost-effective region in which to hold the next training, rather than automatically flying everyone to London. You hope that this new approach based on employee demand rather than management-imposed planning will maximize the HRD budget, as will the more reasonably priced offshore scheduling and programme administration. What type of data do you need to gather to make an informed decision on where and when to hold the training?

MANAGING PEOPLE

The main responsibility of the overall HR function is to maximize and reward the contribution that each employee makes to the organization. In order to do this, organizations choose between a range of policies and practices that can assist in achieving this objective. By this we mean policies and practices such as how to recruit and select employees; how to pay and reward them; what terms and conditions they work under; what HRD opportunities the organization should pay for; how to deal with employees who break organizational rules; and how to ensure that everyone in the organization is treated equally. Specific HRD activities include training and development, career development and talent management. In order to do this, the core skills of those working in the HRD function consist of a combination of efficient training skills such as learning needs identification, designing HRD activities, delivery of HRD activities and evaluation of HRD activities, but also a variety of business and consultancy competencies. These include a broad understanding of the business, an understanding of organizational processes and advanced problem-solving skills. Those working in the HRD function will also be expected to possess strong interpersonal skills and the ability to build strong relationships with managers and clients at all levels within the organization. It is important that the role is performed with credibility, professionalism and confidence. Stakeholder management is a key requirement of the role, and HRD practitioners are usually required to demonstrate value and to convince business unit managers that HRD interventions add value to their business operations.

Since the global financial collapse, many organizations had been reluctant to invest in HRD activities, resorting to short-term cost cutting by freezing pay and other rewards to avoid deeper staff cuts. These cutbacks may seem minor compared with terminating employment contracts, but the effects on the remaining employees can be significant. Employees who survived one or more company lay-offs were found to have higher levels of depression and were more susceptible to workplace injuries (Institute of Behavioral Science, 2003). To take advantage of the somewhat more stable economic climate, HRD functions have begun to focus on improving morale and retaining talented employees. Although investments in HRD activities may seem counterintuitive in a downturn, organizations should recognize the benefits of an engaged workforce. Employees who are properly trained are likely to be more productive, thereby increasing their job satisfaction and improving their commitment to the organization (Edmans, 2011).

BUILDING YOUR SKILLS

If you were in charge of the HRD function in a large call centre with a high volume of staff turnover you might find it more cost effective to outsource their recruitment and training processes, whereas if you were working for an organization operating in a knowledge-intensive market with an advanced HR function you might wish to keep these functions in-house, as they are often seen as important mechanisms for shaping the organizational culture. How would your approach to managing the HRD function differ between the two types of organizations?

THE DIFFERENCE IN APPROACHES BETWEEN SMES AND LARGE ORGANIZATIONS

Lack of familiarity with the term 'HRD' within SMEs is commonplace (Hill, 2004), as HRD is more likely to be perceived and talked about within SMEs as 'training and development' (Sambrook, 2000). A strategic approach to HRD or training and development in SMEs is challenging. Entrepreneurs repeatedly complain that they cannot hire the right people because universities are failing to keep pace with a fast-changing job market. Small firms lack the resources to provide training and are consequently making do with fewer people working longer hours. The owner-manager plays a vital role in developing any kind of a strategic approach towards HRD, and has considerable freedom and influence in making strategic decisions and their role in strategy implementation (Ling *et al.*, 2008). Owner-managers often react to unpredictable changes in the environment and make frequent modifications and refinements to cope with dynamic environments (Barnes, 2002), and focus on 'fire-fighting' activities and operational problems, which is likely to be counterproductive to any type of strategic approach being adopted by the HRD function.

Owner-manager attitudes and values represent a potential barrier (Coetzer *et al.*, 2012) to the operation of the HRD function, and this is evident in the lack of an HRD orientation in SMEs (Bishop, 2008). Keogh *et al.* (2005) found that owner-managers frequently neglected their HRD needs, which in turn influenced their beliefs about the development of the skills of their employees. This may be due to fears that, if they invest in the development of employees, these individuals will become more employable in the wider labour market and are at risk of being poached by another employer.

Benefit or Cost?

ACTIVE CASE STUDY

Two weeks ago, Sinead Donnelly, the senior vice president of HR with responsibility for HRD for a US pharmaceutical organization, Zydtak Medicines, had routinely turned in her budget requirements to her boss, Tom Davies, the COO and executive vice president of administration. Davies had sent the papers back to her that morning, and she was stunned to find that Davies had cut her HRD budget by more than 75 per cent.

That afternoon, as Donnelly set out to draft a memo to Davies, she could not help wondering what she could have done to avoid this crisis. When she had joined the organization five years earlier, she had taken a more proactive attitude to training than her predecessor. Rather than waiting to be approached, she had met with senior managers every quarter to discuss their employees' learning needs. Donnelly then started several training initiatives aimed at two types of employees: new hires, who had to be brought up to speed quickly, and first-level supervisors who had been identified as high-potential performers. Many of these programmes proved to be popular, with average enrolments of between 25 and 30 employees.

However, Donnelly had initially adopted a low-key approach to learning and development. Her team collected information on programmes at various business schools, which she sent to all the managers. If a manager showed interest in a particular programme, the HR function provided additional information and arranged enrolment. Donnelly usually encouraged managers to speak to previous attendees first and look over the course materials those people had brought back. That, she believed, was a good way to determine whether the manager's needs fitted with the programme's theme. If the company's managers rated a programme as 'poor' or 'below average' three times in a row, Donnelly would discourage managers from enrolling in it.

When a manager returned to work after completing a programme, Donnelly would assess its value to the individual and the company. She asked each participant to fill out a two-page form that included questions like:

1 How confident are you that you will be able to use what you have learned in your current job?
2 To what extent do you think the materials covered will help you to improve your performance?
3 To what extent do you think the programme will prepare you for future jobs in the company?

The HRD function did not usually conduct anything more formally by way of follow-up, and left it to participants to transfer what they had learned into their jobs. It was also the participants' responsibility to contact colleagues and subordinates if they wanted anyone else to attend the same programme.

Until five years ago, only about ten of Zydtak's managers each year had attended programmes at universities or industries. Since then the company had sponsored an average of 20 managers in each of the past three years. Noticing the trend, Donnelly had started thinking more proactively about learning and development. Around the same time, administrators at two business schools had approached her and offered to design specialized programmes for Zydtak's managers. In fact, she had been on her way to meet with one of them the previous day.

The more she learned about the opportunities to customize learning and development, the more Donnelly liked the idea. Her plan was to conduct two programmes a year, each consisting of two six-day sessions, with a month's break between them. She obtained tentative commitment from several faculty members at the business schools, who agreed to help design courses, develop materials and serve as classroom facilitators. Eventually, Donnelly hoped, the programme would be a facilitator for the creation of Zydtak's corporate university.

When Donnelly calculated the figures, she estimated the cost of a customized programme at around $12,000 per participant. That was less expensive than the $15,000 to $20,000 in tuition Zydtak spent, on average, to send a manager to a university programme. Nevertheless, the overall costs would be significantly higher, since the plan called for 40 to 50 of Zydtak's managers from all over the world to attend the programmes. That's why Donnelly had asked for a budget outlay of $650,000 for the next year – double the previous year's budget.

Donnelly stared at the blank pad of her desk. She wished she had a plan for responding to Davies, but all she could think of were questions. Should she give up on the customized programme for the moment?

Questions

1 What do you think informed the CEO's decision to cut the HRD budget?
2 Make your case to the CEO to reinstate the HRD budget.
3 Formulate an HRD strategy for this organization.

SUMMARY

This chapter highlights the issues involved in managing the HRD function in organizations. It is important to highlight that the role of the HRD function is to facilitate and enable learning rather than to be the sole provider of learning. In order to obtain commitment from line managers and senior management to this approach, the HRD function plays a key role in formulating HRD strategy by adopting an ongoing collaborative approach that involves engagement with these stakeholders. Being able to articulate this strategy is essential to managing the HRD function as it serves as a supporter and enabler of the overall business strategy.

CHAPTER REVIEW QUESTIONS

1 What role does the line manager play in assisting the HRD function?
2 Outline the role of the HRD function in developing an HRD strategy.
3 What are the steps to formulating an HRD strategy?
4 What should a learning strategy articulate?
5 Suggest some metrics that the HRD function can use to demonstrate its value to the organization.
6 What is the difference between a cost centre and a service centre?
7 Why do some organizations choose to outsource their HRD activities?
8 How is the HRD function viewed in SMEs?

FURTHER READING

Clardy, A. (2008) The Strategic Role of Human Resource Development in Managing Core Competencies, *Human Resource Development International*, 11(2), 183–197.
Cooke, F. L., Shen, J. and McBride, A. (2005) Outsourcing HR as a Competitive Strategy? A Literature Review

and an Assessment of Implications, *Human Resource Management*, 44(4), 413–432.
Economist Intelligence Group (2009) *The Role of HR in Uncertain Times*, London: Economist Intelligence Group.
Mafi, S. L. (2000) Managing the HRD Function and Service Quality: A Call for a New Approach, *Human Resource Development Quarterly*, 11(1), 81–86.

USEFUL WEBSITES

Bersin by Deloitte https://www.bersin.com/practice/Browse.aspx?p=Learning-@-Development
This is an excellent resource detailing up-to-date research on industry trends in HRD, benchmarking standards, and case studies and factbooks.
SHRM Organizational and Employee Development: http://www.shrm.org/hrdisciplines/orgempdev/pages/default.aspx
This section of the SHRM website provides excellent links to current research and guides for those working in HRD functions.
CIPD Costing and benchmarking learning and development http://www.cipd.co.uk/hr-resources/factsheets/costing-benchmarking-learning-development.aspx
CIPD's guide to costing HRD activities gives useful information on budgeting for HRD activities.
CIPD HR Function page http://www.cipd.co.uk/hr-topics/hr-function.aspx
This provides a lot of information on how to manage the overall HR function.
Bureau of Labor Statistics, US Department of Labor http://www.bls.gov/ooh/management/human-resources-managers.htm
This site provides information on what skills people working in the HR function require, the working environment, and how to get a job in a HR function.

BIBLIOGRAPHY

Anderson, V. (2007) *The Value of Learning: From Return on Investment to Return on Expectation*, London: Chartered Institute of Personnel and Development.

Barnes, D. (2002) The Manufacturing Strategy Formation Process in Small and Medium-sized Enterprises, *Journal of Small Business and Enterprise Development*, 9(2), 130–149.

Bishop, D. (2008) The Small Enterprise in the Training Market, *Education and Training*, 50(8/9), 661–673.

Cardon, M. C. and Stevens, C. E. (2004) Managing Human Resources in Small Organizations: What Do We Know?, *Human Resource Management Journal*, 14(3), 295–323.

Clardy, A. (2008) The Strategic Role of Human Resource Development in Managing Core Competencies, *Human Resource Development International*, 11(2), 183–197.

Coetzer, A., Redmond, J. and Sharafizad, J. (2012) Using the Critical Incident Technique to Research Decision Making Regarding Access to Training and Development in Medium-sized Enterprises, *International Journal of Training Research*, 10(3), 164–178.

Cooke, F. L., Shen, J. and McBride, A. (2005) Outsourcing HR as a Competitive Strategy? A Literature Review and an Assessment of Implications, *Human Resource Management*, 44(4), 413–432.

Edmans, A. (2011) Does the Stock Market Fully Value Intangibles? Employee Satisfaction and Equity Prices, *Journal of Financial Economics*, 101(3), 621–640.

Erasmus, B. and Loedolff, P. (2012) Managing Human Resource Development Functions and Services, In J. Wilson (Ed.), *International Human Resource Development: Learning, Education and Training for Individuals and Organisations* (3rd ed.), London: Kogan (407–428).

Garavan, T. N., Shanahan, V. and Carbery, R. (2008) *Training & Development in Ireland: Results of the Biennial National Survey of Benchmarks*, Dublin: Chartered Institute of Personnel and Development in Ireland.

Harrison, R. (2009) *Learning and Development* (5th ed.), London: Chartered Institute of Personnel and Development.

Hill, R. (2004). Why HRD in Small Organisations May Have Become a Neglected Field of Study, In J. Stewart and G. Beaver (Eds), *HRD in Small Organisations*, London: Routledge (8–25).

Institute of Behavioral Science (2003) *Physical and Mental Health Effects of Surviving Layoffs: A Longitudinal Examination*.

Kahaner, L. (1996) *Competitive Intelligence, How to Gather, Analyze and Use Information to Move Your Business to the Top*, New York: Simon and Schuster.

Keogh, W., Mulvie, A., & Cooper, S. (2005) The Identification and Application of Knowledge Capital within Small Firms, *Journal of Small Business and Enterprise Development*, 12(1), 76–91.

Kock, H., Wallo, A., Nilsson, B. and Höglund, C. (2012) Outsourcing HR Services: the Role of Human Resource Intermediaries, *European Journal of Training and Development*, 36(8), 772–790.

Ling, Y., Simsek, Z., Lubatkin, M. H. and Veiga, J. F. (2008) The Impact of Transformational CEOs on the Performance of Small-to Medium-sized Firms: Does Organizational Context Matter?, *Journal of Applied Psychology*, 93, 923–934.

Lovell, K. (2009) *KnowledgePool Learning Outsource Survey 2009: Results*, Berkshire: KnowledgePool Group Limited.

Mayo, A. (2004) *Creating a Learning and Development Strategy: The HR Partners Guide to Developing People*, London: Chartered Institute of Personnel and Development.

McCord, P. (2014) How Netflix Reinvented HR, *Harvard Business Review*, 92(1/2), 71–76.

O'Leonard, K. (2013) *The Corporate Learning Factbook 2013: Benchmarks, Trends and Analysis of the US Training Market*, Deloitte Development LLC.

Sambrook, S. (2000) Talking of HRD, *Human Resource Development International*, 3(2), 159–178.

Stewart, J., Gold, G., Holden, R. and Rodgers, H. (2013) Strategic HRD and the Learning and Development Function, In J. Gold, R. Holden, P. Iles, J. Stewart and J. Beardwell (Eds), *Human Resource Development: Theory and Practice* (2nd ed.), Basingstoke: Palgrave Macmillan (25–48).

Ulrich, D., Younger, J. and Brockbank, W. (2008) The Twenty-First-Century HR Organization, *Human Resource Management*, 47(4), 829–850.

4

INDIVIDUAL–LEVEL LEARNING

Linda Dowling-Hetherington

By the end of this chapter you should be able to:

LEARNING OUTCOMES

- Explain learning and the different types of learning
- Recognize how learning is affected by human and dispositional factors and identify the barriers to effective learning
- Demonstrate an understanding of learning theories and how adults learn

- Describe the steps in the learning process and explain what is meant by experiential learning
- Outline the various types of learning styles
- Appreciate the growing importance of e-learning and how individuals engaging in e-learning might be supported

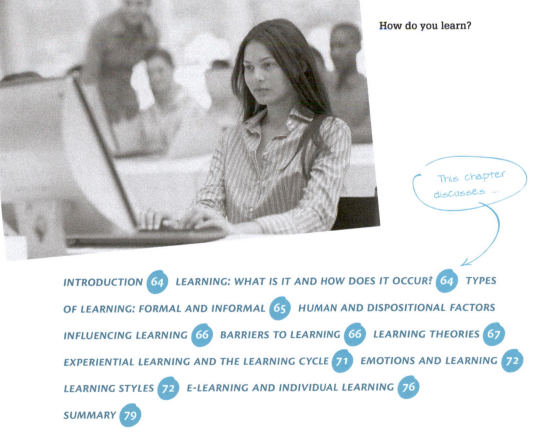

How do you learn?

This chapter discusses ...

INTRODUCTION

Have you ever wondered how you gained some new piece of knowledge or how you learned a new skill? This chapter provides an introduction to the complex topic of how individuals learn. The chapter begins with an explanation of what we mean by 'learning' and explains the different types of learning, formal and informal. An overview of the **human and dispositional factors** influencing learning is provided, along with the main barriers to learning that individuals sometimes encounter. A range of learning theories are introduced, including adult learning. The chapter also introduces you to the important concept of experiential learning. An explanation of the different steps in the learning process is provided, along with an overview of the learning styles that learners may display. The chapter concludes with a discussion on e-learning, its benefits and the kinds of support individuals need while engaging in this kind of learning.

human and dispositional factors individual traits or attributes, e.g. personality

LEARNING: WHAT IS IT AND HOW DOES IT OCCUR?

To facilitate effective HRD, it is essential to understand learning and how it occurs. Learning is a voluntary, natural and lifelong process engaged in by all individuals. Hoekstra *et al.* (2007: 190) define learning as 'being consciously or unconsciously involved in activities that lead to a change in behaviour and/or cognition'. It involves the acquisition and development of behaviours and memories, including skills, knowledge and understanding ▶ Chapter 1. Learning could be considered the overall aim of education. In the 70/20/10 model developed by Lombardo and Eichinger (1996), it is suggested that 70 per cent of what we learn comes from experience, 20 per cent comes from social learning and 10 per cent comes from reading and taking courses. Learning is a relatively abstract concept; it is complex and cannot be observed directly. In determining whether learning has taken place, we can observe changes in an individual's behaviour and we can infer that learning has taken place where such changes are evident. For example, after a training session, a hotel receptionist is able to accurately and efficiently check in a guest for an overnight stay and has, therefore, demonstrated that he/she has learned the

hotel's check-in procedure. Honey and Mumford (1992) suggest that learning has taken place when an individual has gained knowledge that they did not previously have and is able to demonstrate this, and where an individual is able to do something they were unable to do previously.

Learning is an active process. It would be a mistake for HRD practitioners and trainers to assume that an individual learned something just because they sat in a classroom when a trainer presented information or 'content' and when they participated in a learning situation in some way. Equally, HRD practitioners and trainers cannot assume that individuals know how to apply what they have learned in a work setting. For individuals to learn effectively, they must be actively involved during the learning process itself, for example, by engaging in discussions and class activities. After the learning activity, the individual applies that learning to a task or set of tasks that will ultimately change their behaviour and improve their performance at work. Therefore, learning must be an active process, emotionally and intellectually, and the design and delivery of learning activities should reflect this important principle (see Prince, 2004) ▶ Chapters 8 and 9. As suggested by Payne and Whittaker (2006: 11):

> *Learning to learn requires an ability and willingness on your part to assume responsibility for directing and controlling the learning process. Active involvement in the learning process is empowering and engenders curiosity, enthusiasm and a thirst or desire for knowledge.*

Learning is based on experience. It is an individual process and, while the instructor or trainer can help to facilitate and support learning through careful HRD design, learning can only be undertaken by the individual themselves. An individual's knowledge and skills are based on experience. Previous experience conditions an individual to respond to some things and to ignore others. Even when engaging in the same learning activity, individuals react differently to that activity and may learn different things depending on their own individual needs. Learning is complex in that individuals approach learning activities and tasks with preconceived ideas and feelings. Yet, for many individuals, these ideas may change as a result of experience. For example, you might begin preparation for your first-year university examinations by reading your class notes and textbook.

However, over time, you have gained some experience of sitting examinations in first year and have obtained some average grades. Based on this experience, you have come to realize that your examination preparation needs to include reflection on the application of the course concepts to real-life organizational situations so that you are in a better position to demonstrate your learning.

Learning situations may focus on the achievement of a particular learning objective or outcome, for example, the acquisition of verbal information, intellectual skills, motor skills, attitudes and cognitive strategies ▶ Chapter 7. However, while a learner is focused on achieving a particular learning outcome, for example, how to respond effectively to customer complaints, he/she may very well learn other things, such as how to improve customer service levels. Also, learners may develop particular attitudes (good or bad) as a result of a learning situation depending on what they experience during the learning situation itself. This is often referred to as incidental learning, yet it may have a significant impact on the entire development of the learner (see Conlon, 2004; Marsick et al., 2006).

In the past, the focus has tended to be on 'training' and 'training interventions'.

However, in recent years, the focus of attention has been increasingly moving away from 'training' and training 'courses', towards a much greater focus on the development of learning capabilities and assisting individuals in learning how to learn. While this change in focus places different demands on the HRD function, it also creates the possibility for improved outcomes for individuals. It involves a more shared responsibility for learning on the part of employees and the organization and requires individuals to take greater responsibility for their own learning ▶ Chapter 1.

TYPES OF LEARNING: FORMAL AND INFORMAL

Before considering the characteristics of learning situations and 'how' individuals learn in practice, it is important to be familiar with the distinction between formal and informal learning (see Ainsworth and Eaton, 2010). Formal learning is what those of you undertaking a diploma, degree or master's programme

training interventions any event that is undertaken specifically to promote learning.

formal learning occurs in universities, colleges and training institutions and leads to formal, recognized qualifications

informal learning 'informal learning is the unofficial, unscheduled, impromptu way people learn to do their jobs' (Cross, 2007: 15)

may be most familiar with. Such learning is planned and gained in a structured learning environment, for example, in a classroom setting. Formal learning and training activities tend to be used to prepare individuals for a particular role or set of tasks, for example, studying to become an accountant. Despite the considerable focus sometimes placed on formal learning, Boustedt et al. (2011) note that most workplace learning occurs outside formal HRD situations. Indeed, much of the learning that occurs in the workplace is considered informal learning (see Livingstone, 2006). Informal learning occurs regularly in the course of everyday life and at work (Ellström, 2011) and is an integral part of many of our everyday activities (Merriam et al., 2012). The development of knowledge and skills through informal learning occurs in a much more natural setting compared with formal learning, and Zhang et al. (2013: 108) acknowledge that individuals

learn throughout their lives but much of this learning is hardly recognized because it happens informally without conscious awareness.

The growing importance of informal learning and the business world's increasing interest in this type of learning have been noted by Attwell (2007). However, as individuals, we rarely acknowledge that learning occurs in such a manner, yet it is useful to recognize that informal learning is important for individuals and it is of considerable value for organizations when captured and disseminated in a systematic way ▶ Chapter 5. The benefits of informal learning include: retention of learning gained in informal settings is often better; it can facilitate formal learning; it involves greater flexibility in terms of when and where the learning is undertaken; and it can enhance the individual's motivation and sense of satisfaction (Boustedt et al., 2011). Interest in informal learning has become even more apparent with the development of social media and collaborative learning-type tools.

Three types of non-formal learning have been put forward by Eraut (2004), who prefers the term 'non-formal' rather than 'informal' learning. Table 4.1 provides an explanation of each type of non-formal learning and includes an example of each.

Table 4.1 Types of non-formal learning

Implicit learning	Reactive learning	Deliberative learning
Meaning: The unintentional learning that occurs, becomes a part of the learner's experience and is used subconsciously over time.	*Meaning:* Occurs in response to some event or activity (often during the event), but there is little time for reflection on this learning.	*Meaning:* Occurs where time is purposefully set aside for reflection on events or actions.
Example: Learning how to ride a bicycle.	*Example:* Richard works in a busy restaurant in Sydney. During Friday evening service, a customer complains that he has received the wrong order. Richard immediately corrects the order and makes a mental note to take more care in avoiding such errors, but does not have sufficient time to reflect on how this error occurred.	*Example:* The launch of a new product in the US marketplace has failed. Michelle, as marketing manager for the company, takes some time to reflect on why this has occurred and how a similar failure could be avoided in the future.

CONSIDER THIS...

Think about the learning activities you have engaged in over the past few years. Describe the formal learning activities you have participated in. What kinds of informal learning have you engaged in? How might you continue to engage in informal learning activities after graduation? How might your employer encourage you to engage in informal learning?

HUMAN AND DISPOSITIONAL FACTORS INFLUENCING LEARNING

All learners are unique, and the purpose of a particular learning situation may vary from one learner to another. The past learning experiences and backgrounds of individuals influence their readiness to learn, and learners often see a learning situation from different perspectives. Learning is influenced by many factors, including those related specifically to the individual learner themselves (Garavan *et al.*, 2003; Buckley and Caple, 2009). These factors include: an individual's *age* (some of our abilities, physical and mental, deteriorate with age along with our short-term memory and ability to process information) and the individual's *intelligence and ability* level – learners with lower ability levels often prefer to move from 'concrete examples to general principles' (Buckley and Caple, 2009: 171), whereas individuals with higher ability prefer to work in the reverse way. Indeed, the

rate at which individuals learn varies from one person to the next. You may be familiar with the term 'the learning curve', which is often used to illustrate the rate of learning. Furthermore, the individual's *background and emotional disposition* are also important factors that can help or hinder their learning. For example, their earlier experiences in school and their general anxieties around the learning process itself play a role. Individuals' *motivation* to learn and their *learning styles* are also important factors in enhancing the likelihood of a positive outcome from learning. An individual's *trainability* and their general *attitudes* and *personality* are also factors influencing whether learning occurs or not (Werner and De Simone, 2009). Trainability relates to an individual's 'readiness to learn' along with their motivation to learn and their general ability (Werner and De Simone, 2009: 69).

BARRIERS TO LEARNING

We have already noted that learning is a natural process. Yet, despite this, individual learners can encounter a range of barriers that prevent learning in the workplace or that hinder its effectiveness (see Collin, 2010). Some of the factors that can act as barriers to learning have already been touched upon in the above section on the human and dispositional factors influencing learning. In general, the many barriers that relate to the individual learner might include: poor learning capabilities; lack of personal confidence; over-reliance on a particular type of learning style; a lack of inherent motivation or interest in learning; general anxiety and insecurity, perhaps, as a result of a previous learning and education experience;

Table 4.2 Workplace learning – facilitators and barriers

Facilitators	Barriers
• Collaboration and interaction: learning with and from others	• Resource limitations (e.g. lack of time, financial resources)
• Support from management and the organization	• Accessibility constraints (e.g. geographic location of the learner)
• Resources (e.g. technology)	• Individual's high workload
• Personal attributes (e.g. individual learner's use of initiative, prioritization, reflection, motivation, recognition of learning need)	• Personal barriers (e.g. lack of interest in learning)
• Job-related issues	• Insufficient technological infrastructure

and the absence of clear or valued rewards for engaging in learning activities. In research conducted among HRM practitioners, Crouse *et al.* (2011) found a range of facilitators and inhibitors of workplace learning, and these are summarized in Table 4.2. Should you have a particular interest in this area, the Crouse *et al.* reading provides a very useful summary of the body of literature available on the barriers and facilitators of workplace learning (see Table 2 and Table 3 in that reading). While many of the barriers to effective learning may stem from the individual learner themselves, others relate to the organization, and it is, therefore, important that both types of barriers are adequately addressed and that ways of overcoming them are found ▸ **Chapter 5**.

LEARNING THEORIES

Learning theories have received much attention over the years. These theories help us understand the complex process involved

learning theories explain how individuals learn

motivation to learn the reasons individuals engage in learning

in learning. There are a wide range of learning theories and each relates to a different aspect of learning. Some learning theories consider *why* individuals learn, whereas others consider *how* individuals learn (Rogers and Horrocks, 2010). Indeed, many learning theories relate specifically to an individual's **motivation to learn**. Two theories of learning are presented in this chapter – social

learning theory and adult learning theory – along with four motivation theories that impact on motivation to learn – reinforcement theory, goal theory, need theory and expectancy theory (see Noe, 2010).

Social learning theory: Based on the work of Albert Bandura, social learning theory suggests that individuals learn by observing the behaviour of others, i.e. models, who are considered 'credible and knowledgeable' (Noe, 2010: 143). This theory recognizes that individuals learn from, and with, others (Rogers and Horrocks, 2010). The theory acknowledges that behaviour that is rewarded by organizations will tend to be replicated by individuals observing this behaviour. The theory would suggest that learning involves four processes (see Figure 4.1):

Attention: The first step in the process calls for individuals to be attentive to the aspects of the model's behaviour that are considered important and those behaviours that the individual is expected to observe. This step also requires the individual to know who the model is and the individual must have the physical ability to observe the model.

Retention: To be effective, the learner must retain the knowledge and skills gained through observing the model and must find some means of coding and organizing the skills and behaviours observed into memory.

Figure 4.1 Social learning theory processes

Source: Adapted from Noe (2010)

Motor reproduction: This stage of the social learning process calls for the individual to put into practice the behaviours and skills learned by observing the model in an effort to see if he/she will receive the same reinforcement as that obtained by the model.

Motivational processes: If the observed behaviour is copied or applied by the individual and this leads to positive reinforcement and feedback from the organization, then this behaviour is likely to be repeated.

Let's consider an example of social learning theory. Lucy has just starting working for a coffee house in her hometown of Barcelona. Her first few days are spent engaged in on-the-job training where she learns how to use the coffee machines and cash register and how to make the large range of specialist coffees available. During the training, her supervisor, i.e. the model in this instance, demonstrates how each task is performed. Lucy carefully observes and takes note of the different steps involved in each task and then replicates the tasks herself under the watchful eye of her supervisor.

Adult learning theory: Pedagogy places great emphasis on the teacher having primary responsibility for, and control over, the learning content and classroom delivery. Children are generally seen as passive recipients of knowledge and they bring little experience to the classroom situation. Adult learning theory was developed in response to a need to understand how adults learn. Andragogy has been very much influenced by Malcolm Knowles (Smith, 2002) (see Knowles *et al.* (2011) for a comprehensive overview of andragogy and adult learning theory). What we can be certain about is that 'adults can be ordered into a classroom and prodded into seats, but they can't be forced to learn' (Zemke and Zemke, 1995: 41). The learning and motivation theories outlined in this chapter provide us with a basic set of learning principles that can be used to guide the design of HRD activities to meet the needs of adult learners. Table 4.3 provides an overview of three important dimensions of adult learning: basic assumptions of adult learning; motivation to learn as a prerequisite for effective engagement in learning; and the implications of adult learning theory for the design of HRD interventions. While the table addresses some basic assumptions around adult learning, we should also appreciate that not every adult learns in exactly the same way. As highlighted by Newstrom and Lengnick-Hall (1991: 46):

adult learners are a heterogeneous group requiring different approaches to training and development

pedagogy the art of teaching children

andragogy the art of helping adults to learn

depending on individual differences across important characteristics.

Having outlined two learning theories, we now turn our attention to the four theories of motivation outlined by Noe (2010) that impact on motivation to learn.

Reinforcement theory: This theory suggests that the past behaviours of individuals and the outcomes of these behaviours will serve to motivate individuals to either adopt or avoid certain types of behaviours. A pleasant or satisfying outcome resulting from past behaviour is referred to as *positive reinforcement*. For example, an organization receives positive feedback from a client about a customer service agent's level of efficiency and customer orientation which is acknowledged during the agent's performance appraisal. The removal of an unpleasant behaviour outcome is referred to as negative reinforcement. For example, an organization receives feedback from a client in relation to the failure of a particular customer service agent to meet the 24-hour response time for dealing with sales queries. This feedback should be raised during the individual's performance appraisal review and, while it may initially result in a poor review, the performance of the individual should improve as soon as the negative feedback is addressed. HRD practitioners need to understand the kinds of behaviours that individuals consider positive and negative and ensure a clear link between the acquisition of knowledge, skills and behaviour change and these particular outcomes.

Goal theory: Goal setting theory recognizes that an individual's conscious goals influence their behaviour by focusing their efforts and attention over a period of time and by encouraging the individual to develop appropriate strategies to support the attainment of those goals. In attempting to achieve these goals, the theory recognizes the importance of setting realistic and achievable goals. The commitment of the individual to the achievement of the goals is essential. Goal orientation influences the degree of effort individuals may exert during a learning situation or HRD activity. When we consider the goal orientation of individual learners, i.e. the goals learners hold in an HRD situation, two dimensions are important: learning orientation and performance orientation (see Noe, 2010). *Learning orientation* refers to the individual's attempts to improve their competence when performing a particular task. Individuals who possess such an

Table 4.3 Adult learning – assumptions, prerequisites and guidelines

Basic assumptions of adult learning
• *Objective:* Adults need to know why they are learning particular knowledge/skills. Learning is often sought out in response to a life-changing incident, e.g. promotion. • *Control:* Adults are self-directed. • *Background:* Adults bring past life, education and work experiences into the learning situation and these represent rich resources for learning. Past educational experiences may help or hinder future learning. • *Approach:* Adults adopt a problem-centred approach to learning and learn through experience, observation and interaction with others. • *Motivation:* Adults are motivated by intrinsic factors, e.g. self-esteem, personal satisfaction, and extrinsic factors, e.g. increased pay, promotion. • *Application:* The opportunity to apply knowledge and skills gained is important for learning retention purposes.

$\downarrow$

Prerequisites – motivated learners
• *Basic Necessity:* For learning to take place, adults must be motivated to learn. We need to understand what motivates individuals to learn. Adults can be motivated to learn by appealing to their personal development or gain. • *Openness:* There is a window of opportunity for learning, beyond which adults will be less receptive to learning, e.g. on appointment to a new position. • *Increase Learner Involvement and Improve Motivation:* Learning should be viewed as an active process and motivation to learn can be increased, e.g. through involvement in the design of, and participation in, the learning activity.

$\downarrow$

Guidelines for adult learning design
• *Needs and Focus:* Learning activities should be problem-centred and be relevant to the learners' needs and goals. HRD activities should be designed to facilitate adult learners' continued growth and changing values. • *Level of Knowledge/Skill:* Pre-learning activity assessment of learners' knowledge/skill level is essential. The learning activity should be designed around the learners' entry-level knowledge/skills. • *Information Integration:* Learners relate all new learning content to their existing knowledge and experience. Learning content should be designed to promote the integration of information presented during the HRD activity. There should be some overlap between the presentation of new information and information already known by learners. Such overlap promotes the integration and retention of knowledge and information. • *Learning Activities:* Activities should be realistic, meaningful, interesting and challenging, and allow reflection on the part of learners. • *Learning Styles:* The design of HRD activities should account for adults' differing learning styles (we will return to this later in the chapter). • *Application of Learning:* As learning is engaged in for a specific purpose, it is necessary to give consideration to the design of transfer of learning strategies and the provision of opportunities to put the learning gained into practice ▶ Chapter 9. Individuals need to commit the content of what they have learned to memory. • *Feedback, Support and Learning Climate:* These are important elements for effective learning to occur. Learners need to be aware of what learning outcomes they should be striving to achieve and how well they are doing on achieving these outcomes, and to be supported along the way in a conducive learning culture and climate.

Source: Based on ideas presented by Brookfield (1986), Zemke and Zemke (1995), Rogers and Horrocks (2010) and Knowles *et al.* (2011)

orientation consider the success of an HRD activity in terms of how they have improved in their learning and the progress they have made regarding this learning, i.e. the focus tends to be on their learning, rather than on their performance as a result of the learning. Learning-orientated individuals see mistakes as part of the process of learning. *Performance orientation* refers to individuals engaged in learning who focus on the performance of a task or activity and how their performance might compare with others. Individuals demonstrating this latter orientation define success in terms of their performance relative to others and they see mistakes as a source of worry, rather than a possible source of learning. For example, university students will often judge their own performance in their studies and learning activities relative to their friends and how their overall diploma/degree honours grade compares with their classmates.

Need theory: Readers of this textbook may already be familiar with the various needs theories from other modules undertaken in the field of organizational behaviour, e.g. Maslow and Alderfer's needs theories. Both Maslow and Alderfer argue that individuals will attempt to satisfy their lower-order needs first, e.g. physiological and safety needs, before they begin to focus on the achievement of higher-order needs, e.g. esteem and self-actualization. These theories suggest that individuals are unlikely to learn where lower-order needs have not been fulfilled. In the context of HRD, need theories suggest that, to motivate learning, HRD practitioners should identify the learning needs of individuals and ensure they are aware of how the content of the HRD or learning activity will assist them in meeting these needs. For example, a newly appointed team leader who is attending a management and supervisory skills training programme should be made aware of how this training will facilitate them in developing the various people management skills needed to successfully manage the sales team they are responsible for. As we will see later in this chapter, individuals learn in different ways and may seek out particular types of learning activities to meet their needs. It is, therefore, important for organizations to provide a range of learning programmes to meet the varying needs of individuals ▶ Chapter 8.

Expectancy theory: This theory suggests that three particular factors influence an individual's behaviour: expectancy, instrumentality and valence. *Expectancy* relates to the belief or understanding that exhibiting certain behaviours and performing well are related. In the context of HRD, we might ask: does the individual have the learning 'know how' or ability to learn? *Instrumentality* is the expectation that performing a particular type of behaviour, for example, undertaking a Bachelor degree in Accountancy, will lead to a particular outcome, for example, obtaining a traineeship with an accountancy firm. In the context of HRD, we might ask: does the individual believe that the outcomes identified for a learning or development activity will be achieved? *Valence* relates to the actual value an individual puts on a particular outcome. In the context of HRD, we might ask: are these learning outcomes valued by the individual? Individuals face various behavioural choices which they assess depending on their expectancy, instrumentality and valence. If we apply expectancy theory to HRD situations, we can say that learning is likely to occur where individuals are confident in the belief that they have the ability to learn the knowledge, skills or attitudes the HRD activity is designed to address (expectancy); this learning is related to certain outcomes, such as improved performance or enhanced rewards (instrumentality); and the individuals value these particular outcomes (valence). Figure 4.2 provides an overview of the expectancy theory of motivation.

CONSIDER THIS ...

Think about a module on your certificate, diploma or degree programme. How did the lecturer incorporate the features of adult learning theory into the design and delivery of the module? Could the lecturer incorporate any other adult learning principles into the module to enhance your learning? How did the approach taken by the lecturer differ from that taken by your primary school teachers?

Figure 4.2 Expectancy theory of motivation

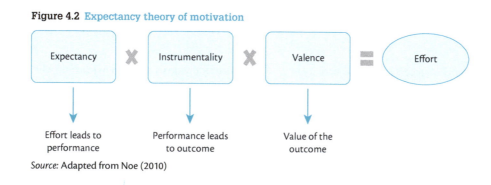

Source: Adapted from Noe (2010)

EXPERIENTIAL LEARNING AND THE LEARNING CYCLE

A key principle of learning is that individuals learn best through experience. The impetus for engaging in learning can be the result of a gap between an individual's past experience and their current experience (Rogers and Horrocks, 2010). In other words, the knowledge and skills gained as a result of an individual's past experience may no longer meet the knowledge and skills needed now to cope with current role requirements and the kinds of experiences an individual will engage in as part of this role. The concept of experiential learning was founded by writers such as John Dewey, Jean Piaget and Kurt

 experiential learning learning through action and reflection

Lewin (Miettinen, 2000), and was further developed in the 1980s by David Kolb (see Kolb, 1984). Experiential learning theory (ELT) is based around a number of important principles (Kolb and Kolb, 2009):

- Learning is best seen as a process, rather than a series of potential outcomes.
- Learning involves the creation of knowledge on the part of the individual.
- Learning involves 're-learning' in that the learning process should seek to explore learners' underlying 'beliefs and ideas' and to consider the integration of these with new and more developed ideas.
- Learning involves the whole person, i.e. 'thinking, feeling, perceiving and behaving' (p. 43).
- Learning occurs through the interaction between an individual and his/her environment.

Much of the focus in the context of experiential learning is on the learning process itself. Kolb's work in this area resulted in the development of a four-step 'learning cycle' (see Figure 4.3). This cycle should not be confused with the Process of HRD cycle discussed elsewhere in this textbook. He suggests that learning occurs in a step-by-step cycle and that individual learners should engage in all four steps in this cycle to become effective learners. Kolb argues that effective learning will occur where individuals display a degree of flexibility by adopting a learning approach that is appropriate in a given situation. Each step in the cycle does not make sense on its own and is not particularly useful if undertaken in isolation from the other steps. The learning cycle is just that – a cycle: the learner can begin at any one of the four steps and the process itself should be viewed as a continuous one.

The learning process very often begins with an individual undertaking a particular action or task and then seeing the effect of this particular action or task (concrete experience). Following the execution of the action, the individual would typically attempt to reflect on the resulting effects of the action and to determine whether he/she could anticipate what might happen if the same action was taken again in the same circumstances (reflective observation). The third step involves the individual in trying to understand the general principle under which the particular instance falls and in generating new ideas and drawing conclusions from his/her previous actions (abstract conceptualization). The last step in the learning cycle involves the application or testing of these new ideas through action in a new circumstance, i.e. we attempt to do things better or differently the next time around (active experimentation). Let's imagine you have been asked to make a presentation during your HRD class. You spend some time preparing the presentation and then make the presentation in class today (concrete experience). After finishing the presentation, you reflect on how it went and the feedback received from your lecturer and fellow classmates (reflective observation). You then give some thought to your experience of making this particular presentation, relate it to your previous presentations in college and consider any theories or knowledge on how to make an effective presentation (abstract conceptualization). Finally, you consider how you might improve your presentation skills by trying out a different approach to the preparation and delivery of your next presentation (active experimentation).

Figure 4.3 Kolb's learning cycle

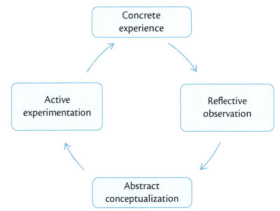

Source: Adapted from Kolb (1984)

Kolb's cycle highlights two particularly useful issues: the importance of incorporating real, concrete experiences into the learning process; and the value to be gained by individuals and organizations from allocating adequate time for learners to reflect on what has been learned and how this learning might be used to facilitate future behaviour change and performance improvement on the part of individuals. The cycle also highlights a number of implications for HRD practitioners to consider when delivering learning and development interventions, particularly the need to identify learners who spend too much time on one particular step in the cycle and/or avoid spending time on others.

curious or very interested in a new area or topic and move through the material with ease, or in quadrant II, where they are motivated to reduce confusion or puzzlement on a particular topic. Either way, the learner is concerned with constructing knowledge. If they have failed to adequately resolve any puzzlement regarding what they are learning, the learner may move into quadrant III and may begin to feel frustrated. The learner amalgamates their knowledge and becomes aware of how their learning is progressing, i.e. what they know and don't know, and moves into quadrant IV, where they develop fresh ideas and enthusiasm for learning, which may push them back into quadrant I again, where the spiral continues.

EMOTIONS AND LEARNING

Kort *et al.* (2001) suggest the existence of a complex relationship between emotions and learning. They have developed a four-quadrant learning spiral model that incorporates a range of emotions that individuals may exhibit during learning (see Figure 4.4). Emotions are shown on the horizontal axis, with positive, pleasurable outcomes on the right and negative, unpleasant outcomes on the left. Learning is shown on the vertical axis, with the construction of learning at the top and un-learning at the bottom. The learner would preferably begin in either quadrant I, where they are

learning styles the methods and approaches individuals use during the learning process

LEARNING STYLES

When we consider each of the learning theories presented in this chapter, there is a danger of assuming that all individuals learn in much the same way. Individuals may vary in their **learning styles** and preferences. An understanding of learning styles is an important consideration when delivering HRD interventions and activities. As individuals, understanding our own learning style allows us to select learning opportunities and activities that best match our style and provide us

Figure 4.4 Kort's learning spiral model

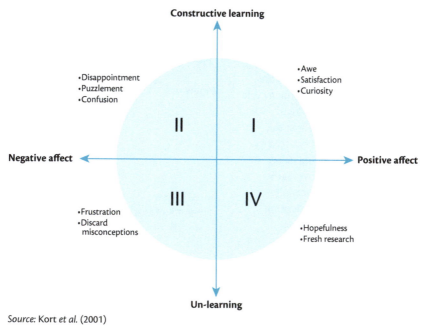

Source: Kort *et al.* (2001)

with the chance to develop or improve other aspects of our learning approach (Torrington *et al.*, 2011). A large number of learning style frameworks exist and Coffield *et al.* (2004) reviewed 13 such models, grouping them into families of learning styles and placing them on a continuum from fixed learning styles to those of a more flexible nature. While a discussion of each of these models is beyond the scope of this chapter, three learning style frameworks will be presented here: the VARK sensory learning styles inventory (Fleming, 1995); Honey and Mumford's (1992) learning styles; and Felder and Silverman's (1988) learning style model.

VARK sensory learning styles

We receive information through our various senses (e.g. through hearing, seeing, touching). Understanding how these senses contribute to learning is an important step in identifying how an individual learner might improve their learning process. Figure 4.5 provides an explanation of each of the VARK learning styles developed by Fleming (1995).

While a learner may have a preference for one particular sensory learning style, other styles should be explored also. Why not complete the VARK learning styles questionnaire online and see what kind of sensory learner you are (see http://www.vark-learn.com)? Interestingly, Flanagan (1997) suggests that individual learners recall 20 per cent of what they read; 30 per cent of what they hear; 40 per cent of what they see; 50 per cent of what they say; 60 per cent of what they do; and 90 per cent of what they read, hear, see, say and do. Learning style preferences influence the kinds of day-to-day activities

from which individuals learn best, and this has important implications for the design of HRD activities. Knowledge of an individual's learning style is very useful information as it allows us to begin to consider how HRD practitioners and trainers might design effective HRD activities to appeal to adults with different sensory learning styles ▶ Chapter 8. HRD practitioners should develop approaches that allow learners to fully draw upon their own style of learning (Rogers and Horrocks, 2010).

Honey and Mumford's learning styles

Another well-recognized set of learning styles are those developed by Honey and Mumford (1992). They have identified four styles of learning that can broadly be categorized into two groups: 'thinkers' and 'doers'. Figure 4.6 provides an explanation of each group and the four styles evident across these groups. As you review these, you are encouraged to reflect on the learning style that you tend to exhibit most often.

Honey and Mumford (1992) suggest that individuals tend to have a preference for particular learning styles over others. Such preferences can lead to a distortion of the learning process as presented in Kolb's learning cycle so that greater emphasis is placed on some stages of the cycle to the detriment of others. Individuals who effectively learn from experience possess and utilize all four learning styles. One of the aims of helping individuals to understand their learning is to facilitate them in reviewing their learning style so that they can begin to explore how they might become better equipped to work through all four stages of the learning cycle. Honey and Mumford suggest that 'no single style has an overwhelming advantage over any other.

Figure 4.5 VARK sensory learning styles

Visual	• individuals who learn best by **seeing** – i.e. through written / visual information, e.g. text / notes, mind maps, diagrams.
Auditory	• individuals who learn best by **hearing** – e.g. through listening to others or hearing themselves read aloud.
Read/write	• individuals who learn best through information presented as **words.**
Kinaesthetic	• individuals who learn best by **doing** and engaging in concrete experiences (these learners draw on all senses).

Figure 4.6 Honey and Mumford's learning styles

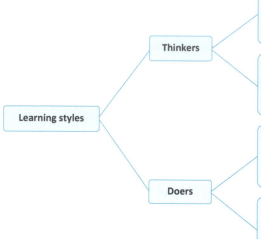

Theorists: learn best when they can relate new information to concepts or theories . . . they adopt a step-by-step approach when dealing with problems.

Reflectors: learn best through reviewing and reflecting on what has happened and what they have done . . . they tend to adopt a passive approach in meetings and discussions.

Activists: learn best when they are actively involved in concrete tasks . . . their time is spent on activities . . . they deal with problems through brainstorming.

Pragmatists: learn best when they can try out new ideas to see if they work in practice . . . they view work-related problems as a challenge.

Source: Adapted from Mumford (1995)

Each has strengths and weaknesses but the strengths may be especially important in one situation, but not in another instance' (2006: 43). Figure 4.7 illustrates how Honey and Mumford's learning styles relate to each of the four stages in Kolb's learning cycle.

Think about your own studies and how you might display one or more of the four learning styles. If you were a *theorist*, one might expect that you would prefer to understand the theories and concepts you are learning. In so doing, you would likely set out to understand the theory and to gather information and facts that would facilitate this understanding. For example, if you were studying the topic of e-learning, you might set out to carefully read your

class notes and textbook and you might then gather some additional information available on the topic through sources such as the Chartered Institute of Personnel and Development or other academic journals and readings. If you were a *reflector*, you might not participate in class discussions on e-learning. Instead, you might attempt to internalize and reflect on the key elements of that topic and to make sense of the topic for yourself in your own time. If you were an *activist*, you would engage in activities during your studies that would allow you to learn by doing. For example, you might engage in discussions, brainstorming and problem-solving exercises on e-learning with your classmates. If you were a *pragmatist*, you might think about how to apply what you have learned about e-learning to a real situation. For example, if the university decided to offer your diploma/degree programme of studies in an online/e-learning format from next year, how might you apply what you have learned regarding the various e-learning design considerations to be taken into consideration when re-designing this programme?

Figure 4.7 Kolb's learning cycle and Honey and Mumford's learning styles

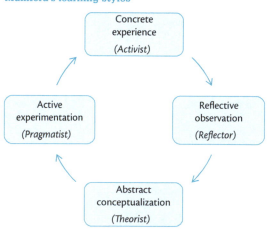

Felder–Silverman's learning style model

According to the Felder and Silverman (1988) model of learning styles, individuals display strong, moderate or mild learning preferences along four continua:

- *Active* (individuals learn by doing things and by working with others) or *reflective* (individuals learn by thinking about things and prefer working on their own)

- *Sensing* (individuals prefer facts and procedures and are concrete thinkers) or *intuitive* (individuals prefer theories and are abstract thinkers)
- *Visual* (individuals prefer visual illustrations of material, such as diagrams and pictures) or *verbal* (individuals prefer the spoken and written word)
- *Sequential* (individuals learn in small incremental steps and in a linear manner) or *global* (individuals learn in large steps and engage in a holistic thinking process)

Having considered the human and dispositional factors that influence learning and also the above models of learning styles, it is important to consider some other issues that may have an influence on learning style. We might expect that the 'cultural conditioning' individuals experience through the education system they have participated in will have an influence in moulding their preferences for certain learning styles (De Vita, 2001: 167). Research conducted by Joy and Kolb (2009: 83) highlights a number of variables, including culture, that impact on learning style. They suggest that culture influences an individual's preferences for 'abstract conceptualization versus concrete experience', but only marginally influences an individual's preferences for 'active experimentation and reflective observation'. Joy and Kolb's findings also suggest that the discipline or area of study being undertaken by an individual may also influence 'a person's liking for abstraction or concreteness' and that level of education may also be an influencing factor. In research conducted by Charlesworth (2008) on Indonesian, Chinese and French students in their first semester in higher education, Eastern students were found to have stronger preferences for the reflector style and weaker preferences for the activist style compared with Western students, at least at the beginning of their studies. Cuthbert (2005: 244) suggests that learning style 'represents part of the "baggage" that the learner brings to the learning situation'.

In concluding the above discussion, while learning styles have been popular among HRD practitioners, some criticisms of learning styles and learning models are evident in the literature. The weak theorization of learning styles (Coffield *et al.*, 2004) and the absence of empirical research that proves how learning styles impact on learning and teaching (Hall and Moseley, 2005) have been noted. In research conducted by Peterson *et al.* (2009: 521), researchers in the learning styles field were concerned with the 'lack of validity, confusion in definitions, fragmented theory and

abundance of concepts and tests'. The measurements used to identify learner styles and preferences are largely subjective in nature, with learners making these judgements themselves (Coffield *et al.*, 2004). It has also been suggested that the theory on learning styles remains relatively silent on how cognitive skills are developed, and considerable differences remain among theorists on the various components of learning styles (Hall and Moseley, 2005). Furthermore, the 'mere process models (e.g. "the learning cycle")' and the 'simple dichotomies' sometimes presented in learning styles models often fail to adequately capture the importance of developing an ability to both process information and learn in 'versatile and integrative ways' (Sadler-Smith, 2014: 86). The dearth of research on how learning styles impact on learning outcomes has also been noted (Menaker and Coleman, 2007). Finally, Felder and Spurlin (2005: 105) suggest that 'the point of identifying learning styles is not to label individual students and modify instruction to fit their labels'. Instead, they argue against teaching exclusively to facilitate particular student preferences for learning styles.

SPOTLIGHT ON SKILLS

You are the HRD executive for a financial services company in Stockholm. Ten new employees, primarily recent graduates, will be joining the organization in the coming months. You will need to design and deliver a two-day induction training programme for these new hires. How would you go about identifying the new team members' learning styles and incorporating learning activities into induction that draw on the various styles?

To help you answer the questions above, visit www.macmillanihe.com/companion/carbery-hrd and watch the video of Noreen Clifford talking about learning styles.

Improving Individual Learning at The Courtyard Hotel in Tokyo

You have recently been appointed to the position of HRD manager at The Courtyard Hotel in Tokyo. The hotel has been experiencing falling bed occupancy rates and fewer bookings for conferences, weddings and other similar events. While some of these business problems may stem from the difficult economic environment many organizations are facing, others relate more to the Courtyard's current HRD practices. For example, the number of customer complaints regarding the level of service from staff in a number of areas has been growing (including complaints about the knowledge and skills of the reception desk staff and the general organization and management of various wedding and conference events). The level of turnover among the more experienced staff in the hotel has also increased recently, much to the concern of management.

One of your initial tasks is to evaluate the effectiveness of the hotel's current approach to HRD and, particularly, how it facilitates learning on the part of all employees. The employees and department managers you have spoken with are critical of the opportunities currently available for staff to enhance their own learning in the workplace. From these informal discussions with employees and department managers, it appears that: the hotel management have not previously invested in employees' learning and development to any significant extent; employee turnover may, in part, be explained by the lack of opportunities for individual learning; and the only training or learning activity that employees are expected to attend is the two-hour induction programme upon their appointment.

In general, opportunities for individual learning are not currently provided in a planned or systematic manner and do not draw upon the full range of possible formal and informal learning activities. Apart from induction, the only other opportunities for individual learning provided are: financial support for staff willing to undertake formal qualifications in hotel management; and some short ad-hoc half-day courses on customer service skills, event management, and food and beverage operations. These training courses are generally delivered in a classroom setting where an outside trainer presents the training content largely in a one-way, non-interactive manner using a PowerPoint presentation. There is no evidence of any discussions with the employees regarding the objectives of this training or of any follow-up with employees after the training to determine the extent to which they are practising and applying what they have learned.

Questions

1 Describe the weaknesses of the hotel's current approach to HRD with respect to its individual learning and development activities.

2 What suggestions could you make about how the underlying principles of both social learning and adult learning theories might be used to improve the effectiveness of individual learning?

3 How might the four steps in Kolb's learning cycle be useful to the hotel in improving its approach to individual learning?

E-LEARNING AND INDIVIDUAL LEARNING

We turn our attention now to the topic of e-learning. In recent years, organizations have been utilizing a much wider range of new technologies to facilitate formal, informal and blended learning and development activities (CIPD, 2013a). While e-learning methods tend to be used for specific types of training, including information technology skills, induction for new staff, customer service skills, and health and safety training, there has been much debate about whether it is appropriate for the development of 'soft' skills, such as interpersonal communication (Derouin et al., 2005; CIPD, 2013a).

There is no doubt that technology is having a major impact on the activities of HRD functions, but also in meeting the needs of individuals for more flexible, customized, engaging and interactive learning opportunities. Although traditional classroom instruction is still used by almost all companies, the growing use of emerging technologies in learning and development activities is increasingly evident. Many of the new technologies that have emerged in recent years will serve as a supplement to the more traditional forms of learning you will be reading about in this textbook.

BUILDING YOUR SKILLS

As a student, you may have already developed a particular set of learning skills or a certain learning style over the years and become comfortable with this style. However, the adoption of this learning style may not necessarily result in the best use of your study time or lead to the most effective outcomes from the perspective of your learning and grades achieved. Consider the VARK sensory learning styles described earlier in this chapter.

- Which learning style do you tend to exhibit most often?
- How might you draw upon other learning styles?
- How might your learning skills be enhanced by drawing on a wider range of sensory learning styles?
- What might your lecturers need to do, or change, to facilitate your use of the full range of learning styles?

While e-learning allows organizations to deliver training and development activities in an entirely online format, it is not expected that e-learning will replace the more traditional, face-to-face ways of learning we are all familiar with. Indeed, e-learning is often utilized in combination with face-to-face classroom learning, what is often referred to as 'blended learning'.

Benefits of E-learning: The increased use of technology has allowed learning to become a much more dynamic process and it leads to several benefits for individuals (see, for example, Welsh *et al.*, 2003; Brown *et al.*, 2006; Bondarouk and Ruël, 2010): individuals can more easily access knowledge and learning opportunities to suit their own needs, i.e. where and when they want; and learners can also interact with, and customize, the learning content to meet their own needs. The use of technology can also facilitate a greater level of digital collaboration between learners, i.e. technology can be used to enhance and extend the ability of individuals to work together irrespective of their geographic location. Digital collaboration can take place in two ways: (i) in a *synchronous* manner where HRD practitioners/trainers and individual learners interact with each other in a live or real-time way; and (ii) in an *asynchronous* manner

where the interactions between the HRD practitioners/ trainers and individual learners occur in a non-real-time way, i.e. learners access the learning information and resources at a time that best suits them (see Hrastinski, 2008). Training and learning can be delivered more quickly to geographically dispersed individuals and in a shorter period of time; updating of content is relatively easy; many of the principles of effective learning set out earlier in this chapter apply – for example, the provision of feedback to learners, the opportunity to practice what has been learned; and clarity on the learning aims and expected outcomes can be built into e-learning activities. E-learning programmes can also be used to create online networks with other learners and subject matter experts.

Social Learning: Earlier in this chapter, we considered the growing attention being paid to informal learning activities. In their factsheet on e-learning, the CIPD (2013a) highlight both the formal and informal nature of e-learning activities:

> The development of e-learning has in subsequent years progressed rapidly to encompass a wide range of both formal course-based e-learning packages and products together with a huge variety of complementary or alternative e-learning techniques, such as sharing knowledge or links to resources via social/interactive media sites and viewing/ participating in online lectures, web seminars (webinars), podcasts or microblogging.

Attention to social learning has considerably deepened in recent years as a result of the growing interest in, and use of, social media and collaborative learning tools such as Twitter, YouTube, Facebook, LinkedIn, blogs, chat rooms and discussion boards (see Carliner, 2013; Thomas and Akdere, 2013). Such social media and interactive learning tools are often referred to as Web 2.0 technologies and, as CIPD (2013a) suggest, they provide individuals with new opportunities for 'collaboration, co-creation and sharing of content'. Indeed, the more widespread use of smartphones, accompanying applications (or 'apps') and cloud computing now provides individuals with much greater access to information and learning content while on the move.

Learner Control: Traditionally, the delivery of training and learning occurred in a very linear or ordered way. For example, trainers first presented the content of a training programme to learners and afterwards they, perhaps, spent time practising and applying what had been learned during the training. The HRD practitioner or trainer tended to be in control and learners were expected to follow the content in the order it was presented by the HRD practitioner. This is much like what you might be experiencing during your studies where Topic 1 is presented first, followed by Topic 2 and so forth. Traditional forms of HRD delivery placed the individual learner in a very passive role during the learning process, with little control over what was being learned, how it was being learned and the pace of the learning itself. E-learning has begun to change this by giving the learner much greater control over the learning process and allowing them to tailor their learning to meet their own individual needs (see London and Hall, 2011). Learning in this way now allows the individual learner to skip the parts of the learning content that he/she is already familiar with and to engage in a much more active process of learning by exercising much greater control over learning content. E-learning also allows the individual learner to control the pace of learning (Derouin et al., 2005).

Learner Support: E-learning can pose a number of drawbacks for individual learners. Learning in this manner is often seen as a 'solitary activity' (Torrington et al., 2009: 146) and depends to a large extent on one's motivation and level of self-directedness and the availability of well-designed learning content. The motivation of individuals to actively engage with and complete a programme delivered in an e-learning format is fundamental. One of the challenges in designing e-learning activities is the development of adequate support for individual learners (Tynjälä and Häkkinen, 2005). Support is important at three key points: *before* commencing the e-learning programme, where an introduction to the technology or learning platform being utilized is needed; *during* the e-learning activity, where guidance on how to navigate the course and related activities, assistance in addressing any questions the learner may have during the learning process, and feedback on progress being made are needed; and *after* the e-learning activity, where support on how to apply the learning gained to change behaviour or improve work-related performance may be needed. E-learning is unlikely to be effective if made available to learners who are inadequately prepared for this kind of learning and who are not sufficiently supported (CIPD, 2013a).

Chapter 1 provided you with an introduction to MOOCs and their growing prominence through a range of independent providers, in association with leading universities, across the world. The emphasis with MOOCs is on individual, self-managed learning that occurs in a more informal manner. While many individuals enrol to MOOCs to meet their professional needs, others participate in these courses out of personal interest in a particular subject. MOOCs offer individuals relatively easy access to learning opportunities and provide them with another path to achieve their own personal learning goals. Such courses place the responsibility for learning on the individual, who identifies what they would like to learn and selects a suitable course that meets their learning needs and interests. As with all kinds of e-learning, MOOCs afford learners a considerable degree of flexibility in terms of how, where and when they engage in learning. They also incorporate an element of social learning through Web 2.0 technologies, such as Twitter and blogs. They involve minimal academic support and draw upon peer-to-peer learning and support. While incorporating the usual benefits associated with e-learning, MOOCs also come with some challenges, including the difficulty for individuals of maintaining motivation in an online setting and handling the online learning platform itself. The completion rate for MOOCs currently stands anywhere between 5 per cent and 20 per cent, and this may be due, in part, to information overload and the lack of any reward or certification at the end of the course.

The question of whether MOOCs result in learning on the part of the individual has received little attention so far. Some commentators suggest that the learning experience may be somewhat undermined by the absence of individual support and feedback for learners. What we do

HRD - IN THE NEWS

know is that four types of MOOC learner archetypes have been emerging: (1) *lurkers*, who enrol but at most only sample a small number of items in the MOOC; (2) *passive participants*, who view the course as consisting of consumable content and who do not participate in any course activities, such as online discussions; (3) *active participants*, who fully engage in all course activities, e.g. class discussions, exercises, social media interactions etc.; and (4) *drop-ins*, who engage in some way with a particular course topic, but who do not try to complete the remainder of the course.

To conclude, we can see that, despite the possible drawbacks of this kind of learning, MOOCs have opened up further opportunities for informal learning on the part of individuals.

1 Why have MOOCs received so much attention recently and why might they be attractive to learners?

2 How might a more active approach to learning in MOOCs be encouraged?

3 What kind of support might be put in place for a learner undertaking a MOOC?

Sources

http://competence.wordpress.com/2013/03/13/how-moocs-change-the-world-do-they-starting-a-list-of-myths-about-moocs/

http://journalistsresource.org/studies/society/education/moocs-online-learning-research-roundup

http://www.insidehighered.com/views/2013/06/03/essay-questioning-evidence-moocs-and-learning

http://www.learningsolutionsmag.com/articles/721/

http://mfeldstein.com/the-four-student-archetypes-emerging-in-moocs/

http://www.universitiesuk.ac.uk/highereducation/Documents/2013/MassiveOpenOnlineCourses.pdf

Effectiveness of E-learning: Of course, the big question for HRD practitioners to consider is whether e-learning is more, less or just as effective as other more traditional forms of learning. DeRouin *et al.* (2005) note the general dearth of research in this area. However, they point to research elsewhere that highlights the generally positive reactions of individuals to e-learning. However, they report mixed results from other research studies on the important question of whether improved learning outcomes occur where e-learning is used as the mode of delivery. They note that some studies suggest that there is no difference in learning outcomes between e-learning and more traditional delivery methods. DeRouin *et al.* (2005) highlight the other research reports that suggest e-learning can improve learning, while others report poorer learning outcomes as a result of e-learning. De Rouin *et al.* also highlight that there is some suggestion that e-learning improves work behaviours; however, there are few studies that explore this in any great detail. The findings of the CIPD (2013b) annual learning and talent development survey indicate that the vast majority of those surveyed (91 per cent) believed that the effectiveness of e-learning is enhanced where it is combined with other forms of learning. The survey also found that 72 per cent of those surveyed believe that e-learning does not serve as a replacement for traditional classroom-type learning.

BUILDING YOUR SKILLS

You have recently been appointed e-learning specialist in a travel company in Berlin called Dolphin International. Your manager is interested in your view on how best to increase informal learning among employees using technology and social media tools. Develop a one-page proposal for your manager on how Dolphin International might go about this task.

SUMMARY

This chapter aimed to deepen the reader's understanding of the complex process of learning. An understanding of the many human and dispositional factors that influence learning, the various learning theories presented and the stages in the learning process provided the reader with a good basis for designing and delivering effective learning and development activities in the workplace ▶ Chapters 8 and 9. It is hoped that that the chapter has also encouraged you to reflect on how you might improve your own learning and on how you might broaden the range of learning styles you draw upon during the course of your studies and beyond.

 CHAPTER REVIEW QUESTIONS

1 Consider the three types of non-formal learning identified by Eraut (2004) – implicit, reactive and deliberative. Can you think of a time when you engaged in each of these types of non-formal learning?
2 Describe the human and dispositional factors that influence learning.
3 Why is an understanding of adult learning theory important for HRD practitioners? What value would it be to know that you were training a group aged between 25 and 40 years?
4 How useful is an understanding of how the application of social learning theory might work in practice?
5 What could a line manager do to encourage employees to more actively engage with all four stages in the learning cycle?
6 Why is the concept of 'learning styles' important for both HRD practitioners and individual learners to understand? What are the likely implications for learners of over-reliance on one particular learning style?
7 How might the effectiveness of an e-learning programme be enhanced from the perspective of: an individual's learning; and the programme's learning outcomes?
8 What barriers might prevent an individual from learning?

 FURTHER READING

Carbery, R. and Cross, C. (Eds) (2013) *Human Resource Management: A Concise Introduction*, Basingstoke: Palgrave Macmillan (Chapter 9).
Coffield, F., Moseley, D., Hall, E. and Ecclestone, K. (2004) *Learning Styles and Pedagogy in Post-16 Learning: A Systematic and Critical Review*, London: Learning and Skills Research Centre.
Derouin, R. E., Fritzsche, B. A. and Salas, E. (2005) E-Learning in Organizations, *Journal of Management*, 31(6), 920–940.
Knowles, M. S., Holton III, E. F. and Swanson, R. A. (2011) *The Adult Learner: The Definitive Classic in Adult Education and Human Resource Development* (7th ed.), Oxford: Butterworth-Heinemann.

Rogers, A. and Horrocks, N. (2010) *Teaching Adults* (4th ed.), Maidenhead: Open University Press/McGraw Hill.
Zemke, R. and Zemke, S. (1995) Adult Learning: What Do We Know for Sure? *Training*, June, 31–38.

USEFUL WEBSITES

http://www.oecd.org/edu/skills-beyond-school/recognitionofnon-formalandinformallearning-home.htm
This OECD webpage provides a concise explanation of both formal and informal learning and provides a link to a report on the recognition of informal learning in various countries.
http://www.vark-learn.com
This website contains information on the VARK learning styles questionnaire. Why not complete the questionnaire and see what learning style you tend to exhibit most often? A number of interviews with the designer of VARK can be found on the website also.
http://www.cipd.co.uk/hr-topics/e-learning.aspx
The Chartered Institute of Personnel and Development (CIPD) website contains a number of useful articles on e-learning, including a factsheet and a survey report on trends in e-learning. If you are not a member of the CIPD, you will need to register as a guest to access these materials.
http://podcasts.cipd.co.uk/resources/podcasts/CIPD-Learning-Development-2010-podcast-42.mp3
This podcast discusses the role of technology in learning and considers what good and bad e-learning might look like. The podcast includes interviews with executives from two organizations.
http://reviewing.co.uk/research/experiential.learning.htm#axzz2UsrLcWE2
This website examines experiential learning and provides a number of links to other websites on the topic. It also includes some critiques of Kolb's learning cycle.

BIBLIOGRAPHY

Ainsworth, H. L. and Eaton, S. E. (2010) *Formal, Non-Formal and Informal Learning in the Sciences*, Calgary: Onate Press.
Armstrong, M. and Taylor, S. (2014) *Armstrong's Handbook of Human Resource Management Practice*, London: Kogan Page.
Attwell, G. (2007) Personal Learning Environments – the future of eLearning?. *eLearning Papers*, 2(1), 1–8. Retrieved 10 April 2014 from: http://www.openeducationeuropa.

eu/en/article/Personal-Learning-Environments---the-future-of-eLearning%3F

Bondarouk, T. and Ruël, H. (2010) Dynamics of e-Learning: Theoretical and Practical Perspectives, *International Journal of Training and Development*, 14(3), 149–154.

Boustedt, J., Eckerdal, A., McCartney, R., Sanders, K., Thomas, L. and Zander, C. (2011) Students' Perceptions of the Differences between Formal and Informal Learning, In *Proceedings of the Seventh International Workshop on Computing Education Research*, August, ACM, 61–68.

Brookfield, S. (1986) *Understanding and Facilitating Adult Learning: A Comprehensive Analysis of Principles and Effective Practices*, Milton Keynes: Open University Press.

Brown, L., Murphy, E. and Wade, V. (2006) Corporate eLearning: Human Resource Development Implications for Large and Small Organizations, *Human Resource Development International*, 9(3), 415–427.

Buckley, R. and Caple, J. (2009) *The Theory & Practice of Training* (6th ed.), London: Kogan Page.

Carliner, S. (2013) How Have Concepts of Informal Learning Developed over Time?, *Performance Improvement*, 52(3), 5–11.

Cassidy, S. (2004) Learning Styles: An Overview of Theories, Models, and Measures, *Educational Psychology*, 24(4), 419–444.

Charlesworth, Z. M. (2008) Learning Styles across Cultures: Suggestions for Educators, *Education+ Training*, 50(2), 115–127.

CIPD (2013a) E-Learning Factsheet. London CIPD (http://www.cipd.co.uk/hr-resources/factsheets/e-learning.aspx). Accessed 30 May 2013.

CIPD (2013b) *Learning and Talent Development: Annual Survey Report 2013*, London: CIPD.

Coffield, F., Moseley, D., Hall, E. and Ecclestone, K. (2004) *Learning Styles and Pedagogy in Post-16 Learning: A Systematic and Critical Review*, London: Learning and Skills Research Centre.

Collin, A. (2010) Learning and Development, In J. Beardwell and T. Claydon (Eds) *Human Resource Management: A Contemporary Approach* (6th ed.), Harlow: Financial Times/Prentice Hall (235–282).

Conlon, T. J. (2004) A Review of Informal Learning Literature, Theory and Implications for Practice in Developing Global Professional Competence, *Journal of European Industrial Training*, 28(2/3/4), 283–295.

Cross, J. (2007) *Informal Learning: Rediscovering the Natural Pathways That Inspire Innovation and Performance*, San Francisco, CA: Pfeiffer.

Crouse, P., Doyle, W. and Young, J. D. (2011) Workplace Learning Strategies, Barriers, Facilitators and Outcomes: A Qualitative Study among Human Resource Management Practitioners, *Human Resource Development International*, 14(1), 39–55.

Cuthbert, P. F. (2005) The Student Learning Process: Learning Styles or Learning Approaches?, *Teaching in Higher Education*, 10(2), 235–249.

Daines, J., Daines, C. and Graham, B. (1993) *Adult Learning, Adult Teaching* (3rd ed.), Cardiff: Ashley Drake.

De Vita, G. (2001) Learning Styles, Culture and Inclusive Instruction in the Multicultural Classroom: A Business and Management Perspective, *Innovations in Education and Teaching International*, 38(2), 165–174.

Derouin, R. E., Fritzsche, B. A. and Salas, E. (2005) E-learning in Organizations, *Journal of Management*, 31(6), 920–940.

Ellström, P. E. (2011) Informal Learning at Work: Conditions, Processes and Logics, In M. Malloch, L. Cairns, K. Evans and B. N. O'Connor (Eds) *The SAGE Handbook of Workplace Learning*, London: Sage (105–120).

Eraut, M. (2004) Informal Learning in the Workplace, *Studies in Continuing Education*, 26(2), 247–273.

Felder, R. M. and Silverman, L. K. (1988) Learning and Teaching Styles in Engineering Education, *Engineering Education*, 78(7), 674–681.

Felder, R. M. and Spurlin, J. (2005) Applications, Reliability and Validity of the Index of Learning Styles, *International Journal of Engineering Education*, 21(1), 103–112.

Flanagan, K. (1997) *Maximum Points – Minimum Panic: The Essential Guide to Surviving Exams*, Dublin: Marino Books.

Fleming, N. D. (1995) I'm Different; Not Dumb. Modes of Presentation (VARK) in the Tertiary Classroom, In *Research and Development in Higher Education*, Proceedings of the 1995 Annual Conference of the Higher Education and Research Development Society of Australasia (HERDSA), HERDSA, July, 18, 308–313.

Garavan, T., Collins, E. and Brady, S. (2003) *Training and Development in Ireland*, Dublin: CIPD.

Gibbs, S. (2011) *Human Resource Development: Foundations, Process, Contexts* (3rd ed.), Basingstoke: Palgrave Macmillan.

Granger, B. P. and Levine, E. L. (2010) The Perplexing Role of Learner Control in E-learning: will Learning and Transfer Benefit or Suffer?, *International Journal of Training and Development*, 14(3), 180–197.

Gutiérrez, K. D. and Rogoff, B. (2003) Cultural ways of Learning: Individual Traits or Repertoires of Practice, *Educational Researcher*, 32(5), 19–25.

Hall, E. and Moseley, D. (2005) Is there a Role for Learning Styles in Personalised Education and Training?, *International Journal of Lifelong Education*, 24(3), 243–255.

Harrison, R. (2000) *Employee Development* (2nd ed.), London: Chartered Institute of Personnel and Development.

Hawk, T. F. and Shah, A. J. (2007) Using Learning Style Instruments to Enhance Student Learning, *Decision Sciences Journal of Innovative Education*, 5(1), 1–19.

Hoekstra, A., Beijaard, D., Brekelmans, M. and Korthagen, F. (2007) Experienced Teachers' Informal Learning from Classroom Teaching, *Teachers and Teaching: Theory and Practice*, 13(2), 191–208.

Honey, P. and Mumford, A. (1992) *The Manual of Learning Styles* (3rd ed.), Maidenhead: Peter Honey Publications Ltd.

Honey, P. and Mumford, A. (2006) *The Learning Styles Questionnaire: 80 Item Version*, Maidenhead: Peter Honey Publications Ltd.

Hrastinski, S. (2008) Asynchronous and Synchronous E-learning, *Educause Quarterly*, 31(4), 51–55.

Hurdle, L. H. (2010) Adult Learning Principles to Consider When Using Web 2.0, *Training and Development*, July, 64(7), 76–77.

Johnson, R. D., Hornik, S. and Salas, E. (2008) An Empirical Examination of Factors Contributing to the Creation of Successful E-learning Environments, *International Journal of Human-Computer Studies*, 66(5), 356–369.

Joy, S. and Kolb, D. A. (2009) Are There Cultural Differences in Learning Style?, *International Journal of Intercultural Relations*, 33(1), 69–85.

Knowles, M. S. (1984) *The Adult Learner: A Neglected Species*, Houston: Gulf.

Knowles, M. S., Holton III, E. F. and Swanson, R. A. (2011) *The Adult Learner: The Definitive Classic in Adult Education and Human Resource Development* (7th ed.), Oxford: Routledge.

Kolb, A. Y. and Kolb, D. A. (2009) Experiential Learning Theory: A Dynamic, Holistic Approach to Management Learning, Education and Development, In J. Armstrong and C. V. Fukami (Eds), *The SAGE Handbook of Management Learning, Education and Development*, London: SAGE (42–68).

Kolb, D. A. (1984) *Experiential Learning*, New York: Prentice Hall.

Kort, B., Reilly, R. and Picard, R. W. (2001) An Affective Model of Interplay between Emotions and Learning: Reengineering Educational Pedagogy – Building a Learning Companion, In *Proceedings of International Conference on Advanced Learning Technologies (ICALT)*, August, Madison, Wisconsin.

Livingstone, D. (2006) Informal Learning: Conceptual Distinctions and Preliminary Findings, In Z. Bekerman, N. C. Burbules and D. Silberman-Keller (Eds), *Learning in Places: The Informal Education Reader*, New York: Peter Lang.

Lombardo, M. M. and Eichinger, R. W. (1996) *The Course Architect Development Planner*, Minneapolis: Lominger.

London, M. and Hall, M. J. (2011) Unlocking the Value of Web 2.0 Technologies for Training and Development: The Shift from Instructor-Controlled, Adaptive Learning to Learner-Driven, Generative Learning, *Human Resource Management*, 50(6), 757–775.

Marsick, V. J., Watkins, K. E., Callahan, M. W. and Volpe, M. (2006) Reviewing Theory and Research on Informal and Incidental Learning, *Proceedings of the Academy of Human Resource Development International Research Conference in the Americas*, 794–800.

Mayer, R. E. (2004) Should There Be a Three-Strikes Rule against Pure Discovery Learning?, *American Psychologist*, 59(1), 14.

Menaker, E. S. and Coleman, S. L. (2007) Learning Styles Again: Where is Empirical Evidence?, In *The Interservice/Industry Training, Simulation & Education Conference (I/ITSEC)*, 2007 (1), National Training Systems Association.

Merriam, S. B. (2001) Andragogy and Self-Directed Learning: Pillars of Adult Learning Theory, *New Directions for Adult and Continuing Education*, 89, 3–14.

Merriam, S. B., Caffarella, R. S. and Baumgartner, L. M. (2012) *Learning in Adulthood: A Comprehensive Guide* (3rd ed.), San Francisco: John Wiley and Sons.

Miettinen, R. (2000) The Concept of Experiential Learning and John Dewey's Theory of Reflective Thought and Action, *International Journal of Lifelong Education*, 19(1), November–December: 54–72.

Mumford, A. (1995) Learning Styles and Mentoring, *Industrial and Commercial Training*, 27(8), 4–7.

Newstrom, J. W. and Lengnick-Hall, M. L. (1991) One Size Does Not Fit All, *Training and Development*, 45(6), 43–46.

Noe, R. A. (2010) *Employee Training and Development* (5th ed.), New York: McGraw-Hill.

Payne, E. and Whittaker, L. (2006) *Developing Essential Study Skills* (2nd ed.), Harlow: Pearson Education.

Peterson, E. R., Rayner, S. G. and Armstrong, S. J. (2009) Researching the Psychology of Cognitive Style and Learning Style: Is There Really a Future?, *Learning and Individual Differences*, 19(4), 518–523.

Prince, M. (2004) Does Active Learning Work? A Review of the Research, *Journal of Engineering Education*, 93(3), 223–231.

Reynolds, M. (1997) Learning Styles: A Critique, *Management Learning*, 28(2), 115–133.

Richardson, J. T. (2011). Approaches to Studying, Conceptions of Learning and Learning Styles in Higher Education, *Learning and Individual Differences*, 21(3), 288–293.

Riding, R. and Rayner, S. (2012) *Cognitive Styles and Learning Strategies: Understanding Style Differences in Learning and Behavior*, Oxon: Routledge.

Rogers, A. and Horrocks, N. (2010) *Teaching Adults*, Berkshire: McGraw Hill/Open University Press.

Sadler-Smith, E. (2014) Learning Styles and Cognitive Styles in Human Resource Development, In J. Walton and C. Valentin (Eds) *Human Resource Development: Practices and Orthodoxies*, Basingstoke: Palgrave Macmillan (85–106).

Sinha, A. (2012) The Learning Continuum: Formal and Informal Learning Experiences–Enabling Learning and Creation of New Knowledge in an Organization, *International Journal of Advanced Corporate Learning*, 5(2), 10–14.

Smith, M. K. (2002) *Malcolm Knowles, Informal Adult Education, Self-Direction and Andragogy*, Harlow: Infed, the Encyclopedia of Informal Education. Retrieved 10 April 2014 from: www.infed.org/thinkers/et-knowl.htm

Thomas, K. J. and Akdere, M. (2013) Social Media as Collaborative Media in Workplace Learning, *Human Resource Development Review*, 12(3), 329–344.

Thompson, N. and McGill, T. J. (2012) Affective Tutoring Systems: Enhancing E-Learning with the Emotional Awareness of a Human Tutor, *International Journal of Information and Communication Technology Education*, 8(4), 75–89.

Torrington, D., Hall, L., Taylor, S. and Atkinson, C. (2009) *Fundamentals of Human Resource Management: Managing People at Work* (1st ed.), Harlow: Financial Times/ Prentice Hall.

Torrington, D., Hall, L., Taylor, S. and Atkinson, C. (2011) *Human Resource Management* (8th ed.), Harlow: Financial Times/Prentice Hall.

Tynjälä, P. and Häkkinen, P. (2005) E-Learning at Work: Theoretical Underpinnings and Pedagogical Challenges, *Journal of Workplace Learning*, 17(5/6), 318–336.

Welsh, E. T., Wanberg, C. R., Brown, K. G. and Simmering, M. J. (2003) E-Learning: Emerging Uses, Empirical Results and Future Directions, *International Journal of Training and Development*, 7(4), 245–258.

Werner, J. M. and De Simone, R. L. (2009) *Human Resource Development* (5th ed.), Ohio: Cengage Learning.

Yamazaki, Y. (2005) Learning Styles and Typologies of Cultural Differences: A Theoretical and Empirical Comparison, *International Journal of Intercultural Relations*, 29(5), 521–548.

Zemke, R. and Zemke, S. (1995) Adult Learning: What Do We Know For Sure?, *Training*, 32(6), 31–38.

Zhang, C. L., Kyriakidou, N. and Chesley, D. (2013) Learning Theories and Principles, In J. Gold, R. Holden, P. Iles, J. Stewart and J. Beardwell (Eds) *Human Resource Development: Theory and Practice*, Basingstoke: Palgrave Macmillan (107–130).

5 ORGANIZATIONAL LEARNING

Ronan Carbery

By the end of this chapter you will be able to:

LEARNING OUTCOMES

- Define organizational learning
- Identify how the concept of the learning organization differs from organizational learning
- Recognize the difference between tacit and explicit knowledge
- Describe the challenges of organizational learning

- Explain the relationship between knowledge management and organizational learning
- Recognize how organizational learning can be supported
- Assess barriers to organizational learning

  Identify how a culture of learning can be supported in organizations

Capturing bright ideas

This chapter discusses ...

INTRODUCTION

We have just looked at how people learn ▶Chapter 4, but what about organizations? Can they learn? Take the case of a host in a restaurant who, after years of learning and gaining knowledge on the job, knows the regular customers' names, where they like to sit and what their favourite drinks are. If this employee decides to leave the restaurant and work elsewhere, what happens to the knowledge they have? Do they take it with them or can the organization tap into it somehow?

Or have you ever wondered why some ideas catch on and others don't, or why some innovations spread quickly while others never catch on? Usually it depends on the conditions required for application of the idea or what has been learnt to be successful. For example, the first documented use of surgical anaesthesia was recorded in Boston in October 1846. Prior to this, even minor surgery left people in excruciating pain, with surgeons having to work fast while attendants pinned patients down to prevent them from writhing in agony. Anaesthesia was a revelation, and by February 1847 it was being used in nearly all European cities and by June the same year in most regions in the world. Around the same period, infection during surgery was the single biggest killer of surgical patients, with up to 50 per cent of patients succumbing to sepsis after major operations. In 1867 a Scottish surgeon discovered that using carbolic acid, an antiseptic agent, to clean hands, wounds and surgical tools destroyed the germs that caused these infections and published his findings in *The Lancet*, the world's leading medical journal. Unlike the fast adoption of anaesthesia, it was 40 years later before antiseptics became widely used. One possible reason behind the slow take up is that anaesthesia addressed a tangible and immediate problem – pain – whereas antiseptics targeted an intangible problem whose effects would not be noticed until well after the operation – infectious germs. Also, while anaesthesia made life easier for both patients and surgeons, antiseptics primarily benefited patients, with surgeons required to rethink their approach to work by doing tasks they previously had never done before, such as sterilizing instruments, changing their uniforms between operations, and using fresh surgical gauze during each procedure instead of reusing sponges from one patient to the next without cleaning them. Even though these scenarios occurred almost 150 years ago, the principles behind organizational learning are pretty much the same. Sharing ideas and spreading knowledge are very much dependent on the conditions that are created within organizations: are new ideas and new ways of doing things encouraged; are people rewarded for sharing knowledge; does the adoption of new knowledge make things easier for employees to carry out their roles?

This chapter looks at what we mean by organizational learning, and then considers the concept of the learning organization, much of which requires an understanding of knowledge management. How organizations actually go about learning is then examined, followed by looking at steps that can be taken to develop a culture that supports learning. Group or team-based learning will be distinguished from individual and organizational learning, and we will finally look at how SMEs go about organizational learning.

ORGANIZATIONAL LEARNING DEFINITIONS AND THEORIES

There has been an increasing emphasis on the concept of learning in organizations in recent years. An ever-changing business environment in terms of global competition and increased customer sophistication has focused organizations on the need to develop a culture of learning in order to gain competitive advantage. This competitive advantage is based on the belief that it is people (human resources) and not capital that provide organizations with their competitive edge (O'Keefe and Harington, 2001). This notion can be traced back to Drucker's (1993) belief that the extent to which individuals, organizations, industries and countries effectively acquire and apply knowledge would become a key competitive factor.

organizational learning how an organization actually learns and adapts to new knowledge

Definitions of **organizational learning** usually incorporate some reference to knowledge creation and exchange as well as use of existing knowledge (Nahapiet and Ghoshal, 1998; Qureshi, 2000; DeNisi *et al.*, 2003). Probst and Buchel (1997) see organizational learning as 'the process by which the organization's knowledge and value base changes, leading to improved problem solving ability and capacity for action' (p. 15). However, Nonaka and Takeuchi (1995) argue that the success of this learning process depends on the 'recognition that creating new knowledge is not simply a matter of "processing" objective information. Rather, it depends on tapping the internal and often highly objective insights, intuitions and hunches of individual employees and making those insights available for testing and use by the company as a whole' (p. 19). In other words, organizations can actually learn.

There are, however, some critics of the concept that organizations can learn. Prange (1999) describes the way in which learning might be considered organizational as one of the greatest myths of organizational learning and argues that there is an unclear distinction in the literature between individual and organizational learning. There have also been concerns expressed that there is no clear justification for applying ideas of individual learning to the collective organizational level and that groups or teams should be the primary level of analysis when exploring organizational learning. There is some agreement that organizational learning incorporates four steps: becoming aware of and identifying new knowledge, transferring or interpreting new knowledge, using knowledge by adjusting behaviour to achieve intended outcomes, and institutionalizing knowledge by reflecting on what is happening and by adjusting behaviour. Table 5.1 presents these phases and the challenges associated with them.

To understand the dynamics of learning in organizations, we can look at three distinct approaches that organizations can adopt: single-loop learning,

CONSIDER THIS ...

With the advent of digital photography, the global market for camera film has collapsed by over 90 per cent from an all-time peak in 2000. The two main companies in the camera film business were Kodak and Fujifilm. Kodak filed for bankruptcy in 2012 but Fujifilm survived by rethinking their business model by expanding their product offerings and investing in new business areas. One of these areas is skincare.

Fujifilm looked at what skills and competencies their employees possessed and what knowledge already existed in the organization and subsequently made the unlikely connection between camera film technology and skincare. Fujifilm realized that the knowledge acquired over 70 years preventing film from degrading could also be applied to skincare. For example, they were already using collagen (50 per cent of film emulsion is collagen), and they knew how to control oxidization, which is very damaging to both film and skin. The knowledge that the company had gained in making people look good on film could now be applied to making their skin look good. In 2007, Fujifilm launched their own skincare brand, Astalift, in Japan. By 2010, they had approximately €100m in sales and are one of Japan's top selling skincare brands.

Table 5.1 Phases of organizational learning and their challenges

Phase	Challenges
Becoming aware of and identifying new knowledge	• How is the environment scanned? • How is new knowledge identified? • What sources and forms of knowledge are deemed legitimate and illegitimate? • What filters exist to screen out potential new knowledge?
Transferring/interpreting new knowledge	• How is new knowledge transferred across the different parts of the organization? • How is tacit knowledge transferred? • What happens to knowledge as it is transferred? • How likely are multiple interpretations to arise? • How are multiple interpretations addressed? • Whose interpretations will be deemed legitimate?
Using knowledge by adjusting behaviour to achieve intended outcomes	• How is knowledge transformed into action? • What is the absorptive capacity of the organization to adopt new ideas? • How is collective action orchestrated? • What forms of organizational resistance to changes in behaviour exist? • How can they be overcome?
Institutionalizing knowledge by reflecting on what is happening and by adjusting behaviour	• How can knowledge be institutionalized? • Is there an organizational equivalent of memory in which experience can be deposited? • What are the internal results of institutionalizing knowledge? • How can institutionalization be reconciled with future learning?

Source: Partially adapted from Levinson and Asahi (1995)

double-loop learning and triple-loop learning. First, single-loop learning, sometimes referred to as adaptive learning, is often seen as a basic form of learning which occurs within a set of recognized and unrecognized constraints that reflect the organization's assumptions about its environment and itself (Argyris and Schön, 1974). The constraints can limit an organization's learning to the adaptive variety, which is usually sequential, incremental and focused on issues within the traditional scope of the organization's activities or within the enterprise's pre-existing track record of successes. For example, consider a thermostat in a room. In single-loop learning, a thermostat set to 22 degrees Celsius turns up the heat whenever the temperature drops below 22 and turns off the heat if the temperature rises above 22. In other words, the system includes one automatic and limited type of reaction – little or no learning occurs.

In single-loop learning, when problems occur, or the result did not go as planned, small changes are made to specific practices or behaviours, based on what has or has not worked in the past. This involves doing things better without necessarily examining or challenging underlying beliefs and assumptions. The goal is improvements and fixes that often take the form of procedures or rules. Single-loop learning leads to making minor fixes or adjustments, by concentrating on changing actions that can often be guided by a strict set of rules.

Double-loop learning sometimes known as generative learning, occurs when an organization is willing to question long-held assumptions about the way it does things, and seeks to develop new ways of looking at the world based on an understanding of systems and relationships that link key issues and events (Argyris, 1977). In our thermostat example above, under a double-loop learning approach, the people in the room might decide to question what is the optimum temperature or ask why it has been set to 22 Celsius in the first place. Double-loop learning is a collaborative method of learning and encourages employees to engage with organizational goals and objectives. Employees are involved in the identification and setting of strategic goals and are encouraged to challenge existing goals with new ideas. Employees become highly engaged in the organization as they are encouraged to contribute to the long-term goals and possible outcomes of these goals. This method improves

single-loop learning the correction of error within a given set of governing variables, norms, policies, objectives etc.

double-loop learning the correction of error in ways that change the governing variables themselves

learning in an organization, as employees are engaged in decision making and respectful of co-workers' mistakes. Control is shared, which gives employees greater freedom within their role and authority to make decisions. Under this learning method best practices are established among employees. It is argued that double-loop learning is the basis for innovation and more likely to lead to an organization's competitive advantage than single-loop learning.

For an example of this, consider the contrasting fortunes of smartphone producers. In 2008, BlackBerry (formerly known as Research In Motion) controlled almost 50 per cent of the smartphone market and had a peak share price of $149.90 in June 2008. By September 2013, its share price had fallen by 94 per cent to $8.80 and it controlled 2.1 per cent of the smartphone market. One criticism of the company is that it had become complacent about its remarkably loyal customers and did not recognize the threat posed by rival companies such as Samsung and Apple. Rather than engage in double-loop learning and attempting to keep up, or lead with technological innovations, BlackBerry smartphones evolved at a very slow pace and were reluctant to embrace many technological features commonly available on other smartphones. Even BlackBerry's attempts to enter the tablet market dominated by Apple and Samsung were characterized by single-loop learning – the PlayBook tablet was first launched in 2011 and required the user to own a BlackBerry smartphone in order to use e-mail and calendar applications, rendering it unpopular with non-BlackBerry users. Six months after its launch, the company announced that it was taking a half billion-dollar loss on unsold stock of the tablet.

Similarly, in 1998, Nokia was the leading mobile phone handset maker in the world, with more than 22 per cent of the global marketplace. It peaked at around 40 per cent in 2008. At the time, Nokia's popularity was built upon doing one thing well and concentrating on that – offering customers phones that were more advanced and more visually appealing than the competition's. Like BlackBerry, Nokia was engaged in single-loop learning: doing the same thing over and over and expecting the same results, i.e. to remain the world's most popular mobile phone manufacturer. Unfortunately for Nokia, it was not ready to engage in double-loop learning when it came to the next transformation of the mobile industry towards smartphones – and its decline can arguably be traced to the launch in 2007 of Apple's first iPhone. Between 2007 and 2013 Nokia lost over €70 billion in market value, and in September 2013 was bought by Microsoft after making a loss of €1.3 billion in 2012.

Triple-loop learning occurs when organizations reflect on previous episodes of learning to discover what facilitated or inhibited it, then develop new strategies for learning, and evaluate what these new strategies have produced (Swieringa and Wierdsma, 1992). It is basically double-loop learning about double-loop learning! What is being reflected upon does not necessarily have to be determined by learning from successes. It is argued that organizations learn more effectively from failures than successes, and that knowledge from failure actually lasts longer than knowledge from success (Madsen and Desai, 2010). Figure 5.1 presents the differences between the three types of organizational learning.

There has been relatively little research conducted to date on the organizational learning strategies in SMEs. However, Chaston et al. (2001) surveyed 168 small UK manufacturing firms to determine the learning systems used and found that firms that adopt double- and triple-loop learning were likely to be more innovative. They also sought to determine whether a relationship exists between learning style and the competences displayed by the organizations. Organizations that adopted some characteristics of learning organizations reported statistically significantly higher capabilities in the areas of developing new products, a greater number of product launches, reduced time to market and developing products to enter new markets. Even for SMEs, attempting to adopt double-loop learning increased their ability to develop innovative capabilities, thereby increasing competitive advantage.

triple-loop learning involves learning how to learn by reflecting on how organizations learn in the first place

learning organization an organization that enables the learning of all its employees and continually changes itself

BUILDING YOUR SKILLS

Think about how you study for any of your modules. Say you receive a grade in your mid-term exam that you are unhappy with. Would you study in the exact same way for your end-of-term exam and hope that the result will be different? This is essentially the single-loop learning approach. Einstein claimed that the definition of insanity was doing the same thing over and over again and hoping for different results. Taking a double-loop learning approach, you could ask yourself: why did I not do well on the exam? Did I do enough study? Did I revise the correct material? Do I need to rethink how I study? You could also seek feedback from your lecturer or tutor to see how you could improve for the final exam. You might just find that adopting a double-loop learning approach could be beneficial for your studies!

The learning organization

The concept of the learning organization is also based around the idea that learning is a key source of competitive advantage (Sloman, 2010). The learning organization model adopts a number of the principles behind double-loop learning, including learning how to learn; enabling employees' learning to generate outcomes such as creativity, innovation, change and transformation; facilitating learning that focuses on changing the behaviour of the organization;

Figure 5.1 Types of organizational learning

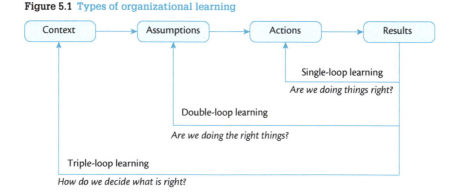

Table 5.2 Characteristic features of the learning organization

• Learning is derived from a multiplicity of experiences: planned/unplanned, deliberate/accidental, successes/failures and is used to shape future behaviour.
• Learning how to learn is a critical aspect of the learning organization.
• Organizations learn from both the external and internal environment and this occurs at all times within the organization.
• Learning is continuous, habitual and internalized.
• Learning is utilized by an organization to enable organizational transformation.
• Learning occurs because it is facilitated by managers and employees and it occurs naturally within an organization.

Source: Adapted from Garavan (1997); Sun and Scott (2006)

and viewing learning as an end in itself. Table 5.2 summarizes the characteristic features of the learning organization.

The idea that organizations could create a climate with all of these characteristics is very much aspirational, and the learning organization model is a difficult one to realize in organizations. At best, it represents a progressive process simply because the conditions necessary for it to flourish are difficult to find in many organizations. It visualizes an organization that is continually transforming itself, and in reality very few organizations meet this condition. It is difficult to find examples of organizations that identify themselves as learning organizations; however, organizations that have features of a learning organization include Apple, Samsung and Merck. What some organizations try to do is create 'mini learning organizations' within specific teams or departments. Important HRD activities that may help in the creation of a learning organization include activities that facilitate the emergence of a learning culture, such as recognition and rewards for learning, the allocation of resources to HRD, and role modelling by senior leaders of openness to learning. A variety of processes can also be implemented, such as structures and routines for knowledge sharing, the facilitation of communities of practice and redesigning organizational structures to facilitate collaboration and teamwork. Evaluation is viewed as a vital

SPOTLIGHT ON SKILLS

You have been asked to develop a framework to capture knowledge in your company. What can organizations do to tap into the individual knowledge that people possess to make tacit knowledge explicit?

To help you answer the questions above, visit www.macmillanihe.com/companion/carbery-hrd and watch the video of Brian Naicker talking about organizational learning.

continuous process to ensure that decisions about HRD are informed by evidence.

Differences between organizational learning and the learning organization

Much of the research carried out on organizational learning has been concerned with highlighting the importance of facilitating a learning culture in organizations. There has been less attention paid thus far to identifying and understanding the practical characteristics of learning organizations and the processes that can be employed for organizations to improve their learning systems.

The debate on the distinction between organizational learning and the learning organization suggests that organizational learning is a descriptive process that explains and quantifies learning activities and events. Consequently, it can be categorized under the wider concept of the learning organization, which refers to a philosophical purpose and direction of an organization and its members (Garavan and Carbery, 2012). Table 5.3 summarizes these differences.

Table 5.3 Main differences between organizational learning and the learning organization

Organizational learning	The learning organization
Descriptive	Prescriptive
Asks 'How does an organization learn?'	Asks 'How should an organization learn?'
Draws from psychology and organization development; management sciences; sociology and organization theory; strategy; production management; cultural anthropology.	Originates from mainly management science and organization development disciplines. First tradition starts from management science perspective and then adds insights from organizational development. Second tradition takes as a starting point models of human development, and then distinguishes between cyclical and evolutionary models of learning.
Authors focus on conceptualization and answering questions, such as: What does OL mean? How is OL at all feasible? What kinds of OL are desirable, and for whom and with what chance of actual occurrence? Literature is intentionally distant from practice and value-neutral.	Authors focus on continuous improvement, competence acquisition, experimentation and boundary spanning. They stress the need for visible commitment from managers to learning by incorporating it and giving it symbolic expression.

Source: Adapted from Argyris and Schön (1996: 181–188), Easterby Smith (1997, 1087–1107), Tsang (1997, 74–76)

BUILDING YOUR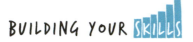

You are working as a training and development manager in a large organization and your boss asks you to assess the extent to which the organization can be classified as a learning organization. How would you go about this? What organizations would you benchmark yourself against? What measures would you use to assess whether or not you meet some of the common characteristics of learning organizations?

GROUP LEARNING

Distinct from both individual learning and organizational learning, group learning focuses on the processes that a group uses to acquire new skills, knowledge, ways of interacting, change patterns between group members, standard operating procedures and behavioural routines. Individual learning tends to be conceptualized as an information system in which learning is interpreted, retained and retrieved by individuals. Group or collective learning is viewed as a more macro-level concept that emphasizes the synergy and advantages of the collective element. Collective learning is assumed to occur when a collective engages in behaviour such as asking questions, seeking feedback, experimenting, reflecting and discussing

options and errors (Garavan and Carbery, 2010). Nonaka and Takeuchi (1995) refer to a number of conditions that stimulate collective learning, including the presence of a vision which directs the processes of knowledge creation, an avoidance of information and a creative focus which stimulates interaction with the environment. Recent theories on innovation, mainly from cultural–individual perspectives, focus on supportive conditions for collective learning, including learning skills, learning motivation and collective foreknowledge.

KNOWLEDGE MANAGEMENT AND ORGANIZATIONAL LEARNING

One of the contextual factors we discussed in Chapter 1 was the knowledge economy. Business practices build on an ever-increasing body of past knowledge, which in itself increases the frequency of new knowledge generation and hastens the obsolescence of old knowledge value. This makes the business environment, which is built on knowledge, increasingly unbalanced. New knowledge demands to be applied. In the event of one business applying new knowledge in a valuable way, others tend to follow, where possible.

When new knowledge is applied, it introduces change into the environment, thereby generating a value. When the value is positive, the resulting change is termed 'innovation' (Amadon, 1997). One of the key determinants of an organization's ability to innovate in a continuously changing environment is dependent on **knowledge management**. This means having the knowledge in a specific individual's head rather than in an online repository, a corporate library or a written document. Technology can enable employees to find resources that help them acquire knowledge, but this is neither a substitute for nor an alternative to an individual learning something.

In knowledge-intensive industries, the ability to capture knowledge and translate it into products or services provides the opportunity for greater business outcomes in the form of increased market share, sales and profits, and enhanced stakeholder satisfaction due to better overall performance. According to the resource-based view of the firm, however, the knowledge must be unique, protected, sustainable and embodied in a product (Barney, 1991). The importance of the human dimension of the resource-based view framework was significantly influenced by human capital theory ▸Chapter 1. Human capital theory emphasizes the potential relationship between the quality and skills of the workforce and organizational performance (Becker, 1964). To understand how knowledge has value, we need to consider the difference between tacit and explicit knowledge.

Polanyi (1966) introduced the notion of **tacit knowledge**, when he found that much human knowledge could not be articulated and turned easily into **explicit knowledge**. Tacit knowledge, which is stored in people's brains as experiences and skills, is difficult to communicate externally (Vail, 1999); for example, imagine trying to describe how to speak a language. Nonaka and von Krogh (2009) described tacit knowledge as knowledge tied to our senses, skills or implicit rules of thumb. It is embedded in the background and experience of an individual or a group (Smith *et al.*, 1997). For organizations, it is context-bound and highly specific to a firm (Almeida *et al.*, 2009), containing insights, intuitions and hunches of the individual (Adel *et al.*, 2010). There are elements of tacit knowledge, which can only be transferred successfully through a process of demonstration, or facilitated through face-to-face contact (O'Toole, 2011). It is a prerequisite for the application of explicit knowledge (Nonaka and von Krogh, 2009) and is a crucial component in the innovation process. Research suggests that tacit knowledge is a sustainable competitive advantage (Wang and Noe, 2010). The strategy for transforming knowledge into capital and assets is to make it explicit. Externalizing internal thought transforms what was previously tacit knowledge into explicit knowledge. Tacit knowledge can be captured through reflective practice and shared with others on an organizational level (Schön, 1983). The most common forms of explicit knowledge are manuals, documents, procedures and how-to videos.

knowledge management having the right knowledge in the right place at the right time

tacit knowledge knowledge in our heads that is difficult to write down, articulate or visualize

explicit knowledge knowledge that can be easily transmitted to others

---

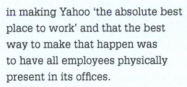
HRD — IN THE NEWS

In February 2013, the recently appointed CEO of Yahoo, Marissa Mayer, introduced a new policy that telecommuting (i.e. working from home) was no longer an option for Yahoo employees. The news of the ban on telecommuting came from a memo to employees sent by Yahoo's head of HR. It was then leaked to *All Things D*, a technology-industry blog. The memo stated that collaboration and communication were critical in making Yahoo 'the absolute best place to work' and that the best way to make that happen was to have all employees physically present in its offices.

In an unprecedented amount of media coverage for HR-related issues, Mayer's move was criticized as 'idiotic' and 'a backward step', and even Richard Branson, founder of the Virgin Group, weighed in, claiming: 'Yours truly has never worked out of an office, and never will.' On the opposite side of the debate, Donald Trump, a US property entrepreneur, tweeted that Mayer was 'right to expect Yahoo employees to come to the workplace vs. working at home'. It probably didn't help Mayer's case when it emerged that she had had a nursery built in her office so that she could bring her child to work prior to the memo being sent out.

Advocates of telecommuting suggest that it allows employees to use their time more efficiently. They can spend more time with their families and less time is wasted in cars or public transport travelling to work. In 2009, Cisco claimed that it was saving $277 million a year by allowing its employees to telecommute. A study by researchers at Stanford and Beijing Universities of a large Chinese travel company compared the performance of employees allowed to work from home with those who were stuck in the office: among the home-workers job satisfaction rose, staff turnover fell by half and productivity went up by 13 per cent. Unsurprisingly, people don't always spend their time at work in the most productive ways – in 2012, J.C. Penney, an American retailer, reported that a third of its headquarters' bandwidth was taken up by employees watching YouTube videos!

But, while telecommuting may offer plenty of benefits for employees, what about organizations themselves? In the absence of people working together face-to-face in one location, it makes it much harder to have any kind of meaningful interaction that is fundamental to the way knowledge moves through an organization. Mayer acknowledged this when explaining the reason for the new policy by highlighting that 'people are more productive when they're alone, but they're

more collaborative and innovative when they're together. Some of the best ideas come from pulling two different ideas together.' As an example of this type of collaboration, Mayer highlighted the new Yahoo Weather app for iOS, which uses built-in geo-location technology in Flickr photo albums that allows users to get a more accurate image of local weather – an idea, she explained, that originated with two software engineers who work in the same office chatting to one another.

The idea that knowledge becomes explicit when employees work more closely together has been validated elsewhere too. In 2010, a professor at Harvard Medical School analysed 35,000 biomedical papers published between 1999 and 2003, each with at least one Harvard author. He then measured how influential the papers were, based on how often they had been cited by other academics. The more physically close the first author listed on the paper was to the last, the more influential their paper became. Sociometric Solutions, a company founded by MIT students and their professor, has developed a digital tagging system to measure workforce interactions. In call centres where employees had close face-to-face networks, employees were twice as productive as

those where workers were more disconnected from each other. As a result of this, one of the main things they changed was the work schedule, so that workers could take coffee breaks at the same time.

Balancing the increasing demand for more flexible working hours with an organization's need for greater flow of knowledge presents a challenge in a knowledge-intensive environment. One possible solution may be for organizations to offer a mix of the two approaches. For example, in the mobile-music-app company Smule, employees must work in the office three days a week during traditional business hours; otherwise they can work from wherever they want.

Sources

Marissa Mayer breaks her silence on Yahoo's telecommuting policy

http://tech.fortune.cnn.com/2013/04/19/marissa-mayer-telecommuting/

The future of telecommuting: Corralling the Yahoos

http://www.economist.com/news/business/21572804-technology-allows-millions-people-work-home-big-tech-firm-trying-stop

Yahoo: Mayer culpa

http://www.economist.com/news/leaders/21572767-forcing-workers-come-office-symptom-ya-hoos-problems-not-solution

Sharing knowledge in organizations

The amount and complexity of information available to people working in organizations are ever increasing, but the methods used to acquire, present and apply this information have remained relatively unchanged (Salisbury and Plass, 2001). Even though knowledge assets are critical resources that provide organizations with competitive advantage (Grover and Davenport, 2001), many knowledge management initiatives do not deliver on expectations (Beaumont and Hunter, 2002). Organizations manage explicit knowledge well, but frequently struggle when seeking to capture tacit knowledge embedded in experienced and skilled people. This high-value-added knowledge is particularly difficult to share using an information technology approach (Gourlay, 2001). An alternative explanation, the people perspective, advocates that individuals in organizations have knowledge that must move to the level of groups and the organization as a whole if it is to be of value for competitive purposes. A central focus of the people perspective concerns knowledge sharing. Knowledge sharing is conceptualized as a natural activity in organizations, something that occurs automatically. However, it is underestimated and underutilized by many organizations, primarily because of the difficulty in capturing it (Burkhard *et al.*, 2011). The evolution of jobs from transactional roles to more complex environments requires more reflection from employees. In multinational companies that have subsidiaries around the world, knowledge developed in one place can be applied in other locations, thereby sharing knowledge internally to expand the knowledge beyond what one employee knows (Nonaka and von Krogh, 2009).

One way organizations can do this is through collaborative learning. Collaborative learning can be defined as the interaction of two or more people engaged in value-creating activities based on improving, practising and transferring learning skills both within the group and to the organization or group of organizations to which a group belongs (Digenti, 1999). Collaborative learning has become very popular in recent years due to the unprecedented levels of change that individuals, organizations and nations who seek to be adaptive and flourish under circumstances where ongoing change is the norm are engaged in. One of the most profound changes in organizations is the flattening of traditional, hierarchical structures in favour of groups of individuals working collaboratively as teams (Axtell *et al.*, 2004).

Digenti (1999) suggests three reasons for the prioritization of collaborative learning in organizations. First, it enables organizations to deal with the pace and direction of change as it occurs. Second, it builds boundary-spanning skills, i.e. cross-disciplinary skills as opposed to the separate management of functional, national culture and subculture boundaries. Third, she suggests that the difference between success and failure in the face of discontinuous change will be the ability to learn and collaborate.

Many employees view sharing tacit knowledge as ethical (Wang, 2004); however, their willingness to share knowledge is dependent on the extent to which they believe they are treated fairly compared with their colleagues (Wang, 2004). Lin (2007) goes so far as to suggest that employees' unwillingness to share knowledge that may hurt an organization's survival is seriously unethical, whereas other commentators have questioned whether tapping into employees' knowledge can be considered ethical behaviour.

Xerox, an American multinational company that produces and sells printers and copiers, wanted to find out ways of improving the productivity of its copier repairmen and sent an observer to see what they actually did on-the-job. The employees were observed spending a lot of time with each other, rather than with customers. They would gather in common areas, such as the local parts warehouse, hang around the canteen, and swap stories about problems that they encountered on the job. Rather than simply trying to eliminate the time employees spent talking instead of carrying out repairs, Xerox took the view that employees were having highly productive conversations by sharing knowledge with each other. The employees weren't just repairing machines; they were also collaboratively producing insights about how to repair machines more effectively. These conversations were crucial in transferring knowledge across the organization. Xerox then created an online database to capture this knowledge in a way that organizes and categorizes a list of tips generated by the repairmen on an ongoing basis. Any employee can submit a tip; the 'reward' is the incentive to be a good colleague, to contribute and receive knowledge as a member of the community.

Tacit knowledge acquisition and transfer methods

Knowledge transfer requires absorption, which can take place through socialization, education or learning. Sharing tacit knowledge is about understanding the purpose, meaning and consequences of actions. Software programs exist that code tacit knowledge into formulated knowledge and upload this data onto a knowledge base for sharing; but it needs to be interpreted by people, requiring prior acquisition of specialized tacit knowledge (Cowan *et al.*, 2000). Since multinational companies (MNCs) can develop knowledge in one place and apply it in others with relative ease nowadays, their competitive advantage depends on their ability to coordinate knowledge transfer within the overall organization (Schreiber *et al.*, 2011).

Individuals acquire tacit knowledge through action, practice and reflection (Nonaka and von Krogh, 2009). Action can take the form of guided learning-by-doing and by walking around in the workplace (Nonaka and Konno, 1998). Practising what we learn in a classroom reinforces knowledge and allows us to internalize the information so that it becomes tacit. Reflection allows us to challenge existing assumptions, which has proven to be a more creative way of learning, leading to organizations reassessing strategic goals (Thorpe *et al.*, 2009). Reflective practice facilitates the process of converting tacit knowledge into words, by helping to generate mental models to make sense of the world, which can then be shared with others on an organizational level and developed through interaction (Schön, 1983; Anderson and Boocock, 2002).

Sources and recipients of knowledge prefer it when the information is simplified by categorizing it into different sections (Smith *et al.*, 2007). It is crucial to select the appropriate people to capture and share tacit knowledge, considering training motivation, cognitive ability, personality traits and self-efficacy (Liebermann and Hoffmann, 2008). The more supportive an organization is towards HRD activities, the more likely it is that employees will participate and share knowledge (Carbery, 2010). The source needs to be reliable in order for the recipient to accept the knowledge (Hölste and Fields, 2010).

In practice, the lack of knowledge sharing has proved to be a major barrier to the effective management of knowledge in organizations (Ipe, 2003). Organizational culture is increasingly being recognized as a major barrier to effective knowledge creation, sharing and use (Ipe, 2003). Individuals can decide whether or not to share or use tacit knowledge (Holste and Fields, 2010). Individual knowledge is linked to status, career prospects and individual reputations, which may prevent employees from being forthcoming with knowledge-sharing initiatives. Employee motivation to learn and motivation to transfer knowledge need to be considered when aspiring to capture tacit knowledge (Bock *et al.*, 2005).

Apprenticeships and communities of practice (CoPs) are two methods of acquiring and sharing tacit knowledge. In addition, we will also consider corporate universities.

Apprenticeships

Apprenticeship is based on the relationship between the master and the apprentice, which is more commonly replicated in coaching and mentoring processes in the current working environment. A mentor is a subject matter expert who interacts on a one-to-one basis with an apprentice in real assignments to share valuable knowledge, skills and experience and develop specific competencies in the apprentice (Marshall, 2005). This face-to-face interaction is fundamental to sharing tacit knowledge through experience and thought processes (Wang and Noe, 2010; O'Toole, 2011). A coach is usually a task-centred expert in human motivation who focuses on turning problems into opportunities, rather than the acquisition of knowledge (Marshall, 2005).

Communities of practice

A community of practice is considered a form of collective learning (Knapp, 2010) at an organizational level. CoPs are defined as 'groups of people informally bound together by shared expertise and passion for a joint enterprise', are an important collaborative learning mechanism, and have received a lot of research attention (Ardichvili, 2008). They are different from traditional teams in that they are driven by value rather than deliverables; defined by opportunities to learn rather than managerially allocated tasks; bound by a shared identity rather than commitment; and often cross the restrictive organizational boundaries to incorporate people from the outside (Brown and Duguid, 1991). A CoP emerges when people with similar interests seek each other for discourse, experience sharing, and problem-solving assistance. Dove (1999) suggests that this self-motivated continuous learning has always been present to some degree in the workplace, but it now gets significant leverage from the corporate intranet and even more so from the internet.

According to Brown and Duguid (1991), 'the way forward is paradoxically to look not ahead, but to look around' (p. 8). The premise of this is because learning occurs when members of a CoP socially acquire their understanding of some issue or event and then share this understanding with others. Learning is facilitated not through the provision of instruction, but through the granting of access to a shared community and the provision of opportunities to engage in increasingly more demanding 'real-work' tasks in conjunction with other community members.

> **communities of practice (CoPs)** a group of individuals who share a common interest in a topic, and who deepen their knowledge of it through ongoing interaction and relationship building in their group

A notable feature of CoPs is the absence of a formal learning facilitator or instructor. Lave and Wenger (1991) argue that an instructor's role is secondary to the role of the community as a whole in offering learners opportunities for co-participation. Newcomers to a community should learn primarily by observing more experienced members and by attempting simple, manageable tasks in collaborative engagements with their peers, gradually developing their skill base through the experiences of everyday work activities. Lave and Wenger (1991) claim that the development of skill in such a setting is an almost inevitable process, since few newcomers fail to attain expert status, despite the absence of a formal instructor and the community's lack of dependence on a formal curriculum. They promote the belief that successful progression along a community's learning trajectory is helped by community empowerment through the granting of opportunities for participation.

According to Wenger et al. (2002), each CoP is a 'unique combination of three fundamental elements: a domain of knowledge, which defines a set of issues; a community of people who care about this domain; and the shared practice that they are developing to be effective in their domain' (p. 27). The domain is the field or discipline that creates common value and a sense of common identity. A shared domain instils a sense of accountability to a body of knowledge and the development of a practice. When well defined, the domain lends legitimacy to the community by articulating its purpose and value to the community members and other stakeholders. The community creates the social structure for learning, fostering interactions and relationships based on mutual trust and respect. It is not simply a website, database or report. It is a group of people who interact, learn together, build relationships and subsequently foster a sense of mutual belonging and commitment. Another element that characterizes the COP process, shared practice, refers to a set of socially defined ways of doing things in a specific domain. It is a set of common approaches and shared standards that create a basis for action, communication, problem solving, performance and accountability. An effective practice evolves as a collective product of the community and is integrated into members' work. When these three elements function cohesively, they allow the creation of a social structure that can assume responsibility for developing and sharing knowledge.

One organization that uses CoPs successfully is Electronic Arts (EA), an entertainment software company that develops, publishes and distributes interactive software worldwide for video game systems, personal computers, wireless devices and the web. EA launched CoPs in 2009 across its globally distributed workforce to try to gain the efficiencies of a large enterprise without compromising local teams' creativity. The concept was based on an analogy described by EA's CEO, John Riccitiello, as the difference between swimmers and water polo players. At a swimming event, each group competes by having its swimmers compete individually in different events and by swimming in their own lanes with little interaction between team-mates. Water polo players, on the other hand, features two teams, each comprised of individuals working together by collaboratively passing the ball to score goals. Members were empowered to make decisions and to take action to achieve specific goals. EA's CoPs could recommend the next technology roadmap, or they could change a business process to become more effective or efficient. Over 20 per cent of EA's staff are active members of CoPs, with numerous benefits, including faster resolution of issues, reduced learning curve for new hires, and increased sharing of knowledge. One way in which EA has tried to measure the financial impact of CoPs is through return on investment calculations ▶ Chapter 10. Specifically, teams at EA use a code in their animation system that controls movement of humans. This code is particularly advanced technology that took a team of programmers and artists to initially create and develop at a cost of approximately $250,000. This code has now been used by over ten teams at EA, with each team making minor modifications to the original work. This means that a $2.5 million dollar saving has occurred through sharing, fostered by CoPs.

Corporate universities

A corporate university is an organization-specific educational provider. It is created and owned by a specific company and provides job-specific and organization-specific training to the organization's employees. There are over 2,000 corporate universities in existence, with famous examples including the Disney University, Hamburger University belonging to MacDonalds, and General Electric's Crotonville. Crotonville is the world's oldest corporate university, having been established in 1956, and Hamburger University followed shortly afterwards in 1962. Apple University and Pixar University are relatively recent additions to the field of corporate universities. These institutes have developed a strong reputation for maintaining a focus on corporate culture and history, while also identifying the importance of training students in creativity, flexibility, innovation and adaptability. In most countries, the ability to award an academic degree is regulated by law and can only be offered by accredited institutes such as a college or university; in the UK, for example, only institutes authorized by either Royal Charter or Act of Parliament can legally award degrees. Given that corporations lack the ability to do this, there has been a movement towards education partnerships, with organizations partnering with third-level institutes to provide recognized and accredited awards to employees. In the US, for example, Chevron's University Partnership Program partners with several major universities, including the Colorado School of Mines; Louisiana State University; Massachusetts Institute of Technology; Stanford University; Texas A&M University; University of California, Davis; and the University of Texas at Austin to offer a range of education programmes. Ostensibly, having a group of individuals for one organization working and studying together is believed to develop a shared culture of learning and foster the sharing of knowledge.

DEVELOPING A CULTURE THAT SUPPORTS LEARNING

With the correct learning environment, organizations can learn faster than the speed at which change occurs in their industry. A supportive and respectful environment is essential for learning. Organizations need to ensure that the **psychological safety** of their staff is protected. An environment that does not interfere with employees' psychological safety encourages risk taking, open discussion on problems, creativity and involvement. An open and error-tolerant learning environment needs to be established in order to have employees who are willing to acquire, transfer and retain new knowledge (Van Wijk *et al.*, 2008). For this to happen, employee involvement is crucial. Employees should be involved in the setting of learning objectives within the organization. These learning objectives should be aligned with the strategic goals of the organization so that employees are committed to meeting goals, thus meeting learning objectives. Learning should be viewed as an asset to both the employees and the organization.

psychological safety people's beliefs that they are able to speak up without there being negative consequences to their job or career

Similarly, clear and transparent processes and procedures are required. Garvin *et al.* (2008) suggest that:

- Clear processes and procedures need to be established so learning can be carried out effectively. These procedures should be aligned with the long-term plans of the organization. Learning must be a continual and proactive process.
- Processes within the organization need to be clear, concise and open to employee discussion. If employees feel a part of the learning process they will be more willing to acquire, transfer and retain new knowledge.
- Employees need to be encouraged to take responsibility for their own learning; an andragogical approach to learning ▸Chapter 4 should be used.
- Learning can be implemented through coaching, job shadowing, on-the-job training, e-learning, assessment centres etc. Deciding on the form of learning depends on the learner and their type of learning ability.
- Employees need to reflect on and review what they have learned, in order to learn from mistakes made. They can undertake an after-action review (see Active Case Study) where they discuss: (a) What goal was set out to be achieved? (b) What actually happened? (c) Why was there a difference between performance and goal set? (d) What can we take or eliminate from our work, in order to improve performance next time?

Table 5.4 presents some common barriers and facilitators to developing a culture of organizational learning.

At a wider HR level, it is now commonly accepted that HR activities needed to be devolved to line managers ▸Chapter 2. The rationale is that the line manager is the person who works most closely with the employee. Just like HRM, however, it is the overall vision, values and managerial ideology of the owner which have the critical influence on the way in which HRD operates in an organization. In larger organizations, it is still the managing director or senior management team who create the environment for the operation of HRD and organizational learning policies. The status, role and profile of the HRD function are influenced by the strength of the belief of senior management in the added value that HRD can contribute to the organization. For

Table 5.4 Barriers and facilitators to developing a culture of organizational learning

Barriers	Facilitators
• Lack of resources, incentives and training • Pressure to meet deadlines • Fragmented and hierarchical structure • Top-down leadership and conflicting strategic priorities • Lack of multi-functional teams or domination of multi-functional initiatives by particular functions • Communication bottlenecks and poor communication • Role constraints, role complexity, role ambiguity • Organizational policies • Fear of change • Low employee morale • Defencive routines where people say they learn but do not manifest it in their behaviour and resist admitting any inconsistency, making it difficult to challenge the status quo • Inability to deal with tacit knowledge • The activities associated with learning and change, e.g. risk taking, making mistakes, are deemed illegitimate in the larger organization • Highly institutionalized cultures	• Hiring key individuals • Training and continuous development • Individual (e.g. compensation) and organizational (e.g. patents) incentives • Motivation, including high cost of errors, need for continuous improvement, performance gap • Curiosity about the environment • Concern for measurement of learning activities and outputs • Committed, involved leadership and multiple advocates • Involvement of middle managers • Decentralized structure and diffusion of information • Cross-cutting, open communication and coordination mechanisms • High levels of trust • A strong culture that values learning and high organizational commitment • High absorptive capacity – ability to pick up new ideas • Willingness to experiment; variety of methods to facilitate experimentation • Centrality of R&D function • Total Quality Management (TQM), reverse engineering, benchmarking and customer input • Systems perspective • Diversification, strategic and cross-national alliances, outsourcing

those responsible for HRD in all organizations, there are a number of steps that can be taken to reinforce a learning culture:

● There is a need for organizations wishing to foster a learning culture to consider developing programmes that embed the work experiences and work tasks of employees; for example, including work-based components directly related to employees' jobs within HRD activities. This is beneficial to the organization as well as to the individual.

● Creation of a learning culture is aligned closely to the development of a more communicative work environment and the use of working relationships as a source of learning, e.g. making information available about performance through either quality data systems or performance review systems and mentoring approaches. Management and supervisory styles of management-level employees can foster a more collaborative, interactive workplace.

● A more open climate of communication in which learners/employees are able to access information and have opportunities sanctioned and supported by the organization, enabling them to work collaboratively on work-based problems, can promote a type of learning valued by organizations and employees.

● An ethos of employees accepting greater responsibility for learning places an onus on individuals to actively seek out HRD activities.

Organizational learning in SMEs

For SMEs, the effect of the owner is even more pronounced. Research in Ireland, for example, found that owners of SMEs were 'self-made' individuals who built their organization from the ground up with little assistance from others (Garavan *et al.*, 2008). In a large number of cases, the owners did not have any formal education qualifications or participation in any type of HRD activities. These individuals had the belief that, if they could develop a successful business without training or development, there was no need to spend money on HRD activities for their employees.

After-Action Reviews in the US Army

The US Army uses a technique called after-action reviews (AAR) as a means to capture knowledge and make learning permanent. An AAR is an evaluation conducted after a project or major activity that allows employees to discover and learn what happened, why it happened and what could be done differently the next time.

The technique spread throughout the army slowly, and it took a long time before AARs became practised on a regular basis. The turning point was the Gulf War – AARs came about spontaneously as small groups of soldiers gathered together, in trenches or around tanks in the middle of the desert, to review their most recent missions and identify possible improvements. Soon after, AARs become commonplace in all army activities and continue to be used extensively to capture and share critical organizational knowledge.

AARs involve all participants getting together immediately after an important activity or event to review their assignments, identify successes and failures, and look for ways to perform better the next time around. The process can be formal or informal, may involve large or small groups, and may last for minutes, hours or even days depending on the scale of the mission or activity. Formal AARs require a lot of resources and involve more detailed planning, coordination, logistical support, supplies, and time for facilitation and report preparation. A facilitator guides the review discussion and notes are recorded on flip charts with the help of a dedicated scribe. The review should follow an agenda, using the four guiding questions outlined below to guide the discussion. Following the AAR session itself, a formal report is presented. Recommendations and actionable items are later brought to the attention of management.

Informal AARs are usually conducted on-site immediately following an event, activity or programme. An informal AAR is generally carried out by those responsible for the activity, and, if necessary, the discussion leader or facilitator can either be identified beforehand or chosen by the team itself. As with a formal AAR, the standard format and questions guide the discussion.

Regardless of the scope, the army uses the same four-step approach when carrying out any AAR:

1 Review what was supposed to occur. A facilitator such as a unit leader, along with the participants, reviews what was supposed to happen. This review is based on members agreeing on the purpose of their mission and the definition of success. Otherwise, if people don't know what exactly is expected of them, there will be no basis for evaluating performance or comparing plans with results. In the army, objectives are normally defined with great precision, e.g. 'at a range of 2,000 yards, hit an enemy tank moving at 20 miles per hour over uneven terrain at night with an 80% success rate'. With specific objectives like this, it is relatively easy to determine whether the objective was achieved satisfactorily or poorly.

2 Establish what actually happened. The facilitator and participants determine as clearly as is possible what actually occurred during the operation. The facilitator attempts to gather as many views or perspectives as possible. The key to an AAR is openness and honesty, which allows all the participants in the organization to participate. This helps to establish a common understanding, and if employees feel that their opinion is valued they are more likely to commit to the learning outcomes of the activity.

3 Determine what was right or wrong with what happened. Participants then establish the strong and weak points of their performance based on the commander's intent and performance measures. The facilitator guides discussions to ensure input from everyone. For example, if a tank was 20 minutes late reaching a critical checkpoint, what caused the delay? Honesty is essential here; individuals are required to face up to their own deficiencies, avoiding the tendency be oblivious to personal errors or weaknesses being highlighted. This is particularly true of leaders. One commander in the army suggests: 'If you are not willing to hear criticism, you probably shouldn't be doing an AAR.'

4 Determine how the task should be done differently next time. The facilitator guides the group in determining how the activity might be performed more effectively in the future. Additionally, the facilitator guides the discussion to

determine whether there is a more effective way to improve the tasks to achieve the commander's intent. It is particularly important that participants focus on the things they can fix, rather than external forces outside their control. Otherwise, the process is likely to have little immediate impact.

According to army guidelines, roughly 25 per cent of the time should be devoted to the first two questions, 25 per cent to the third and 50 per cent to the fourth.

On a US mission to Haiti in the 1990s, the first wave of soldiers deployed there faced a range of unfamiliar challenges, such as keeping the peace, delivering food, overseeing elections, even collecting rubbish. They were asked to review the majority

of these activities and develop a set of standard operating procedures for the units that would follow them. AARs were the primary tool they used to develop these procedures. Small squads conducted AARs daily, often informally; larger sections conducted them after every critical mission, presenting the results in a formal report; and platoon leaders conducted them weekly, submitting their findings to commanders for further refinement and review. Quick feedback led to quick implementation, sharply increasing the rate of learning.

Initially, soldiers found many areas for improvement and strove only to make each effort better than its predecessor. But, with experience, there were fewer and fewer problems, and attention shifted to sustaining successes. Eventually, the unit developed

a series of what they called 'cookbook recipes' that captured their own best practices, wrote them up and submitted them for review. Capturing what had been learned in this way allowed the practices to be adopted as formal army guidelines and to be used by both the army's Center for Army Lessons Learned and their National Training Centers to prepare subsequent units for their upcoming assignments.

Questions

1 How easily can AARs be applied to organizations? Do you think you could apply the same four-step approach to your studies, even?
2 How often should AARs be carried out?
3 Why do not all organizations carry out AARs?

SUMMARY

This chapter highlights the concept of organizational learning and the role that it plays in facilitating organizations to capture the knowledge of its employees and use that as a source of competitive advantage. By looking at the characteristics of organizational learning and contrasting it with the concept of the learning organization, we see the actual process by which organizations can learn. HRD policies and practices play an important role in creating a culture of learning and facilitating knowledge management within organizations. By recognizing both the facilitators of and potential barriers to learning that exist in organizations, we can see how the HRD function can help organizations to tap into the knowledge of their employees and use this as a competitive advantage.

 CHAPTER REVIEW QUESTIONS

1 How does organizational learning differ from the concept of the learning organization?
2 Suggest three ways in which organizations can learn.

3 Distinguish between single, double and triple-loop learning
4 Distinguish between tacit knowledge and explicit knowledge.
5 In what way can organizations adopt an effective knowledge management strategy?
6 How can organizations capture tacit knowledge?
7 Describe three characteristics of communities of practice (CoPs).
8 What can organizations do to foster a culture of learning?

FURTHER READING

Easterby-Smith, M. and Lyles, M. A. (2011) *Handbook of Organizational Learning and Knowledge Management* (2nd ed.), Chichester: Wiley.
Garvin, D. A., Edmondson, A. C. and Gino, F. (2008) Is Yours a Learning Organization?, *Harvard Business Review*, March, 109–116.
Gibb, S. (2011) *Human Resource Development: Processes, Practices and Perspectives* (3rd ed.), Basingstoke: Palgrave Macmillan (Chapter 3).

USEFUL WEBSITES

https://itunes.apple.com/us/app/aar-us-army-after-action-review/id414811775?mt=8

For more information on after-action reviews as used by the US Army, there is a useful app available with instructions and video examples for carrying out an AAR that is worth checking out.

http://youtu.be/IUP4WcfNyAA

This Harvard Business Review video discusses how organizations can take steps to become a learning organization.

http://los.hbs.edu

For those of you currently in employment, you can take the Harvard Business Review learning organization survey to benchmark your current workplace.

BIBLIOGRAPHY

Adel, H. M., Maher, A. H. and Alia, T. S. (2010) Developing a Theoretical Framework for Knowledge Acquisition, *European Journal of Scientific Research*, 42(3), 439–449.

Almeida, F., Oliveira J. and Cruz, J. (2009) Paths to Accomplish a Successful Open Innovation 2.0 Strategy, *International Journal of Innovation Science*, 1(3), 131–140.

Amadon, D. (1997): *Innovation Strategy for the Knowledge Economy*, Stoneham, MA: Butterworth-Heinemann.

Anderson, V. and Boocock, G. (2002) Small Firms and Internationalisation: Learning to Manage and Managing to Learn, *Human Resource Management Journal*, 12(3), 5–24.

Ardichvili, A. (2008), Learning and Knowledge Sharing in Virtual Communities of Practice: Motivators, Barriers and Enablers, *Advances in Developing Human Resources*, 10(4), 541–554.

Argyris, C. (1977) Double Loop Learning in Organizations, *Harvard Business Review*, 55(5), 115–125.

Argyris, C. and Schön, D. (1974) *Theory in Practice: Increasing Professional Effectiveness*, San Francisco: Jossey-Bass.

Argyris, C. and Schön, D. A. (1996) *Organizational Learning II: Theory, Method and Practice*. Reading, MA: Addison-Wesley.

Axtell, C. M., Fleck, S. J. and Turner, N. (2004): Virtual Teams: Collaborating across Distance, *International Review of Industrial and Organizational Psychology*, 19, 205–248.

Barney, J. (1991) Firm Resources and Sustained Competitive Advantage, *Journal of Management*, 17(1), 99–120.

Beaumont, P. and Hunter, L. C. (2002) *Managing Knowledge Workers*. London: CIPD.

Becker, G. (1964), *Human Capital* (1st ed.), New York: Columbia University Press for the National Bureau of Economic Research.

Bock, G., Zmud, R., Young-Gul, K. and Lee, J. N. (2005) Behavioral Intention Formation in Knowledge Sharing: Examining the Roles of Extrinsic Motivators, Social-Psychological Forces, and Organizational Climate, *MIS Quarterly*, 29(1), 87–111.

Brown, J. S. and Duguid, P. (1991), Organizational Learning and Communities of Practice, *Organization Science*, 2(1), 40–57.

Burkhard, R. J., Hill, T. R. and Venkatsubramanyan, S. (2011) The Emerging Challenge of Knowledge Management Ecosystems: A Silicon Valley High Tech Company Signals the Future, *Information Systems Management*, 28(1), 5–18.

Carbery, R. (2010) Explaining Managers Participation in Career-Focused Learning and Development, unpublished thesis (PhD), University of Limerick.

Chaston, I., Badger, B. and Sadler-Smith, E. (2001). Organizational Learning: An Empirical Assessment of Process in Small UK Manufacturing Firms, *Journal of Small Business Management*, 39, 139–151.

Cowan, R., David, P. A. and Foray, D. (2000) The Explicit Economics of Knowledge Codification and Tacitness, *Industrial and Corporate Change*, 9(2), 211–253.

DeNisi, A., Hitt, M. A. and Jackson, S. E. (2003) The Knowledge-Based Approach to Sustaining Competitive Advantage, In S. E. Jackson, M. A. Hitt and A. DeNisi (Eds), *Managing Knowledge for Sustained Competitive Advantage*, San Francisco, CA: John Wiley and Sons (3–33).

Digenti, D. (1999) Collaborative Learning: A Core Capability for Organizations in the New Economy, *Reflections*, 1(2), 45–57.

Dove, R. (1999) Knowledge Management Response Ability, and the Agile Enterprise, *Journal of Knowledge Management*, 3(1), 18–35.

Drucker, P. F. (1993) *Postcapitalist Society*, Oxford: Butterworth-Heinemann.

Easterby-Smith, M. (1997) Disciplines of Organizational Learning: Contributions and Critiques, *Human Relations*, 50(9), 1085–1113.

Garavan, T. N. (1997) The Learning Organisation: A Review and Evaluation. *The Learning Organisation*, 4(1), 18–30.

Garavan, T. N. and Carbery, R. (2012) Collective Learning, In N. M. Seel (Ed.), *Encyclopedia of the Sciences of Learning*, Berlin: Springer Science+Business Media, LLC (646–649).

Garavan, T. N., Shanahan, V. and Carbery, R. (2008) *Training & Development in Ireland: Results of the Biennial National*

Survey of Benchmarks, Dublin: Chartered Institute of Personnel and Development in Ireland.

Garvin, D. A. (2000) *Learning in Action, a Guide to Putting the Learning Organization to Work*, Boston: Harvard Business School Press.

Garvin, D. A., Edmondson, A. C. and Gino, F. (2008) Is yours a Learning Organization?, *Harvard Business Review*, March, 109–116.

Gourlay, S. (2001) Knowledge Management and HRD, *Human Resource Development International*, 4(1), 27–46.

Grover, V. and Davenport, T. H. (2001) General Perspectives on Knowledge Management: Fostering a Research Agenda, *Journal of Management Information Systems*, 18(1), 5–21.

Holste, J. S. and Fields, D. (2010) Trust and Tacit Knowledge Sharing and Use, *Journal of Knowledge Management*, 14(1), 128–140.

Ipe, M. (2003) Knowledge Sharing in Organizations: A Conceptual Framework, *Human Resource Development Review*, 2(4), 337–359.

Knapp, R. (2010) Collective (Team) Learning Process Models: A Conceptual Review, *Human Resource Development Review*, 9(3), 285–299.

Lave, J. and Wenger, E. (1991) *Situated Learning: Legitimate Peripheral Participation*, New York: Cambridge University Press.

Levinson, N. S. and Asahi, M. (1995) Cross-National Alliances and Interorganizational Learning, *Organizational Dynamics*, 24(2), 50–63.

Liebermann, S. and Hoffmann, S. (2008) The Impact of Practical Relevance on Training Transfer: Evidence from a Service Quality Training Program for German Bank Clerks, *International Journal of Training and Development*, 12(2), 74–86.

Lin, C. P. (2007) To Share or Not to Share: Modeling Tacit Knowledge Sharing, Its Mediators and Antecedents, *Journal of Business Ethics*, 70(4), 411–428.

Madsen, P. M. and Desai, V. (2010) Failing to Learn? The Effects of Failure and Success on Organizational Learning in the Global Orbital Launch Vehicle Industry, *Academy of Management Journal*, 53(3), 451–476.

Marshall, P. (2005) Coaching – More Membership Benefits, *Human Resources Magazine*, 10(1), 14–15.

Nahapiet, J. and Ghoshal, S. (1998) Social Capital, Intellectual Capital, and the Organizational Advantage, *Academy of Management Review*, 23(2), 242–266.

Nonaka, I. and Konno, N. (1998) The Concept of 'Ba': Building a Foundation for Knowledge Creation, *California Management Review*, 40(3), 40–54.

Nonaka, I. and Takeuchi, H. (1995) *The Knowledge-Creating Company*, New York: Oxford University Press.

Nonaka, I. and von Krogh, G. (2009) Tacit Knowledge and Knowledge Conversion: Controversy and Advancement in Organizational Knowledge Creation Theory, *Organization Science*, 20(3), 635–652.

O'Keefe, T. and Harrington, D. (2001) Learning to Learn: an Examination of Organisational Learning in Selected Irish Multinationals, *Journal of European Industrial Training*, 25(2), 137–147.

O'Toole, P. (2011) *How Organizations Remember: Retaining Knowledge through Organizational Action, Change and Innovation*, Berlin: Springer Science+Business Media.

Polanyi, M. (1966) *The Tacit Dimension*, New York: Doubleday.

Prange, C. (1999). Organisational Learning: Desperately Seeking Theory? In M. Easterby-Smith, J. Burgoyne and L. Araujo (Eds), *Organisational Learning and the Learning Organisation*, London: Sage, (22–43).

Probst, G. and Buchel, B. (1997) *Organizational Learning: The Competitive Advantage of the Future*, London: Prentice Hall Europe.

Qureshi, S. (2000) Organizational Change through Collaborative Learning in a Network Firm. *Group Decision and Negotiation*, 9, 129–147.

Salisbury, M. and Plass, J. (2001) A Conceptual Framework for a Knowledge Management System, *Human Resource Development International*, 4(4), 451–464.

Schön, D. (1983) *The Reflective Practitioner*, New York: Basic Books.

Schreiber, D., Vilela, D., Vargas, L. and Maçada, A. (2011) Knowledge Transfer in Product Development: An Analysis of Brazilian Subsidiaries of Multinational Corporations, *Brazilian Administration Review*, 8(3), 288–304.

Sloman, M. (2010) *L&D 2020*, Cambridgeshire: Training Journal.

Smith, E. M., Ford, J. K. and Kozlowski, S. W. J. (1997) Building Adaptive Expertise: Implications for Training Design, In M. A. Quinones and A. Ehrenstein (Eds), *Training for a Rapidly Changing Workplace: Applications of Psychological Research*, Washington, DC: APA Books (89–118).

Sun, P. Y. T. and Scott, J. L. (2006) Process Level Integration of Organisational Learning, Learning Organisation and Knowledge Management, *International Journal of Knowledge and Learning*, 2(3), 308–319.

Swieringa, J. and Wierdsma, A. (1992) *Becoming a Learning Organization: Beyond the Learning Curve*, Wokingham: Addison-Wesley.

Thorpe, R., Cope, J., Ram, M. and Pedler, M. (2009) Leadership Development in Small-and Medium-Sized Enterprises: The Case for Action Learning, *Action Learning: Research & Practice*, 6(3), 201–208.

Tsang, E. W. K. (1997) Organizational Learning and the Learning Organization: A Dichotomy between Descriptive and Prescriptive Research, *Human Relations*, 50(1), 73–89.

Vail, E. F. (1999) Knowledge Mapping: Getting Started with Knowledge Management, *Information Systems Management*, 16(4), 16–23.

Van Wijk, R., Jansen, J. and Lyles, M. (2008) Inter- and Intra-Organizational Knowledge Transfer: a Meta-Analytic Review and Assessment of its Antecedents and Consequences, *Journal of Management Studies*, 45, 815–838.

Wang, C. C. (2004) The Influence of Ethical and Self-interest Concerns on Knowledge Sharing Intentions among Managers: An Empirical Study, *International Journal of Management*, 21(3), 370–381.

Wang, S. and Noe, R. S. (2010) Knowledge Sharing: A Review and Directions for Future Research, *Human Resource Management Review*, 20(2), 115–131.

Wenger, E., McDermott, R. and Snyder, W. (2002) *Cultivating Communities of Practice: A Guide to Managing Knowledge*, Boston, MA: Harvard Business School Press.

6 ORGANIZATION DEVELOPMENT

Claire Armstrong

By the end of this chapter you will be able to:

LEARNING OUTCOMES

- Understand the nature and importance of OD
- Discuss the values and principles that underpin the practice of OD
- Examine the process of carrying out an OD intervention
- Identify the differences between HRD and OD and explain how each contributes to the other
- Explain the relationship between OD and change management

OD can result in **organizational transformation**, much like a small acorn becoming a huge oak tree

This chapter discusses ...

INTRODUCTION

In this chapter, we look at the concept of Organization Development (OD) and explain how it works in contemporary organizations. OD is an increasingly influential field of practice, especially in large organizations, in both the private and the public sector. One reason for this is that there is an ever-growing need for organizations to be able to respond quickly to the changes in their external environments. However, this is easier said than done. An organization is a social system – not a mechanical system, like a machine. When a machine becomes outdated, we find the obsolete part and replace it. Such a simplistic approach cannot work for organizations, however, because social systems are inherently complex and contain numerous interpersonal relationships. In social systems, the relationship between cause and effect can often only be clearly seen in hindsight. Facilitating organizational change which requires employees to change, for example, the way they work, make decisions or problem solve is a challenging endeavour – one that requires a considered, concerted and step-by-step approach, such as that proposed by OD. This chapter looks at the concept of OD; its values and principles; its goals and how it relates to other organizational functions and processes such as HRD and change management. First, we will explain OD.

> **behavioural science** a field of study that includes all the disciplines that explore the activities of and interactions among humans including psychology, sociology, social psychology and communication science, among others

For our purposes, we will describe OD as being a practice that applies human **behavioural science**. Its goal is to help organizations learn, improve and even transform, so that they can achieve sustained effectiveness ▶ Chapter 5.

However, behind this apparently straightforward definition, there is much research and also disagreement. There are numerous definitions of OD in both practical and academic writing. In general, they are broadly similar, but tend to emphasize different aspects depending on the viewpoint and experience of the creator of the definition. Some are broad and all-encompassing, such as Beckhard's (1969: 9) classic academic definition:

> *Organization Development is an effort [that is] (1) planned, (2) organization-wide, and (3) managed from the top, to (4) increase organization effectiveness and health through (5) planned interventions in the organization's 'processes', using behavioural-science knowledge.*

Other academic definitions are oriented towards a specific type of outcome, such as Burke's (1982) focus on culture change, French's (1969) focus on improvement in problem-solving capability and adaptation to change, and Bass and Avolio's (1994) focus on changing belief systems, attitudes and values.

More practitioner-oriented definitions include:

> *OD is a field directed at interventions in the processes of human systems (formal and informal groups, organizations, communities, and societies) in order to increase their effectiveness and health using a variety of disciplines, principally applied behavioural sciences. OD requires practitioners to be conscious about the values guiding their practice and focuses on achieving its results through people. (Minors, 2011)*
> *OD is a 'planned and systematic approach to enabling sustained organisation performance through the involvement of its people'. (CIPD, 2012)*

WHAT IS OD?

From the dawn of the Industrial Revolution until the 1940s, most work was considered to be a mechanistic process, whereby each action or task was broken into small and simple segments which could be easily taught and carried out. Although successful in many ways, this approach was rightly criticized for alienating workers by treating them as unthinking and unfeeling, easily replicable factors of production. However, mindsets started to change during the 1930s/1940s, when some research started to show that human factors were important in producing quality work. Effectively managing people and groups was linked to attitude change, greater commitment and higher performance. Thus, the ideas that were the forerunners of what we today consider OD began to emerge.

So, whether classical or modern, or academic or practitioner oriented, there appear to be a number of agreed-upon aspects. First, OD involves a planned change of some kind within organizations, the ultimate aim of which is to improve organizational effectiveness. To effect the change, OD uses principles of human behavioural science and addresses issues holistically with the organizational 'system' in mind ▶Chapter 5.

During the 1990s, OD began to be seen as a 'fad' (Porras and Bradford, 2004; Greiner and Cummings, 2005) and was criticized for not achieving the required outcomes. It was seen to be too emotionally oriented and more interested in meeting the needs of the individual than the organization. Despite such concerns, there has been a more recent resurgence of interest in OD – particularly in the UK – because of the current climate of rapid change. This is because OD, when well implemented, is particularly adept at helping organizations understand how to develop and exploit their capabilities while adjusting and accommodating themselves to rapidly changing environmental conditions (CIPD, 2012).

Garrow *et al.* (2009) conducted an investigation on the nature of OD among OD practitioners and made a number of interesting findings, including that OD is seen as a field of practice and not a functional discipline. It is context dependent and can vary according to the organizational situation. While OD is systematic, it is not formulaic and contrived. It does not have a specific location within most organizations and often operates across traditional boundaries. While often physically based within HRM offices, OD has many similarities with strategic HRM but few with operational HRM.

OD values and principles

One of the many challenges in delivering OD work is that it is not just what is done that is important, but also the values and principles that are brought to bear on how the work is done. It is these values and principles, in particular, that distinguish OD from other types of organizational interventions. Andersen (2012) describes the core values of the field of OD as consisting of the following:

○ **Participation, involvement and empowerment:** Efforts are concentrated on supporting everyone in the client organization to increase their levels of autonomy and empowerment to make the workplace more engaging and productive.

○ **The importance of groups and teams:** Organizations comprise a variety of formal and informal groups and teams. Therefore, clients are encouraged to acknowledge the norms and beliefs that belong to them in order to help those groups and teams contribute most effectively to the organization.

○ **Growth, development and learning:** OD practitioners believe that their work with organizations should help people to learn the skills needed to help them navigate change in the future. OD practitioners themselves should engage in personal and professional development through lifelong learning.

○ **Valuing the whole person:** This involves equitably valuing the perspective and opinions of everyone in the organization. Therefore, OD practitioners must strive to understand the diversity of individual needs, skills, and feelings and respect those differences in their work with them.

○ **Dialogue and collaboration:** This involves building collaborative relationships between the practitioner and the client, as well as encouraging collaboration throughout the client system. It also recognizes that conflict is inevitable in teams and organizations. Therefore, dialogue is used to address conflict in a healthy, open manner.

○ **Authenticity, openness and trust:** In order to create trusting workplaces, organizational leaders and members must consistently demonstrate honesty, transparency and congruence in all that they do. OD practitioners encourage these qualities in their clients and strive to achieve them themselves.

As is evident from the aforementioned, at least on the face of it, these values appear to be very ethical and concerned with the well-being of all ▶Chapter 14. It is relatively easy to see how such values might be used in an organizational intervention when resources are plentiful, but can they or should they be used in times of organizational crisis? We will consider this point a little later in the chapter in the section on OD and planned organizational change.

So what do these core OD values mean in practice? How are they manifest? The OD Network (2011) asserts that OD is grounded in a distinctive set of

---

organizational interventions are initiatives, projects or programmes associated with fixing organizational problems, maintaining good performance, consolidating and building on strengths and adapting to future changes

collaborative relationships relationships that occur where two or more people work together with a deep, collective, determination to reach an identical objective

dialogue the giving and receiving of voice, practised within a framework where participants speak simply, authentically and from the heart, and listen openly, attentively and with respect

Table 6.1 OD principles

Principle	Description
• Values-based	The practice of OD is grounded in a distinctive set of core values (such as those described above) that guide behaviour and actions.
• Supported by theory	Draws from multiple academic disciplines that inform an understanding of human systems, in particular, human behavioural science.
• Systems focused	Recognizes organizations as open systems; it acknowledges that change in one area of a system always results in changes in other areas and change in one area cannot be sustained without supporting changes in other areas of the system. This is also referred to as 'systems thinking'. Importantly, all elements within the organizational system must be aligned for optimum performance.
• Follows action research principles	Continuously re-examines, reflects and integrates discoveries throughout the process of change in order to achieve desired outcomes. In this way, the client members are involved both in doing their work and reflecting on it and learning from those reflections in order to achieve shared results.
• Process focused	Intervenes in organizational processes to help bring about positive change and help the client work towards desired outcomes.
• Informed by data	Involves rigorous assessment of the internal environment in order to discover and create a compelling need for change and the achievement of a desired future state of the organization. Some methods include survey feedback, assessment tools, interviewing, focus groups, process consultation and observation.
• Client centred	Focuses on the needs of the client in order to continually promote client ownership of all phases of the work and support the client's ability to sustain change after the consultant engagement ends.
• Focused on organizational effectiveness and health	Helps to create and sustain a healthy effective human system as an interdependent part of its larger environment.

principles that guide practice. Table 6.1 presents these principles.

According to the CIPD (2012), what makes an organizational intervention distinctively OD is its focus on aligning the work of various parts of the organization (systems focused) as well as building the capability of the organization to monitor its own health and performance, and address any issues itself without need for frequent recourse to the OD specialist (developing 'learning organization'-type capabilities). Thus, some examples of OD interventions might be an OD specialist working with the HR and business planning teams to develop a performance management system that properly aligns individual and organizational goals, HR business partners working with their manufacturing floor colleagues to embed a programme of job enrichment or the HR team working with organizational leaders to develop their reflective listening skills before together engaging in a process of major organizational change.

systems thinking a holistic approach to looking at the way that the organization's constituent parts (e.g. the employees, technology, structures etc.) interrelate and how they work over time and within the context of larger systems, such as the economy. The systems thinking approach contrasts with the traditional approach, which studies systems by breaking them down into their separate elements

WHAT IS THE VALUE OF OD AND WHAT ARE ITS GOALS?

It is difficult to distinguish the goals of OD from the value which they bring to the organization, because, almost by definition, it is the achievement of OD goals that are, of themselves, the value-adding factors. Nonetheless, what is clear is that the overall goal of OD is to achieve sustainable improvement in organizational performance. As described earlier, OD is a data-driven process. The data that is generated can be fed back into a variety of situations, for example, enabling individuals within organizations to collaborate in identifying and ranking specific problems (or opportunities), in devising methods for finding their real causes (or exploiting them), and in developing plans for coping with them (or managing them) realistically and practically. This is what

CONSIDER THIS...

In May 2011, Slough Borough Council (UK) put out a tender for strategic HR and OD advice, in an outsourcing arrangement which it believed would provide better value for money than having an in-house HR director. The council sought to appoint an organization that would supply a comparable level of advice as a head of the HR function, but in a contract that would initially last up to two years. Do you think this was a good idea? See if you can find out what has happened to HR services in Slough Borough Council since then.

Table 6.2 Desired results of OD interventions

Organizational renewal	Improved problem solving
Organization culture change	Increased effectiveness
Increased health and well-being of organizations and employees	Strengthen system and process improvement
Increased profitability and competitiveness	Effective change initiation/management
Improved learning and development	Support adaptation to change

enables organizations to develop more sustainable and robust solutions/opportunities to exploit and to engage in a continuous cycle of diagnosis and review which informs future strategy and enables them to develop the capacity to continuously adapt to change (CIPD, 2010). Some of the broad areas in which the value that OD can bring to organizations is most visible relate to organizational change and growth, improvement in work processes and product innovation.

OD specialists or the application of OD principles are often used to solve problems once they have occurred. However, for OD to be used to its best effect, it should also operate proactively, developing processes and procedures to ensure the best possible functioning of an organization before problems occur. Because OD is such a wide-ranging field and works in so many aspects of organizations, it is impossible to mention all of the goals or values-adding properties of OD. However, Egan (2002), examining 27 OD definitions, identified ten 'macro-level' groups of desired results contained within the definitions. These are presented in Table 6.2.

According to McLean (2006), the breadth of issues that OD is expected to address makes OD a challenging area in which to work, because the expectations of both clients and practitioners of OD can vary considerably. At a more micro level, some of the types of goals that OD practitioners would be tasked with achieving might include building and developing a high-quality executive team ▶ Chapters 11 and 12; developing, enhancing or refining an organization's mission and vision; helping an organization to align an organizations processes to ensure they are all acting holistically to achieve organizational success; introducing or improving performance and reward management

processes; restructuring organizations; process re-engineering; career planning ▶ Chapter 13; improving communication; conflict management and developing 'learning organizations'.

BUILDING YOUR SKILLS

You want members of the HRD team in your organization to undertake a course in OD. There is a lot of grumbling about this, with people claiming to be too busy doing 'real' HRD work to participate in some 'touchy-feely new-age' course. 'Will we all have to have a big group hug at the end?' was one sarcastic query which came from a particularly reluctant candidate. By focusing on the value that OD can bring to employees and organizations, convince your team members to undertake the course. Read the earlier parts of Chapter 3 of this book to help you in carrying out this exercise.

THE PROCESS OF CARRYING OUT AN OD INTERVENTION: THE OD CYCLE

There are a number of approaches to OD interventions, but, in general, most include the important steps as shown in the diagram below (Figure 6.1).

1 **Entry and contracting** – This phase involves developing the relationship between the OD practitioner (whether they are an OD specialist or a member of the HR team) and the client or

Figure 6.1 The process of an OD intervention

commissioner of the OD assistance (usually a leader/manager). It is the time for clarification of the issues to be addressed as well as the expectations of the client(s) regarding project outcomes, deliverables and schedule. This is also where agreement is established regarding the role of the practitioner, as well as that of the client(s) in the project.

2　**Data Gathering and Diagnosis** – Collecting the necessary data and analysing it allows the practitioner and leader to understand what is happening and how to move forward from there ▶Chapter 7. Diagnosis is vital because, without a proper understanding of the situation and issues involved, any planned intervention is unlikely to succeed. It is also important to remember that carrying out the diagnosis is in itself an intervention, because people will react to what is discovered during the data collection process.

3　**Feedback** – Presenting the analysis, findings and any preliminary recommendations to the leader. At the entry and contracting stage, the practitioner should also have agreed the role (if any) of the leader in the process of analysing the information. In giving feedback, the practitioner should also be prepared to encounter resistance. This tends to be a crucial point in the OD process and the resistance must be addressed before proceeding.

4　**Planning Change** – Identifying specific courses of action (i.e. the interventions) that address the situation and developing action plans for implementation. At this phase of the process, the role of the practitioner is facilitative. Ideally, here, they should help the leader to identify the steps that can be taken to achieve the goal. In designing the interventions, three aspects must be considered (Schmuck and Miles, 1976):
   ○ The issue at hand (e.g. culture, communication or work processes)
   ○ The level at which the intervention is to be focused (e.g. an individual, team or total organization)
   ○ The mode of intervention (e.g. coaching, training, task force establishment)

It is also necessary to consider the potential results of technique, the potential implementation of technique including costs versus benefit and the potential political acceptance of technique.

5　**Intervention** – Implementing the specific intervention to the organization. This is where application of high-quality change management practices is important.

6　**Evaluation** – Assessing the results of the intervention and determining future courses of action ▶Chapter 10. Although evaluation is often placed as the final phase of the OD process, it is in reality a cycle that includes a feedback loop. It is also vital that the method of evaluation is decided upon during the entry and contracting phase.

BUILDING YOUR SKILLS

You have been tasked by senior management with a project to work out the 'bottom line' effects of using an OD specialist to develop an organization-wide performance management system. Using an established evaluation model as your basis, e.g. Kirkpatrick and Kirkpatrick's (2006) Four Level Model or Phillips' (2003) ROI model, present a plan to the organization's board explaining how you are going to do this. How might your evaluation differ if you were carrying it out for an HRD specialist rather than an OD specialist? See Chapter 10 to help you carry out this exercise.

SPOTLIGHT ON SKILLS

You are an OD specialist. You have been hired by the managing director of an engineering consultancy company with 100 employees to help them with their performance management system (PMS). Earlier this year, the company introduced team working, whereby each client's case is discussed and worked on by a team of engineers. Prior to this, each client's case was dealt with by just one engineer unless there was a specific problem that necessitated additional help. Thus, the old individually based PMS is no longer fit for purpose. Having asked around your colleagues, though, you've discovered that the employees of this engineering consultancy are generally unhappy with the new team-working system, so you think this is going to be a pretty tough assignment.

Following a typical OD process, such as detailed in this chapter, prepare notes for yourself on what you expect might happen, the particular barriers you might encounter and how you would try to overcome them, at each stage of the process. How might an HRD specialist have helped the engineers to prepare for team working in advance of its introduction?

To help you answer the questions above, visit www.macmillanihe.com/companion/carbery-hrd and watch the video of Noelette Ensko talking about OD.

OD AND HRD: THE SAME, DIFFERENT OR SUBSETS OF EACH OTHER?

This is a difficult question to answer because there is little agreement as to whether OD and HRD are completely different or are subsets of each other.

To some extent, it is like the question of the chicken and the egg; which came first? In the literature, there is a lot of discussion about this topic, with some strongly opposing views in evidence. Two professional groups that exclusively represent the interests of OD practitioners, the OD Network and the OD Institute, argue that they are completely distinct fields. However, many other well-known organizations, such as the Academy of Human Resource Development (AHRD), the Academy of Management (AOM) (especially the ODC – Organization Development and Change – Division), the Society for Human Resource Management (SHRM) and the University Forum of Human Resource Development (UFHRD) consider OD to be a subset of HRD. However, yet others argue that, particularly in Europe, OD has had a major influence on the development of HRD, so much so that HRD could be described as 'living in the shadow of OD' (Grieves and Redman, 1999: 82).

Arguably, a more balanced approach is espoused by the CIPD (2012), where they suggest that, because OD is rooted in the concept of a systemic, organization-wide approach to the pursuit of effectiveness, it would be limiting for OD to be seen only as part of HRD. Nonetheless, it is fair to say that, because OD has developed from a focus on people, is based on traditional humanistic values and concentrates on development and learning, it is logical that there is a strong relationship between it and HRD. In fact, many of the techniques of OD are also used by HRD specialists. Some working in HRD are pleased to adopt the remit of OD because OD's focus on the whole structure and process of the organization enhances the strategic nature of HRD and provides it with a more important role within the organization as a whole. In fact, over the last few years, the use of OD principles and techniques has provided the HRD function with a more strategic, proactive, commercial and professional focus, allowing practitioners not only to deliver short-term HRD functional activity, but to equip the organization for sustainable performance in the long term, through its people (CIPD, 2011).

Thus, today, HRD and OD have a number of things in common, and, according to Foster (2012), as HRD takes on an increasingly strategic and transformational role, OD skills will enable HRD professionals to support transformation, work on organization design, design and deliver learning and development interventions, support clients in major change and organization design projects, analyse and improve the overall health of the organization, and maintain organizational health and fitness for future challenges. So, while there is little agreement as to how embedded HRD and OD are within each other, there does seem to be a growing convergence between the two. It appears that the line between HRD and OD is becoming increasingly blurred, particularly as the field of HRD strives to achieve a more strategic and valued role within organizations.

Organization Development in Netflix

In 2009, Lynn McCord, Netflix's chief talent officer from 1998 to 2012, and Netflix CEO Reed Hastings documented the approaches used in Netflix to develop a very specific organization culture. A 127-slide PowerPoint deck posted on Slideshare.net explained how they shaped the culture and motivated performance in the organization. The slides were viewed more than eight million times between 2009 and 2014, and are considered among the most influential guides for startups and progressive firms. Sheryl Sandberg, Facebook's chief operating officer (COO), said it 'may well be the most important document ever to come out of (Silicon) Valley'.

Hastings and McCord outlined some of the more unusual aspects of working at Netflix, such as the lack of any type of holiday recording. Time off is based on an honour system: employees take whatever holidays they think is appropriate, working out the details with their bosses. The goal is to shift responsibility back to the managers, instead of controlling it from a HR standpoint. McCord described this approach as follows:

Over the years we learned that if we asked people to rely on logic and common sense instead of on formal policies, most of the time we would get better results, and at lower cost ... 97% of your employees will do the right thing. Most companies spend endless time and money writing and enforcing HR policies to deal with problems the other 3% might cause. Instead, we tried really hard to not hire those people, and we let them go if it turned out we'd made a hiring mistake.

Performance appraisals are another thing that Netflix does differently. They eliminated formal reviews in favour of encouraging employees to have conversations about performance as a typical part of their work. According to McCord, 'Traditional corporate performance reviews are driven largely by fear of litigation. The theory is that if you want to get rid of someone, you need a paper trail documenting a history of poor achievement. At many companies, low performers are placed on "Performance Improvement Plans." I detest PIPs. I think they're fundamentally dishonest: They never accomplish what their name implies.'

Other things in the presentation that were crucial in creating a culture of high performance were their approach to on-the-job performance – Netflix doesn't accept anyone who does an 'adequate' job, with this leading to a 'generous severance package'. Employees get to make decisions; managers just give them the right context to do so. Also, it doesn't matter how good you are at the job. If you're considered a 'jerk', you won't stick around Netflix for long.

Since the slides first appeared, Netflix itself has adjusted some of the specific elements to meet the changing times, though it hasn't wavered from the seven cultural aspects enumerated in the original slides:

1. Values are what we value – the company values are the behaviours and skills that are valued in fellow employees.
2. High performance – Netflix believe in a culture where every employee is someone you both respect and learn from.
3. Freedom & responsibility – flexibility is more important than efficiency in the long-run.
4. Context, not control – the best managers figure out how to get great outcomes by setting the appropriate context, rather than trying to control people.
5. Highly aligned, loosely coupled – strategies and goals across the organization should be clear, but teams should be allowed autonomy to get things done fast.
6. Pay top of market – this is crucial to a high performance culture.
7. Promotions & development – Netflix avoid formalized development and allow people to manage their own careers.

McCord says HR puts too little effort into explaining to workers how business works. 'How can we help every worker understand what we mean by high performance?' she suggests. 'At Netflix I worked with colleagues who were changing the way people consume filmed entertainment, which is an incredibly innovative pursuit … There's no reason the HR team can't be innovative too.'

The basic idea of the Netflix culture is that, if a company hires correctly, workers will want to be star performers, and they can be managed through honest communication and common sense. Most companies focus too much on formal policies aimed at the small

number of employees whose interests aren't fully aligned with those of the organization. Therefore, organizations should hire, reward and tolerate only responsible adults. Be honest about performance. It should be made clear to managers that their top priority is building great teams. Leaders should create the company culture, and the HR function should think like innovative businesspeople.

Questions

1 How easily can this type of culture be applied to organizations in other industries, such as the manufacturing industry?
2 Is there a role for an HRD function in an organization like this?
3 If an organization wanted to adopt a similar culture to Netflix, what steps could they take from an OD point of view?

OD STRATEGY

An OD strategy draws together the strategic objectives, priorities and values of an organization and interprets them as a model for the design, development and operation of the organization. It also, therefore, determines the desired performance and behaviour of its staff. At its centre is the development of a culture through which the organization will achieve sustainable success.

According to Brown (2010), there are three basic types of OD strategy, developing activities that focus on solving problems or building on strengths that are:

(a) Structural – these are changes that specifically involve altering how the elements of organization relate to one another. Interventions might involve removing or adding layers to hierarchy and increasing or decreasing centralization.
(b) Behavioural – such strategies concentrate on improved utilization of human resources by improving elements such as employee morale, motivation, engagement etc. OD is traditionally associated with these types of strategies. The kinds of interventions that might be considered under this heading are coaching, training and development, process consultation.
(c) Technical – these strategies relate to changes in technology, machinery, work methods, automation and job design.

OD AND ORGANIZATIONAL CHANGE MANAGEMENT

OD has been, and conceivably continues to be, the major approach to planned organizational change, at least across Western cultures (Piotrowski and Armstrong,

2005; Burnes, 2007; Boje *et al.*, 2011; Rees, 2011; Burnes and Cooke, 2012). Arguably, because of this, it is sometimes suggested that OD and change management are one and the same, and, undoubtedly, at times there is overlap. However, this is not always the case. Sometimes, there are rapid and dramatic changes in an organization's external environment, such as the global recession that began in the mid–late 2000s. At times like these, almost instant change, such as radical downsizing or salary reductions, is required for organizational survival. As such, change cannot rely on the use of usual OD processes, principles or values. Beer and Nohria (2000) drew a useful distinction between change processes that can and cannot use OD principles. They termed these two types of change E-change – which is a change based entirely on economic value – and O-change – change which is related to increasing an organization's human capability. As such, O-change is planned and follows OD principles, while E-change is market driven and does not follow OD principles. Nonetheless, both are included in what many people call change management.

While long-term, system-wide planning that results in change (the OD model) can be very beneficial for an organization and its bottom line, when there is a sudden and significant change in an organization's external environment, failure to act quickly and to make immediate decisions, even when those processes violate OD principles, may well result in the demise of the organization (Dunphy and Stace, 1988). Another way of conceptualizing O-change management (the type that OD is normally concerned with) is that it is an important element of an OD plan. OD practitioners recognize that company-wide changes, while ultimately intended to improve things for the company and employees, create uncertainty and are often perceived as threatening and stressful. OD change management typically includes group and individual coaching and training with employees at all levels, including executives, front-line managers and employees. New work processes, reporting relationships and job functions are explained. Employees are coached on them and their concerns are discussed and generally managed.

Another model which examines the nature of change was developed by Burke and Litwin (1992). It relies on a highly significant distinction regarding organizational change, that is to say, between 'transactional' changes and 'transformative' changes. In the case of 'transactional' changes, the identity of the organization remains unchanged, its fundamental nature stays the same; only certain features of the organization are modified. In 'transformational' change, the organization's identity, its fundamental nature, is changed. Organization development is concerned with both types of changes, but with an emphasis on the latter. A further factor that distinguishes OD from other change interventions is the emphasis on learning though action and building on the knowledge that this generates to improve the planning process for the future.

While acknowledging that the terms 'OD' and 'change management' ought not to be used interchangeably, the skilled use of OD principles and practices is key to achieving major and sustainable changes.

Matt Minihan writing about OD practitioners …

We've been playing small ball, under the cover of the HR function and limited by our own ambivalence about power. It's time to step forward … we serve the field, our organisations, our HR colleagues, and ourselves by establishing the OD function independently, declaring our boundaries, and then working together across them, but separately. (Minihan, 2010)

What do you think of this line of thought? Is it in an organization's best interest?

The World's Greatest OD Challenge?

Not many people realize just what a large organization the NHS (National Health Service – UK) is. With approximately 1.3 million employees, it ranks third in the world, only lagging behind the People's Liberation Army of China and Indian Railways. Thus, if a culture change is required across the NHS, it can reasonably be considered to be one of the world's greatest OD challenges.

On 6 February 2013, the Report of the Public Inquiry into the events at Mid Staffordshire NHS Foundation Trust (aka The Francis Report) was published, making 290 detailed recommendations. This report, which made for disturbing reading, concerned unusually high

mortality rates among patients at the Stafford Hospital, Stafford, England in the late 2000s. It raised important questions about the way NHS care was regulated and the roles of the different bodies that oversaw the system.

The report repeatedly arrived at the conclusion that, at its most basic, the problems seen were the product of a dysfunctional organizational culture. Practices and behaviours appeared to have developed within the hospital that were at odds with the obligations of NHS employees, as set out in the NHS constitution – as well as being inconsistent with the professional duties of regulated care providers working at the hospital.

As a result of the Inquiry, all NHS organizations are taking a look at some of their core HR approaches and working on OD plans that will affect employees and the millions of people using NHS services each week. They will be looking at policies and procedures such as how staff members raise concerns and the need to embed improved approaches to health, work and wellbeing.

Despite the disturbing nature of many aspects of the report, it does provide an opportunity for the board of Mid-Staffordshire NHS Foundation Trust and all Boards across the NHS to re-engage with staff at all levels, not just from the top down but, very importantly, from the bottom up. It is a chance to genuinely involve people, from those serving tea in the staff canteen, through the junior doctors, to the chief executives, in achieving cultural change to ensure that patients get the best possible compassionate care.

On 3 April 2013, UK Health Secretary Jeremy Hunt said:

The health and care system must change. We cannot merely tinker around the edges – we need a radical overhaul with high quality care and compassion at its heart ... this is ... the start of a fundamental change to the system.

So who is going to change the culture in the NHS? The Francis Report provides solid foundations for change in the management and clinical practice of the health service – but someone has to actually accept the challenge, take genuine responsibility for it and do it. The report's recommendations offer tools for improvement in the NHS, but they will not cure all ills. They will create their own pressures, contradictions and problems, and the cultural change to deliver them is likely to take many years.

Sources

Cook, E. (2010). Neglected hospital patients were left starving, sobbing and humiliated. Available at: http://www.mirror.co.uk/news/uk-news/neglected-hospital-patients-were-left-203797. Retrieved 25 November 2013.

Department of Health (2013) Putting patients first: Government publishes response to Francis report, Press Release. Available at: https://www.gov.uk/government/news/putting-patients-first-government-publishes-response-to-francis-report. Retrieved 10 October 2013.

Dorrell, S. (2013) Francis report: care quality needs to be part of the natural culture of the NHS. Available at http://www.theguardian.com/healthcare-network/2013/sep/18/francis-report-care-quality-nhs. Retrieved 30 November 2013.

Francis, R. QC (2013). Report of the Mid Staffordshire NHS Foundation Trust Public Inquiry (Report). House of Commons. ISBN 9780102981476. Available at: http://www.midstaffspublicinquiry.com/report. Retrieved 6 May 3013.

Haq, Lubna (2013) Creating a culture of compassion in the NHS after the Francis report. Available at: http://www.theguardian.com/healthcare-network/2013/mar/27/create-culture-compassion-nhs-francis-report. Retrieved 30 November 2013.

NHS (2013) The NHS Constitution for England. Available at: http://www.nhs.uk/choiceintheNHS/Rightsandpledges/NHSConstitution/Documents/2013/the-nhs-constitution-for-england-2013.pdf. Retrieved 12 October 2013.

Vize, R. (2013) Francis report: culture change in the NHS will take years. The Guardian-Healthcare Professionals Network. Available at http://www.theguardian.com/healthcare-network/2013/feb/07/francis-report-culture-change-nhs. Retrieved 30 November 2013.

Questions

1 Which type(s) of OD strategy will be most useful in changing the culture here?
2 Suggest particular changes that you think are necessary to improve the situation. Are they E changes or O changes? Explain your conclusion.
3 Try to find out what steps the NHS is planning to take to address the Francis Report. Do you think they are the right steps? Is 'systems thinking' in evidence?

SUMMARY

This chapter has demonstrated the distinctive nature of OD. It is a field of study and practice in organizations that is often overlooked because it is considered to be part of the HRD function and not a field in its own right. We have looked at the principles and values that guide the practice of OD, and it is clear that, in many ways, they are different from those of either HRM or HRD. That said, there are a number of parallels between these areas; foremost among them, their focus on people. We have explored the origins of OD, and the various streams which have, over time, added to its richness and explain its distinctive character. We have explored the value that OD can bring to organizations and the process that is involved in any OD intervention. Finally, we examined the role that OD can play in creating successful and sustainable change in organizations and in achieving what some believe to be the 'holy grail' in organizations, a truly learning organization.

CHAPTER REVIEW QUESTIONS

1 What do you understand by the term 'organization development'?
2 What is human behavioural science and which subjects form part of it?
3 What are the principles of OD?
4 According to Andersen (2012), what are the six guiding values behind OD?
5 What are the three types of OD strategy?

6 What are the main phases in the OD cycle (process of an organization development intervention)?

7 Distinguish between HRD and OD.

8 Distinguish between E-change and O-change.

FURTHER READING

Burnes, B. and Cooke, B. (2012) The Past, Present and Future of Organization Development: Taking the Long View, *Human Relations*, 65(11), 1395–1429.

Cummings, T. and Worley, C. (2005) *Organisational Development and Change* (8th ed.), Mason, OH: Thomson South-Western.

Francis, H., Holbeche, L. and Reddington, M. (2012) *People and Organisational Development: A New Agenda for Organisational Effectiveness*, London: CIPD.

Garrow, V. and Varney, S. (April 2011) *Learning to Swim, Learning to Fly? A Career in Organisational Development*, Report 481, London: Institute for Employment Studies.

Rothwell, W., Stavros, J., Sullivan, R. and Sullivan, A. (2009) *Practicing Organization Development: A Guide for Leading Change*, San Francisco: Wiley.

Senge, P. (2006) *The Fifth Discipline: The Art & Practice of The Learning Organisation* (2nd ed.), New York: Doubleday/Currency.

 USEFUL WEBSITES

http://www.odnetwork.org

The OD Network is a North American-based grouping of OD practitioners and academics, dedicated to advancing both the practice and the theory of OD. The website contains lots of information about OD as well as case studies, tool kits, a job directory and many other resources.

http://organisationdevelopment.org/

These guys describe themselves as 'The ultimate practitioners guide for all things OD'. This is a website full of very accessible information including news, tool kits, jobs and interesting features on the requisite skills and competencies of OD practitioners and evaluating OD. This website places OD firmly within the HR function.

http://www.cipd.co.uk/hr-resources/factsheets/organisation-development.aspx

The CIPD provides a broad range of resources on various people management policies and practices. Follow this link to see its fact sheet on OD.

http://www.employment-studies.co.uk/main/index.php

The Institute for Employment Studies is the UK's leading independent centre for research and evidence-based consultancy in employment, labour market and human resource policy and practice. The website has lots of interesting resources in many areas relevant to OD.

BIBLIOGRAPHY

Andersen, D. (2012) *The Process of Leading Organizational Change* (2nd ed.), Thousand Oaks, CA: Sage.

Bass, B. and Avolio, B. (1994) *Improving Organizational Effectiveness through Transformational Leadership*, Thousand Oaks, CA: Sage Publications.

Beckhard, R. (1969) *Organization Development: Strategies and Models*, Reading, MA: Addison Wesley.

Beer, M. and Nohria, N. (2000) Cracking the Code of Change, *Harvard Business Review*, May/June 2000, 133–141.

Boje, D., Burnes, B. and Hassard, J. (Eds) (2011) *The Routledge Companion to Organizational Change*, London: Routledge.

Brown, D. (2010) *An Experiential Approach to Organization Development* (8th ed.), Boston, MA: Prentice Hall.

Burke, W. (1982) *Organization Development: Principles and Practice*, Boston: Little, Brown.

Burke, W. W. and Litwin, G. H. (1992) A Causal Model of Organisation Performance and Change, *Journal of Management*, 18(3), 523–545.

Burnes, B. (2007) Kurt Lewin and the Harwood Studies: The Foundations of OD, *Journal of Applied Behavioral Science*, 43(2), 213–231.

Burnes, B. and Cooke, B. (2012) The Past, Present and Future of Organization Development: Taking the Long View, *Human Relations*, 65(11), 1395–1429.

CIPD (2010) HR's Role in Developing OD Solutions to Manage Change. Available at: http://www.cipd.co.uk/hr-resources/research/hrs-role-developing-od-solutions-manage-change.aspx. Retrieved 28 November 2013.

CIPD (2011) *Learning and Talent Development Survey 2011*, London: Chartered Institute for Personnel and Development.

CIPD (2012) Factsheet: Organisation Development. Available at: http://www.cipd.co.uk/hr-resources/factsheets/organisation-development.aspx. Retrieved 3 November 2013.

Dunphy, D. and Stace, D. (1988). Transformational and Coercive Strategies for Planned Organizational Change: Beyond the OD Model, *Organisation Studies*, 9(3), 317–334.

Egan, T. M. (2002) Organization Development: An Examination of Definitions and Dependent Variables, *Organization Development Journal*, 20(2), 59–70.

Foster, C. (2012) OD and HRM. Available at http://organisationdevelopment.org/history-of-od/od-hrm/. Retrieved 12 December 2013.

French, W. (1969) Organization Development: Objectives, Assumptions and Strategies, *California Management Review*, 12(2), 23–34.

Garrow, V., Varney, S. and Lloyd, C. (2009) *Fish or Bird? Perspectives on Organisational Development*, Brighton, UK: Institute for Employment Studies.

Greiner, L. E. and Cummings, T. G. (2005) OD: Wanted More Alive Than Dead, In: D. Bradford and W. Burke (Eds), *Reinventing Organizational Development*, San Francisco: Pfeiffer (87–112).

Grieves, T. and Redman, T. (1999) Living in the Shadow of OD: HRD and the Search for Identity, *Human Resource Development International*, 2(2), 81–102.

Kirkpatrick, D. and Kirkpatrick, J. (2006) *Evaluating Training Programmes: The Four Levels* (3rd ed.), San Francisco, CA: Berrett-Koehler Publishers.

McLean, G. N. (2006) *Organization Development: Principles, Processes, Performance*, San Francisco, CA: Berrett-Koehler.

Minihan, M. (2010) OD and HR: Do We Want the Lady or the Tiger?, *OD Practitioner*, 42(4), 17–22.

Minors, A. (2011) *What is Organization Development?*, Available at http://www.odnetwork.org/?page=WhatIsOD. Retrieved 1 October 2013.

OD Network (2011) Principles of OD Practice, Available at: http://www.odnetwork.org/?page=PrinciplesOfODPracti. Retrieved 30 November 2013.

Phillips, J. (2003) *Return on Investment in Training and Performance Improvement Programs* (2nd ed.), Waltham, MA: Butterworth-Heinemann.

Piotrowski, C. and Armstrong, T. R. (2005) Major Research Areas in Organization Development, *Organization Development Journal*, 23(4), 86–91.

Porras, J. I. and Bradford, D. L. (2004) A Historical View of the Future of OD: An Interview with Jerry Porras, *The Journal of Applied Behavioural Science*, 40(4), 392–402.

Rees, C. J. (2011) Organisation Development and International Contexts: Values, Controversies and Challenges, In D. Boje, B. Burnes and J. Hassard (Eds) *The Routledge Companion to Organizational Change*, London: Routledge (74–86).

Schmuck, R. and Miles, M. (1976) *Organizational Development in Schools*, San Diego, CA: University Associates.

PART

II

PROCESS OF HRD

**Human Resource Development:
A Concise Introduction**

Fundamentals of HRD
2. Strategic HRD
3. Managing the HRD function
4. Individual-level learning
5. Organizational learning
6. Organization development

Contemporary challenges
11. Managing talented employees
12. Leadership development
13. Graduate employability
14. Ethics, corporate social
    responsibility, sustainability and HRD

Process of HRD
7. Identifying learning needs
8. Designing HRD programmes
9. Delivering HRD programmes
10. Evaluating HRD programmes

This next section deals with the *Process of HRD*. There are four stages to this process and it is important to note that all four stages operate interdependently, and not separately. Yet, it is a systematic process in which all four elements must be included.

Chapter 7 looks at the first stage in the process: identifying learning needs. This focuses on identifying and prioritizing the learning needs of both individuals and groups in the organization in order to assist the organization in meeting its strategic goals. This is often referred to in textbooks as training needs analysis. Here we have taken a broader perspective, following our discussion of the differences between training and learning discussed in Chapter 1.

Prioritization is important, as resource allocation usually dictates that not all identified needs can be met. This first stage should take place before learning interventions such as training courses are either decided on or designed.

Chapter 8 details the second stage of the process and moves from identifying learning needs towards designing an HRD programme or activity that will meet these learning needs. The design phase is key in ensuring that HRD programmes and activities are both effective and successful. If HRD programmes are not well designed, they are likely to fail, or, at best, be problematic in meeting identified learning needs. This chapter identifies the key stages in the design of HRD programmes and activities, and considers who is responsible for the design of the programmes and activities in both small to medium enterprises (SMEs) and larger organizations.

Chapter 9 focuses on the third stage in the process and deals with the issue of delivering HRD programmes. There are many details that must be organized and planned for in relation to the delivery of any HRD activity. These include the choice of delivery method; identification of learner needs; location, timing and duration of the event; room layout; and presentation medium. It is critical that the delivery methods chosen match the learner's needs and that the intervention is skilfully delivered. If not, then even the best designed HRD intervention will fail to achieve the desired outcome. This chapter discusses the various learning, training and development delivery methods available. It also focuses on the role of the person who delivers the intervention and identifies issues related to creating effective delivery.

Chapter 10 presents the fourth and final stage in the process cycle: evaluating HRD programmes. There should be a strong and clear relationship between the previous three phases and the final stage in the Process of HRD cycle. Evaluation closes the cycle and its outcome becomes the input to any future learning needs analyses. It should, therefore, be an integral feature of the HRD cycle, occurring before, during and after each learning event, highlighting the continuous, ongoing nature of the evaluation process.

7 IDENTIFYING LEARNING NEEDS

Paul Donovan

At the end of this chapter you should be able to:

LEARNING OUTCOMES

- Explain what learning needs assessment is and why this is important to organizations
- Show how a well-conducted learning needs assessment can contribute to overall organizational effectiveness
- Justify why organizations need to invest carefully in the effective assessment of employee learning needs
- Distinguish between the various terms used by authors and practitioners in this area
- Outline how the learning needs assessment is a critical part of the Process of HRD cycle
- Identify specific steps in conducting a learning needs assessment
- Describe how learning needs assessment is important from a strategic perspective
- Explain how learning needs may be prioritized

Identifying learning needs affects everyone in the organization

This chapter discusses ...

INTRODUCTION

The current climate of globalization and competition has led organizations to the search for advantage in terms of intellectual assets. Indeed, the critical role of knowledge and skills in creating competitive advantage in the modern economy is expressed emphatically in the literature (Jeung *et al.*, 2011). Accordingly, the development of people and their skills is of significant importance to organizations; however, organizations and managers are increasingly uncertain about the value they get in return for their investment in training. In the US, the American Society for Training and Development estimates that organizations invest $156 billion annually in training (ASTD, 2012). Chapter 1 describes the considerable value that HRD delivers to organizations. There have, however, been criticisms that a lot of this investment is wasted, because it is suggested that after just one year employees retain only 10 per cent to 15 per cent of what they have learned (Wexley and Latham, 2007).

The root causes of these problems may have something to do with how training, as a **learning solution**, is initiated and used in organizations. In an ideal world, every learning solution would arise from real learning needs. In this situation, managers would consider carefully what their employees need to learn and would provide learning solutions as appropriate. However, the world is not ideal and sometimes learning solutions have scant relationship with the needs of the organization or the employee. For example, if we look at performance problems, in many cases poor performance may be caused by a lack of training and may be solved by introducing some form of learning solution. However, not all performance problems are caused by a lack of training; nonetheless, some managers use learning solutions as a 'knee jerk' reaction to organizational problems – problems that perhaps might be solved by actions other than training. In this chapter we will begin by defining and examining the area of learning needs assessment (LNA) in organizations today. We then examine the steps required to conduct an effective LNA and the resultant benefits to organizations and individuals. We will also show how organizations prioritize learning needs and will contrast approaches in larger organizations and SMEs.

> **learning solution** any activity, formal or otherwise, that is used to enable the employee to acquire the necessary learning
>
> **learning needs assessment (LNA)** is the first stage in the Process of HRD cycle

SPOTLIGHT ON SKILLS

To begin to effectively manage the LNA, HR professionals need to ask the following questions:

1 What their organization's business is – what business are you in? How is it different from other businesses?

2 What is their organization's strategy? How does the organization plan to achieve a competitive advantage over its rivals?

3 What internal organizational issues have to be considered on a regular basis – culture, size, stability etc.?

4 Who are its people? What are the firm's demographics, skills, diversities, supply etc.?

Think about how knowing the business could be of benefit to you in assessing the learning needs of your organization's people. How would you go about acquiring the knowledge described above? How would you keep in touch with the changes that are taking place in the business? How would you develop an early warning system to tell you when the learning needs of the organization might be changing? How can you bring employees into the LNA process?

To help you answer the questions above, visit www. macmillanihe.com/companion/carbery-hrd and watch the video of Clodagh Blighe talking about identifying learning needs.

WHAT IS LEARNING NEEDS ASSESSMENT?

Identifying learning needs or **learning needs assessment (LNA)** ▶ Chapter 1 is about deciding and prioritizing the learning needs of individuals and groups so that

Figure 7.1 Process of HRD cycle

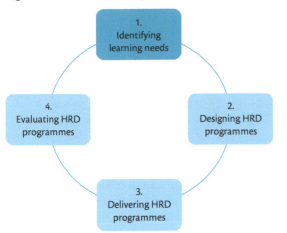

the organization may achieve its short, medium and long-term goals (see Figure 7.1). It appears early in the Process of HRD cycle as it is an essential foundation for organizational growth and development. LNA is sometimes referred to as identifying learning needs, or training needs analysis. The assessment of learning needs takes place (or should take place)

before learning solutions, such as training courses or programmes of learning, are decided upon or designed. It should also occur before the delivery of these learning solutions and, naturally enough, it pre-dates their

formal learning that we have experienced during the early years of our lives, e.g. classroom-type events

lifelong learning a concept that stresses that individuals need to continue to learn at all phases of their lives, young and old and both in and out of the workplace

evaluation. The results from these evaluations should, however, feed in to future LNAs to help inform future assessments of learning and, ultimately, future learning solutions.

LNA is usually directed towards the performance of individuals and teams. All organizations need their people to perform effectively. As a result, every employee needs to have the required complement of knowledge, skills and attitudes to deliver on their part of the bargain. But what happens when there are changes, such as the introduction of new technology or a change in the law, which directly affect an employee's work? In these instances the employees have to adapt to these changes and to perform in a different way. Take Audi AG, for example, a successful automobile producer, which needed a recruitment system to deal with employment bottlenecks. Because of the novelty and unfamiliarity of the new system, an LNA was required. Indeed, an LNA is required in most cases when people need to learn something new. Another example is MasterCard,

which needed to train its staff to keep up with changing technology in financial services (Doran-Houlihan, 2013). In our towns and cities we can all see stores that previously sold music CDs but have now seen their business decimated by technology, i.e. the use of the internet by customers to download music, bypassing the store. As a result, the management and staff of these stores have had to learn new ways of attracting customers, e.g. selling video games, in order to stay in business. These new activities required new learning on their part, which had to be carefully defined using an effective LNA.

You can see how critical it is, from a strategic perspective, to get LNA right. If a business needs to grow and to develop, its people need to learn all the time. If they can learn better and faster than the competition, this may be a source of significant competitive advantage (Bush, 2012). As the example above portrays, however, an effective LNA may also be vital to sustain the very existence of a business.

In considering LNA we need to take a broad view of learning in terms of how it is achieved and over what period of time. When we think of learning we often think of **formal learning** ▶ Chapter 4. Formal learning is usually a highly structured, off-the-job process which takes place as part of an academic programme, carrying recognized academic accreditation. But there are many other types of learning that take place outside formal settings and outside the workplace that impact on the performance of human beings. Indeed, society recognizes this by accepting the idea of **lifelong learning**. Think about your own situation. The knowledge and skills that got you by three or four years ago just won't cut it today. Nor will what you now know be sufficient in five years' time. Accordingly, you have a lifelong need and a 'lifewide' (not merely at work) need to assess your learning needs. So, we need to think broadly about learning, in terms of both how it is achieved and over what period of time.

Individuals and organizations can also take different perspectives on learning. Whereas an organization might place emphasis on the bottom-line benefits that employee learning might bring, employees often focus on the effect of learning on their careers, e.g. how much more marketable they may become if they learn new things. As a result of these conflicting interests, LNA can be challenging.

As mentioned previously, LNA is often used as a synonym for the terms 'training needs assessment', 'training needs analysis' and 'training needs identification'. This can lead to confusion, not only for students, but for practitioners also. The terms 'assessment', 'identification' and 'analysis' are often used interchangeably, at least in practice, with only a slight difference in emphasis. LNA is about discovering what is the organizational need for learning and how this is connected to learning activities. The organizational need is the critical element in LNA, as it provides the justification for what may be considerable expenditure by the organization. The steps in conducting an LNA effectively are quite simple to state, but are more challenging, however, to implement (Price *et al.*, 2010). These steps are as follows:

(a) Identify the organizational need – the why. What is happening in the organization to warrant the need for action? It is critical to show why we should commit precious resources to any learning activity.

(b) Relate the organizational need to knowledge, skills and/or attitudes deficiencies of employees. In the next section we will show five areas where we can connect organizational needs to the learning needs of employees.

(c) Determine which employees need what kinds of learning. Rather than train everyone in the same topics, we must identify the exact learning required by each different employee. In a later section we show a set of tools for this purpose.

These steps may take place in many different forms in organizations. But the basic principles underpinning them will remain the same. What may be essentially different is how organizations prioritize the learning needs of staff. In most organizations there are not enough resources to meet the needs of all employees. Accordingly, the HRD function must have some basis for prioritizing the needs of employees. They usually do this through their HRD policy document ▶ Chapter 2. In most organizations, especially large ones, HRD practitioners create a learning and development policy document to help show the rest of the organization where the resources of the HRD function will be placed. For example, in Ryanair, such a document would show a major emphasis on learning in the main areas of safety and cost reduction – two essential elements of Ryanair's strategy. In a highly regulated pharmaceutical organization, such as Pfizer, the emphasis would be on learning activities related to product quality and compliance with industry standards – important strategic issues for this pharmaceutical giant.

Sometimes you will come across textbooks that talk about the levels of LNA (McGehee and Thayer, 1961). They represent a group of researchers whose authors believe that you may examine learning needs through looking at different levels of the firm, such as at organization level, at task level, and at person/individual level (Ostroff and Ford, 1989; Cekada, 2011). Several academic writers find it useful to categorize learning needs in this way as it offers a structure to what is a very broad topic (Di Milia and Birdi, 2010). These levels are sometimes depicted as follows:

Organizational level – needs derived from issues that affect the whole organization and everyone in it, e.g. a major change initiative. For example, the mergers of major banks following the recent economic crisis will require LNA across the entire business for all employees as two entities work closely to synthesize their activities. Recently the Danish Football Association engaged a local consulting firm to help them understand how to work better as a team – the whole organization! This initiative uncovered specific learning needs, including how to better understand and appreciate each team member's unique personality and skills in order to increase collaboration internally within the team. A five-month development programme, coaching and work-based assignments made a big difference to their internal communication and understanding.

Task or operations level – needs derived from issues that affect aspects of the job. For example, the introduction of new software programmes for managing merchandise in a department store will change the way that the tasks of stocking and selling goods are executed by staff. LNA will have to be carried out at this level to establish the specifics of what is required by an individual undertaking the task.

Individual level – needs derived from issues that affect an individual worker, e.g. the need for time management training for one person. Not all individuals are the same or have the same learning needs. People develop in different ways. LNA at this level recognizes individual differences and creates different learning solutions for each person.

These levels are rarely referred to by practitioners, who find, by experience, that the levels 'leak' into each other in practice and that the levels approach does not offer much utility in their day-to-day work. Accordingly, practitioners tend to concentrate on the business need when tackling LNA and to accept that, while the levels exist, they are not the best lens through which learning may be identified in practice.

BUILDING YOUR

You are the manager of a fashion boutique with ten employees in a busy shopping mall in your local area. You have just recruited a new sales assistant who has very little experience in retail. How would you go about finding out this person's learning needs with a view to setting up an effective orientation programme for them?

LNA *and the needs of the business*

LNA should be based upon the business need (Reay, 1994). This may seem an obvious thing to say, but it is amazing how many organizations (even quite advanced ones) can fall into habits and routines that do not prioritize business needs ▶ Chapter 2. For example, in large organizations, it is still quite common to find a training catalogue. Its creators will defend it, saying that it is the result of careful LNA. However, that assessment may have taken place a long time ago. Learning needs are so dynamic that it is hard to believe that these catalogues of programmes and their trainers are keeping up with the ever-changing business needs. Organizations often discover that when a training programme is approved and is put into the catalogue it is very difficult to remove it. This is because it becomes someone's property and so takes on a life and purpose of its own, despite what the business might need. This is not to say that all training catalogues are like that, but you can see the point. If a trainer sets up a programme and delivers it successfully a few times, then that represents a considerable investment of time and energy on their part. It may be frustrating for them to learn that the business has moved on and needs something new. So they might resist changing or removing it. This behaviour, however, has only short-term benefits. In the long run the HRD function is damaged if senior management believe that HRD no longer remains relevant to the success of the business. Where this belief persists, the support of senior management for HRD can no longer be guaranteed.

LNA requires a proactive and a strategic approach if the HRD function is to play a central role in the business. For this to happen, the HRD professionals in the firm need to both conduct an effective LNA and to design and deliver effective learning solutions to meet these needs. Let us use a very practical example to show why this is important. Imagine a street in your town where there are two newly qualified doctors, A and B. Doctor A decides to continue assessing her learning needs by constantly assessing her knowledge and skills against the top standards in her profession. Doctor B decides that there is no need to do this because she has learned enough from university and will learn anything else she needs on the job. It is likely that the following will happen – Doctor A will deliver a better service and will attract more patients and grow her business. Doctor B, over time, will not have the knowledge and skills to offer the same service as Doctor A and will lose patients, literally. Organizations are quite similar. They need to be proactive, restless even, in seeking to understand what their staff members need to know for their business to grow. They need to ensure that their employees have an edge over the competition in terms of their knowledge, skills and attitudes. At the very least their people must be comparable to the competition in terms of competence. This can be achieved only by conducting an effective LNA.

HRD practitioners must be proactive in understanding the needs of the organization first, so that they may then capture its learning needs. In getting to know a business the HRD professional should first understand the general environment in which the business operates. What industry is it in? What is the purpose of its operation? Who are the suppliers and customers? What is the system of regulation, e.g. laws, industry regulator, collective bargaining etc.? For example, an organization producing drugs for medical care will be highly regulated and will have significantly different needs in terms of learning than a bus company. If the HRD practitioner has a good grasp of these areas, they are in a strong position to have a meaningful engagement with the organization's senior management in determining the learning needs of employees and how these needs are to be met.

An effective LNA may have important consequences. Consider the case of the United Airways Airbus plane that landed in the Hudson River in January 2009, shortly after take-off. The plane suffered what is termed a 'bird strike', in which a flock of birds inadvertently becomes drawn into the plane's engines, causing them to fail. The

> **training catalogue** a list of training programmes that allows employees to know courses/activities which are available to them to pursue and are paid for by the organization

prompt actions of the flight crew led to all those on board being rescued. The subsequent report into the incident demonstrated two interesting issues. First, the training for the flight crew was transferred by them into the work situation, i.e. in the emergency the flight crew acted as they had been trained to do (NTSB, 2010). Conversely, only ten of the 150 passengers on board exited the plane on to the wings wearing safety jackets, suggesting that the training for the passengers in safety measures is much less effective, as, for various reasons, people do not pay much attention to the safety announcements which happen before take-off (NTSB, 2010). It seems, from this incident, that an important passenger learning need is not being achieved by airlines – the recognition of the importance of the life vest. This example shows how casual people can become even when their own lives are at stake. Accordingly, organizations need to constantly examine and improve the ways in which they determine what people need to learn and how they learn it.

The Impact of Downsizing on Learning Needs

Any reduction in headcount in an organization has learning implications. In Ireland, under the National Recovery Plan 2011–2014, and in accordance with the Programme of Financial Support for Ireland agreed with the EU/IMF, the government is committed to reducing the cost of the public sector pay bill. As part of this there is an Employment Control Framework in place. Basically, this means that, in order to protect the government's budget, public sector organizations are pressurized to reduce staffing levels through a ban on hiring and non-replacement of leavers. Although this certainly reduces payroll costs in the short term, it does have implications for performance and, for our purposes in this chapter, for learning needs, as recent media reports suggest regarding Enterprise Ireland (EI), a statutory business development organization in Ireland. EI is an Irish government organization, which is responsible for the development and growth of Irish enterprises in world markets.

The national broadcaster reported in 2013 that EI had conducted an internal audit which showed that the government-imposed ban on recruitment had a significant impact on its staffing levels, with consequent shortages of skills in certain areas. The agency claimed that it had lost more than 16 per cent of its staff due to the hiring moratorium and normal staff attrition. EI is mandated with the task of promoting Irish firms throughout the globe in order to support exports. Record exports for EI-supported firms were achieved in 2012, but the agency believed that its gains are threatened by the constant loss of skilled personnel.

The report states that EI has maintained its output through redeployment of staff, noting that one in four of its 740 employees had moved into a different role to fill gaps in essential services. Some of these roles were already vacant, so there was no one to guide the new incumbent in their duties. Accordingly, many of these staff members have limited knowledge, skills and experience in their new jobs.

Politicians have entered into the debate, with the opposition spokesperson on Jobs and Enterprise calling for the report to be debated and challenging the minister on the issue. 'The loss of knowledge and experience at the agency is very serious and the need for upskilling ... is compelling,' he said. An agency spokesperson said that the departures of staff constituted a 'loss of intellectual property' and that a 'wealth of knowledge and experience' was being lost.

Sources

http://www.irishtimes.com/business/economy/report-on-ei-shows-major-flaws-in-jobs-strategy-fianna-fail-1.1552034, accessed 10 August 2013

http://www.independent.ie/business/irish/enterprise-ireland-hiring-ban-puts-agency-services-at-risk-29639246.html#sthash.fm3RGV3m.dpuf, accessed 10 August 2013

Enterprise Ireland struggling due to loss of staff – RTÉ News http://www.rte.ie/news/2013/1006/478688-enterprise-ireland-staffing, accessed 10 August 2013

Questions

1 How should EI go about prioritizing the learning needs for staff in redeployment?
2 What lessons does this situation teach us regarding LNA for staff?

FUNDAMENTAL 'WINDOWS' THROUGH WHICH TO IDENTIFY LEARNING NEEDS

There are certain fundamental areas where learning needs can identified and assessed, and these have been described as learning needs 'windows' (Bee, 1997). These are as follows:

● Human resource planning
● Succession planning
● Critical incidents
● Management information systems
● Performance appraisal systems

As we work through these areas it will become clear how, far from being a stand-alone area, LNA is inextricably linked with the topics of the other chapters in this book, with HRM topics in general, and, indeed, with effective management of the organization.

Human resource planning

Human resource planning is often described as being 'the right people, in the right place, and at the right time'. So it is quite a simple concept to describe, but perhaps a rather challenging one to put into practice, given the rate of change in organizations today. However, it has a significant impact on LNA. As the numbers and categories of staff change, there is an immediate effect on the learning needs of the organization and its individual employees. This may be the case whether employee numbers are expanding or contracting. Take the case of the public sector in Ireland. By the end of 2012 the total number of employees was approximately 291,000, a number which is around 30,000 lower than the peak of 320,000 in 2008. That is significantly fewer people. At first glance we should reduce training and development input, right? This is because we have fewer staff to train and therefore we can save both effort and money. But immediately you begin to realize that the workload facing these organizations has probably not diminished at all. In order to cope with the expanding demand for services such as education and health provision, employees and their duties are being redeployed in nearly every area. This is because there are fewer staff, but also greater demand for services. This means that people are doing more with fewer staff. Staff members are taking on more duties and responsibilities that their departed colleagues once did. For example, retirements

Table 7.1 Sample of projected demand for call agents

2016	2017	2018	2019	2020
1,000	1,250	1,500	1,750	2,000

and attrition at supervisory management level mean that managers are often responsible for even greater numbers of people. These changes require those managers to have new managerial skills. So, far from believing that there is a reduction in learning needs of this group of employees, there has, most likely, been an increase in their learning needs. Throughout this four-year period, learning professionals have been working to make sure that the right learning opportunities have been afforded to the appropriate staff to keep the wheels of the public sector in Ireland turning.

In a situation of expansion there is much more clarity that learning needs will be growing and that the required training input will grow in tandem. Sometimes, however, organizations underestimate the numbers required. For example, let's say you work in HRD for eBay and it wants to open a call centre in your city catering solely for the Chinese market. It estimates the number of call agents it will need at the beginning of each year for the next five years (Table 7.1).

As you can see from Table 7.1, a simple calculation tells you that you will need to train up 250 call agents per year to keep pace with demand. If you did that, however, you would fall considerably short of the actual employee headcount need. Why is this? First, you have to factor in labour turnover. If this was just 10 per cent you would still need an extra 100 recruits trained in the first year alone. In addition, some employees will not successfully pass through their training due to lack of ability and will lose their jobs. Even if this failure rate was as low as 2 per cent, you would be looking for an extra 20 recruits to train in the first year. If the HRD function fails in any way to assess the correct numbers of trainees required for training, the business may have difficulty in acquiring enough staff.

Succession planning

When David Moyes was sacked as manager of Manchester United Football Club in 2014, the club's fans, the world over, were talking about succession planning. Who would succeed him? Similarly, Steve Jobs, founder of Apple, passed away in 2011 amidst much speculation about who his replacement would be.

Figure 7.2 Sample organizational chart

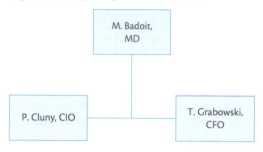

Figure 7.3 Organizational chart with ages and years to retirement

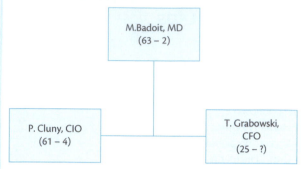

People are fascinated by the quest to replace the seemingly irreplaceable. But once they have been replaced the discussion turns to another pressing topic. How will the new person perform in their new role? Will the replacement have the necessary competencies to sustain the success of the previous job holder? Talent is difficult to replace. And most organizations can't just go out to the market to buy a ready-made replacement in the way large sporting organizations such as Manchester United can. Often, there just aren't the resources available to do this. In these instances it is vital to have an internal source of replacement.

To assist with the issue of succession planning, HRD practitioners should keep a copy of the **organization chart** nearby so they can plan for the learning needs of employees. An organization chart does not specifically identify learning needs, but, if properly used, it can be a source of this information (Figure 7.2).

At first glance Figure 7.2 does not tell us much apart from the information about names and titles. Badoit is managing director, Cluny is chief information officer and Grabowski is the chief finance officer. But what if we put in their age and number of years to retirement (at age 65)? We might get something like Figure 7.3.

Figure 7.3 shows us that the MD is going to retire in two years' time on reaching retiring age. It is likely that Cluny will simply be a 'stop-gap' replacement, perhaps having only two years left to retirement at that time. Grabowski might be identified as a possible replacement if the necessary competencies to perform the role can be acquired over the next five years. Of course, this is a decision for senior management; however, a proactive HRD practitioner will assess what Grabowski needs to learn in order to prepare for the MD role. This will give senior management the opportunity to make the best choice about whom to

organization chart is a graphical description of the hierarchical structure of the organization and its reporting relationships

appoint. Given that the search for an executive usually costs about 25 per cent of the person's annual salary, this action on the part of the HRD professional could help save the organization considerable resources. The proactive HRD professional will also be looking to see who will take over from Badoit and Cluny in two and four years' time respectively, either internally or externally.

BUILDING YOUR SKILLS

Consider a small to medium-sized organization in the locality in which you live and with which you are familiar. You might have a family member or friend working there to help you with some of the data needed for this exercise. It could be a local supermarket, garage, or public sector or community office. Examine the structure of this organization. Try to find out the different people running it, their ages, their service in terms of years remaining and their skills requirement. Try to work out the logical succession activity over the next five years. If no one is close to retirement you will have to imagine some likely turnover of staff. Now consider what you might do if you were responsible for HRD in this firm. Who might succeed whom? What skills are they deficient in? What training might they need?

Critical incidents

These are often defined, from an HRD perspective, as a sudden and negative departure from expected business performance, usually due to group or individual behaviour (Bee, 1997). We use the word 'critical' to describe the urgent nature of the matter – it is usually something important. The word 'incident' reflects that it is reasonably contained in timescale – it is either one single event or a series of events within a short timeframe. When a critical incident occurs, such as a serious accident in a manufacturing plant or a sharp downturn in performance of the sales team in a service organization, it is not unusual to hear calls for extra training to be provided to deal with the problem.

In times of great stress in organizations there is often a great deal of pressure to take action – any action, as long as it shows that something is being done. Training is the easiest action for some managers, especially for non-HRD personnel, to recommend. But this may be 'sticking plaster' thinking. What is needed is to identify whether the problem is linked to learning at all. Or are these calls for training merely a diversionary tactic – a distraction from the real cause of the problem, which could be management inattention or negligence? In most cases, hard evidence, and only this, will provide the answers. Let's take an example of a call centre sales team in one of the large telecom carriers, such as Vodafone or O2. Imagine what would happen if the performance of the sales team had dropped by 50 per cent. This incident is critical. Operations people might call HRD for extra training, but the last thing any HRD professional wants to do is to expend precious resources on training that may not be effective. So, HRD will press for an analysis which will identify whether a deficit in learning needs is the cause of the problem. If it is, only then should training be used to resolve the issue.

In this example we should begin by asking five questions. The first is to quantify the problem. *What is the problem exactly?* Here it is a 50 per cent drop in sales. We need to get the exact amounts and to learn also what would be acceptable as an output, to allow us to establish the scale of the problem. Second, we ask: *When did the performance drop happen?* We need to know in which exact period of time the team began to digress from its normal performance. In some situations the problem will become obvious, as the drop in performance will be associated with some other event such as the team being asked to try out new procedures, or being tasked with managing a new software programme. Third, we ask: *Where is it taking place (and where is it not)?* Sometimes, the cause of a problem may reveal itself if we can identify and isolate a subsection that explains the largest share of the problem. For instance, is it happening in the Dublin centre, but not the overseas unit? The fourth question is: *Whom is the problem happening with?* Is it occurring

only with new entrants, or among staff with limited experience? Is it occurring with inductees from the recent orientation programme only, suggesting that there may be something amiss with this training? Lastly, we ask: *Why is it happening?* This should be obvious from the answers to the other four questions. We may then move forward, armed with the information and the knowledge that, if we do decide to implement a learning initiative, it will be for the right reasons. This example also highlights that it might take 'nerves of steel' to take the time to research the answers to these five questions when you are being pressurized to provide training as a solution.

CONSIDER THIS ...

Many organizations use a survey method to find out the learning needs of their staff. This is a simple and usually very inexpensive way of getting the views of people on their individual-level learning needs and, combined with other methods of assessment, it can offer some useful information. But a note of caution should be added here. When people are asked what they would like to learn they usually respond by talking about things they are interested in. For example, what subjects do you like in your programme of study at university? Would you have chosen to take those subjects if given the choice? In organizations, some people will like some things, and like other things a bit less! So, the survey method has to be designed and used carefully so that it elicits the learning *needs* and not simply the learning *wants* of the employee.

Management information systems

The purpose of management information systems (MIS) is to present information to the organization's leaders so that they may make timely decisions about which actions to take to enhance and protect the business. HRD professionals should try to gain access to standing meetings of the organization, such as weekly production meetings and sales meetings where the data of the firm are discussed. The kinds of data to look out for may be quite varied. The obvious ones are sales data and data concerning output of various locations and departments. There are also data regarding waste and quality, and, taken in a time-series manner, these data can tell whether the situation is improving or declining – perhaps a matter for HRD intervention? HR data such as those related to turnover of staff may give an indication of employee dissatisfaction and could indicate a learning need for supervisors and managers in the area of employee engagement. Comparisons over time and between locations and individuals can signal learning issues that are not immediately obvious. The critical issue for HRD is to become involved in such meetings and to contribute from the learning expertise point of view. Other managers will accept this positive approach and will be thankful for the input.

Performance appraisal

Performance management in organizations is defined as a formal approach, usually top down, where line managers assess performance over a certain period of time and, in a performance review meeting, agree a plan for improving performance (Jayam, 2012). In theory, performance management is an ongoing process which takes place on a continuous basis, with managers constantly taking steps to guide, coach and

 CONSIDER THIS ...

The next time you take a flight, consider the work of the cabin attendants. More specifically, consider their learning needs. If you were in HRD, what do you think they would need to learn? You might suggest customer service skills, operation of equipment, basic first aid etc. Now ask yourself: who provides this training? You might assume that their employer does. If you are thinking about Ryanair as the employer, then you would be wrong. Cabin crew who wish to become employed by Ryanair must first be accredited by a secondary organization known as Crewlink. This organization provides training for, and certifies the competence of, candidates for employment in Ryanair. Following a period of training with Crewlink, candidates usually get an offer of a contract of employment with Ryanair. The cost of this training is around €3,000, including accommodation. This cost is met by the applicant. So, in this instance, employees pay for their own basic training. Do you think all airlines operate in this way with regard to basic training?

encourage better performance levels from their staff. The information from the performance management system should be used by HRD professionals to identify specific learning needs, which are agreed between the manager and employee. Employees at Linde Gas in Singapore are encouraged to discuss their development needs during their appraisal meeting, and these discussions help to shape the learning and development initiatives for the following year for these employees.

SPECIFYING PRECISE LEARNING NEEDS

So far we have used tools to identify that a learning need may exist. Some of these produce general evidence of learning needs, such as human resource planning, and others are more specific, such as performance review information. However, the more precise we can be about the exact learning needs at this stage the easier it will be to match the chosen learning solutions to each need. What we are trying to identify is 'who', 'what' and 'when' in terms of learning solutions. To arrive at that point we need to be able to discover what the performance gap is, i.e. what is the difference between actual and desired performance in the target individual or group? Identifying a performance gap requires the use of tools and techniques to gather information. Data collection and data analysis are essential parts of learning needs assessment. Donovan and Townsend (2009) describe a range of commonly used effective data collection methods that are suited to the precise and comprehensive discovery of these specific learning needs. This list includes both quantitative and qualitative methods, which can be used in combination to identify learning needs. Quantitative methods are those which involve numbers or data which can be converted to numerical formats. Qualitative methods, on the other hand, describe data, often in text format.

(a) *Quantitative methods*
   ○ Survey questionnaire
   ○ 360-degree surveys
   ○ Attitude surveys
   ○ Knowledge pre-tests
   ○ Skills matrices
(b) *Qualitative methods*
   ○ Competency profiles/job descriptions
   ○ Structured interviews
   ○ Observation
   ○ Focus groups and interviews

Survey questionnaires

A questionnaire is a survey instrument consisting of a series of questions and other prompts for the purpose of gathering information from respondents. Surveys are usually the least expensive methods of all the learning needs assessment data collection tools in use in organizations today. They may be distributed and submitted online using a system such as SurveyMonkey. An HRD-led approach to a learning needs assessment survey might contain questions on the following areas:

- Technical/job-related training
- Interpersonal skills training
- Information training

When the surveys have been completed, the results can be assessed to identify the specific learning requirements of individuals and groups.

360-degree surveys

This is a type of survey distributed as part of a performance management process to all those involved with the job holder in their role. Thus, the manager, peers, suppliers, customers etc. of a job holder may be surveyed regarding the person's skills and job role effectiveness. To address issues of trust and confidentiality surrounding their use, the surveys are submitted anonymously. The aim is to uncover the perceptions of a specific group of people with respect to the performance of the job holder. This information may be really useful in identifying accurate up-to-date learning needs of the job holder.

Attitude surveys

Attitude surveys are a means of testing the climate in an organization. They are principally used to 'take the temperature' of how people are feeling about a range of issues in their employment. They take the form of a questionnaire, usually online, and are conducted annually so that progress may be measured. HRD executives usually include questions concerning the learning needs of individuals and how these are being met as another method of gleaning critical information about LNA in the firm.

Knowledge pre-tests

Before expensive training solutions are implemented, it may be useful, especially in the case of experienced workers, to conduct a pre-course knowledge assessment to see whether there are parts of the training that are already well understood by the employee. This may be a common occurrence when refresher training is being provided. For example, in manufacturing operations, some employees may be required to attend the same safety or manufacturing operations practice courses every year for the duration of their careers to meet health and safety requirements. This pre-testing can relieve employees of the responsibility to attend those parts of the programme that they are already familiar with. The results of this pre-testing also provide a sharper focus to the training, allowing the trainer to emphasize points that the test results highlighted as needed.

Skills matrices

A skills matrix is a tabular assessment of where a set of employees are located against a set of necessary skills. Table 7.2 provides an example of what a skills matrix looks like and what its purpose is. As you can see in Table 7.2, a person who is Developing (D) is just starting out learning the basic skills in each area. Where a person is identified as Operational (O), the person can already perform the skill to the minimum specification. Where S is indicated, this person can work alone without assistance, while where E, meaning Excellent, is used, this means that the person is at a standard where the skill is developed enough to teach others how to do the job. By using a skills matrix the supervisor of this section can see at a glance the skill level of each member of the group for each skill. The matrix can also provide warning signals about learning needs that are urgent. For example, there is only one person here, M. Delfois, who is highly skilled in book keeping. If this person were to leave the organization, or become ill, there would be a gap in that area. It is, therefore, an urgent learning need that others become more accomplished in the book-keeping task.

Competency profiles/job descriptions

Competencies are the set of behaviours based on knowledge, skills and attitudes that an employee needs to bring to a job in order to carry out certain tasks successfully. A competency profile is that set of competencies which,

Table 7.2 Skills matrix

Skills matrix – administration section					
Legend: D = Developing, O = Operational, S = Strong, E = Excellent					
	Word processing	Spreadsheets	Reception skills	Book keeping	Filing skills
P. Mueller	O	O	O	D	O
L. Grassi	S	S	S	D	O
M. Delfois	E	S	S	E	E
S. Visockaite	D	D	D	D	D
S. Blasi	O	E	O	D	E

when bundled together, make up the requirement for the whole job. Competency profiles are used quite frequently in recruitment to make sure that HR can find the right person for the job. But they are also useful in LNA, because, if you can compare the competencies of the job holder with the desired profile, the observed gaps become learning needs. Similarly, a job description states the tasks that the job holder has to undertake to execute the job successfully. The job description is usually accompanied by a person specification. The person specification tells us the type of person who would likely be successful in the job, e.g. their qualifications, education, experience, attitudes etc. So, taken together, these documents can be examined in respect of each job holder to assess whether the job holder meets the requirements set out in these documents. Where there are gaps we may have identified a learning need.

Structured interviews

Structured interviews are used to gain information from individuals about their learning needs. They are a form of meeting that is planned in advance and which comprises a series of questions regarding the work to be done and the knowledge required to do this work. Typically, this interview is conducted by a member of the HRD team who is trained in conducting such exercises. Careful notes are taken and later these are reviewed to determine the learning needs of the employees under review.

Observation

Managers observe their staff at work in terms of performance on the job. Observation of this kind may actually be covert, or overt. Covert observation, as the name suggests, is done without the person knowing they are being observed. There are clearly problems

associated with this approach, but managers often argue that a person acts more naturally if they don't feel they are being watched over. Overt observation is more open and honest and, in a trusting relationship, is a much more productive approach. The manager can identify aspects of performance that need improvement and can specify learning needs accordingly.

Focus groups and interviews

Focus groups are short workshop sessions conducted by a facilitator where interested stakeholders are encouraged to voice their views about various topics. HRD can use this process to refine and craft the precise learning needs of a group. They are useful in allowing the employees to bring out the nuances of the workplace situation. The resulting training may be much improved by involving these groups in the elaboration of the learning need. Interviews are typically one-to-one exchanges where specific questions are posed to the interviewee following a predetermined structure while still leaving room for individual comments and ideas from the interviewee on their learning needs.

The methods described above involve specific approaches aimed at identifying the individuals who require training and the specific learning needs. Due to the expense and numbers involved, these methods are more likely to be used in larger organizations than in SMEs. This type of organization will be considered in the next section.

SMEs: A DIFFERENT APPROACH?

SMEs often do not have the financial resources to employ full-time HRD staff to assess the learning needs of individual employees. Normally this function is subsumed into the role of the HR manager (if there is one) or the person in charge of finance. Many of the key principles identified in this chapter regarding the assessment of learning needs apply just as much to SMEs as they do in larger organizations. It has been remarked, however, that SMEs are much more varied in their approaches to identifying learning needs than their larger counterparts (Boyd *et al.*, 2003). In a smaller organization, however, there is one critical difference. The smaller organization relies to a much greater extent on the senior management team, principally the CEO. It is often said about SMEs that 'the person is the business'. This is meant to convey that the performance of the owner/director is a key determinant in the success of the enterprise. Accordingly, the assessment of learning needs for the top team, especially the CEO, takes on much greater significance. If this is done well, it will be a major benefit to the firm. If not, the firm is likely to underperform. In addition, there is the paradox that small business persons are less likely to have the time to engage in training, especially the off-the-job variety. This is because such organizations do not have the same slack resources as larger ones do.

As a result of diversity in SMEs, it is difficult to generalize in terms of the specific approaches used in conducting an LNA. Some organizations engage consultants to administer psychometric tests to their key personnel to identify their key learning and development requirements. These tests include, but are not limited to, personality tests, intelligence tests, and tests to assess critical thinking skills. Following these tests, these consultants design programmes of activities to meet the executives' learning and development needs.

The 'Free Hand' Approach to LNA

You have recently been appointed as learning and development manager for a UK private sector manufacturing company, with 7,000 employees. The organization is 40 years old and has a reputation for conservatism, stability and good employment conditions. It has, however, lacked innovation and entrepreneurialism. The new CEO has started her reign and changes are being made all over the organization. You anticipate that the area of learning and training will not be any different.

She recently called a meeting with you to set the scene and to communicate what she expects from you and your team in HRD. At this meeting she told you that the development of the organization had been hampered by a lack of development in its people and that your task was to correct this. Accordingly, she has tasked you with the job of conducting a LNA for all employees in the organization. She has given you a free hand with regard to budget (within reason) and she expects that you will implement as you go. In other words, you are to identify the training required and to execute that training. In addition, she wishes you to evaluate the training that you put in place and, in doing so, to measure its effects on the performance of the organization.

As part of your preparation you conduct a search of all of the best writers in the area of LNA. All the authors seem to suggest a consensus around having wide participation from the workforce in terms of getting their views on their needs. Also, in your research, you are attracted to the idea of building a competency profile for each of the jobs in the organization: that is, a set of skills, knowledge and behaviours required to perform each job being set down. You believe that, if this is done, every employee could be assessed against this profile, leading to the identification of the learning needs of the whole workforce.

Having decided on an approach, you set out to achieve your goal. You engage a wide group of volunteers at all levels to develop these competency profiles for all jobs. When these are completed, you employ each line manager throughout the organization to conduct an assessment of each employee in their area. Using databases, you collect all the information with a view to providing solutions.

Having assessed the information from line managers, you prepare a programme of learning solutions to meet the needs of the employees. Over the following year, a wide-ranging programme of learning and training events takes place. These are conducted by a combination of internal and external experts and you retain tight control over the delivery to ensure the quality of each programme. Anecdotal evidence suggests that the participants enjoyed the learning activities and found them valuable. Finally, you conduct an evaluation exercise to find out the outcomes of the training, as requested by the CEO.

However, little or no improvement in performance has occurred as a result of the training. You have been requested by the CEO to submit a report to her on the entire exercise and she is waiting in her office now to discuss it with you. You hear on the grapevine that she is not pleased!

Questions

1 Would you describe the LNA as outlined above as the correct approach? Why/why not?

2 As learning and development manager, outline what you see as the possible reasons why the training did not have a positive impact on the organization.

3 What changes, if any, would you recommend for future approaches to LNA in the organization?

SUMMARY

This chapter discusses LNA and the role it plays in the early stages of the Process of HRD cycle. By looking at the role LNA plays in organizations, we can see how the correct identification of learning needs can assist in developing a strategic competitive advantage. We can also see how LNA needs to be inextricably connected to the business requirements of the firm to assist in achieving organizational-level goals. You saw evidence of this in Chapter 2 of this text. Examining the steps in LNA highlights the systematic nature of this process, and examining the methods used uncovers the diversity of approaches used by organizations to gather the data needed to make decisions about learning solutions. It is these learning solutions which are required to fill the organization's knowledge and skills gaps. We can also see that, by learning about the strategic aspects of their organizations, HRD professionals can be well placed to play a strategic role in making their organizations more competitive.

 CHAPTER REVIEW QUESTIONS

1 How would you define learning needs assessment and why is this important to organizations?

2 How does a properly conducted learning needs assessment contribute to organizational effectiveness?

3 What is the rationale for investing in a learning needs assessment from a business perspective?

4 What is the difference, if any, between the terms 'learning needs analysis' and 'learning needs assessment'?

5 Where does the learning needs assessment fit in the overall Process of HRD cycle?

6 What are the principal steps in conducting a learning needs assessment?

7 What contribution can a strategic view of learning needs assessment make to an organization's competitive advantage?

8 How do organizations prioritize the learning needs of individuals and groups?

📖 **FURTHER READING**

Berry, J. (2011) Transforming HRD into an Economic Value Add: A Transformation Is Taking Place in Human Resource Development (HRD). It Is Moving from Being Managed as a Cost Center to Being Used as a Source of Competitive Advantage, *T&D*, 65(9), September 2011.

Lee, M. (2003) *HRD in a Complex World*, London: Routledge.

Scannell, E. E. and Donaldson, L. (2000) *Human Resource Development: The New Trainer's Guide*, New York: Perseus Publishing.

Stewart, J. and Beaver, G. (2004) *HRD in Small Organisations: Research and Practice*, London: Routledge.

 **USEFUL WEBSITES**

http://learningspacetoolkit.org/needs-assessment/
This is a fun site with lots of tools to use in conducting a LNA.

http://www.go2itech.org/HTML/TT06/toolkit/assessment/adults.html
A detailed site with many toolkits for assessing the learning needs of adults.

http://www.assetproject.info/learner_methodologies/before/learning_analysis.htm
This site is very informative, with many links to LNA but also to the other parts of the HR cycle.

http://hrweb.mit.edu/ctm/organizational-strategies/
learning-development-strategies/learning-needs-
assessment
This site also links into MIT's Human Resources supports
for employees.

BIBLIOGRAPHY

ASTD (2012) *State of the Industry Report*, Alexandria, VA:
ASTD.

Bee, F. B. R. (1997). *Training Needs Analysis and Evaluation*.
London: Institute of Personnel and Development.

Boyd, E., Knox, H. and Struthers, J. (2003). Work-based
Learning, Theory and Practice: A Case Study of Scottish
SMEs, *Industry & Higher Education*, 17(3), 163–178.

Bush, H. (2012). The Ability to Learn Faster than Your
Competitors May Be the Only Sustainable Advantage.
Retrieved 19 May 2014, from http://www.beingpoint.
com/the-ability-to-learn-faster-than-your-competitors-
may-be-the-only-sustainable-advantage/

Cekada, T. L. (2011). Need Training? *Professional Safety*,
56(12), 28–34.

Di Milia, L. and Birdi, K. (2010). The Relationship between
Multiple Levels of Learning Practices and Objective and
Subjective Organizational Financial Performance, *Journal
of Organizational Behavior*, 31(4), 481–498.

Donovan, P. and Townsend, J. (2009). *Training Needs
Analysis Pocketbook*. Hants, UK: Management
Pocketbooks.

Doran-Houlihan, M. (2013). Skills Training, *Training*, 50(4),
55–56.

Jayam, R. (2012). A General Study on Performance
Management in the Health Care Sectors, *Indian Streams
Research Journal*, 2(10), 1–5.

Jeung, C.-W., Yoon, H. J., Park, S. and Jo, S. J. (2011). The
Contributions of Human Resource Development Research
across Disciplines: A Citation and Content Analysis,
Human Resource Development Quarterly, 22(1), 87–109.
doi: 10.1002/hrdq.20062.

McGehee, W. & Thayer, P. (1961) *Training in Business and
Industry*. New York: Wiley.

NTSB (2010) *Loss of Thrust in Both Engines After Encountering
a Flock of Birds and Subsequent Ditching on the Hudson
River, US Airways Flight 1549, Airbus A320-214, N106US,
Weehawken, New Jersey, January 15, 2009*, accessed
1 August 2013 at http://www.ntsb.gov/doclib/
reports/2010/aar1003.pdf

Ostroff, C. and Ford, J. K. (1989). Assessing Training Needs:
Critical Levels of Analysis, In I. L. Goldstein (Ed.) *Training
and Development in Organizations*, San Francisco: Jossey-
Bass (25–62).

Price, R., Jim, L. and Kozman, T. (2010). Use of Competency-
Based Needs Analysis in Developing Employee Training
Program, *International Journal of Business & Public
Administration*, 7(1), 117–130.

Reay, D. G. (1994). *Identifying Training Needs*, London: Kogan
Page.

Wexley, K. N. and Latham, G. P. (2007). Developing and
Training Human Resources in Organizations, *Journal of
European Industrial Training*, 31(4), 283–296.

8

DESIGNING HRD PROGRAMMES

Jean McCarthy

By the end of this chapter you should be able to:

LEARNING OUTCOMES

- Identify and explain the key stages in the process of designing HRD programmes and activities
- Discuss the difference between SMEs and large organizations in their approach to the design of HRD programmes and activities
- Formulate and write learning outcomes for HRD programmes and activities
- Identify suitable content for inclusion in HRD programmes and activities

- Select and construct an appropriate strategy in designing HRD programmes and activities
- Sequence and structure HRD programmes and activities
- Choose the most appropriate time, location and venue for HRD programmes and activities
- Consider the use of e-learning in HRD programmes and activities
- Examine the resources required for HRD programmes and activities

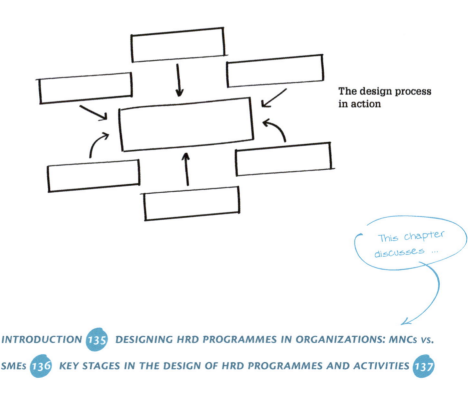

The design process in action

This chapter discusses ...

INTRODUCTION

Having studied the first phase of the Process of HRD cycle – identifying learning needs – in Chapter 7, this chapter now focuses on the second phase of the cycle ▸ Chapter 1 and addresses the design of HRD programmes and activities (see Figure 8.1). We are now moving from considering the learning needs that have been diagnosed for an organization, team or set of individuals towards designing an HRD programme or activity

HRD programmes and activities refer to learning, training and development events which are designed to improve both employee and organizational capabilities through meeting the learning needs of the organization

that will meet these learning needs. The design phase is critical in ensuring that HRD programmes and activities are both effective and successful – just as the design phase is critical to the success of products and appliances, or the construction of buildings. If HRD programmes (or computers or cars) are badly designed, they are likely to fail, or, at best, be problematic in meeting identified needs. It is therefore important that those who are tasked with responsibility for HRD, such as HRD specialists, facilitators and line managers, approach the design and development of learning events with an in-depth understanding of the HRD design process.

It is against this backdrop that we begin to examine this design process. Unlike other HRD textbooks, this chapter adopts a different approach. Rather than simply describing the stages in the design of HRD programmes, we include practical guides, exercises and activities that actually demonstrate *how to* design an HRD programme, which you will have the opportunity to do at the end of this chapter. This chapter will, therefore, help prepare you to design a range of learning, training and development events in the workplace.

We begin by discussing the concept of designing HRD programmes in both large organizations and small and medium enterprises (SMEs), and consider who is responsible for the design of such programmes in these types of organizations. We then identify and discuss the eight key stages in the design of HRD programmes

Figure 8.1 Process of HRD cycle

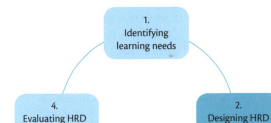

and activities: (1) Gathering data; (2) Seeking feedback; (3) Setting learning outcomes; (4) Developing content; (5) Identifying a learning strategy; (6) Choosing the facilitator(s); (7) Structuring and sequencing; and (8) Setting the location, time and venue. Further, we consider the concepts of e-learning, coaching and mentoring as contemporary approaches to the design of HRD programmes and activities. Finally, we take a look at the resource implications aligned with the design of learning events.

DESIGNING HRD PROGRAMMES IN ORGANIZATIONS: MNCs vs. SMEs

Organizations are increasingly investing in HRD programmes and activities as a means of increasing their overall competitiveness through the improvement of their employees' knowledge, skills and attitudes. For example, Toyota design learning events to improve employees' problem-solving skills, and develop their knowledge on quality and innovation in production. General Electric (GE) design leadership programmes to enhance employees' communication skills, budgeting skills, people management skills, and knowledge about business strategy, in order to prepare them to lead the organization effectively through change. McDonald's even have a 'Hamburger University', which designs training programmes to ensure employees at every one of their restaurants across the globe are consistent in their approach to cooking, hygiene and service, as expected by their customers. HRD programmes and activities can vary widely, from one-day training events to year-long management development programmes. And at the heart of every HRD programme in any organization, regardless of the type of learning event in question, is its design. If a programme is not effectively designed to meet the needs of the organization in terms of improving performance or facilitating change, then that programme is unlikely to benefit the organization in any way ▶ Chapter 7. In other words, if an HRD programme is not designed in such a way as to enhance the effectiveness of the organization at some level through the development of certain knowledge, skills and/or attitudes, then that HRD programme is considered a waste of valuable resources.

A **learning and development HRD specialist**, sometimes called an instructional designer, or an HRD specialist, is responsible for designing, developing and planning HRD programmes and activities

A **facilitator**, on the other hand, is someone who delivers the learning event

Successful HRD programmes accomplish purposeful goals, and are not thrown together on a whim; they are carried out as a result of a solid design process. Of all the responsibilities of HRD professionals, then, the design of HRD programmes represents one fundamental activity.

Inherent in the design process in any organization is the choice of whether to design HRD programmes or activities in-house, or to buy in design expertise from HRD professionals or consultants outside the organization. Organizations can also provide HRD to employees through educational institutions, such as colleges and universities. This choice may depend on the resources available within the organization (e.g. finance, time and available expertise), the type of HRD programme or activity that is required (e.g. a one-day software training programme or a year-long management development programme) and whether the learning event must take place at an organizational, team or individual level (e.g. software training for all employees in the organization, a team-building activity or an individual undertaking a part-time MBA programme). Our focus in this chapter, however, is on the design of HRD programmes and activities in-house. Most large organizations (particularly multinational corporations or MNCs) have formal HRD strategies in place, which include policies and practices that guide the design of learning events in-house. Many of these organizations delegate responsibility for all HRD activities, including design, to a dedicated HRD function or to a department of HRD specialists, led by an HRD manager, often referred to as a chief learning officer (CLO). Depending on their level of knowledge, skill and expertise, as well as the type of learning event in question, **learning and development specialists** can also act as **facilitators** for HRD programmes or activities in large organizations.

It is less likely, however, for SMEs to have a formal HRD function ▶ Chapter 3, and the responsibility for the design of HRD programmes in SMEs can vary considerably, from owner-managers, to HR managers or line managers, and even administrative staff. In general, SMEs are less likely to have dedicated HRD specialists with the necessary expertise to design HRD programmes and activities, when compared with their larger counterparts. As a result, SMEs often send their employees on external learning, training and development courses and events, or they outsource the design of their learning events. SMEs, however, tend to have limited financial resources to dedicate to HRD activities, so it is important to remember that the process of HRD in SMEs, including the design of HRD programmes, is not a 'scaled down version' of the formal process of HRD in larger organizations (Westhead and Storey, 1996). Learning events in SMEs tend to occur in an ad-hoc manner, and are often designed in reaction to immediate work-related problems or external pressures, rather than as a result of a formal learning needs analysis. Moreover, research over the past decade has shown that, because of the limited infrastructure and resources available for HRD, SMEs are less likely to engage in the design of formal learning, training and development activities at all, compared with larger organizations (see, for example, Hill and Stewart, 1999; Johnson, 2002; Stone, 2012). Recognizing this situation, many national-level policies in recent times have placed an emphasis on enabling SMEs to engage in the design of HRD programmes and activities, given the importance of SMEs to the economy. SMEs can now seek guidance and support on the design of HRD activities from a wide range of sources, including trade associations, government-sponsored schemes and private HRD consultancies.

Table 8.1 HRD support available for SMEs

Country	Examples of support organizations for the design of HRD programmes in SMEs
Ireland	Irish Small and Medium Enterprises Association (ISME) Enterprise Ireland
United Kingdom	The Institute for Small Business and Entrepreneurship (ISBE) Regional growth fund
France	Agefos-PME
Germany	Bildungscheck NRW
Finland	New workplace development programme
Sweden	Lifelong learning project
US	Small Business Innovation Research (SBIR) programme
Malaysia	Workforce Development Agency
Luxembourg	National Institute for Vocational Training
Australia	Enterprise connect
Canada	Industrial Research Assistance Program (IRAP)
Japan	Public Industrial Technology Research Institutes (Kohsetsushi Centres)

Regardless of organizational size, however, or the individual(s) in charge, there are a number of key actions and decisions that need be made in order to successfully design any type of HRD programme or activity in-house. We now turn our attention towards these required actions and decisions, focusing on the eight key stages in the design phase of the Process of HRD cycle.

BUILDING YOUR SKILLS

Imagine you are the owner-manager of a high-tech start-up company which employs 30 people. You are keen to ensure that all employees continuously develop the knowledge, skills and attitudes required to keep abreast of the fast-paced change and innovation that characterizes the sector. However, you're not sure how to go about this, given that your area of expertise is in software development. You were told at a recent networking event that there are some organizations in the country that provide assistance to SMEs for training and developing their staff. You must now begin to research these organizations and to compile a report on the services provided by these organizations in your country.

KEY STAGES IN THE DESIGN OF HRD PROGRAMMES AND ACTIVITIES

It is important to remember that HRD is a continuous process, and that each phase in the Process of HRD cycle is intrinsically linked to the phases that come before, and the phases that come after. As such, the design of HRD programmes and activities is based on the results of the learning needs analysis (discussed in Chapter 7), and both the delivery and evaluation phases of these learning events are based on their design (discussed in Chapter 9 and Chapter 10). The design process is, therefore, complex, requiring a comprehensive understanding of identified learning needs, and an acute awareness of design implications for the delivery phase and the evaluation phase. It is also important to remember that learning events should be learner-focused. That is, HRD programmes and activities should be designed with the learner(s) in mind. It is useful at this point to briefly

Figure 8.2 Stages of the HRD design process

Gathering data

Seeking feedback

Setting learning outcomes

Developing content

Identifying a learning strategy

Choosing a facilitator

Structuring and sequencing

Location, time and venue

7 *Structuring and Sequencing:* The programme or activity is planned, structured and sequenced.
8 Selecting the *location, time* and *venue* for the HRD programme or activity.

We will discuss each of these stages in turn, providing information on the important issues to consider at each stage, as well as guidance on how to carry out each stage successfully.

GATHERING DATA

The first stage in the design of any HRD programme or activity is to gather information related to the first phase of the Process of HRD cycle, Identifying Learning Needs ▶Chapter 7. Those charged with the design of learning events need to understand what type of learning needs exist within the organization, and whether they exist at the organizational, team or individual level, before embarking on designing a specific HRD solution. It is important at this stage to consider the priority learning needs identified, based on the evidence from various data sources, and what types of HRD solutions have been recommended to meet these needs. Please revisit Chapter 7 for an in-depth discussion on the identification of learning needs, including data collection.

revisit Chapter 4, Individual-Level Learning, and recall the variety of ways in which adults learn, as well as the principles underlying effective learning. It is necessary to keep these principles in mind as you begin to think about each stage of the design process.

There are eight key stages in designing HRD programmes and activities (see Figure 8.2). While these eight stages are presented in a sequential manner here, it is important to remember that, in the reality of dynamic and chaotic organizational environments, the design phase may not follow such a logical path. Nonetheless, it is important to recognize the interrelatedness of the stages, and that each stage must be completed in order to design a successful learning event.

1 *Gathering Data:* First, data on identified learning needs must be gathered and analysed.
2 *Seeking Feedback:* Next, feedback must be sought from key decision makers regarding the most appropriate HRD programme or activity to meet identified learning needs.
3 *Setting Learning Outcomes:* Identified learning needs must then be translated into explicit learning outcomes for the specific HRD programme or activity.
4 *Developing the Content:* Once these learning outcomes are defined, the appropriate content required to address each learning outcome is selected and developed.
5 *Identifying a Learning Strategy:* Suitable learning strategies through which the programme or activity content can be delivered are then determined.
6 *Choosing the Facilitator(s):* The facilitator(s) who will deliver and/or facilitate the programme or activity is then chosen.

SEEKING FEEDBACK

Once priority learning needs have been identified, it is important to involve other organizational members in the design process at this point, outside the HRD specialism: especially key stakeholders, such as decision makers, executives and managers. The data gathered as part of the learning needs identification phase should be presented to these stakeholders (via reports, meetings or briefings, for example) so that they can provide feedback on their thoughts and perceptions about these learning needs; which needs they feel are priority to the overall effective functioning of the organization; and what types of HRD programmes or activities they feel would be most appropriate in meeting these learning needs. This feedback is critical, not least because it helps inform the design of learning events so that they are aligned with the strategic goals of the organization, but also because these stakeholders often hold authority over the resources to be allocated to the HRD function.

Their involvement in the design of HRD programmes can help foster the support and promotion of these programmes throughout the organization, and provide further validation (over and above the identification of learning needs) for such programmes. As such, resource allocation, or the available HRD budget, will usually be discussed and agreed upon at this point. We return to this issue of resources at the end of this chapter.

SETTING LEARNING OUTCOMES: BEGIN WITH THE END IN MIND

The next key stage in the design phase is to define and articulate specific learning outcomes for the HRD programme or activity. The purpose of developing learning outcomes is threefold:

1　To set out the goals of the HRD programme or activity
2　To signpost to the learner what they should expect to learn from the HRD programme or activity, and what is expected of them upon completion
3　To frame the basis of evaluation for the learner, the facilitator and the HRD programme or activity

> learning outcomes are brief, precise statements that describe and define what a learner is expected to know; be able to do; or be able to understand by the end of the HRD programme or activity
>
> SMART learning outcomes should also be Specific, Measurable, Attainable, Relevant and Time-Framed

Learning outcomes should be derived directly from a learning need that has already been identified ▶Chapter 3, and translated as a specific learning outcome of the HRD programme or activity intended to meet that learning need. Just like learning needs, learning outcomes should relate to required performance on the job. For example, if a learning needs analysis conducted in a chemical manufacturing plant identified that a particular group of employees have little or no knowledge of current health and safety legislation, then one learning outcome of the HRD programme/activity designed to meet this need would be that 'on completion of the programme/activity, learners will be able to identify and explain the specific procedures to be followed on the job in accordance with current health and safety legislation'. It is necessary for this group of employees to be knowledgeable about the health and safety procedures in order to legally perform their job well, so this learning need has been translated into a learning outcome for the HRD programme/activity they will undertake.

Writing learning outcomes

Learning outcomes are usually categorized into three types, or along three dimensions: knowledge-related learning outcomes; skill-related learning outcomes; and attitude-related learning outcomes; in other words, what you want learners to know, be able to do or be able to understand once the programme or activity has been completed. Swart *et al.* (2005: 239) state that knowledge, in terms of learning outcomes, refers to the 'internalization, understanding and application of new information and concepts'; skill refers to 'the incorporation through practice of new ways of responding (i.e. mental, physical and social)'; and attitude refers to 'the adoption of new values, feelings and psychological orientation'. In other words, learning outcomes should be SMART: indicate exactly what the learner will know, be able to do or be able to understand (Specific); be observable or testable at the end of the programme or activity (Measurable); be realistically achieved within the programme or activity (Attainable); be focused on learning needs for job performance (Relevant); and be feasibly accomplished by the end of the programme or activity (Time-framed).

When developing learning outcomes, first consider the learning needs identified. Which needs are knowledge-related, which ones are skill-related and which ones are attitude-related? Write down what the goals are for the HRD programme or activity in meeting these needs. It is helpful to then write the phrase: 'On completion of this HRD programme, learners will be able to …' and add an action verb that describes what the learner will be expected to be knowledgeable about, be able to do or be able to understand (see Table 8.2). Think about the level or standard of performance that is required from the learners in order for the learning needs to be met. Choose action verbs that specify an expected level of performance, and imply measurability upon completion. Finally, ask yourself: if the learner was to achieve these learning outcomes, would the learning need be met?

Here is a list of action verbs that can be used when writing learning outcomes depending on learning required. These verbs indicate that activities are specific and measurable.

Table 8.2 Action verbs for learning outcomes, grouped by meaning

Arrange	Associate	Add	Analyse	Argue	Appraise
Collect	Change	Apply	Appraise	Arrange	Ascertain
Count	Clarify	Assess	Arrange	Assemble	Argue
Define	Classify	Calculate	Break down	Categorize	Assess
Describe	Classify	Change	Categorize	Collect	Choose
Enumerate	Compute	Choose	Classify	Combine	Compare
Examine	Construct	Classify	Compare	Compile	Conclude
Identify	Convert	Collect	Connect	Compose	Consider
Name	Decode	Complete	Contrast	Construct	Convince
Order	Defend	Compute	Criticize	Create	Decide
Outline	Describe	Construct	Debate	Design	Defend
Present	Discuss	Demonstrate	Deduce	Develop	Detect
Point	Distinguish	Develop	Detect	Devise	Determine
Quote	Estimate	Discover	Determine	Establish	Estimate
Recall	Explain	Divide	Develop	Explain	Explain
Recite	Express	Examine	Differentiate	Formulate	Evaluate
Recognize	Extend	Find	Discover	Generalize	Grade
Recollect	Extrapolate	Illustrate	Discriminate	Generate	Interpret
Record	Generalize	Interpret	Distinguish	Integrate	Justify
Recount	Give examples	Interview	Divide	Make	Measure
Relate	Identify	Map	Draw conclusions	Manage	Recommend
Repeat	Illustrate	Modify	Examine	Modify	Select
Reproduce	Indicate	Operate	Experiment	Order	Standardize
	Infer	Organize	Group	Organize	Set up
	Interpret		Identify	Originate	Summarize
	Locate		Illustrate	Plan	Synthesize
				Prepare	
				Rewrite	

Of course, writing learning outcomes for an HRD programme or activity is a prerequisite to guiding the next stage of the design process, Developing the Content, which we turn to now in the next section.

SELECTING THE CONTENT FOR HRD PROGRAMMES AND ACTIVITIES

The next stage in the design phase is to select and develop the content for the HRD programme or activity. Content can come in the form of material, text, images, audio or interaction. **Programme content** is derived directly from the specific learning outcomes of an HRD programme or activity, and learning outcomes provide an initial indication of the programme content. Developing the content is a critical step in the design process. If the content required to achieve a learning objective is not included in an HRD programme or activity, then that programme or activity will not be sufficient to meet

programme content refers to the individual items or topics that must be learnt in order for the learning outcomes to be achieved

CONSIDER THIS...

Let's return to our earlier example in the chemical manufacturing plant, where one learning outcome identified for the HRD programme was: 'on completion of the programme, learners will be able to identify and explain the specific procedures to be followed on the job in accordance with current health and safety legislation'. What content, in the form of facts, procedures, concepts and principles, should be included in the programme to achieve this learning outcome?

the learning needs identified. According to Morrison *et al.* (2010), there are six types of learning content: Facts; Procedures; Concepts; Principles; Interpersonal Skills; and Attitudes (see Table 8.3).

When developing programme content, focus on what type of content must be included in order to achieve each specific learning outcome.

Table 8.3 Types of learning content

Types of learning content	Explanation	Examples
Facts	Specific information that answers the *Who? What? When? Where?* questions	Company history and information, company structure, policies and procedures, turnover and productivity data, legislation
Procedures	Specific information that answers the *How to?* question. A set of clearly defined steps or stages taken in order to perform a task	Instructions for using the cash register, instructions for operating a machine, health and safety procedures, fire drill
Concepts	Specific information that answers the *What is?* question. Concepts are an idea or group of ideas objects, or entities that are defined by a single word or term and share common characteristics	Product design, service delivery, customer service, dignity and respect, equal opportunities, professionalism
Principles	Specific information that answers the *Why?* questions. Principles describe the relationship between two or more concepts	Guidelines for dealing with difficult customers, managing the employment relationship, business ethics, handling a crisis
Interpersonal skills	Verbal and non-verbal communication skills for dealing with people	Solving team conflict, negotiating, interviewing, interacting with clients and customers
Attitudes	Emotional judgements, reactions and categorizations, predispositions to behaviour	Organizational culture, motivation, job satisfaction, team commitment and team building

Adapted from Morrison *et al.* (2010)

Guide to using mind maps to develop content for HRD programmes or activities

Mind maps are often centred on a single word, or concept, from which subcategories of that word or concept are branched out. Mind maps are used to facilitate various activities at work, such as problem solving, brainstorming and note taking. Mind maps can also be used to help HRD specialists develop content for their HRD programmes and activities. For example, the image, below, depicts a mind map of an HR strategy plan. If you were designing a programme on developing an HR strategy, one knowledge-related learning outcome of this programme might be that, 'by the end of the programme, learners will be able to identify and explain the key aspects of the HR strategy planning process'. You could then use a mind map, like the one below, to identify the aspects of the strategy planning process that learners are required to know about on completion of the programme, thereby identifying the content for the programme that relates to this specific learning outcome. So, you might include content related to change management, rewards, recruitment and selection, employee relations, performance management, leadership, culture and communication systems in the programme.

A mind map is a visual diagram used to categorize information

A learning strategy is the overarching approach in which the learning event is framed

SELECTING AN APPROPRIATE STRATEGY IN DESIGNING HRD PROGRAMMES AND ACTIVITIES

The next stage in the design process is to decide on an appropriate learning strategy for the HRD programme or activity. A learning strategy, or, indeed, learning strategies are chosen based on the specific learning outcomes of an HRD programme or activity, and the corresponding content to be included in the programme to achieve that specific learning outcome. Garavan *et al.* (2003) outline six generic learning strategies that can be used in designing HRD programmes and activities: General Theory; Declarative Knowledge; Concept Learning; Rule-Learning; Problem-Solving; Skill Based. Each of these is discussed in turn.

Mind map

culture and communication systems

change management

leadership

HR strategy

rewards

performance management

recruitment and selection

employee relations

General theory learning strategy

A general theory learning strategy approach frames a learning event in such a way that the majority of content is delivered in a largely didactic learning manner. General theory learning events should be relatively short and well structured. Learning new theory, concepts or factual knowledge can cause 'information overload' for learners if poorly timed or badly structured. The introduction section should clearly outline the purpose of the session, highlighting its importance, link this session to any previous event carried out on the programme and, importantly, generate interest among the learners. The content of the session should then be explained in the main body. Having explained the content to the learners, the facilitator should construct some sort of activity which relates the information being explained to its relevance on the job. Taken together, the informative content and

> A general theory learning strategy can be used as an approach to frame content in the form of facts, procedures, concepts or principles that relate to knowledge-based learning outcomes

> Didactic learning occurs when a facilitator explains theory, concepts or factual knowledge to learners, with little interaction from the learners, other than to ask questions

> Similar to a general theory learning strategy, a declarative knowledge learning strategy can be used as an approach to frame content in the form of facts, procedures, concepts or principles that relate to knowledge-based learning outcomes

> A concept learning strategy can be used as an approach to frame content in the form of concepts, principles or attitudes that relate to both knowledge-based and attitude-based learning outcomes

the activity should then be summarized. Finally, the concluding section should review the purpose of the session, measure or test whether the learning outcome has been achieved, link this particular session to any future sessions on the programme, and clarify any remaining questions. For example, a session on employment law for HR professionals could be delivered using a general learning strategy.

Declarative knowledge learning strategy

A declarative knowledge learning strategy, however, is mostly used in facilitating learning of scientific or very technical knowledge, where learners will have high levels of cognitive ability. For example, a declarative knowledge strategy may be used in designing an HRD programme on scientific mathematical models for a group of engineers in an organization.

A concept learning strategy

Many concepts in the workplace, such as 'organizational learning' ▶ Chapter 4 are of an abstract nature, while others, such as 'product branding', can be identified by a set of physical characteristics, including symbols, images, text and policies. A concept learning strategy can be designed in two particular ways in order to facilitate knowledge-based and attitude-based learning outcomes:

1 A *discovery* concept learning strategy presents the learner with examples and non-examples of the concept, thereby prompting the learner to 'discover' the concept relating to the examples. For example, if you were designing a learning session on corporate strategy, you could use discovery learning to highlight examples of two organizations: one which followed a specific plan that failed, and another which followed a specific plan that was successful. The learner would then be prompted to 'discover' the concept of corporate strategic planning, before you explicitly deliver content related to the corporate strategic planning process, and what a successful corporate strategy entails.

2 An *expository* concept learning strategy explicitly presents the learner with the concept itself, examining its critical characteristics and attributes, followed by a discussion of a good or best example of the concept. Learners are then encouraged to present their own examples of the concept. Using the same example above, if you were designing a learning session on corporate strategy, you could use an expository learning strategy to first introduce the

concept of corporate strategy, and follow afterwards with examples of good and bad practice in two organizations.

A *rule learning strategy*

This type of learning strategy uses an *inquiry* approach to facilitate the learning of rules for the iob or in the workplace. For instance, the learners might be first presented with a particular problem or difficult situation which is described or demonstrated. Learners are then encouraged to seek information and gather data in order to correctly solve the problem or situation, being able to understand, appreciate and even demonstrate the rule related to the learning outcome. Rule learning is very common on HRD programmes or activities focused on health and safety, manual handling, customer service, and dignity and respect at work.

A rule learning strategy can be used as an approach to frame content in the form of facts, procedures, concepts, principles, attitudes or interpersonal skills that relate to knowledge-based, skill-based and attitude-based learning outcomes

A problem-solving learning strategy can be used as an approach to frame content in the form of principles, attitudes or interpersonal skills that relate to skill-based and attitude-based learning outcomes

A skill-based learning strategy can be used as an approach to frame content in the form of procedures, principles, attitudes or interpersonal skills that relate to skill-based learning outcomes

A *problem-solving learning strategy*

A problem-solving learning strategy is similar to a rule learning strategy, except that learners have previous knowledge on job or workplace rules. For example, a session on customer service could use a problem-solving strategy to introduce an example of a customer complaint, stating that the learners have to solve this problem by outlining how they would deal with such a complaint. The learners would then be asked to recall their previous knowledge, and associated rules, about dealing with customer complaints. Learners would then be directed to think through this knowledge or these rules in order to deal with the particular complaint example highlighted in the session.

A *skill-based learning strategy*

In HRD programmes and activities, this type of strategy is used to facilitate the learning of skills. The facilitator introduces the session by outlining the skill to be learned and the learning outcomes. They then highlight the importance of learning this particular skill or set of skills for performance on the job, and they assess the current level of the skill among the learners. During the main body of the session, the facilitator demonstrates how the skill is performed. While talking the learners through the skill, they check for understanding and provide the learners with the opportunity to practise the skill. Practice should account for half of the time allocated for the main body of the session. The session should conclude by reviewing the key stages of the skill, answer any questions that learners may have, and explore whether any new techniques or ways of carrying out the skill were discovered along the way. This type of strategy could be used in a session which demonstrates the use of plant machinery, or the use of a computer system in an organization.

CHOOSING THE FACILITATOR(S)

Determining who will deliver the programme is a hugely important next step in the design phase, and it can be a rather difficult one. Depending on the learning outcomes, content and strategies specified within an HRD programme or activity, choosing an appropriate facilitator or set of facilitators will depend on whether HRD specialists and/or line managers with the relevant knowledge, skills and expertise are employed in the organization, or whether the organization is prepared to hire a professional facilitator from an outside organization or consultancy.

Guide to choosing a facilitator

When deciding on an appropriate facilitator or set of facilitators to deliver your HRD programme or activity, the following issues should frame this decision-making process:

1 Consider the learning outcome to be achieved in the session, and the content that is to be delivered. Who has the necessary expertise in this knowledge, skill or attitude?

2 Consider the learning strategy. Who has the ability to instruct via this approach?

3 Consider the credentials of the facilitator(s). Have they undertaken formal learning in instructional strategies and methods? Do they need to have undertaken formal learning to be able to facilitate the learning event? Do they have the necessary verbal and non-verbal skills to deliver the learning event? Have they previous experience in instructing a similar learner or group of learners?

4 Consider the evaluations from previous learning events. Did this facilitator receive positive feedback and results?

5 Are the facilitator(s) both willing and available to facilitate the learning event?

STRUCTURING AND SEQUENCING HRD PROGRAMMES AND ACTIVITIES

Once the learning outcomes have been articulated, the content has been developed, a learning strategy has been chosen, resources have been considered, and the facilitators have been identified, the next stage in the design process is deciding on how best to structure and sequence the HRD programme or activity. Key questions at this point are:

1 How much time should be allocated to each content topic or topics in the HRD programme or activity?

2 How should the HRD programme or activity be sequenced?

Guide to structuring and sequencing HRD programmes and activities

We must consider the learning outcomes and related content again at the outset of this part of the design process. You should think about how much time is realistically required for the learning outcomes to be achieved. The learning event should continue until it can be measured or observed that the learning outcome has been achieved by the learner. Obviously, this will depend on the type of learning outcome and the type of content required to facilitate learning based on this outcome. Truelove (1995) suggests some 'rules of thumb' about knowledge, skills and attitudes: knowledge-related content should be limited to a maximum of approximately one hour at a time; skill and attitude-related content should comprise a ratio of 2:3 in terms of time delivering the knowledge-related content connected with the skill versus the time allocated for learners to practise this skill or reflect on the attitude. It is also useful to remember that learner attention span is generally longer in the morning time, while it slumps later in the afternoon. It is therefore useful to schedule knowledge-related content earlier in the day, and provide time for practice and reflection later in the day, when learners need to be re-energized. Similarly, in any one session, adult attention spans tend to dwindle after 20 minutes, so it is useful to think about ways to re-energize learners every 20 minutes. For example, after 20 minutes of content delivery, there could be a question and answer session, a short video could be played, or some other type of activity related to the content of the session. These, and other methods of delivery, will be considered in detail in the next chapter.

You then need to think about whether some aspects of the content should be logically delivered before others. For example, are there certain learning outcomes that should be achieved before moving to another learning outcome? Broad facts, concepts and principles that have relevance throughout the HRD programme or activity should be delivered early in the programme. Creating logical links between content and content topics helps facilitate continuity in learning, and reinforces learning. Learning events should also be structured in such a way as to provide learners with the opportunity to consider new knowledge, practise new skills or communicate new attitudes. It is also essential that learning content and strategies are interchanged throughout the programme or activity to prevent boredom among the learners, and increase their engagement with the programme and their motivation to learn.

CONSIDER THIS...

Think about the way the content of this book is structured and sequenced – look at the Table of Contents. Scan the learning outcomes on the first page of each chapter, and notice the sequence of the chapters. Why do you think this book was structured and sequenced in this manner?

SELECTING THE LOCATION, VENUE AND TIME FOR HRD PROGRAMMES AND ACTIVITIES

The final stage in the design phase is to select an appropriate location, time and venue for the HRD programme or activity to occur. You should consider the following practical questions when making these choices:

1   Where is the most logical location for the learning event to occur? Should it be held on-site in the workplace (e.g. a skills demonstration on the use of machinery), or off-site at a different location (e.g. a team-building event)?

2   Do the learners work in different locations around the country, or, indeed, around the globe?

3   Where are the facilitators located? Are they willing and available to travel to the location of the learning event?

4   How many learners will be completing the programme or activity? Is there a suitable venue that holds this number of people? Is the venue secure? Does this venue have facilities such as access

to parking, toilets, catering, required hardware and software capabilities, or required specialist equipment and technical support?

5   Is the venue better suited to a large or small group of learners?

6   Does the venue provide freedom to carry out learning strategies without interruption?

7   What are the financial implications of using this venue to roll out the HRD programme of activity?

8   How much time in total is required to carry out the HRD programme or activity?

9   Is the venue available at this time?

10 Are the learners available at this time?

11 Are the facilitators available at this time?

Having answered these questions, it is important to remember that, whatever the location, venue and time chosen for an HRD programme or activity, it must be a space which best facilitates completion of the learning outcomes. Also, the delivery of the content through the chosen learning strategies should be aligned with the HRD programme or activity, while taking into account the practicalities of the location, venue and time for both the learners and the facilitators.

Designing an Induction Programme at McBurger'n'Fries

You have recently been appointed as general manager in a newly established McBurger'n'Fries fast food family restaurant and drive-thru located in a busy commuter town in Ireland. Under McBurger'n'Fries recruitment policy, each individual restaurant is responsible for filling hourly paid positions. Together with the regional manager for the McBurger'n'Fries chain of restaurants, you have recently hired 20 full-time service staff for your restaurant. Fourteen of the new staff are aged 20 or under and, for the majority, this will be their first experience of employment. Three members

ACTIVE CASE STUDY

of the new staff are aged over 40; these applicants have been unemployed for over a year and it will be their first experience working in the fast food industry. The remaining three members of staff previously worked in a city centre chain of McBurger'n'Fries for two years. Each of the staff members will be responsible for the following duties as required at any time during their shift:

- Serving customers at both the counter and drive-thru service facilities, involving use of the cash register, various drink dispensers and various food trays, and acting upon

McBurger'n'Fries methods of quality control

- Preparing and cooking all McBurger'n'Fries menu items in line with demand to a high standard as required by law and McBurger'n'Fries customer expectations, involving various cooking equipment and utensils in a busy kitchen environment

- Maintaining McBurger'n'Fries excellent levels of hygiene and cleanliness as required by law and McBurger'n'Fries customer expectations, involving use of various cleaning equipment, utensils and products

You want to make sure that all members of staff in your restaurant

(continued)

provide 100 per cent customer satisfaction through: helpful, friendly and professional behaviour in a team working environment; timely and accurate counter service; effective verbal and non-verbal communication; high energy levels; a wholehearted commitment to hygiene, cleanliness and the provision of high-quality products; confidence in dealing with a diverse customer base; and an awareness of customer preferences and expectations in line with McBurger'n'Fries company mission and culture.

You have been asked by the regional manager to design a two-week induction HRD programme for all 20 staff, with the help of McBurger'n'Fries regional HRD specialist. Each member of staff must complete this two-week programme before commencing employment. You now need to consider the following important questions before your meeting with the HRD specialist next week:

- What is the purpose of this induction programme?
- What are the specific learning outcomes of this programme?
  - ○ What are the knowledge-related learning outcomes?
  - ○ What are the skill-related learning outcomes?
  - ○ What are the attitude-related learning outcomes?
- What content should be included in the programme in order to achieve these learning outcomes?
- Consider the staff profile. What instructional strategies might be best suited to achieving the learning objectives of the programme for all the employees? Revisit Chapter 3 on Individual-Level Learning to help frame your answer.
- Consider the content. What instructional methods might be used to deliver the content? What materials or equipment are required to deliver the content?
- Could any of the content be delivered via e-learning? If so, how might this be done? If not, why not?
- Where and when should the programme be delivered?
- How should the programme be structured and sequenced?
- Who should deliver each aspect of the programme? Should it be you, the HRD specialist or some other person?
- What other resources are required to deliver the programme?

You should prepare an outline plan of the two-week programme for the HRD specialist to consider, using the following template.

Name of HRD activity:		
Purpose of HRD activity:		
Location(s) of HRD activity:		
Learning objectives for HRD activity:		
Knowledge-related	Skill-related	Attitude-related
Timetable for HRD activity:		
Day 1		

Session 1	Purpose/learning objective(s)	Facilitator/materials/equipment required	Key content	Learning strategy
Session 2...	...	...	...	...

Note: Remember to schedule adequate coffee/tea and lunch breaks

E-LEARNING, COACHING AND MENTORING: CONTEMPORARY PERSPECTIVES ON DESIGNING HRD PROGRAMMES AND ACTIVITIES

E-learning

E-learning is beginning to play an important role in the design and delivery of HRD programmes and activities in the workplace.

Electronic learning, known as e-learning refers to anything delivered, enabled or mediated by electronic technology for the explicit purpose of learning (Hicks, 2000). E-learning is still a relatively new concept in the design of HRD programmes and activities. It is, however, gaining in popularity due to its potential to reduce costs for the HRD function, and because technology now permeates our daily work lives. E-learning is a way of designing HRD programmes or activities that can be delivered to learners anywhere, and at any time, via the internet and other technologies. So, whether the target learners are sitting all together in one venue, are placed in different work sites across the country or, indeed, across the globe, or are working from home or in some other 'virtual' office, they can access HRD programmes and activities via the internet or an internal intranet at any place and any time. There are three types of e-learning:

1 Asynchronous e-learning
2 Synchronous e-learning
3 Blended learning

> **Electronic learning, known as e-learning**, is the appropriate use of electronic technology (usually internet technology) to support the delivery of learning events that enhance knowledge, skills and attitudes

Asynchronous e-learning means that programme content and material can be uploaded online by HRD providers, and downloaded or streamed by learners over the internet, or viewed on DVD or CD-Rom. Learners in asynchronous e-learning environments can begin and complete the programme or activity in their own time, at their own pace. It is, however, a self-directed form of learning, with no interaction with the facilitator, as opposed to traditional 'live' learning programmes and activities. Synchronous e-learning, on the other hand, means that, while programme content and material are uploaded online by HRD providers, just like in asynchronous environments, the HR programme or activity is spaced at particular intervals, whereby learners must begin and complete programme sessions at scheduled times.

Virtual classrooms enabling 'live' interaction with the facilitator and other learners participating in the same programme are often used. Blended learning uses a mix or 'blend' of both asynchronous and synchronous e-learning combined with the traditional 'live' learning format. IBM, a famous American computer hardware manufacturer, developed a four-tier model called 'The E-Learning Model', which blends the traditional 'live' classroom learning environment with e-learning (blended learning). According to IBM, once you know in which tier the learning needs to go, you can efficiently and effectively develop and deliver the learning. Tier 1 is basic knowledge transfer, company strategy and other policy documents. Tier 2 is more advanced knowledge and skills, practise-it-yourself interaction with a computer. Tier 3 involves virtual exercises and online interaction with facilitators and peers. Finally, Tier 4 includes really advanced skills and know-how, real-time demonstrations and face-to-face mentoring.

Tier 4 Learning from collocation	Experience-based learning	Getting together, meet as a community, develop relationships, live it, do it	Mentoring, role-playing, case studies, coaching	Face-to-face
Tier 3 Learning from collaboration	Collaborative learning	Discuss it, practise with others, create virtual communities	Live virtual classrooms, eLabs, eTeams, collaborative sessions, web conferences	Collaborative
Tier 2 Learning from interaction	Interactive learning, games and simulations	Examine it, try it, play at it, interact with it	Interactive games, actual simulations	Multimedia
Tier 1 Learning from information	Reference materials and performance support	Read it, watch it, listen to it, be directed by it	Websites, audio seminars, videos, books, eBooks	Internet

Adapted from IBM (2002) *Source:* ftp://ftp.software.ibm.com/pub/lotusweb/lspace/LSP-2002-022-B.pdf

The choice of whether to use e-learning, or which type of e-learning to use, depends on the learning outcomes, content, strategy and time required to complete the HRD programme or activity. It should be noted that e-learning is increasingly being used, not only to facilitate how employees learn, but to design and facilitate learning for suppliers and customers about the products or services offered by an organization. For example, Microsoft provide training on their website for customers (in the form of video tutorials and product instructions) on how to use their software programs, such as Microsoft Office. Organizations can develop e-learning internally, outsource it, or develop it in collaboration with some other entity or organization. There are a number of advantages and disadvantages associated with using e-learning to design HRD programmes and activities, which should be considered when making the decision about using e-learning:

Advantages

1 Internet technology makes e-learning possible at work and/or at home.
2 E-learning programmes and activities can reach a large number of people based in any location.
3 As such, e-learning has the potential to provide a more cost-effective way of designing and delivering HRD programmes and activities in organizations. It may reduce travel costs, venue costs, facilitator costs and other resources associated with traditional HRD programmes and activities.
4 E-learning offers greater flexibility to learners, often comprising 24/7 access to course content and materials.
5 E-learning offers new tools to facilitate learning strategies, such as simulation.
6 Once e-learning content has been developed, structured and sequenced, it can be repeatedly delivered.

Disadvantages

1 Initially setting-up an e-learning activity can be very costly to the organization, including infrastructure costs; hardware and software costs; technical assistance; time taken to develop the programme online; and marketing the programme.

2 Learners can be quite resistant to e-learning, particularly if they have low levels of skills or competence in the use of the technology being employed.
3 Learners usually require a high-speed internet connection to participate in e-learning, something which is not available in all locations.

SPOTLIGHT ON SKILLS

When designing any type of e-learning activities in an organization, what considerations do you need to take into account? How does e-learning facilitate HRD, for example in a university or college setting?

To help you answer the questions above, visit www.macmillanihe.com/companion/carbery-hrd and watch the video of Brian Naicker talking about organizational learning.

BUILDING YOUR SKILLS

Your manager, the chief learning officer, wants to introduce e-learning into the design of all HRD programmes and activities in your organization. He is unsure, however, whether asynchronous, synchronous or blended e-learning environments work best. He has asked you to make a presentation on the merits and drawbacks of each e-learning environment, providing evidence from existing research on e-learning in organizations.

E-learning Revolutionizing Education in Africa: The First Massive Open Online Course (MOOC) Designed by Africans for Africans

We have considered the use of e-learning in HRD programmes and activities in organizations, but have you considered how e-learning could be used in universities? Let's imagine that, instead of coming into your university every day to attend lectures, meet fellow students, visit the campus library and sit your exams, you could watch lectures, interact with fellow students,  access your reading material, and complete your assignments and exams, all online. This new trend is happening all over the world with the development of massive open online courses (MOOCs). MOOCs are a new form of e-learning, in which courses at universities and other educational institutions are offered solely online, aimed at large-scale enrolment and participation. It is now possible to now take courses at many universities, such as Harvard and Oxford, from anywhere in the world, via the internet.

Interestingly, this recent development has heralded a new era for education in Africa. Developments in technology, coupled with a significant increase in the number of people who have access to the internet across the continent, mean that more Africans than ever before have the option to participate in higher education. The African Management Initiative (AMI) recently made headlines with its introduction of the first MOOC to Africa. The AMI, in conjunction with university business schools, is developing a free, online course in management specifically for entrepreneurs and SMEs – the lifeblood of the African economy. The AMI, a non-profit organization, says:

the existing management education infrastructure is woefully inadequate to meet the scale of the need. Africa currently has about 100 business schools offering an MBA – 1 per 10 million people … Fewer than 10 African business schools measure up to international standard … the majority of African managers and potential managers are unable to access quality and relevant management education and support.

The development of this MOOC has the potential to reach thousands of participants across the African nations who may otherwise be unable to participate in higher-level management education and HRD programmes and activities.

Thomas Friedman of *The New York Times* recently wrote: 'nothing has more potential to enable us to reimagine higher education than the massive open online course (MOOC) … nothing has more potential to unlock a billion more brains to solve the world's biggest problems'. Now, that is food for thought. However, consider the following issues:

- What potential problems might occur with the design of a MOOC?
- What potential problems might occur in the delivery of a MOOC?
- What are the resource implications of a MOOC?

Sources

http://www.theafricareport.com/North-Africa/e-learning-in-africa-massive-online-and-free.html

http://www.timeshighereducation.co.uk/features/africas-mobile-phone-e-learning-transformation/2007120.article

http://www.nytimes.com/2013/01/27/opinion/sunday/friedman-revolution-hits-the-universities.html?pagewanted=2&_r=0

http://www.forbes.com/sites/troy-onink/2013/09/11/want-an-online-college-degree-google-it/

Coaching and mentoring

HRD programmes and activities do not always take place in the form of an 'off-the-job' learning event, where employees develop knowledge, skills and attitudes away from the work environment through the various learning strategies described earlier in this chapter. HRD learning events can also take place 'on the job'. On-the-job learning is an increasingly common method of HRD design, especially in SMEs, that focuses on the development of knowledge, skills and attitudes through hands-on experience while employees are actually working. This type of learning event is typically designed and conducted by experienced employees or managers. These experienced members of the organization demonstrate the necessary knowledge, skills and/or attitudes required for daily work-related tasks, roles and responsibilities, from which employees learn in real time. The two most common strategies through which on-the-job learning is carried out are coaching and mentoring.

The coach, the line manager, identifies the individual learning needs of the subordinate employee, and sets about providing experiential learning events for that employee on the job to meet their individual learning needs ▶Chapter 4. The coach provides opportunities for the employee to work on various tasks and projects, demonstrates best practice to the employee, and allows time for reflection and feedback on the employee's performance. Mentoring is less focused on the development of task-related knowledge, skills and attitudes, and more focused on the development of relationship-orientated learning, such as understanding career advancement, work–life balance skills and developing self-confidence.

coaching an approach to the design of HRD activities based on a relationship between an individual employee and one other more experienced employee, usually a line manager

mentoring similar to coaching, but the mentor, unlike the coach, is usually a more senior-level manager, or a manager from a different function

RESOURCE IMPLICATIONS OF HRD PROGRAMME DESIGN

As a final consideration in the design of any learning event, we turn to the resource implications aligned with designing and delivering HRD programmes and activities. A discussion on HRD budgets was presented in Chapter 3, but is useful to now take a look at the costs that may be incurred as a result of the design phase. There are six main types of costs associated with learning events as listed in Figure 8.3.

Usually, the budget allowance for a chosen HRD programme or activity will have been discussed and agreed upon during the second stage of the design process, *seeking feedback*, but adjustments may have to be made at each stage of the design process, depending on the decisions and actions made. Further discussion on HRD programme cost, as well as the return on investment (ROI) for HRD programmes and activities, is presented in Chapter 10.

Figure 8.3 HRD Program Design Cost

Learner costs: An estimate of time an employee spends undertaking an HRD programme or activity, calculated as a percentage of their annual salary.

HRD personnel and/or facilitator costs: An estimate of the time spent identifying the learning needs associated with an HRD programme or activity: designing and delivering the programme or activity: and other administrative costs, calculated as a percentage of the annual salaries of these personnel.

Equipment and material costs: A calculation of the cost of using various equipment (e.g. machinery or computers) for an HRD programme or activity, as well as materials (e.g. notes, handbooks,pens etc.) and consumables (e.g. water, coffee and tea, lunch etc.) provided as part of the programme or activity.

Facilities costs: A calculation of the cost of renting facilities, such as conference rooms or computer labs, for the purpose of the programme or activity.

Travel accommodation and incidental expenses: An estimate of the average cost per learner multiplied by the number of learners undertaking a programme or activity.

External HRD costs: Consultancy fees, or external course fees (e.g university fees).

SUMMARY

The second phase in the Process of HRD cycle, designing HRD programmes and activities, is a critically important step in facilitating the learning needs of an organization. Those charged with designing such programmes and activities should follow eight stages: (1) gathering data; (2) seeking feedback; (3) setting learning outcomes; (4) developing the content; (5) identifying a learning strategy; (6) choose the facilitator; (7) plan, structure and sequence; and, finally, (8) selecting the location, time and venue for the HRD programme or activity. They should also consider whether a move to e-learning might be appropriate for the learning needs of the organization, and whether on-the-job coaching or mentoring might be appropriate for the learning needs of individuals in the organization. At the same time, the design phase requires careful consideration of previously identified learning needs, at the organizational, group and/or individual level, as well as mindfulness of the next phase of the Process of HRD cycle, *Delivering HRD Programmes*, which is dealt with in the next chapter (Chapter 9). Finally, it is important that whoever is charged with designing HRD programmes in any organization can demonstrate that a learning event is worthwhile to both management (often the gatekeepers of important resources required for HRD) and the employees (who will be taking part in the learning event), and that it will benefit the organization, through the development of important knowledge, skills and/or attitudes required for performance. These issues are considered in the fourth phase of the Process of HRD, *Evaluating HRD Programmes*, in Chapter 10.

 CHAPTER REVIEW QUESTIONS

1 What are the key stages involved in designing HRD programmes and activities?
2 What differences exist between SMEs and large organizations in their approach to the design of HRD programmes and activities?
3 Why is it essential to write learning outcomes for HRD programmes and activities? How should learning outcomes be constructed? Give three examples of learning outcomes for this textbook.
4 Prepare a mind map for the content of this textbook.

5 What choices exist in choosing a learning strategy? What factors need to be taken into account when choosing this learning strategy?
6 Identify the resource implications that need to be considered when designing HRD programmes and activities.
7 What factors do you need to take into account when identifying, structuring and sequencing programme content? What factors do you need to take into account when choosing the most appropriate time, location and venue for HRD programmes and activities?
8 What is e-learning? How can it be used in the design of HRD programmes?

FURTHER READING

Bonk, C. J. and Graham, C. R. (2006) *The Handbook of Blended Learning: Global Perspectives, Local Designs*, San Francisco, CA: John Wiley and Sons.

Hill, R. and Stewart, J. (2000) Human Resource Development in Small Organisations, *Journal of European Industrial Training*, 24(2/3/4), 105–170.

IBM (2002) *The 4-tier Model: Managing the New e-Learning Curve*, available online at ftp://ftp.software.ibm.com/pub/lotusweb/lspace/LSP-2002-022-B.pdf , accessed 20/1/2014.

Liker, J. K. and Franz, J. K. (2011) *The Toyota Way to Continuous Improvement: Linking Strategy and Operational Excellence to Achieve Superior Performance*, New York: McGraw-Hill Companies.

Morrison, G. R., Ross, S. M., Kemp, J. E. and Kalman, H. (2010) *Designing Effective Instruction*, Hoboken: John Wiley and Sons.

USEFUL WEBSITES

http://blogs.hbr.org/2011/10/the-best-approach-to-training/
Read the Harvard Business Review Blog on designing HRD programmes
Check out David Myers' short video on 'Making Things Memorable' on *You Tube*: http://www.youtube.com/watch?v=rFIK5gutHKM – this video provides a useful strategy to help your learners to remember and recall the content delivered in your HRD programme.
https://www.coursera.org/
Visit Coursera and take free classes via e-learning from the world's top universities.
http://office.microsoft.com/en-us/training/
Visit Microsoft.com to see how they provide training for customers on their products via e-learning.

http://www.cipd.co.uk/cipd-training/courses-qualifications/learning-talent/designing-learning-development-activities/
Read the Chartered Institute of Personnel and Development's website section dedicated to designing learning and development activities.

BIBLIOGRAPHY

Bonk, C. J. and Graham, C. R. (2006) *The Handbook of Blended Learning: Global Perspectives, Local Designs*, San Francisco, CA: John Wiley & Sons.

Garavan, T. N., Hogan, C. and Cahir-O'Donnell, A. (2003) *Making Training and Development Work: A Best Practice Guide*, Cork: Oak Tree Press.

Hicks, S. (2000) Evaluating E-learning, *Training and Development*, December, 77–79.

Hill, R. and Stewart, J. (1999) Human Resource Development in Small Organizations, *Human Resource Development International*, 2(2), 103–123.

IBM (2002) *The 4-tier Model: Managing the New e-Learning Curve*, available online at ftp://ftp.software.ibm.com/pub/lotusweb/lspace/LSP-2002-022-B.pdf

Johnson, S. (2002) Lifelong Learning and SMEs: Issues for Research and Policy, *Journal of Small Business and Enterprise*, 9(2), 285–295.

Morrison, G. R., Ross, S. M., Kemp, J. E. and Kalman, H. (2010).*Designing Effective Instruction*, Hoboken: John Wiley and Sons.

Stone, I. (2012) Upgrading Workforce Skills in Small Businesses: Reviewing International Policy and Experience, Report for Workshop on 'Skills Development for SMEs and Entrepreneurship', Copenhagen, 28 November 2012.

Swart, J., Mann, C., Brown, S. and Price, A. (2005) *Human Resource Development: Strategy and Tactics*, Oxford: Elsevier.

Truelove, S. (1995) *Handbook of Training and Development*, Oxford: Blackwell.

Westhead, P. and Storey, D. J. (1996) Management Training and Small Firm Performance: Why Is the Link so Weak?, *International Small Business Journal*, 14(4), 13–24.

9 DELIVERING HRD PROGRAMMES

Christine Cross and Mary Fitzpatrick

By the end of this chapter you should be able to:

LEARNING OUTCOMES

- Explain how learning can be maximized in the delivery stage of HRD activities
- Outline the range of delivery methods available
- Explore the use of different delivery methods for different situations
- Explain how to create an effective HRD intervention
- Discuss the issues involved in creating a positive learning environment
- Describe how motivation to learn can impact on the effectiveness of learning

Delivering HRD activities
in a traditional manner

This chapter discusses ...

INTRODUCTION

The focus of this chapter is on the third stage in the Process of HRD cycle ▶Chapter 1 and looks at the delivery of HRD programmes and activities (see Figure 9.1). A great deal of preparation is involved before any actual training, learning or development event takes place. You may have attended an HRD session where you wondered what you were supposed to be learning or why you could not concentrate on what was being said. Or, you may have attended a lecture and wondered why you were there, as you were learning nothing new. Understanding why these commonly experienced issues occur is central to ensuring the successful delivery of HRD activities. There are many details that must be organized and planned for in relation to the delivery of any HRD activity. These include the choice of delivery method; identification of learner needs; location, timing and duration of the event; room layout; and presentation medium. Even the best possible programme design can fail to achieve its objectives if the programme delivery methods do not match the learner's needs, or if it is not skilfully delivered. We begin this chapter by explaining the role of learning outcomes in the delivery phase of an HRD activity. We then discuss the various delivery methods available and the important role of the person delivering the HRD activity. Issues related to creating effective delivery are then explained, and the chapter ends with a description of the characteristics of effective trainers.

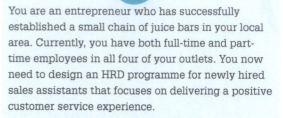

SPOTLIGHT ON SKILLS

You are an entrepreneur who has successfully established a small chain of juice bars in your local area. Currently, you have both full-time and part-time employees in all four of your outlets. You now need to design an HRD programme for newly hired sales assistants that focuses on delivering a positive customer service experience.

What HRD delivery approaches are you going to adopt and why?

Identify potential delivery methods that you will use and provide a rationale for your choices.

To help you answer the questions above, visit www.macmillanihe.com/companion/carbery-hrd and watch the video of Sarah O' Hea talking about HRD delivery.

IMPLEMENTING LEARNING OUTCOMES

Having a clear set of learning outcomes is a key element in designing an effective and meaningful learning and development intervention ▶Chapter 8. This is also the case for the decision about the delivery of the learning event. The choice of delivery methods should be guided by the learning outcomes set out for the event in the design stage (Baume, 2009). The most important criterion for effective delivery of the material is that it should enable participants to achieve the stated learning outcomes. We need to bear in mind that different participants may prefer to learn differently ▶Chapter 3 and they will often have different levels of skill and knowledge. We also need to appreciate that particular

Figure 9.1 Process of HRD cycle

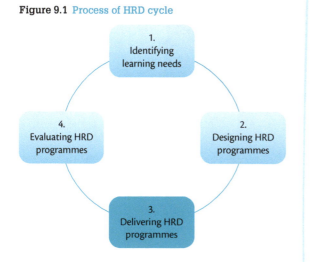

learning outcomes may require specific delivery methods if those outcomes are to be achieved. For example, a learning outcome for a selection interview skills development session could be stated as: 'by the end of the session the participant will (a) know how to use different question types in order to gather information from the interviewee and (b) have practised different questioning techniques in a mock selection interview'. In order to meet the stated outcomes here, the HRD event must include the opportunity to practice the skill development in a mock selection interview.

We should note here that there are reservations about the use of learning outcomes. One of the main concerns is a philosophical one – that academic study should be an open-ended process and, therefore, learning outcomes do not fit in with this liberal view of learning (Adam, 2006).

HRD DELIVERY METHODS

Once an HRD programme has been designed, there are many issues to be considered in deciding on the most appropriate delivery methods required to meet the objectives for the programme. Achieving the stated learning outcomes should be the first priority for those responsible for making the delivery decisions. One of the next considerations relates to cost. Most HRD interventions will have a specific budget allocated for their delivery, and this provides the initial constraints ▶ Chapter 6. Large budgets will allow the use of a variety of delivery methods. This may include the use of an external provider to deliver all or part of the programme. Consultants can be used to deliver more generic content, which can be adapted in the design phase to meet the organization's needs. Examples include

conflict resolution, customer service, and selection interviewing skills. Often, external providers are used if there is insufficient time to develop an HRD intervention, or if the organization lacks expertise in a particular area. The use of external consultants is quite common in organizations (CIPD, 2013).

A second issue relates to the existing level of expertise of the participant group. Yin (2011) developed a useful tool in helping to understand why the existing expertise of the trainee is an important consideration. Figure 9.2 presents this in the form of a learning cube and identifies the basic knowledge and skills needed as prerequisites for the task. Those who are at this stage are likely to be anxious and may be easily confused. Taking this into account, individuals who require these basic skills and this knowledge level will require more directional and instructor-led learning. As the existing level of expertise of the trainee grows, they begin to possess more confidence. The more confident individuals will require more experiential methods in order to maximize learning effectiveness. As a result, a combination approach to methods is often used. For example, if you are deciding on training/learning methods for a group of new hires in a call centre with no previous call centre experience, initial learning and training will begin with providing all the information required to operate the systems in the call centre. This is because the learners are at the bottom of the learning cube. You will most likely provide instructor-led classroom-based training HRD activities in the first few days of training. Then, as they become knowledgeable in the call centre systems, you will introduce more creative delivery methods, such as using role-plays where participants practices, using the systems. Finally, once they have an established level of expertise you may move on to providing them with the opportunity to take 'live' calls as part of the training methods chosen.

Figure 9.2 The learning cube

Expert		
	Focused, confident learners	⟶ Experiential methods
	Anxious, confused learners	⟶ Instructor-led learning
Basic knowledge and skills		

Source: Adapted from Yin (2011)

Table 9.1 Learning and development delivery methods

Large groups didactic	Large groups experiential	Small groups didactic	Small groups experiential	Individuals
Lecture-based format	Case studies	Lecture-based format	Case studies	On-the-job training
Demonstrations	Exercises and games	Discussion and debate	Role-plays	Coaching
Audio-visual	Outdoor learning	E-learning	In-basket exercises	Mentoring
Discussion and debate			Exercises and games	Self-paced
Virtual classroom			Outdoor learning	E-learning
			Audio-visual	Blended learning
			Brainstorming	Virtual classroom

Another issue concerns the location of the HRD activity – should it take place on the job, take place in a classroom-type environment or be delivered at the learner's own pace?

On-the-job training (OJT) is most frequently used in smaller businesses (Blanchard and Thacker, 1999). With this method more skilled and experienced employees are used to train those with lower skill levels, and the training is delivered where the work takes place. Those involved in delivering the training can be co-workers or managers, and this form of training can be supplemented with some classroom-based training.

McDonald's provides new hires with 'crew training', where skills transferable to other industries are the focus. Trainees learn the operational skills necessary to run each of the 11 workstations in a restaurant, from front counter to the grill area.

It is often the case that this is an informal method of delivery, with little real planning having taken place. Those providing the training rarely have any formal training skills and there are no set learning outcomes. For example, in a small-scale retail environment, training on conducting a stocktake is usually provided by another sales assistant while the stocktake is actually taking place. While this is commonplace in smaller organizations, there are implications in relation to how the training is conducted, with the potential for poor habits or short-cuts being passed on. Another issue with this approach is that employees may find themselves in the position of trainer without any preparation for the role (Jacobs and Jones, 1995).

The size of the group is also an important factor in the delivery decision. Experiential learning approaches ▶ Chapter 3 are an important aspect of the informal learning which takes place at work. This

> **On-the-job training (OJT)** describes the process of working alongside a colleague to observe and learn the skills needed for a particular piece of work/job

approach is particularly useful in smaller group settings, as they are more time dependent (and thus have a higher cost) than instructor-led delivery. As can be seen in Table 9.1, different methods of delivery are more suitable than others for particular group sizes. Each of these methods is briefly outlined below.

- **Lecture-based format:** Conveys large amounts of information. This is a fast, efficient forum which allows exploration of content in more detail. However, the audience is largely passive in this method.
- **Demonstrations/presentations:** With this method you can keep participants interested and involved in the learning process. Resources can be discovered and shared by the participants and learning can be observed by the trainer. The main disadvantages can be that time control is more difficult and some participants dominate.
- **Case studies:** In a case study, small groups of participants are presented with a problem situation that they analyse and for which they provide solutions. Participants are actively involved in this method and it provides opportunities both to learn new knowledge and to learn how they contribute in a group situation. This method is most effective when the case study has relevance to the learner's work.
- **Exercises and games:** These encourage participants to work on activities which may be related or unrelated to the topic in question, but the skills and the process are the key focus of the learning. They are very effective when used to develop skills and attitudes following some discussion of theory.
- **Role-plays:** These allow the participants to practise a new skill in a safe and supportive learning environment. Participants are actively involved in the session and learning can be observed. Often participants are nervous in a role-play situation, they are quite time intensive, and

developmental feedback needs to be provided, so the trainer needs to manage the use of this method carefully.

- **In-basket exercises:** An in-basket exercise is a form of case study in which participants are individually presented with a series of e-mails, telephone calls, documents etc. from a normal working environment. They then have a limited time to prioritize and respond to them. This method provides participants with an opportunity to apply knowledge learned to a real situation. The trainer should provide development feedback following this method.

- **In-group discussion:** Short time-specific discussions such as 'buzz groups' are very useful for encouraging all participants to contribute, particularly quieter group members. The trainer needs to be able to collate responses and ensure no one dominates the discussion.

- **Discussion and debate:** This approach asks for and provides different points of view. This can be a method that is thought provoking and engaging for the participants.

- **Outdoor learning:** This is a form of experiential learning that takes place outdoors, often involving an adventure element and including organized team-building activities, which are particularly popular in management development. While outdoor development and experiential learning is quite common in the UK and the US, it has been slow to take off in continental Europe.

- **Audio-visual media:** Includes video clips from the internet, other pre-recorded material and even television programmes. This approach introduces 'entertainment' into the session and can be used to break up the session or to reinforce learning. There is, however, the possibility of some aspect of the equipment not working.

- **Brainstorming:** This can allow the generation of ideas in a way that includes all participants and can generate energy in the session. It is useful when a change of pace is needed or when problem solving is an aspect of the learning process. A clear definition of the problem and good facilitation skills are necessary for this method to work effectively.

- **E-learning:** this method uses computers and networked and web-based technology to deliver material, and is often delivered via the organization's intranet system. Participants can learn at a time that suits them and at their own pace. This delivery method should have both IT support and progression feedback on progress in order to be effective. British Airways' award-winning online learning programme was developed to help British Airways cabin crew to use an on-board point-of-sale system that records in-flight sales and acts as a stock-control system (Little, 2006).

- **On-the-job training:** Is usually delivered by colleagues or supervisors and is often of an informal nature. On-the-job training is often referred to as 'Sitting by Nellie'; this describes the process of working alongside a colleague to observe and learn the skills needed for a particular piece of work/job. This can be a faster and more useful way of learning a job role than studying a written manual. The colleague is on hand to answer any questions and assist in dealing with unexpected learning problems. This training is suited to specific types of work where hands-on skills are required.

- **Coaching:** Is usually delivered on a one-to-one basis and its aim is to improve an employee's performance. Effective coaching focuses on helping the coachee to learn, rather than teaching the individual. The emphasis in coaching is often on tangible issues, such as managing more effectively, and, as such, coaching is often a key element in leadership and management development programmes. Line managers can use coaching techniques in the management and development of team members; for example, in a call centre setting, the team leader coaches team members to achieve call targets.

- **Mentoring:** This involves the specific development of a relationship between two people – mentor and mentee – who usually work in a similar field or share similar experiences. It can be formally organized by the organization or can occur more informally, at the request of a mentee. The mentor provides advice, guidance and support to the mentee. Coaching and mentoring are two individual-level development techniques, which are based on the use of one-to-one discussions. Their purpose is to enhance an individual's skills, knowledge and/or work performance. While it is possible to draw distinctions between coaching and mentoring, in practice, the two terms are often used interchangeably (CIPD, 2014a). One of the key differences is that coaching usually takes place over a relatively short timeframe, while mentoring, which is based on developing a relationship of trust, has a longer timeframe.

- **Self-paced learning:** Is designed to allow the learner to proceed from one topic or section to the next at his/her own speed. This is also known as asynchronous learning and does not require students and instructors to be together or online at the same time. Self-paced learning usually includes e-learning activities which the learner can undertake at their own pace, rather than within a set time limit. This approach has become particularly popular for generic courses at work, such as ergonomics training or Microsoft Office training.

- There is also a move towards the use of **blended learning** ▸ Chapter 8, in which delivery methods can be combined. This is particularly the case when a large part of the intervention can be delivered via e-learning methods, with a much smaller face-to-face methods component involved.

○ The **virtual classroom** has become popular, particularly in the US. These scheduled courses provide participants with live, instructor-led training delivered off-site. By using web conferencing software, participants can interact with the instructor without ever leaving their desk, resulting in reduced costs. Organizations such as Xerox have moved part of their training and learning to a virtual classroom in an effort to reduce costs.

The issue of integrating individual performance with HRD interventions means that training and development activities are moving 'closer to the job' in order to achieve 'real time' learning (Foster and Stephenson, 1998).

It must be remembered that the choice of method is always dependent on the learning aims and outcomes (Simmonds, 2012). Regardless of the particular delivery method/s chosen, there are a number of issues that impact on the effectiveness of every method. The first of these is the style of delivery adopted by the trainer.

STYLES OF DELIVERY

Trainer delivery styles differ greatly, and they can have a significant impact on the level of engagement, participation and motivation of the learners. In the role of trainer it is important to consider your preferred training style before you prepare any training event. It is not uncommon for a trainer to train in the way they like to be trained themselves. This, however, is not always the most appropriate way for all learners to learn, because, as we know, everyone learns differently (Honey and Mumford, 1992). The trainer needs to ensure that all learning styles ▶ Chapter 3 are catered for in the delivery of the training so as to maximize learning and engagement of participants. A trainer's training style preferences, however, should not necessarily dictate the style used for every intervention. Typically, there are two key styles of delivery that are commonly used. They are referred to as instruction style and facilitation style. Each of these is discussed below. While both of these styles are equally valid approaches, they can be useful in different situations and within different contexts, depending on a number of factors:

● The trainees' prior knowledge, motivation, age, experience and learning style. For example, if the participants are highly experienced it can be useful to harness this experience through facilitation of their learning and through an exercise or discussion. However, if the group have little or no experience of the topic, instruction can be most appropriate in order to explain the context and theory of the topic.
● The content/material being delivered. The nature of the material can often dictate the approach adopted. For example, if the content is complex, it can be useful to introduce it using the instructional style and then facilitate a discussion or exercise to make the material more meaningful. Equally, if the material is procedurally based, the instructional approach may be more appropriate, as the trainer will provide a step-by-step approach to the procedure.
● The context of delivery. The rationale and context for the HRD activity can really impact on the delivery strategy. For example, if the activity is mandatory, this can affect the participants' motivation levels, and so the facilitation style may work better at the outset in order to increase participation.
● The number of trainees. The larger the group, the more likely it is that an instructional style will be used, as it is a very effective way of delivering the same message to a large number of people.

Additionally, a mixture of both styles can be used during any one HRD event. One of the greatest challenges for trainers is to identify the delivery method that will enhance the learning process.

The instructor

The instructor style is very direct, typically involving one-way communication, and is quite a straightforward style. This approach is often used with large groups. Normally, an instructor will have a set of objectives to achieve in a relatively short period of time, and so they must ensure that they are comprehensive in approach, yet maintaining simplicity of delivery. They must engage and retain the learners, and, finally, they must ensure that they allow time for practice and feedback in order to encourage retention and learning. It is important that the learners are given time and space to put the theory or demonstration into practice. If this does not happen, the reality is that most of the learning will not be retained after the HRD event has finished. For trainers, it is of critical importance to engage learners and allow them to participate in the process in order to retain the key learning outcomes.

The facilitator

This is a very different style of delivery from instruction. Here, the approach focuses on encouraging the learners to become actively involved in discussing the topic. The facilitator's focus is on providing the time, space and structure for learning to take place. Their role is to allow the learners to discuss and make sense of the key elements of any theory. This is normally achieved through a combination of group-work, discussion and in-class exercises. Gilley *et al.* (2002) advocate that facilitation is more likely to bring about a change in the learner.

This facilitation style is, however, not as straightforward as it sounds. In order to achieve an effective outcome with this approach, the facilitator needs to have a number of skills:

● Excellent communication skills: The trainer's directions must be clear; the questions must be timely and prompted when required. Listening skills are of paramount importance here in confirming the learners' progress.
● Organizational, planning and time management skills: The trainer must fully plan and prepare for all activities to be used during the HRD intervention. In particular, they must allow enough time for each individual within the groups to get fully involved. It is also important to manage the time allocated for the intervention and to get the balance right in terms of group inputs and acknowledgements of those inputs.
● Group management: Where possible, the trainer can divide the groups in advance of the session. Alternatively, it can be useful to use random group

Table 9.2 Trainer delivery styles

Instructor	Facilitator
Direct, one-way communication	Listens and reflects on learners' insights
Suitable for demonstrations/ information giving	Suitable for problem solving and theory application
Large groups	Small groups

selection to encourage broader individual participation with other groups.
● Relationship building/empathy: The facilitator needs to demonstrate empathy and help develop and encourage rapport, both with the groups and within the groups, in order to allow the individuals to benefit fully from the event.

Table 9.2 contains a comparative summary of instructor and facilitator delivery styles.

In making a decision on which delivery style to adopt, a general rule of thumb which is linked to learning retention is proposed by Glasser (1969). He states that as learners we retain information as a consequence of the way in which the information is received. Figure 9.3 highlights that the more participation learners have in the learning experience, the more likely they are to retain information. Facilitation can, therefore, be a very useful way to engage learners, as retention of information is key to **learning transfer**. Of course, there can be

learning transfer transfer of knowledge and skills from a learning situation back to the workplace

Figure 9.3 Linking training style to learning retention

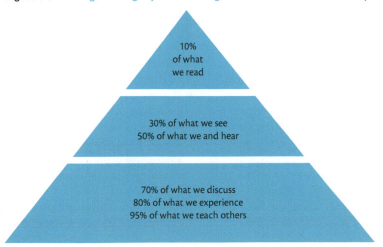

10% of what we read

30% of what we see
50% of what we and hear

70% of what we discuss
80% of what we experience
95% of what we teach others

elements of instruction and of facilitation in any one session, and the trainer can adapt their preferred style where necessary.

The lecture format in third-level education can be considered as an instructor approach to learning. Pick two different subjects and think about the lecturers involved in those subjects. Do these lecturers have the same style of lecturing? Do some try to engage you in the lecture through questions, discussion and debate? Do you like this approach? Do you know other students who don't like that style? The answers to these questions highlight the difficulty in trying to match trainer styles with individual learning styles when dealing with groups in an HRD activity.

MOTIVATION TO LEARN

A learner's motivation to learn is critical to a successful and effective learning event. However, we cannot assume that individuals are motivated just because they are in attendance! Many factors may be taken into account as to why they are there. For example, they may have been sent to the learning event by their manager; they may be required to complete the programme based on mandatory health and safety legislation (for example, manual handling training); they may be part of a new team which is receiving team training; or a new IT system may have been introduced on which they need training. Motivation levels are usually based on previous experience of training and education experiences (Tharenou, 2001). Barriers to motivation for learning can manifest in a number of ways. These can include financial concerns, practical concerns and social/demographic concerns ▸ Chapter 3. The trainer's role is to maximize the level of motivation and to engage as many learners as possible so as to ensure learning and retention of the material.

In this respect the age of the learners is of concern, as there are important differences between older and younger learners (Knowles *et al.*, 1998) ▸ Chapter 3. Knowles *et al.* (1998) highlight that adults have life experiences, which they want to incorporate into their

learning. They are often motivated to learn when they have a problem to solve or need to learn something specific for their work. For adults, being a learner is often secondary to their other life obligations. On the other hand, younger learners' retention rates are much higher; their motivation is focused on a broader end goal such as a career path, or career entry, and the HRD activity can be their key focus at this point. This presents the trainer with delivery-related issues that must be considered for the event to be well received and meet the needs of the adult audience.

There are a number of key areas where the trainer can have an impact on the learner's motivation during the event. These include:

● Delivery style of the trainer. Is it inclusive? Does it reach everyone? Is there variety in terms of activities? Do they actively listen to the participants? Does the trainer use expression and intonation in putting their point across (Abrami *et al.*, 1980; Towler and Dipboye, 2001)?

● Use of on-site versus off-site facilities. There are important advantages to off-site delivery in terms of participants' motivation, as being off-site provides both the time and the space for the learner to fully engage with the learning process. Where the event takes place on-site participants are often called away to deal with issues that arise during the day, or are encouraged to check in at their desk during break times. These issues significantly impact on the learner's motivation. However, it is important to ensure that the off-site venue is near to the workplace, as participants do not welcome additional travel on their working day.

● The content – depth, breadth and level/pitch of the material and how relevant this material is to the learner. This is referred to as the 'what's in it for me' or WIIFM. It is important to view the material from the perspective of the learner. How will they benefit from the learning? How can they use the material that they are learning? Can they apply it to their work? Will it help them develop at their job and, indeed, help their prospects for promotion and their career development at work?

● The rapport within the group and how they interact and engage in their level of participation. Do participants feel at ease to engage within the group? Are all personalities respected? Is there a positive atmosphere in the group which promotes active involvement in the learning?

Three-quarters (76 per cent) of European workers are willing to undertake training in their spare time and 53 per cent would be willing to part-fund it, found a survey of 2,200 employees by learning and development provider Cegos (CIPD, 2014b). When a group of learners are highly motivated the HRD event can result in a very positive outcome and can be a very valuable and energizing experience for all involved. While this is the ideal scenario, it is, however, not necessarily the most common experience. The factors which impact on motivation need to be acknowledged by the trainer, and they can do this through exploring the expectations and motivations of the participants at the beginning of the event. It is important, of course, to consider the learning styles of the trainees, but it is equally important to consider the social and demographic backgrounds and how these can impact on the learners' level of motivation. As learners, we don't appear as blank canvases – we bring with us lots of different experiences, individual backgrounds and differences. For example, do you note any differences when you look at your and your classmates' interactions in class? Are some people more willing to talk than others? Do some people have more examples than others? Are some more realistic than others in their approach?

BUILDING YOUR SKILLS

Trainees can often become disengaged after 25 minutes of a lecture-based session. What suggestions would you incorporate to increase learner engagement and participation? Use your previous experience of attending lectures/training as a basis for your answers.

WHAT MAKES AN HRD INTERVENTION EFFECTIVE?

In order to ensure that an HRD event is effective, the trainer must consider many factors right through from the design and planning to the actual delivery strategy and method. As we saw in Chapter 8, the plan of the event sets out the learning outcomes and the design, so the next stage is to put these into action. The trainer has many tools to use in this regard in

terms of communication skills, organizational skills and interpersonal skills, and needs to draw on each of these to ensure an effective event and engagement of the trainees and participants.

A trainer must be aware of the cultural differences which exist within the training/learning environment. When we are discussing cultural awareness we are referring to awareness both of the culture of the organization and of national cultural characteristics. Care should be taken to ensure that any national cultural differences in a mixed cultural group are identified prior to the learning event. This will allow the material to be designed ▶ Chapter 8 and delivered in an appropriate manner, ensuring that the language is clear and that country-specific jargon is not used (Gay, 2010). It is also important to provide clarity on the structure and manner of the HRD activity to avoid any misunderstandings or confusion on the part of the trainees. The culture of the organization will also have an impact on the delivery of the material. Organizations differ in terms of prevailing learning climates. An innovative software development organization is unlikely to respond as effectively to an instructor-led approach to delivery, whereas a more traditional public sector organization may respond well to this approach. Also, the choice of delivery tools such as media should be examined for cultural appropriateness.

The delivery strategy that the trainer chooses can really set the overall tone for the event and for how learners feel about participating. Therefore, it must be considered very carefully in light of the objectives set out – i.e. will you adopt a didactic strategy whereby communication of the material is primarily one-way and where the participants are largely sitting and listening, or will you adopt an inductive strategy where there is lots of discussion and exploration of the material? Following on from the strategy, the trainer must decide on what delivery methods to employ in order to achieve the highest level of impact on transfer of learning and retention. It can be a challenge to decide how much variety to include in an event and how long to spend on each activity. Sometimes it is tempting to include lots of variety but not allow enough time for participants to really engage in the activity. Therefore, the learning objectives are the guide to activities – what do you want the participants to achieve at the end of the session? How can they best achieve this? How much time should we allocate to this?

Is the Lecture Dead?

The lecture as a means of delivering information to students has been the dominant form of learning delivery in education for about 600 years. The practice began when scholars read aloud from an original source to a class of students who took notes on the lecture. The central idea was that students passively absorbed facts and ideas from their teacher. Little has changed, and today the traditional lecture is a standard means of delivery in higher education. Although it remains the dominant form of instruction, the traditional lecture has received much criticism recently, leading many academics, students and commentators to question: 'Is the lecture dead?'

Digital presentation tools have radically changed many of the central aspects of this delivery method. Lecturers can now not only share the entire text of their lecture if they want to, but they can also enhance that material with audio, video and interactive media.

For many, the value of the lecturer is to provide information beyond the scope of the media presentation. Those skilled in this delivery method can open learners' eyes to new questions, connections and perspectives

HRD IN THE NEWS

that they have not considered before. Adding context, working through examples, sharing relevant experiences or providing an enhancement of the material on the screen all represent ways in which the educator can add value to their lecture. This approach represents an active form of both delivery and learning.

We know that learners retain information as a consequence of the way in which the information is received; therefore, taking active learning seriously means revamping the entire teaching/learning activity – even turning it inside out or upside down. At some universities lecturers post video recordings of lectures online *before* class, thereby freeing class time for more active styles of instruction. The 'flipped classroom' has been suggested by the founder of Khan Academy, Sal Khan. He argued in a TED (http://www.ted.com) talk that videos of lectures can be placed online, and students should be assigned to watch these as homework, to allow class time to be used for discussion and other interactive experiences.

Yet, despite the debate around the death of the traditional lecture, there are a number of benefits to the

organization (the university/college) in the choice of the lecture as a delivery method. We can see that it allows the delivery of information to hundreds of students at the same time, thus making it a low-cost delivery option. Additionally, the majority of classrooms are already designed to facilitate this format of delivery – in a theatre-style setting – with the lecturer at the centre of the 'stage'.

Sources

Lambert, C. (2012) *Twilight of the Lecture*, Harvard Magazine April, http://harvardmagazine.com/2012/03/twilight-of-the-lecture, accessed 22/2/2014.

Hackman, M. (2013) *The College Lecture is Dead – But Microsoft Bob isn't*, PCWorld, 15 July, http://www.pcworld.com/article/2044399/bill-gates-the-college-lecture-is-dead.html

Gunderman, R. (2013) Is the lecture dead? *The Atlantic*, 29th January, http://www.theatlantic.com/health/archive/2013/01/is-the-lecture-dead/272578/

Questions

1 If you were in charge of the Faculty of Business at your university/college, would you ban the use of the traditional lecture? Why/why not?

2 What alternatives to this delivery method are there in the context of third-level education?

Managing participants' engagement

Engaging and maintaining participant interest is a challenge faced by most trainers. **Active learning** relates to activities other than reading and listening which engage the learners. In response to this challenge, trainers incorporate lots

Active learning is the way we can engage and keep learners focused on content and material

of activities, yet they often find that they have too many activities to complete during the session, which then results in rushed activities and confused learners. For example, if you introduce a new topic to the group and want them to apply it to their own experiences or to a case study, you may wish to incorporate some group work into the session. Initially, this may be for 20 minutes, but, if you see that very valuable discussion and outputs are emerging from this discussion, then you may need to allow an additional unscheduled time period before asking the group to debrief. In other situations you may find that you don't need the time allocated, and so you make a judgement based on the level and depth of discussion and whether the group have already noted the key outcomes for full group discussion. This is where the trainer must be flexible and able to read the reactions and actions of the participants. While planning is absolutely necessary, this must be adaptable to both the level and the engagement of the participants and not rigidly adhered to.

Reading audience reaction is one of the key skills a trainer must demonstrate during the HRD event. This skill allows the trainer to establish whether or not they have engaged the audience and whether they need to change the approach to more effectively engage the participants. If the learners seem bored, or, alternatively, have finished an assigned task, it can be useful to change the training or learning approach or introduce a new activity. However, if the learners are uneasy with the task (perhaps it may seem unusual or daunting to the learners) the trainer can take time to explain the purpose and benefit to the groups and give them a time limit for undertaking that activity. Generally speaking, learners may be hesitant to tackle a new or innovative activity, but once they are encouraged and have clear directions they tend to throw themselves into it wholeheartedly. It is important to set ground rules, maintain confidentiality and provide plenty of encouragement at all stages of engaging participants.

Communication skills

Clearly, when we talk about training and learners, communication skills are of paramount importance. The trainer must have excellent communication skills: that is, verbal, listening and non-verbal skills, all of which are central to their role as a trainer. An effective trainer knows that communication is not about simply delivering the words; it is about the message. By this we mean that the importance of what you are trying to say is transmitted not just in the words that are used, but also in the tone and the non-verbal body language used. It is well known that Mehrabian's rule (1971) is critically important for trainers to acknowledge:

- Seven per cent of the meaning of our message is relayed by the words we use.
- Fifty-five per cent of the meaning of our message is relayed through non-verbal behaviour.
- Thirty-eight per cent of the meaning of our message is relayed through our tone of voice.

Interestingly, this breakdown sounds surprising at first glance. How can the words have such little impact on the delivery of a message?

CONSIDER THIS…

When you attend an HRD event you are often given a set of handouts or a training manual which contains the material covered during the course. Many attendees will bring the manual or handouts back to work and put them in a drawer or on a shelf, and never take them out again. Why do you think this happens?

Listening skills are also important here. While often we may assume that it is the trainees' role to listen, this is not the case in reality. The trainer must listen to both what is being said and also what is not being said (Reed, 1985). How engaged are the learners? How participative are they? Are they making sense of the material in their discussions? It is not always the person who answers who is learning, but also the person who is not answering the questions. We must also listen to what they are not saying. In the skills of listening we are listening to the unasked questions, that is, the questions that you would expect but that are not articulated. An effective trainer will ask these questions if they are not raised in order to establish whether the message is being understood and learning is taking place.

BUILDING YOUR SKILLS

Working in pairs, one person is to talk about their love for their hobby to their partner using a monotone, using no facial expression or body language gestures – how enthusiastic do you sound? Try again, being natural, and see how different the reaction is! Think about this issue in terms of the impact on the person receiving the information during an HRD activity.

Questioning

Questions can be invaluable within a training or learning session. Here we mean questions both from the learners and from the trainer. We cannot assume that, if there are no questions from the learners, they understand the material and are following the theme of the session. It is common for trainers to ask the group: 'Are there any questions?' and when there is no response from the learners the trainer assumes that everything is clear. It would be more useful to ask a specific question on the topic. For example, 'so in summary, what do we mean by the term xxx?'; if there is no response, the trainer could ask the learners to work in pairs or in small groups to report back on the answer. This can generate very valuable discussion, and, more importantly, can provide the trainer with an insight into the learners' level of understanding. There are many types of questions that can be asked. These can vary from an open question to a very closed and specific question, each of which can be used for different purposes:

- Use *open questions* to encourage a full response. An open question is one which begins with 'who', 'why', 'where', 'what', 'when' or 'how'. These questions open up the conversation.
- Use *closed questions* to help you to confirm or clarify facts. Questions which begin with 'do', 'are', 'is', 'have' or 'can' are all examples of the use of a closed question. These questions effectively force a yes or no answer.
- Use *probing questions* to get more depth of information. These questions use a combination of both open and closed questions, where the closed questions are used to gather specific information on responses to open questions.
- Use *reflective questions* to summarize key points and check for understanding.
- Use *behaviourally based questions* to assess the candidate against criteria that are identified as key to successful job performance. The focus here is on identifying aspects of past behaviour which are predictive of future performance.
- Use *hypothetical questions* only if they are within the candidate's expertise or experience. A hypothetical question allows the person to say what they would do in a particular situation. For example, 'What would you do if …?'

- Avoid *leading questions*. A leading question is one which either contains its own answer or implies the answer, for example, 'Did you all enjoy that session?'
- Avoid *multiple questions*. This is a common issue and involves asking more than one question at the same time. These questions often involve providing a choice to the person within the question by using the word 'or'.

As we can see, different types of questions have different purposes, and some are more effective in a full group discussion than others. Nevertheless, all the above questions are better than a broad, almost rhetorical, closed question such as 'Any questions?' 'Is that clear?': questions which are often asked by the trainer, but which are generally not answered by the group and are therefore redundant as questions.

Feedback

As we mentioned earlier, the role of the facilitator is to ensure that both feedback and practice are incorporated into the session. Feedback is acknowledged as being an important facilitator of learning (Corno and Snow, 1986). It is important, however, to note that feedback comes from both the learner and the trainer. In order to encourage the learners and engage their participation, it is important for the trainer to provide some feedback. This can be in the form of acknowledgement of inputs, general class feedback on participation, and the summarizing of class material. Learners can also provide feedback through discussion, answering questions and, indeed, asking questions. This can give the trainer a very keen insight into how the learners are progressing and how they are finding the pace and content. It is important, if giving feedback on performance, that the trainer is clear on the ground rules of giving feedback. Giving feedback is, however, a skill that is seldom taught. It is important to note that it is not the same as criticizing. The outcome of criticism is most likely to be negative, while the purpose of feedback is to allow development. Feedback should be both constructive and encouraging. It should also be prompt, in that it should closely follow the event on which feedback is being provided. It should indicate clearly to the learner why something needs development rather than just what the problem is. It should also provide information on how the skill/behaviour can be

feedback Information about performance with the intention of leading to an action to change or to maintain performance. It can be either motivational or corrective

improved. As a general rule, when providing feedback it is important to start with the positive, followed by any areas for improvement, and then finish on a positive or neutral note. Feedback must be timely, clear, specific and to the point in order for it to be regarded as meaningful by the recipient.

One of the critically important factors that trainers must consider all the way through the learning cycle is retention of learning. Therefore, trainers must ensure that they use a variety of tools to reinforce the learning. Some of these include: asking questions of individuals and of the full group; using case study examples/exercises for small group discussion, briefing (explaining what will be delivered before the event) and debriefing (reviewing key learning points at the end of the event); using handouts or summaries; and, finally, use of tests/exercises as a quick way to check retention during the event.

Icebreakers

An icebreaker can be useful at the beginning of the programme to allow participants time to get to know a little about each other, but also can be used during the programme to re-energize the learners (after lunch, for example). There are many examples, ranging from simple small group introductions to puzzles and games which require all learners to be involved in order to solve them.

> icebreaker is a short game or exercise which allows the participants to meet and begin talking to other participants

Rapport

Developing rapport with the participants is a key skill for an effective HRD event. Rapport is essentially the ability to make a connection with another person and to develop a sense of mutual understanding. It is an important skill in many areas of work. A trainer can encourage this positive relationship with the learners from the outset of a session in a number of ways – in how they introduce the session; in how they approach the learners; in how they engage with the learners and how they use personal insights to make the material meaningful to the participants. Given the nature of building rapport, learners respond very positively to relevant personal anecdotes and to the opportunity to offer their own insights and experiences. A trainer can also develop rapport with the participants through getting to know something about the learners and showing some interest in their background, experiences

and motivations. This can be done in many ways. On meeting the group for the first time, the trainer can engage in an open discussion of the programme content, asking the participants to work in small groups or pairs on their expectations/motivations and asking them to provide some personal information. This can also be used as an icebreaker. The pairs can then feed this information back to the full group, introducing their partner, their background and their overall expectations of the programme. The trainer can then refer to some of these where appropriate throughout the programme, demonstrating that they were listening to the participants' introductions, and also that they had remembered them. Using learners' names is hugely valuable, and learners respond much more positively in this regard. This allows the participants to feel that there is a personal element to the HRD activity and that the trainer is truly engaged and interested in their individual learning and progress. The trainer also benefits by gaining an insight into the needs and background of participants, putting themselves in a position to modify or adapt the material to suit the specific needs of the individuals, which increases the meaningfulness of the material for the learner.

HRD activity environment and room layout

While all the above factors are critical to the development of a positive environment for learning, there are other more practical elements which must also be considered. The temperature, noise level, location, seating and layout of the room itself are all important factors. The room must not be too hot or too cold, as this can prove distracting to learners. There should be some ventilation to ensure that the learners stay alert! Additionally, the trainer should have enough space to move around the room during the session. This does not mean pacing back and forth, but, rather, having the room to walk and talk between rows/sections of the room.

The room should be located away from any loud noises (such as manufacturing) and comfortable seating should be available. It is also recommended that drinking water is provided in the room. In addition, the room layout can have a significant impact on the effectiveness of the event. There are many options which can be considered, depending on the content being delivered and, indeed, the number of participants.

Figure 9.4 Lecture-style room layout

Figure 9.5 Bistro-style room layout

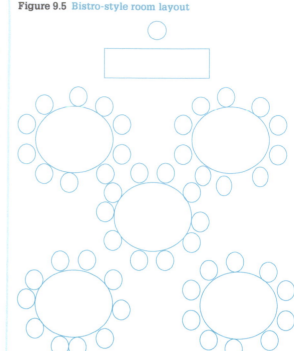

The lecture style

This is where the seats are all placed in rows facing the front of the room with a podium or screen as a focal point. This layout is most suitable for large groups and for information-giving sessions, as it is quite trainer centred. The advantage of this is that everyone is facing the same way, the trainer can make eye contact with all participants and the room is orderly. The disadvantage of this layout is that participants are unable to make eye contact with everyone else and there is an enforced distance between them and the trainer. It can also make the organization of group work more cumbersome (Figure 9.4).

The bistro style

Seats are placed in small circles (usually around tables) around the room. This layout is particularly useful for both large and medium-sized groups where discussion will be a key activity. The advantages are that everyone in the group can make eye contact with each other and group work is easily facilitated. However, not everyone can make direct eye contact with the trainer unless the trainer moves around the room (Figure 9.5).

U-shaped

Seats are placed in a U shape with the trainer as a focal point at the top. This can work really well for small to medium-sized groups as the group can all see each other and the trainer. It also provides good scope for movement and group work. Generally, there are no tables used in this format, so as to maximize space and ease of movement. However, with small groups, tables can also be used.

The trainer should decide which room layout will best meet the objectives of the session. For example, if you have a lecture-style room with everyone sitting in rows there is a limitation on how much movement and group work you can develop. However, if you have a bistro layout which involves round tables there is more scope for movement and group discussion. This is also true for a U-shaped layout, where the trainer can see all participants and all participants can see the trainer. This layout also allows ease of movement and group work, and is a preferred layout for HRD events with up to 30 people.

Figure 9.6 U-shaped room layout

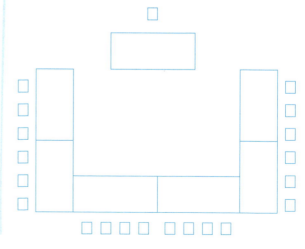

Environmental factors

There are a number of additional factors related to the environment and room layout which need to be considered. Noe (2002) and Mankin (2009) identify a number of issues as important in this regard. These include that the lighting in the room is adequate and adjustable; the need for enough electrical outlets to avoid having cables running along the floor; the need to check for noise from outside, from nearby rooms or inside the room itself; and that the chairs and tables can be moved easily if needed to facilitate group discussion.

Managing time and content

The first issue in dealing with time is related to scheduling the activity. If the HRD activity is not one that can be delivered solely online this can be a difficult decision, as it raises a number of issues. The first question to be dealt with is whether the programme should take place during the working day or be scheduled outside working hours. Both have advantages and disadvantages. For example, if the HRD event takes place during the working day, will people be called away from the session to deal with problems that arise during the day. If it is to happen outside working hours, such as after work, before work or at a weekend, will participants have to be compensated for the time spent on a work-related activity? However, holding the event during scheduled working hours demonstrates that learning is an important aspect of their work. The second question relates to the time of the day. Should the event take place in the morning or the afternoon, or be an all-day event? If it takes place in the afternoon, will some participants opt out of the session after a busy morning at work?

In terms of managing the time versus the content, flexibility is an important aspect. While each activity or content block is allocated a specific amount of time in the design stage, the trainer must ensure the best use of the time available. Sometimes an activity may run over time due to the level and depth of engagement, and that is a valuable outcome. However, if the trainer is not managing the inputs and contributions of the participants and keeping the discussion on track, then time may be wasted and frustrations may arise as 'catch-up' time will be needed and other activities may have to be left out.

Managing expectations

At the outset it can be a very good idea to set out the agenda for the day at the beginning of the session and to ask the participants to discuss the agenda in pairs or small groups. This allows them to assess the relevance and meaning of the day's content. This approach can be beneficial for both the trainer and the learners – the trainer gains an insight into the level, perspective and attitude of the trainees from the outset and the trainees believe that that their input is valued from an early stage, instilling a positive atmosphere in the session. The trainer can manage this process by asking the pairs to comment on their own expectations and noting all comments on a flipchart. These comments are then compared with the set agenda, making adaptations where possible, but also highlighting any constraints that may exist. This can also be a useful way to get any concerns out in the open and allow the learners time to discuss their expectations, and identify the benefits for them, or what is commonly referred to as the 'what's in it for me' (WIIFM).

Presentation skills

For the majority of HRD events, there are supports such as visual aids, handouts, demonstrations etc., and so the trainer must consider his/her presentation skills in deciding which ones to use. Presentation skills are key to effective delivery and include areas such as:

- Importance of eye contact throughout the event. Trainers should look at the audience where possible and engage in eye contact, rather than looking at the presentation screen.
- Using the voice to engage and enthuse the learners. Varying the tone and pitch is an important aspect in generating learners' interest. A flat monotone delivery is more likely to cause participants to lose interest than to engage them. Enthusiasm is a critical part of effective delivery regardless of how many times you have delivered the same material (Blanchard and Thacker, 1999).
- Awareness of mannerisms and habits which can be distracting for the learners. For example, if you are someone who clicks a pen when talking, hold a pencil instead!
- Always double checking you have all your HRD materials/presentations and that all the equipment is working before the event will create a professional approach to delivery.

DELIVERY COSTS

Regardless of the delivery method chosen for the HRD intervention, there is likely to be a set of associated costs which are incurred to facilitate the training, learning or development activity. We can differentiate between direct and indirect costs:

Direct Costs: these are directly associated with the delivery of a specific HRD activity. Direct costs generally include salaries and wages; consultant services contracted; travel costs and materials, supplies and equipment costs.

Indirect Costs: These costs cannot be directly related to the activity, but are necessary for the organisation to function. The term 'overhead' is often used to describe these costs (Garavan *et al.*, 2003). Salaries of administrative and clerical staff providing normal support activities, lighting, heating and office equipment are identified as indirect costs.

CHARACTERISTICS OF EFFECTIVE TRAINERS

What do trainers need to do in order to be effective? An effective trainer is an expert at instructional techniques but is not necessarily a subject specialist. 'There is a visceral "moment of truth" when engaging an audience is … a relatively unpredictable process of question and answer and give and take that leads learners to the objectives that were established at an earlier time' (Korte, 2006: 514). Trainers must have the competencies to carry out their role, must have the subject matter expertise and must also be motivated. In addition, they need to have the necessary communication skills and organizational skills discussed earlier in this chapter. Train the trainer programmes, provided either internally or externally, can be useful in upskilling new HRD personnel. In deciding on the most effective person for the HRD role, the areas to be included are identified in Table 9.3.

Table 9.3 Characteristics of effective trainers

• Demonstrating enthusiasm about the material
• Pitching material at the right level – not too high and not too low for the time allocated
• Punctuality in starting and finishing the session
• Being supportive of the learners' needs
• Listening to and acknowledging all inputs and guiding learners to alternative viewpoints
• Clarity in delivery of material and explanation – little use of jargon, and if it is used it must be explained
• Continuous review of the learning objectives
• Using a variety of activities to engage the various learning styles and personalities of the learners
• Providing feedback and exercises to encourage retention. Summarizing at regular intervals and questioning participants
• Allowing learners to engage and not assuming that teaching is all about doing the talking
• Preparedness for what potentially could go awry and knowing how to use the technology etc.
• Using anecdotes and stories to make the material relevant and real for the learners and asking the learners for their views and inputs or applications of the theory

Training the Taxman!

You are a management consultant hired to deliver an HRD activity to a group of middle managers from a public sector organization in your country, responsible for income tax. The organization employs 300 staff – 55 per cent female and 45 per cent male. The ages range from 25 years to 60 years of age, with the largest percentage of employees in the 45–60 age bracket. In recent times, there has been an increase in the number of customer complaints which have been escalated to senior management.

In addition, a new initiative based on improving communication within the public sector has been launched at national level, and, as a result, the organization's senior management team has engaged your consultancy firm to design a management development programme aimed at middle managers. Learning and development opportunities are rare within the organization, as much of the learning is on the job and employees learn 'how we do things around here' from one another.

There are 45 middle managers in total, who, for the most part, do not see the benefit of the training/learning and see it as a criticism of their management skills to date.

Their view is: if it is not broken, why fix it? They believe that the real need for training/learning lies with their staff and those who report to them. Surely they are the people who need to improve their communication, as they are in the front line and many of the complaints relate to them and their work?

Overall, within the organization there is general lack of engagement with the idea of training, learning and development. A recent organization-wide survey found that 70 per cent of employees were quite negative towards training, learning and development, with the remainder expressing positivity and lots of new ideas in this regard. Customer-facing

employees are welcoming the initiative, as they see they can only benefit from their managers taking part in the HRD activity. Morale is, however, quite low among employees 'at the front line' and there is a significant degree of absenteeism as a result. These employees see middle managers as very fixed in their ways, with little innovation evident in their organization. They also believe that managers do not welcome any new initiatives or ideas from their staff. Training can only be a good thing as far as they are concerned.

1 What delivery methods might you consider here? Explain your rationale and outline how they might work in action.
2 The trainees arrive and are all seated in a U-shaped table

setting. You introduce yourself and your agenda for the day. You then ask them to work in pairs and discuss their expectations for the day, and why they are there. There is a stunned silence as a sea of blank faces look at you in disbelief. One participant addresses you, saying: 'Surely it is your job to teach and ours to listen.' What do you do?

3 How will you address the differing levels of motivation to learn throughout the programme?
4 Would your approach to delivery be any different if this was a private organization rather than a public organization? Why/why not?

SUMMARY

This chapter has identified some of the key issues related to the delivery of HRD activities. The other steps in the Process of HRD cycle focus on creating the content of the learning and training activities, while the delivery or implementation phase is concerned with delivering the content in a way that maximizes learning effectiveness. Successful learning and training delivery depends on carefully chosen and implemented delivery methods. This chapter has looked at the important considerations involved in making those choices. Those responsible for HRD delivery must choose the delivery method that matches learning and training outcomes, participant learning styles, and budget. We have identified some of the main issues involved in creating a positive learning environment and have explained how an individual's motivation to learn can impact on the effectiveness of learning and training interventions. The next chapter focuses on the fourth and final stage in the Process of HRD cycle – evaluation.

 CHAPTER REVIEW QUESTIONS

1 What are the key differences between the facilitator and instructor styles of delivery?
2 How can the trainer maximize the effectiveness of the learning experience for the individual learner?

3 Explain why some delivery methods are more suitable for large group instruction than for smaller groups.
4 Discuss the importance of learning outcomes in delivery of HRD activities. Why should learning outcomes be matched with delivery methods?
5 What must a trainer consider in relation to delivering an HRD activity to a culturally diverse group of learners?
6 Explain how individual levels of motivation can positively or negatively impact on learning.
7 Identify three ways in which you would maximize learner engagement in a small group learning environment.
8 What combination of delivery methods would you use for sales staff in a car dealership?

 FURTHER READING

Agochiya, D. (2009) *Every Trainer's Handbook* (2nd ed.), London: Sage.

Beevers, K. and Rea, A. (2010) *Learning and Development Practice*, London: CIPD.

Carliner, S. (2005) *Training Design Basics*, Alexandria, VA: ASTD Press.

Fisher Chan, J. (2010) *Designing and Developing Training Programs*, CA: Wiley.

USEFUL WEBSITES

http://web.mit.edu/training/trainers/guide/index.html
This MIT website contains information for trainers on design and delivery of training. It includes a very useful matrix which assists with the decision about the choice of delivery method.

http://www.learningsolutionsmag.com/
This is a source of practical information on the strategies, tools, technologies, services and best practices for the management, design, development and implementation of enterprise-wide e-learning programmes.

http://www.trainingzone.co.uk/
This website contains a wealth of information and resources related to training.

http://www.go2itech.org/HTML/TT06/toolkit/delivery/index.html
This website contains resources that provide information on delivering training to your target audience. The website is divided into two main sections: Training Methods and Effective Communication Skills.

BIBLIOGRAPHY

Abrami, P. C., Dickens, W. J., Perry, R. P. and Leventhal, L. (1980) Do Teacher Standards for Assigning Grades Affect Student Evaluations of Instruction?, *Journal of Educational Psychology*, 72(1), 107–118.

Adam, S. (2006) An Introduction to Learning Outcomes, In E. Froment, J. Kohler, L. Purser, and L. Wilson (Eds) *EUA Bologna Handbook*, article B.2.3-1, Berlin: Raabe. Available at http://sss.dcu.ie/afi/docs/bologna/writing_and_using_learning_outcomes.pdf

Baume, D. (2009) *Writing and Using Good Learning Outcomes*, Leeds: Leeds Metropolitan University.

Blanchard, N. and Thacker, J. (1999) *Effective Training Systems, Strategies, and Practices*, Upper Saddle River, NJ: Prentice Hall.

CIPD (2014a) Coaching and Mentoring Factsheet. Available at http://www.cipd.co.uk/hr-resources/factsheets/coaching-mentoring.aspx

CIPD (2014b) Learners Highly Motivated for Training, Survey Finds, *People Management*, Available at http://www.cipd.co.uk/pm/peoplemanagement/b/weblog/archive/2013/01/29/learners-highly-motivated-for-training-survey-finds-2010-06.aspx

CIPD (2013) *Learning and Talent Development Survey 2013*, CIPD, available at https://www.cipd.co.uk/hr-resources/survey-reports/learning-talent-development-2013.aspx accessed 21/1/2014.

Corno, L. and Snow, R. E. (1986) Adapting Teaching to Individual Differences among Learners, In M. C. Wittrock

(Ed.) *Handbook of Research on Teaching* (3rd ed.), New York: Macmillan (605–629).

Foster, E. and Stephenson, J. (1998) Work-Based Learning and Universities in the UK: A Review of Current Practice and Trends, *Higher Education Research and Development*, 17(2), 155–170.

Garavan, T. N., Hogan, C. and Cahir-O'Donnell, A. (2003) *Making Training and Development Work: A Best Practice Guide*, Cork: Oak Tree Press.

Gay, G. (2010) *Culturally Responsive Teaching* (2nd ed.), New York: Teachers College Press.

Gilley, J. W., Eggland, S. A. and Maycunich Gilley, A. (2002) *Principles of Human Resource Development*, Cambridge, MA: Persus Publishing.

Glasser, W. (1969) *Schools without failure*, New York: Harper & Row.

Honey, P. and Mumford, A. (1992) *Manual of Learning Styles*, Maidenhead: Honey Publications.

Jacobs, R. L. and Jones, M. J. (1995) *Structured on-the-Job Training*, San Francisco: Berrett-Koehler.

Knowles, M. S., Holton, E. F. and Swanson, R. A. (1998) *The Adult Learner*, Houston-Tex: Gulf.

Korte, R. F. (2006) Training Implementation – Variations Affecting Delivery, *Advances in Developing Human Resources*, 8(4), 514–527.

Little, B. (2006) British Airways Flies High with Online Learning System: Cabin Crew Can Top Up Their Training from Across the World, *Human Resource Management International Digest*, 14(4), 20–22.

Mankin, D. (2009) *Human Resource Development*, Oxford: Oxford University Press.

Mehrabian, A. (1971) *Silent Messages* (1st ed.), Belmont, CA: Wadsworth.

Noe, R. A. (2002) *Employee Training and Development*, New York: McGraw-Hill.

Reed, Warren H. (1985) *Positive Listening: Learning to Hear What People Are Really Saying*, New York: F. Watts.

Simmonds, D. (2012) Designing Learning Events, In J. P. Wilson, *International Human Resource Development: Learning, Education and Training for Individuals and Organisations* (3rd ed.), London: Kogan Page, 267–293.

Tharenou, P. (2001) The Relationship of Training Motivation to Participation in Training and Development, *Journal of Occupational and Organizational Psychology*, 74, 599–621.

Towler, A. J. and Dipboye, R. L. (2001) Effects of Trainer Expressiveness, Organization, and Trainee Goal Orientation on Training Outcomes, *Journal of Applied Psychology*, 86(4), 664–673.

Yin, L., Crews, R., Brookshire, T.B., R.G., and Norris, D.T. (2005) Lifelong e-learning: A foundation for technology education and professional success. *Issues in Information Systems*, VI(1).

10 EVALUATING HRD PROGRAMMES

Sue Mulhall

LEARNING OUTCOMES

- Explain the concept and purpose of HRD evaluation
- Know why it is important to evaluate
- Discuss the different philosophical approaches to evaluation and the associated models

- Explain when evaluation should take place
- Identify what can be evaluated in HRD
- Describe how evaluation can take place
- Outline how learning transfer can occur in the workplace

Take time out to evaluate

This chapter discusses ...

INTRODUCTION

In this chapter we look at the concept of evaluation. Without realizing it, we evaluate events all the time. Before a potentially difficult encounter we may consider what to say and do, and anticipate the possible reactions of the other person. During the interaction we try to remember our pre-planned objectives so as not to become too involved in the actuality of the occurrence. After the experience we reflect on what happened, what was said and by whom, how it was stated, and why the incident unfolded as it did. We also deliberate on whether we achieved what we set out to accomplish and consider the implications for our future dealings with the individual. Evaluating HRD programmes in a company is similar to how we gauge the interpersonal relationships in our own lives. We focus on the '5 W's and 1 H' (who, what, when, where, why and how), that is, questions whose answers are deemed essential in preparing for, participating in, and then assessing the outcome of a situation. Despite this apparently logical approach to evaluation, many organizations do not evaluate their HRD activities. They put forward a host of reasons for not evaluating, including that it is overly time consuming, excessively costly, and unnecessary as everyone has to have some training for their job. Given the time and money involved in HRD, however, providing evidence of the value of this activity to the organization is important from a return on investment (ROI) perspective. This chapter commences with the 'where' of evaluation by locating it within an organizational setting, and then relating the 'what' and the 'why' by explaining the concept and the basis for its use. We then discuss 'when' evaluation should occur and 'who' may be concerned with the information emanating from the process. We place a strong emphasis on the 'how' of evaluation by detailing the main models available and their associated measures. The chapter ends with a discussion of how to create a culture of effective evaluation.

evaluation the systematic determination of a subject's merit, worth and significance, using criteria governed by a set of standards, which assist in the identification of changes to future programmes

EXPLAINING THE CONCEPT OF EVALUATION (WHERE, WHAT AND WHY)

We begin by explaining what evaluation is and outline the background to evaluation, thereby linking it in with strategic HRD ▶ Chapter 2. We also explore the purpose of evaluation by summarizing the rationale underpinning the process of assessing HRD interventions.

In the previous three chapters, we discussed how to identify HRD needs and then design and deliver a programme to satisfy those requirements ▶ Chapters 7, 8 and 9. There should be a strong and clear relationship between these three phases and the final stage in the Process of HRD cycle (see Figure 10.1). Evaluation influences the design and the delivery of HRD interventions because the output from an evaluation exercise becomes the input to any future learning needs analyses (LNA). It should, therefore, be an integral feature of the HRD cycle, occurring before, during and after each learning event, highlighting the continuous, ongoing nature of the evaluation process.

This chapter interprets the term 'evaluation' in its broadest sense by using Hamblin's (1974) definition, describing evaluation as 'any attempt to obtain information (feedback) on the effects of a training programme and to assess the value of the training in the light of that information' (p. 8). Evaluation involves the measurement and use of data concerning the outcome, that is, the effectiveness, of an HRD intervention (McGuire and Mølbjerg Jørgensen, 2011; Blanchard and Thacker, 2013; Armstrong, 2014). Good management practice indicates that all organizational activities are routinely examined to ensure that they occur as planned and produce the anticipated results. Without such a review, corrective action cannot be taken to address situations that do not transpire as intended, and, thus, generate the expected effects. Similarly to all other functional areas, the HRD

Figure 10.1 Process of HRD cycle

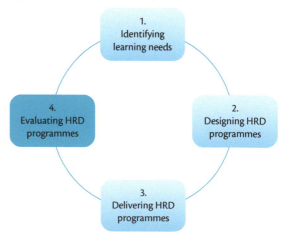

function is obliged to engage in an audit of its practice to demonstrate that it is contributing to organizational effectiveness through aligning its activities with the business strategy (Swart *et al.*, 2005). The term 'effectiveness' is a relative concept, typically determined with respect to

SPOTLIGHT ON SKILLS

As the HRD director of a multinational mobile phone company, you are responsible for the learning needs of 5,000 staff in the Europe, Middle East and Africa (EMEA) region of the business. Your department coordinates the needs assessment, design, delivery and evaluation of learning programmes for all organizational grades, from production operative to chief executive, and for all functional areas, including manufacturing, logistics and supply chain, sales and marketing, retail, finance and HR. At a recent board meeting you presented an evaluation review noting that the ROI for learning activities during the current financial year was 10 per cent lower than the previous period, despite the same expenditure level. The board has asked you to prepare a report recommending initiatives to ensure that the learning ROI improves for the forthcoming year, without decreasing either the budget (€1.5 million per annum) or the annual allowance per employee (€300). Consider the following issues:

- Where will you access the information to inform your decisions?
- Whom will you liaise with?
- What will you recommend to the board?
- How will you rationalize your proposals?

To help you answer the questions above, visit www.macmillanihe.com/companion/carbery-hrd and watch the video of Linda Edgeworth talking about ROI.

the achievement of a goal or a set of goals (Werner and DeSimone, 2012). HRD effectiveness must be viewed in relation to the goals of the learning programme(s) being assessed. It entails the comparison of objectives with outcomes to identify whether the intervention has achieved its purpose (Armstrong, 2014). The formulation of objectives and the establishment of methods to measure the ensuing results are an essential element of the design phase of a learning programme (first stage in the HRD cycle). The evaluation phase of the HRD cycle (fourth and final stage) provides guidance on what is required to ascertain whether these learning events are effective.

Purpose of evaluation

Learning activities are not ends in themselves. Organizations need to establish whether these activities are successful, what worked well and whether the cost was justified by the outcome of the activity. This means that we should evaluate to discover whether the learning activities add value and enhance employee capability (Martin *et al.*, 2010). Evaluation can, therefore, be **summative** (Easterby-Smith, 1986), **formative** or oriented to **learning**.

All three forms of evaluation (summative, formative and learning assessment) entail gathering information and generating knowledge to facilitate decision making within companies (Bramley, 2003; McGuire and Mølbjerg Jørgensen, 2011; Werner and DeSimone, 2012; Blanchard and Thacker, 2013; Phillips and Gully, 2014). The evaluation of HRD programmes is, consequently, situated within the wider organizational context (Swart *et al.*, 2005; Harrison, 2009). It attempts to understand the process of cause and effect by analysing how learning can impact on individual behaviour, group and departmental targets, and, ultimately, corporate efficiency and effectiveness. For example, Simmonds (2003) argues that evaluation can provide firms with answers to the following questions:

- How effective was the LNA?
- How useful were the learning strategies and methods that were used?

summative assessing the effectiveness of the outcomes against those specified when the activity was planned; usually takes place at the end of an intervention

formative focuses on continual improvement, indicating where improvements or changes are necessary to make the programme more effective

learning assessing the extent to which the person can transfer the content of the programme to the job and improve performance

- What was the reaction of the learners and facilitators to the activities?
- To what extent have those who participated in the intervention acquired the intended knowledge, skills and attitudes (KSA)?
- What changes in workplace performance and behaviour are attributable to the learning programme?
- To what degree have the learning events contributed to the attainment of organizational goals?

HRD evaluation involves the collection of information necessary to make effective learning decisions related to the selection, adoption, value and modification of various instructional activities (Werner and DeSimone, 2012). This type of information allows managers to make informed decisions about various aspects of the HRD process, including:

- Determining whether a programme is accomplishing its objectives
- Identifying the strengths and weaknesses of the initiative, which can lead to adjustments as required
- Ascertaining which participants benefited the most, or the least, from an activity
- Discovering which participants are transferring what they learned to their job
- Deciding who should participate in future programmes
- Collating data to promote future programmes
- Establishing the cost–benefit ratio of a programme
- Justifying resource allocation
- Building the credibility of the HRD process with key internal and external customers (Bramley, 2003; Martin et al., 2010; Phillips, 2011; Werner and DeSimone, 2012; Phillips and Gully, 2014).

ESTABLISHING THE OUTPUT OF EVALUATION (WHEN AND WHO)

In this section we explore the information (output) generated through the evaluation process that assists corporate decision making, with particular reference to when the evaluation should occur and who may be interested in the resultant data.

CONSIDER THIS ...

Take the example of a fictitious international car components company. The firm manufactures its products in China and ships them to a large warehouse situated at its European headquarters in Dublin. From this central location, the organization distributes the car parts throughout Europe. During a recent stock audit, a marked increase in the number of breakages was detected, particularly glass-based products, such as windscreens, mirrors, headlamps, indicator casings and bulbs. The root cause was identified as human error, mainly due to inappropriate practices by the fork-lift drivers when stacking the merchandise. The firm scheduled a training course on the correct loading/unloading procedures for all of the warehouse fork-lift drivers. How will the training course cause a change in the number of breakages? What information will the company need to determine the effectiveness of this programme?

Information: Type and timing

The two types of information (output) from the evaluation phase of the HRD cycle that aid organizational decision making are referred to as process and outcome data (Blanchard and Thacker, 2013). Evaluation designed to provide feedback so that improvement of the programme can take place is called process evaluation. It coincides with evaluation conducted before and during a learning event. In contrast, evaluation constructed as a terminal activity to represent success or failure, akin to a report card, is termed outcome evaluation. This occurs when an assessment is carried out upon completion of a learning initiative and on return to the workplace.

In relation to the first type of data, process evaluation, the actual intervention is assessed against the expected (as planned) programme to provide an appraisal of the effectiveness of the learning implementation (Swart et al., 2005). This facilitates a review of the learning process and the intended outcomes. The analysis is divided into two

process evaluation compares the designed and developed intervention with what actually takes place in the real-life experience

outcome evaluation finds out about the effect of the learning on the participant, the job and the organization by investigating how well the HRD activity has achieved its objectives

timeframes – before and during the learning (Blanchard and Thacker, 2013). The 'before' element involves investigating the steps used to develop the activity, that is, prior to delivery. For example, exploring:

● Were learning needs diagnosed correctly?
● Were needs correctly translated into learning objectives?
● Was an evaluation system devised to measure the accomplishment of the learning objectives?
● Was the programme formulated to meet all of the learning objectives?
● Were the methods employed suitable for each of the learning objectives?

The 'during' component entails determining whether all of the systems planned into the programme were actually carried out. For example, examining:

● Were the facilitator, learning techniques and learning objectives well matched?
● Were the teaching portions of the learning effective?
● Did the facilitator utilize the various learning methodologies appropriately (e.g. case studies, role-plays, individual exercises and group activities)?
● Did the facilitator adhere to the learning design and lesson plans?

Looking at the second type of data, outcome evaluation, various end result measures are studied to establish the degree to which the learning met or is meeting its goals (Blanchard and Thacker, 2013). The four outcome evaluation results that are probably the best known are reaction, learning, behaviour and organizational data (Kirkpatrick, 1959), which are explored in greater detail in the section on 'Models of Evaluation' later in this chapter:

● *Reaction outcomes* influence how much can be learned and provide information on the participant's perceptions, emotions and subjective interpretations of the learning experience.
● *Learning outcomes* affect how much behaviour can alter on return to the job and supply information on how well the learning objectives were achieved.
● *Behaviour outcomes* are the changes of performance and behaviour on the job that will influence company results and present information on the degree to which the learnt behaviour has transferred to the job.
● *Organizational outcomes* are the variations in corporate **metrics** related to the rationale for the

> **metrics** measures of a firm's activities and operational functioning
>
> **return on investment (ROI)** involves a comparison of the costs and pay-offs of the learning event

learning intervention in the first place. They provide information on the organizational performance gaps identified in the LNA so that any divergence can be utilized as the baseline for calculating an improvement in results following the completion of the learning programme.

People: Interest and importance

To determine what evaluation data (process or outcome) should be used when assessing the effectiveness of a learning event, we ask the question: 'Who is interested in the information collected?' In response, the HRD function is primarily concerned with process information to analyse how they are doing. The customers of training (defined as anyone with a vested interest in the HRD function's activities, such as learners and their supervisors), however, usually pay more attention to outcome evaluation than to process evaluation (Blanchard and Thacker, 2013). The output of evaluation (process and outcome data) can, therefore, be viewed as important from three different perspectives: gauging the success of learning initiatives; assessing the design effectiveness of the associated activities; and judging the **return on investment (ROI)** from these interventions. The key participants in the HRD process will attach varying levels of importance to these three positions (Swart *et al.*, 2005). In the first case (gauging success), the persons attuned to this form of evaluation will most likely be the learners who took part in the actual process (and possibly their supervisors and colleagues). They will place an emphasis on identifying the degree of success at obtaining the learning objectives. The second position (effectiveness of design) would generally be aligned with the standpoint of the designers and facilitators of the intervention, plus the HRD function. Their focus will centre on taking action to improve the planning and delivery of the programme and to consider the results of the learning, rather than concentrating simply on activities (Garavan *et al.*, 2003). Moving onto the third evaluation position (ROI), those drawn to this would probably be the people who made the learning possible, that is, the decision makers at organizational level who secured the budgetary resources (Swart *et al.*, 2005).

CONSIDER THIS ...

Returning to the learning requirements of the previously mentioned car components company, when devising the evaluation process for the fork-lift driver lifting procedures course, the firm has to take into account the information needs of the various participants. It has to ascertain the appropriateness, or otherwise, of the learning objectives, pedagogical methods and facilitator approach utilized during the learning activity. Additionally, it has to determine the fork-lift drivers' opinion of the course and what additional knowledge and skills they acquired and applied in their jobs after undergoing the training. Identifying the number of car component breakages, particularly with regard to glass-based products, would also be beneficial. Would you have the same issues to consider if the fork-lift drivers worked in a warehouse in a large electrical and white-goods retailer?

EXPLORING THE MODELS OF EVALUATION (HOW)

How should a company manage the process of evaluating an HRD programme? There is no overall agreement to this question, with Anderson (2007) maintaining that a narrow solution to evaluation is unsuitable because firms should introduce bespoke solutions aligned to their own specific requirements. It has been suggested that there are two different philosophical approaches to conducting HRD evaluations (Pilbeam and Corbridge, 2010). Hierarchical models, focusing on levels of outcomes within an organization, can be distinguished from contextual models, incorporating a broader situational perspective on evaluation. By examining a company's HRD strategic plan, it is possible to identify what learning interventions should be assessed, at what levels, how they should be reviewed, and what evaluation models are applicable (Blanchard and Thacker, 2013) ▶ Chapter 2.

Hierarchical models

Hierarchical approaches are sometimes referred to as scientific/quantitative models, and rely on techniques that focus on objective measurement so that the costs

and benefits of any learning activity can be measured, thereby calculating a ROI (Pilbeam and Corbridge, 2010). Such frameworks assess the economic benefits of learning (Phillips, 2011), which may include generating cost savings (e.g. decreasing unit costs), creating time savings (e.g. achieving enhanced order response rates), facilitating productive work habits (e.g. reducing absenteeism), developing the skills base of learners (e.g. resulting in fewer product defects) and improving the workplace climate (e.g. engendering greater job satisfaction).

The most popular approaches within hierarchical evaluation models are ones that emphasize levels of measurement, which outline the contributions that learning can make for the different constituents in an organization (Pilbeam and Corbridge, 2010). Such frameworks require that data be quantifiable and based on predetermined aims (Gunnigle *et al.*, 2011), and the evaluation process is constructed to meet those objectives (Bramley, 2003). These approaches envisage that, if each level is evaluated, it is possible to have a more complete understanding of the full effects of HRD interventions. For example, if participants enjoy the programme (level 1), they are likely to learn (level 2). If participants learn, they are predisposed to change their on-the-job performance and behaviour (level 3). If participants alter their work performance and behaviour, the learning is liable to have a business impact (levels 4 and 5). Every level necessitates a different evaluation strategy and is seen as a measure of the progressive transfer and application of learning content. As Table 10.1 indicates, numerous hierarchical models incorporating levels of measurement have been proposed. The most widely used hierarchical approach is the Kirkpatrick model, with the majority of frameworks incorporating his four levels of evaluation to a greater or lesser extent, either as explicit steps in the process or as information collected within these steps. Examples of companies using these models are found across the globe. A large retail chain in Latvia utilizes the Kirkpatrick model (Enkuzena and Kliedere, 2011); a major garment exporter draws upon the Phillips model to evaluate its management training initiatives (De Alwis and Rajaratne, 2011); and an executive coaching programme in South Africa was assessed with Brinkerhoff's model (Beets and Goodman, 2012).

Difficulties have been identified with this category of models (Werner and DeSimone, 2012; Blanchard and Thacker, 2013). For example, research suggests that there is a poor relationship between positive reaction-level assessments, learning, changes in job

Table 10.1 Summary of key hierarchical evaluation models

Model	Description	Comments
Kirkpatrick's (1959, 1979, 2007)	Proposes evaluation along a hierarchy of learning outcomes:	
Four-Level Model	Level 1 (reactions) – the response of learners to the content and methods of the intervention is elicited.	This measures the satisfaction of the participants with the learning context, programme structure, content and methods, facilitator style, and assessment type. It constitutes a formative evaluation.
	Level 2 (learning) – the actual learning of participants achieved during a programme is measured and an assessment is made regarding how well they have advanced in their level of knowledge and skills.	This level examines the knowledge and skill progression of participants arising from the intervention. The overall degree of learning can be shaped by a number of factors, such as participant motivation, prior learning experiences, learning design, learning delivery, and perceived relevance of the material. It constitutes a formative evaluation.
	Level 3 (behaviour, also known as transfer of learning) – the effect of the event on the performance and behaviour of the learner on his/her return to the workplace is measured.	The transfer level assesses how well learning is employed in the workplace. The scale of transfer may be increased by improving the connection between the learning context and the performance context, in addition to enhancing workplace support. This level constitutes a summative evaluation.
	Level 4 (results) – the impact of the learning on the business is examined.	The results level gauges the consequence of learning on organizational metrics, such as productivity and profitability. This level constitutes a summative evaluation.
Hamblin's (1974) Five-Level Evaluation Framework	Bears some similarities to Kirkpatrick's model, but places greater emphasis on the higher levels of the hierarchy with a keener focus on results:	
	Level 1 – reaction level measures employee opinions regarding the nature of the learning initiative.	It explores the usefulness of the learning, plus participant perceptions in relation to the content of the programme and the approach of the facilitator.
	Level 2 – learning level measures what knowledge and skills the participants have acquired.	The emphasis is on KSA acquisition.
	Level 3 – job behaviour level measures the outcome of the learning event on the performance and behaviour of the participants in the workplace.	It seeks to establish the level of learning transfer.
	Level 4 – organization level measures the effect of learning on company metrics.	It assesses how changes in job performance and behaviour have influenced the functioning of the organization.
	Level 5 – ultimate value measures how the company has benefited as a totality from the learning intervention.	This is analysed in terms of organizational ratios, such as growth, profitability and productivity.
Phillips' (1991, 1997, 2011) ROI Model	Incorporates a fifth level of ROI to Kirkpatrick's four-level model by measuring the monetary value of the results and costs of a learning programme. The five levels are called reaction and planned action, learning, applied learning on the job, business results and ROI.	Establishing the ROI of learning justifies current and future budget spends, facilitates the tracking of costs, increases the prediction of revenue based on improved service and product selection, and enhances the organization's understanding of corporate measures (e.g. number of accidents, turnover and absenteeism).

Model	Description	Comments
Brinkerhoff's (1987) Six-Stage Model	Explores how a learning programme can be modified to become more successful; thus, it differs in focus from the previous three frameworks by suggesting a cycle of six overlapping steps, appreciating that difficulties identified in a particular phase are possibly caused by occurrences in a previous stage. This six-stage model is also known as the Success Case Method (SCM):	The earlier stages of the systematic HRD cycle (needs assessment, design and delivery) are explicitly incorporated into this approach, thereby assisting HRD professionals to recognize that evaluation is an ongoing activity, not just an endeavour that is carried out post-implementation.
	Step 1 – goal setting to determine what is the need.	
	Step 2 – programme design to establish what will work to meet this need.	
	Step 3 – programme implementation to identify whether the design is appropriate.	
	Step 4 – immediate outcomes to ascertain whether the participants learned.	
	Step 5 – intermediate or usage outcomes to discover whether the participants are using what they have learned.	
	Step 6 – impacts and worth to find out whether the programme made a useful contribution to the organization.	

Based on ideas presented by Garavan *et al.* (2003), Martin *et al.* (2010), McGuire and Mølbjerg Jørgensen (2011), Marchington and Wilkinson (2012) and Werner and DeSimone (2012).

performance/behaviour, and the application of learning to the workplace (Devins and Smith, 2013). Studies have identified some linkages (for example, Alliger *et al.*, 1997; Colquitt *et al.*, 2000; Liebermann and Hoffmann, 2008) demonstrating that reactions affect learning outcomes, and learning outcomes influence transfer to the job. Few investigations, however, have attempted to link these transmission effects to organizational metrics due to the difficulty of factoring out other variables, particularly external elements, related to these outcomes (Blanchard and Thacker, 2013).

Contextual models

The limited scope of hierarchical models has led to the development of another group of frameworks – contextual perspectives – that adopt a more expansive approach to evaluation. They emphasize the enhancement of learning processes, in contrast to simply focusing on validating the worth of learning programmes. Contextual models include tangible and intangible benefits, such as learner expectation, and corporate culture and values, so that the long-term consequences of learning can be assessed.

Models that adopt a contextual philosophical approach take into account the situation in which a company operates. Systems theory refers to the way in which organized collectives respond in an adaptive manner to cope with transformation in their external environments to ensure that their basic structures remain intact. It offers HRD practitioners a contextual evaluation framework. For example, such models have been used by Korean companies when evaluating web-based and classroom-based management training programmes (Kong and Jacobs, 2012). The CIRO model, developed by Warr *et al.* (1970), explores four aspects of learning evaluation – context, inputs, reactions and outputs:

- Context analyses factors such as the identification of needs and objective setting in relation to the company's culture, thereby positioning the programme within a broader setting. It involves deciding whether a particular issue has a learning solution, rather than, for example, relating to a resource constraint.

- Input examines the design and delivery of the activity and how individual interventions are framed. It can occur during the actual event, or following the completion of the initiative.
- Reaction explores the process of collating and reviewing the feedback received with regard to the learning experience. The participants' responses to the learning event are central to this element.
- Output gauges outcomes along three dimensions (immediate post-intervention modifications, learning transfer to the workplace, and impact on departmental and organizational performance). It assesses the extent to which the planned objectives were achieved.

A systems-oriented framework to evaluation is also advocated by Easterby-Smith (1986, 1994), who suggests considering the following issues:

return on expectations the extent to which stakeholder expectations have been met by the HRD programme, while simultaneously assessing the associated potential monetary value of those expectations

- Context assesses the features surrounding the learning intervention, such as organizational culture, values, the provision of appropriate support, and the availability of technology.
- Administration considers how the event is promoted and communicated to potential participants. It reviews pre-programme instructions, location of the course and expectations conveyed to learners.
- Input investigates the various components of the initiative, such as learning techniques to be used, topics to be covered and layout of the classroom.
- Process studies the content of the programme and the mechanisms by which the syllabus is delivered. It focuses on how learning is structured and the experiences of the participants.
- Output examines the developments that occur as a result of the HRD activity. At the individual level this centres on KSA change, and at the organizational level it explores corporate metrics.

Anderson (2007) maintains that the traditional hierarchical models of evaluation concentrate on the reactions and consequences for learners and facilitators resulting from discrete and individual interventions. She argues for a strategic perspective stressing the aggregate value contribution made by a more diverse range of learning processes and stakeholders. This stance has been termed a responsive approach to evaluation, that is, it considers how the intervention is perceived by various concerned parties (Bramley, 2003). Designed

in conjunction with the Chartered Institute of Personnel and Development (CIPD), the Partnership Model of Learning (Anderson, 2007) highlights the interconnections and responsibilities of the learner, the learner's supervisor, senior management and the HRD function. The model is concerned with ensuring that learning and organizational strategies are aligned, and it views the purpose of evaluation as establishing this strategic integration. Internal factors (learning and ROI) and external elements (benchmarking and capacity indicators, that is, corporate metrics) are included in the evaluation process. This framework also recognizes the subjective nature of evaluation by considering **return on expectations**. The Partnership Model of Learning concentrates on four main areas of evaluation:

- Learning function emphasizes the efficiency and effectiveness of the HRD function. It assesses how the learning intervention is provided and the competence of the personnel within the function.
- Return on expectations (ROE) explores the anticipated benefits of the programme and whether these have been achieved. It identifies what progress, if any, has occurred as a result of the programme.
- ROI examines the benefits arising from the initiative relative to the costs incurred over a specific timeframe. It analyses how learning is contributing to the attainment of key performance targets.
- Benchmark and capacity indicators compare the learning activity with a set of internal and external standards. This enables a company to gauge its performance against established in-house and industry norms, thus promoting a climate of continuous improvement.

EXAMINING MEASURES OF EVALUATION (HOW)

Regardless of the model employed for evaluation, the difficulty for most organizations lies in identifying a set of tools that can facilitate the effective evaluation of learning interventions. The methods used must accurately and fairly measure what they are intended to measure (be valid), in addition to exhibiting preciseness in measurement over time (being reliable).

It is possible for a company to draw upon two different types of measurement approaches:

o **Quantitative methodologies:** investigations of phenomena that can be counted and enumerated using statistical, mathematical or computational techniques provide an account of the 'what' of the learning (e.g. the number of people involved and the size of the learning investment). This form of evaluation data is gathered by calculating outcomes and by scoring behaviours on predetermined scales (Swart *et al.*, 2005).

o **Qualitative methodologies:** exploration of phenomena based on individual interpretation and meaning using interviewing and observational techniques offers a sense of how a programme functions and the implications that this may generate for all the parties involved. It is related to how people 'feel' and how they have 'experienced' the process. This form of evaluation data is accessed by asking people questions that allow them to express their opinions, or by monitoring their behaviour (Swart *et al.*, 2005).

Quantitative and qualitative information can be collected through the deployment of a varied array of measurement instruments. These devices can be employed with both hierarchical and contextual models of evaluation.

Measures for hierarchical models

The measurement tools that can be drawn upon to gauge outcomes at the various levels of the Kirkpatrick, Hamblin, Phillips and Brinkerhoff frameworks are outlined in Table 10.2. The decision relating to what method to adopt should be made during the early stages of the systematic HRD cycle because many of the mechanisms require a baseline of current performance against which to assess the impact of the intervention (a 'before and after' comparison). The measurement approach to be used, therefore, should be selected prior to the commencement of a learning intervention, ideally at the design phase of the cycle.

Level 1

Instruments at the first level of an evaluation hierarchy (reactions) measure whether learners perceive that a particular initiative was of benefit to them as individuals. They investigate the view of the participants regarding the value and relevance of the learning, their enjoyment of the endeavour, the competence levels of the facilitators, and their

satisfaction ratings of the content, structure and delivery of the activity. Opinions may also be sought about the facilities, including location, transport arrangements, room size and layout, technological supports, and catering services. Gathering information about the participant's reactions to the learning event is usually achieved by using a quantitative technique like a questionnaire (Garavan *et al.*, 2003; Swart *et al.*, 2005; Marchington and Wilkinson, 2012); however, other qualitative media, such as interviews and group discussions, are equally valid.

There are two types of reactions-level questionnaires available at stage one of an evaluation hierarchy – affective and utility (Blanchard and Thacker, 2013). An affective questionnaire assesses feelings about the learning programme (e.g. 'I found this training enjoyable'), whereas a utility questionnaire appraises beliefs about the relevance of the intervention (e.g. 'This training was beneficial for me'). The following steps have been suggested when compiling either an affective or utility reactions-level questionnaire (Blanchard and Thacker, 2013):

● Determine what issues need to be measured.
● Develop a written set of questions to obtain the information.
● Construct a scale to quantify the participants' answers.
● Make the survey anonymous so that learners feel free to respond honestly.

Table 10.2 Summary of hierarchical measures of evaluation

Level	Measures
Level 1 (reactions)	Questionnaires, feedback sheets (sometimes called happy sheets, smile sheets or reactionnaires), oral discussions, surveys, interviews and checklists
Level 2 (learning)	Before and after tests, examinations, portfolios, projects, learning logs and simulations
Level 3 (behaviour)	Interviews, observation, critical incident techniques, pre- and post-programme testing, reflective journals, performance appraisals and attitude surveys
Level 4 (results)	General workplace metrics (e.g. profits and turnover) and specific workplace indicators (e.g. levels of absenteeism and accidents)
Level 5 (ROI)	Cost benefit analysis techniques

Based on ideas presented by Garavan *et al.* (2003), Gunnigle *et al.* (2011), Marchington and Wilkinson (2012), Martin *et al.* (2010), McGuire and Mølbjerg Jørgensen (2011) and Phillips and Gully (2014).

- Ask for details that might be useful in ascertaining differences in reactions by subgroup, such as age, gender, occupation and grade.
- Provide space for additional comments to allow learners the opportunity to mention topics that the questionnaire designer may not have considered.
- Decide the most appropriate time to distribute the survey to collect the information required.
  - If the questionnaire is handed out immediately after the learning event, it is good practice to ask someone other than the facilitator to administer and collate the information.
  - If handed out some time later, it is recommended that a mechanism to promote a high response rate be incorporated (e.g. encourage the learner's supervisor to allow him/her to complete the questionnaire on company time).

Level 2

At this level, measurement tools are employed to determine the degree of learning achieved and to assess the design of the programme to identify whether it accomplished the objectives set (Garavan *et al.*, 2003).

BUILDING YOUR SKILLS

The design of a reactions-level questionnaire is not an easy task. It requires that you carefully consider what data you want to collect, the content and wording of the questions, the use of appropriate types of questions, and the format and layout of the survey. As the HRD manager of our fictitious international car components company, devise a questionnaire to establish the views of the warehouse fork-lift drivers after they have completed a course on the correct loading/unloading procedures. Consider what questions you would pose about the structure and content of the programme, in addition to inquiring about the delivery methods and techniques utilized by the facilitator. Figure 10.2 may assist your deliberations, as it outlines a generic format for a post-programme reactions-level questionnaire.

Figure 10.2 Example of a reactions-level post-programme questionnaire

We would be grateful if you would complete this questionnaire to help us improve the learning event that you have just attended. Your honest and constructive comments will enable us to build an improved programme for future participants.

Please indicate how you would rate the following elements of the programme:

	Excellent	Good	Average	Poor	Comments
Topic 1					
Topic 2					
Topic 3					
Topic 4					
Usefulness of overall content					
Structure of programme					
Length of programme					
Standard of slides and handouts					
Timing of programme					
Suitability of venue					

(continued)

Figure 10.2 *continued*

Please indicate how you would rate the programme facilitator:

	Excellent	Good	Average	Poor	Comments
Knowledge of subject					
Presentation skills					
Dealing with questions					
Controlling the programme					
Interpersonal skills					
Enthusiasm					
Support provided					

Did you find the programme of benefit to you?   Yes ☐ No ☐

Please elaborate on your response:

_____

_____

_____

Could you please indicate the learning points from the programme that you are most likely to apply in your work:

_____

_____

_____

_____

_____

Please use the space provided to indicate if you have any suggestions that could be incorporated into future programmes (e.g. expanding, omitting and/or adding topics):

_____

_____

_____

_____

Please use the space provided to include additional comments that you would like to make on any aspect of the programme:

_____

_____

_____

_____

_____

(continued)

Figure 10.2 *continued*

Signed (optional): _____

Department: _____

Name of programme: _____

Facilitator: _____

Date: _____

This entails utilizing methods that gauge the acquisition of before and after knowledge and skills. The learning objectives that were developed in the design phase specify the outcomes that will signify whether the learning has been successful; thus, the appropriate measurement instruments were determined during the identification of HRD needs ▶ Chapter 7. Evaluation at the learning level should appraise the same things in the same way as in the LNA. The needs analysis is, therefore, the 'pre-test'. A similar analysis at the conclusion of the programme will indicate the 'gain' in learning.

transfer of learning occurs when learning in one situation impacts on a related performance in another context

The devices available for pre- and post-testing of learning are participant self-assessment (e.g. learning logs), written tests (e.g. examinations), practical tests (e.g. simulations) and questionnaires. Mechanisms applied at this stage should demonstrate that the achievement of the new knowledge and skills is directly linked to the learning experience. Bramley (2003) recommends that a learner's knowledge of facts can be gauged with objective tests (e.g. requesting the participant to select the correct alternative from a number offered). To determine a person's knowledge of procedures, open-ended, short-answer questions can be posed, and to ascertain their ability to analyse situations it is recommended that open-ended, free expression questions are asked (e.g. identifying his/her decision-making process). Skills are generally evaluated by means of practical tests in which either the learner is set a task and the finished product is graded at the end of the programme, or the learner's performance is reviewed throughout the activity so that the methods deployed can be appraised. Such tests could entail establishing the learner's ability to conduct simple procedures (usually with the aid of notes and instructions), to perform proficient actions (often requiring considerable practice), or to judge whether a piece of accomplished work is of acceptable quality.

Level 3

Measurement at this level (behaviour) is concerned with identifying the degree of improvement in the learner's performance and behaviour on the job as a result of the intervention. This process is called transfer of learning, a phenomenon that we explore in greater detail later in the chapter (see section on 'Enabling a Culture of Effective Evaluation'). According to Garavan *et al.* (2003), the aim of evaluation at this stage (level 3) is to:

- Examine the analysed learning needs to ascertain whether these were accurate in their assessment of what was required to augment the individual's performance and behaviour
- Review the effectiveness of a particular learning event and the methods used, taking account of the passage of time, which should assist the participant to make an objective appraisal
- Explore how successful the jobholder has been in applying what he/she learned to the workplace
- Determine whether the learning has had an impact on overall organizational goals

The tools used should provide the learner with an opportunity to reflect on the completed programme and ascertain how he/she intends to utilize the learning in his/her employment situation. This entails gauging the learner's attitude, their feelings, values, beliefs and opinions that support or inhibit behaviour, and, consequently, influence motivation towards incorporating newly acquired knowledge and skills into normal work routines ▶ Chapter 4. Interviews, questionnaires, observation, performance records, performance appraisals, reflective diaries and attitude surveys can all be relied upon to evaluate this transfer. The relevant method can be administered when the learner returns to the workplace and at agreed periodic timeframes thereafter. The time lag for assessing application of learning depends on the learning objectives. It is suggested that the more complex the objective(s), the longer the interval should be between the cessation of the intervention and the behaviour-level assessment (Blanchard and Thacker, 2013).

Level 4

At the fourth level of an evaluation hierarchy (results) the focus shifts from post-programme consequences to the effect of the HRD process on the firm as a whole. Examining the impact of a learning programme on corporate effectiveness can be conducted using a variety of performance indices, such as productivity, cost savings and timeliness. The interconnections between organizational outcomes, job performance and behaviour, and the learner's KSA should be clearly articulated in the LNA ▶Chapter 7. This creates a causal relationship specifying that if certain KSAs are developed, and learners employ them on the job, then particular corporate metrics will occur. Tracking performance indices over time allows a company to assess whether the learning produced the desired changes to organizational outcomes. Examples include analysing customer complaint records, customer retention rates, accident statistics, absenteeism percentages and staff attrition quotients.

Level 5

The final level is focused on ascertaining a ROI. This tool assists HRD professionals and management to identify whether learning programmes are beneficial to the organization by calculating the financial return on the firm's investment. ROI is calculated as the ratio of money gained or lost on a venture relative to the amount of money expended. According to Phillips and Gully (2014), the basic definition of a percentage ROI is:

$$\text{ROI (\%)} = \frac{\text{Learning Benefits} - \text{Learning Costs}}{\text{Learning Costs}} \times 100$$

A positive ROI indicates that the benefits outweigh the costs; thus, the intervention should be continued (although further enhancement may also be possible). A negative ROI means that costs outweigh benefits and suggests that the undertaking should be changed or discontinued unless additional advantages exist that have not been considered (e.g. heightened employee morale). Translating learning initiatives into monetary terms indicates that such events are investments and will generate future gains (Werner and DeSimone, 2012). Engaging in ROI analysis can also improve the image of the HRD function by demonstrating that its activities make a financial contribution to corporate effectiveness. Additionally, it can confirm that the HRD function operates on a value-for-money basis, and its staff possess budgetary management skills and cost containment abilities (Blanchard and Thacker, 2013).

Bringing Evaluation into Play in the Field of Football

Sir Alex Ferguson's 26-year reign as manager of Manchester United Football Club came to an end on Sunday 19 May 2013, with a dramatic 5:5 draw against West Bromwich Albion. This thrilling match, culminating in United being crowned the 2012/2013 English Premier League champions, epitomized Ferguson's tenure. Glowing accolades were penned about this man's career following his retirement. Legends from the football community past and present, music celebrities, Hollywood actors and even prime ministers added their voices to an extensive roll of honour. But how would HRD professionals assess Ferguson's time as the man responsible for ensuring that soccer training sessions resulted in ongoing on-field success, and, ultimately, soaring shareholder value? Using the hierarchical models of HRD evaluation, we can analyse both his and the Manchester United team's accomplishments.

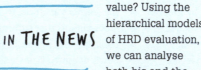 HRD IN THE NEWS

At the reactions level, tributes were offered by a variety of prominent personalities from all walks of life about Sir Alex's spectacular record. According to Richard Scudamore (English Premier League chief executive), 'No one's made as great a contribution to the Premier League.' A contemporary peer, André Villas-Boas (football manager), referred to Ferguson as 'The finest manager in world football', a sentiment echoed by another managerial colleague, Roy Hodgson, who noted that 'No one will be able to match his achievements.'

When examining the learning level, attention needs to be paid to the skills development (technical and tactical nous), winning mentality, work ethic and team spirit that Ferguson instilled in his players through his unique style of coaching. Continuing the tradition of promoting juvenile talent, and providing gifted young players with opportunities to prove themselves, Ferguson motivated his team. This professionalism is exemplified by Ryan Giggs, who joined United's Academy as a teenage soccer prodigy and worked his way through the ranks. Making his senior debut for the club in March 1991, he was subsequently appointed player-coach by Sir Alex's initial successor, David Moyes, in June 2013. Less than one year later, in April 2014, he was promoted by the club to the position of interim manager upon Moyes' departure.

Turning to the next stage of the evaluation hierarchy, the behaviour level, this was epitomized by the action that Ferguson took when his team were runners-up in the 2011/2012 English Premier League. Losing the title in the last minute of the season on goal difference to their derby rivals, Manchester City, prompted him to buy the league's leading goal scorer, Robin van Persie (RVP). Commenting on the importance of van Persie's goals in the following campaign's triumph, which resulted in Ferguson's final championship success, David Moyes declared that 'Probably what won the league were the goal scorers, Robin especially.'

The results level is typified by the number of national, European and international trophies adorning the cabinet room at Manchester United Football Club during Ferguson's term. He won 13 Premier League titles, five FA Cups, four League Cups, two Champions Leagues, one Cup Winners Cup, one FIFA Club World Cup, one UEFA Super Cup, one Inter-Continental Cup and ten FA Charity/Community Shields. Being a serial title winner was enabled by the stability, consistency and cohesiveness of Ferguson's reign, engendering a high-performance culture of success at the club. The adverse impact of a climate of instability was obvious in the season following Ferguson's departure, when his immediate replacement, David Moyes, presided over a turbulent, unpredictable and divisive campaign in 2013/2014.

When considering the final level, ROI, Manchester United is one of the wealthiest and most widely supported soccer clubs in the world. After being floated on the London Stock Exchange in 1991, the club was purchased by Malcolm Glazer (chief executive of First Allied Corporation) in May 2005 in a deal pricing the company at almost £800 million. In August 2012 Manchester United made an initial public offering on the New York Stock Exchange. Eight months later, in January 2013, United became the first sports team in the world to be worth $3 billion. *Forbes Magazine* valued the club at $3.3 billion – $1.2 billion higher than the next most valuable sports team (the Dallas Cowboys American football team).

Sources

http://www.bbc.co.uk/sport/0/football/22505640

http://www.bbc.co.uk/sport/0/football/23177876

http://www.bbc.com/sport/0/football/27114788

http://en.wikipedia.org/wiki/Manchester_United_F.C.

Northcroft, J. (2013) 'I've Given Them the Hairdryer', *Sunday Times Sport Supplement*, 14 July: 11.

Questions

1 Apply the Phillips five-level ROI hierarchical evaluation model (reactions, learning, behaviour, results, ROI) to any pursuit that you are interested in.
2 Describe each level of this framework as it relates to your chosen activity.
3 Illustrate the measurement tools that you could use for each of the five levels in this framework.

Measures for contextual models

The difficulty with measuring at levels four and five on a hierarchical model has been recognized by numerous authors (for example, Martin *et al.*, 2010; Armstrong, 2014). This is because individual, team, departmental and/or firm performance occurs within a wide-ranging environment of which learning forms only one part. For example, a low rate of staff turnover may be indicative of high levels of unemployment, a factor external to the circumstances of the company, rather than being connected to any internal activities, such as learning programmes. Consequently, many organizations, particularly SMEs, confine their measurement activities to the lower levels of the hierarchical models of evaluation. The CIPD (2013) Learning and Talent Development Survey found that, of their 880 respondents, more than half use the Kirkpatrick model, or limited stages of it, at least some of the time, although fewer than a fifth employ the full model always or frequently. The incidence of deployment is contingent upon the size of the organization, with 56 per cent of companies employing fewer than 1,000 employees never drawing upon the full model compared with 34 per cent of those with more than 1,000 employees. A quarter report that they use limited stages of this model frequently or always, mainly at the reaction level (21 per cent of those with fewer than 1,000 employees, in contrast to 34 per cent of those with more than 1,000 employees). A minority of respondents (14 per cent) always or frequently utilize a contextual system to collate HRD metrics, with over half (55 per cent) of firms employing fewer than 1,000 staff never availing themselves of such a framework.

There has been a move towards the use of overall measurement tools that are aligned to contextual models of evaluation, which explore mechanisms to improve corporate performance. Questionnaires, interviews and observational techniques are also pertinent to contextual models. Unlike the hierarchical tradition, however, contextual frameworks adopt an integrated perspective on learning. For example, Warr *et al.*'s (1970) CIRO model scrutinizes the manner in which needs are identified, learning objectives are devised, and the way that objectives link to, and support, pre-planned competences and competencies. Additionally, it considers how these components reflect the culture and structure of the company. This type of evaluation confirms (or refutes) the need for capacity building, i.e. whether those involved in a learning initiative require further strengthening of their skills, competencies and abilities. For example, Fuchs, a global organization based in Germany producing and distributing lubricants, takes account of HRD metrics when evaluating its social sustainability ▶ Chapter 14. The company sets human resource-related measurement tools, called key performance indicators (KPIs), and reports on their achievement in their annual accounts. It has increased the average number of further education hours per employee continuously since 2010. In 2010 each staff member attended an average of nine hours of further education, but by 201, this had risen to 17 hours (Fuchs, 2013).

The CIPD Partnership Model of Learning (Anderson, 2007) mentioned previously incorporates the perspective of all stakeholders in the development of metrics that typify the distinctive characteristics of the company. This measurement approach advocates:
- Taking stock of the extent to which learning activities are aligned with the firm's strategic priorities
- Reviewing the evaluation and reporting mechanisms that are currently used

- Ascertaining the most appropriate and timely methods to assess the significance of learning for the organization under four categories of measurement – learning function, ROI, ROE, and benchmark and capacity indicators

The Partnership Model considers the use of scorecard techniques to quantify the value of learning. An example of such a benchmark tool is the stakeholder scorecard (Nickols, 2005), a methodology that contends that the sustained success of a firm is a function of the extent to which the needs of its different stakeholders are balanced, without sacrificing any one to the others. With regard to an HRD intervention, Nickols (2005) maintains that there are four key stakeholders (senior management, learners, facilitators and the learner's supervisor). The steps involved in preparing a stakeholder scorecard are to:
- Identify the stakeholder groups
- Determine the contributions received from, and the inducements provided to, each stakeholder group
- Prioritize the contributions from the perspective of the organization, and prioritize the inducements from the standpoint of the stakeholders
- Establish measures of the contributions and inducements
- Apply the measures

Employing this approach to an HRD evaluation indicates that stakeholders attach different values to the various aspects of learning evaluation; therefore, a ROI approach, which is the key focus of the hierarchical models, may not satisfy all constituents equally. Consequently, it is argued that a contextual perspective to measurement is more relevant (Anderson, 2007). We will now examine how to take into account the needs of the key participants in the learning process when conducting an HRD evaluation.

ENABLING A CULTURE OF EFFECTIVE EVALUATION (HOW)

Learning evaluation provides information that is critical to the successful operation of an organization. It is, however, often conceived of as a weak link in the systematic HRD cycle. According to Gibb (2002: 107), 'it is the step most likely to be neglected or underdone'. Lack of an assessment procedure, or an inappropriate approach to appraisal, can result in learning that is wasteful of financial and human resources, and, furthermore, generate inadequate data for executive decision making. To enable learning interventions to enhance organizational functioning, it is recommended that companies create a culture of effective evaluation by:

- Appreciating that organizational blockages exist and the major stakeholders in the HRD process may inadvertently augment these barriers and inhibit the application of learning to the workplace
- Developing a climate of collaboration so that the principal stakeholders work in partnership and adopt a coherent approach to surmount any potential difficulties regarding learning transfer

Appreciate the existence of organizational blockages

Organizations should recognize that conducting an evaluation can be a challenging exercise. Numerous reasons for not adequately assessing learning interventions have been identified. It has been argued that many of the shortcomings associated with measurement difficulties can be traced to the main HRD stakeholders. As previously noted, evaluation can be conceived from three different stakeholder perspectives. Table 10.3 provides a summary of the possible barriers that impinge on creating an appropriate corporate culture for effective evaluation. It explores these potential organizational blockages from the perspective of the main stakeholders in the HRD domain.

When examining the consequences of not conducting a systematic appraisal of the HRD process from each of these points of view, Garavan *et al.* (2003) note that the:

- Learner reaction, plus their development and progress, is not recorded
- Facilitator performance is not measured
- Learning event efficiency and effectiveness are not assessed
- Changes in KSA levels are not linked to the learning intervention
- Transfer of learning to the work environment is not quantified
- Organization is unable to carry out a cost–benefit analysis

Considering evaluation from the standpoint of the key personnel involved in the HRD process (learners, facilitators, HRD professionals, supervisors and colleagues, and decision makers) helps us to understand where potential blockages may occur and how they may be surmounted. This assists the firm to formulate and implement learning initiatives that support individual, team, departmental and organizational effectiveness, including learning transfer.

Develop transfer of learning among key stakeholders

The importance of building a partnership approach between the main stakeholders in the HRD process has been recognized by many commentators (for example, Anderson, 2007; Harrison, 2009; McGuire and Mølbjerg Jørgensen, 2011). This involves assessing what the company's business priorities are and how the principal constituents involved in learning can contribute to meeting these objectives (top-down approach to strategic HRD) ▶ Chapter 2. It also necessitates facilitating learners to manage the move from being in an education environment, obtaining new knowledge and skills, to performing the job on an enhanced basis in the workplace (bottom-up approach to strategic HRD) ▶ Chapter 2.

This transition is called learning transfer, and it entails the application of the KSA gained from the learning event to the job, and subsequent maintenance of them over a defined period of time. Garavan *et al.* (2003) distinguish between two types of learning transfer. Specific or pure transfer happens when newly acquired skills practised during the learning event are carried out in precisely the same manner in the work setting, such as operating proprietary software packages customized to the company's requirements; while generalizable transfer occurs when the participant learns in a classroom situation to execute tasks in ways that are similar, but not identical, to the sequence in which they are performed in the workplace, such as using off-the-shelf software packages. Brinkerhoff (1987) maintains that learning events alone typically result in only 15 to 20 per cent of learning being applied to on-the-job performance and behaviour. According to Baldwin and Ford (1988), the factors affecting the successful application of learning to the workplace can be divided into three categories: learner characteristics (personality, ability and motivation effects); programme issues (pedagogical principles of design, content, structure, sequencing and delivery); and work environment features (organizational supports, continuous learning culture and task constraints). Figure 10.3 graphically depicts the alignment of these activities carried out by the actors in the HRD sphere with the firm's strategic objectives.

Table 10.3 Summary of potential organizational blockages to evaluation from perspective of key stakeholders

Stakeholder	Examples	Author(s)
Learners	Learners may exhibit a lack of motivation, which could delimit the success of the programme and the transmission of learning to the workplace.	McGuire and Mølbjerg Jørgensen (2011)
Facilitators	If the objectives of the learning intervention have not been defined, it will be difficult to measure what has actually been achieved (example also relates to HRD professionals).	Armstrong (2014) Martin *et al.* (2010)
	It can be challenging to establish a direct link between the learning and the associated results because there are many other factors that may impinge on improvement (example also relates to HRD professionals).	Martin *et al.* (2010)
HRD professionals	HRD practitioners may possess incomplete knowledge, skills and expertise to conduct an evaluation.	Armstrong (2014) McGuire and Mølbjerg Jørgensen (2011)
	They may not consider their work within the context of corporate learning, performance and change.	McGuire and Mølbjerg Jørgensen (2011)
	The HRD function may be reluctant to receive feedback that could potentially lead to budgetary cuts and programme restrictions, particularly if the review reveals that the initiative has had limited impact (example also relates to facilitators).	Armstrong (2014) Werner and DeSimone (2012)
	Constrained HRD funding may mean that resources are devoted to learning provision rather than evaluation (example also relates to organizational decision makers).	Armstrong (2014)
Supervisor and colleagues	An absence of appropriate support mechanisms for the learner may occur, such as a dearth of practice opportunities, and a lack of constructive feedback.	Garavan *et al.* (2003) McGuire and Mølbjerg Jørgensen (2011)
Organizational decision makers	Senior management may not request information on the effect of the learning that was delivered.	Armstrong (2014)
	Costs may outweigh benefits, particularly as considerable resources are expended to assess learning thoroughly, so any outlay has to be balanced against what is learned from the analysis.	Martin *et al.* (2010)
	Gains from learning are often intangible and materialize gradually, particularly with developmental activities, because such skills are built over a protracted period of time and may not become immediately apparent on completion of the original activity.	Martin *et al.* (2010)

Based on ideas presented by Garavan *et al.* (2003), Martin *et al.* (2010), McGuire and Mølbjerg Jørgensen (2011), Werner and DeSimone (2012) and Armstrong (2014).

For evaluation to make a significant contribution to improving the quality of learning and positively impact on firm performance, it should be supported by an appropriate corporate culture (Harrison, 2009). An important foundation stone is usually an organizational learning strategy, which articulates core values and policies ▶ Chapter 2. At the heart of such an ethos the key partners take joint ownership for learning, work in collaboration to identify learning needs, ensure that the most suitable learning solution is provided,

and promote the application of relevant KSA to the workplace. This entails developing strategies to facilitate learning transfer, including the following (Garavan *et al.*, 2003; McGuire and Mølbjerg Jørgensen, 2011):

- Involvement of the learner, supervisor and colleagues, HRD function, and facilitator in the four stages of the HRD cycle
- Provision of information detailing the benefits of the learning and the rationale for attending the programme prior to commencement of the intervention

Figure 10.3 Aligning strategic objectives and HRD activities among collaborative constituents

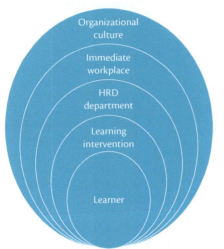

Organizational culture

Immediate workplace

HRD department

Learning intervention

Learner

- Use of relapse prevention strategies that reinforce learning outcomes and minimize skill erosion, such as learner log books, reflective journals, support groups and refresher sessions
- Access to appropriate resources (equipment, facilities, money, time) before, during and after the learning endeavour

When a firm is designing, implementing and reviewing its HRD evaluation process with a view to facilitating transfer of learning, it needs to recognize the factors that are relevant to its specific set of circumstances. This entails developing a strategic perspective to reinforce learning transfer by integrating the evaluation of learning programmes with the company's HRD strategy, which, in turn, is linked to the overall business strategy.

- Utilization of appropriate evaluation models and measurement tools before, during and after the learning initiative
- Similarity between the learning and performance contexts to assist effective application, as a positive correlation has been found between these two areas
- Opportunities for learners to practise their skills in a safe, constructive environment, both during the event and on return to the workplace
- Emphasis on colleagues attending learning events on a group basis, rather than as individuals, as peers can provide post-programme assistance, and even be considered potential coaches
- Focus on devising realistic action plans on completion of a learning activity, which can then be monitored and reviewed on an ongoing, periodic basis in the work environment
- Encouragement offered, particularly from supervisors, to learners on return to the work setting

BUILDING YOUR SKILLS

For most organizations, assisting the transfer of learning does not mean introducing new processes, but usually requires combining current HRD policies, procedures and practices. As the HRD manager of our fictitious international car components company, consider the issue of learning transfer in relation to the warehouse fork-lift drivers participating in a loading/unloading procedures course. What actions should you take before, during and after the training to ensure positive application from the programme to the workplace? Whom do you need to liaise with? What difficulties would you expect to encounter? How do you anticipate you will overcome these challenges?

Applying HRD Principles to the Cosmetics Industry: Case Study from Oriflame's Research and Development Subsidiary

The Oriflame Group is an international beauty company selling direct in more than 60 countries worldwide. Its portfolio of nature-inspired innovative beauty products 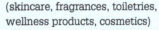 (skincare, fragrances, toiletries, wellness products, cosmetics) are marketed through a global sales force of 3.4 million independent consultants, who together create annual sales of €1.5 billion. Respect for people and nature underpins the company's philosophy, mission statement and operating principles, which, in turn, is reflected in its social and environmental policies. For example, Oriflame supports numerous national and international charities and is a co-founder of the World Childhood Foundation.

ACTIVE CASE STUDY

Having its origin in Sweden, Oriflame provides a global human resource management (HRM) service to its 7,500 employees, offering expertise in the areas of talent recruitment, people development and rewards. It also operates a HR Shared Service, with the subsidiaries in each country supported by centralized expertise in learning and development (L&D), compensation and benefits, and administration, delivered through in-country business partners.

All research and development (R&D) relating to Oriflame's products emanates from its Irish operation. This unit employs 165 professional staff in chemistry, biology and general business, with over one tenth educated to doctoral level (12 per cent), one fifth to Master's level (22 per cent) and more than half (53 per cent) to degree standard. To complement and supplement the company's product innovation, the R&D subsidiary devises, develops and implements pioneering HRM projects. These are initially formulated for Ireland, with successful programmes being adapted for global use in the Oriflame group. The foundation stone of these initiatives is the Capability Framework, which advises the company what capabilities staff should have (or aspire to have) to enable them to do an effective job. By defining these capabilities, Oriflame ensures that it recruits the right people, clarifies to employees what is expected of them, identifies any skills gaps and learning needs, generates individual learner plans, and assists internal career management and success planning.

Integral to Oriflame's Capability Framework is a commitment to continuous learning and improvement. This concept is embodied in the company's L&D Programme, which facilitates learning in its broadest sense, reinforces effectiveness and motivation through appropriate actions, and systematically develops knowledge, skills, technical competence and behavioural competencies of staff. It aims to promote an organizational culture that fosters leadership and staff profiles that are dynamic and aligned with the organization's values (togetherness, spirit, passion) and evolving needs. This is achieved by embedding L&D in five underlying principles:

1 Regarding learning as a strategic activity
2 Integrating learning with the short- and long-term needs of the organization
3 Aiming to develop the 'whole' employee
4 Providing equitable access to all employees
5 Evaluating learning effectiveness by its ability to satisfy organizational requirements

The areas of L&D considered a corporate priority are those that are:

- Mandatory to perform a function or a role within the organization, such as:
  ○ Safety training and/or safety awareness
  ○ Technical skills improvement programmes, including language training
  ○ Programmes to improve leadership skills, supervisory skills and the required managerial capabilities

- Necessary to ensure successful integration into Oriflame and/or the local area, such as:
  ○ Induction so that all employees have a common understanding of the corporate mission
  ○ Software training to enable personnel at all levels to effectively utilize the company's systems
  ○ Basic language and safety training

- Aimed at fostering mutual understanding within the organization, such as:
  ○ Core communication programmes
  ○ Actions to raise awareness of workplace diversity issues

Decisions relating to budget allocation are determined by balancing the subsidiary's business priorities, the individual needs of its employees, and the appropriateness and cost effectiveness of the learning. Learning interventions are the responsibility of both the functional departments and the HR department, with ultimate accountability contingent upon strategic and operational imperatives. Such interventions are provided through participation in internal formal programmes, external training programmes and/or other appropriate formal or informal actions. Learning is evaluated according to the four levels of Kirkpatrick's model and the feedback generated improves the four stages of the systematic HRD cycle (needs analysis, design, delivery, evaluation).

Questions

As the HR director of Oriflame's R&D operation in Ireland, consider your responses to the following questions that the global HR manager from Corporate Head Office has posed regarding the roll-out of the new L&D Programme to all the company's worldwide subsidiaries by:

1 Providing examples of the learning interventions that could be included in the:
a. Internal formal training programmes

   b. External training
      programmes
   c. Other appropriate formal or
      informal training actions

2 Explaining how the learning
   interventions could be
   assessed using Kirkpatrick's
   four-level model of evaluation

3 Considering how the L&D
   budget could be structured
   and allocated to satisfy
   Corporate Head Office and
   local subsidiary needs

SUMMARY

This chapter highlights the importance of evaluating HRD programmes, because evaluation can directly contribute to improving corporate effectiveness ▸Chapter 2. HRD professionals need to provide evidence to the organization of the benefits of their learning, training and development activities; thus, the HRD function has to consistently assess and measure its HRD programmes ▸Chapters 7, 8 and 9. The evaluation phase of the systematic HRD cycle should, therefore, prove worth and impact; control for quality and efficiency; and lead to improvements for future initiatives. To achieve these aims, HRD staff must understand the distinction between the two different philosophical perspectives on evaluation (hierarchical and contextual models) and apply appropriate measurement tools (such as reactions-level post-evaluation questionnaires, interviews, examinations, before and after tests, and calculations to gauge monetary return). It is also important that the organization creates a culture of effective evaluation by assisting the HRD stakeholders to collaborate and work in partnership to successfully transfer learning from the classroom situation to the workplace.

⟳ CHAPTER REVIEW QUESTIONS

1 Explain the purpose of evaluating HRD programmes, making specific reference to the benefits accruing to an organization from engaging in such an activity.
2 Compare and contrast hierarchical models of evaluation with contextual models of evaluation.
3 Describe the stages in Kirkpatrick's four-level model of evaluation.
4 Distinguish between the two key outputs from the evaluation process, that is, process data and outcome data, clearly outlining the stage in the HRD cycle when each output occurs.
5 Discuss any three evaluation measurement tools available to a company and provide an example of the learning intervention that each tool could evaluate.

6 Identify the basic definition of a percentage ROI formula and include examples of the potential benefits and costs that could be contained in this ratio.
7 Compare and contrast specific (pure) transfer of learning with generalizable transfer of learning.
8 List seven strategies that an organization could utilize to assist learning transfer.

📖 FURTHER READING

Hutchins, H. M., Burke, L. A. and Berthelsen, A. M. (2010) A Missing Link in the Transfer Problem? Examining How Trainers Learn about Training Transfer, *Human Resource Management*, 49(4), 599–618.

Kirkpatrick, D. L. and Kirkpatrick, J. D. (2006) *Evaluating Training Programs* (3rd ed.), San Francisco, CA: Berrett-Koehler Publishers.

Laker, D. R. and Powell, J. L. (2011) The Differences between Hard and Soft Skills and Their Relative Impact on Training Transfer, *Human Resource Development Quarterly*, 22(1), 111–122.

Phillips, J. J. (2011) *Handbook of Training Evaluation and Measurement Methods* (3rd ed.), Oxon: Routledge.

Saks, A. M. and Burke, L. A. (2012) An Investigation into the Relationship between Training Evaluation and the Transfer of Training, *International Journal of Training and Development*, 16(2), 118–127.

Tomé, E. (2009) The Evaluation of HRD: A Critical Study with Applications, *Journal of European Industrial Training*, 33(6), 513–538.

⟨www⟩ USEFUL WEBSITES

http://www.cipd.co.uk/NR/rdonlyres/94842E50-F775-4154-975F-8D4BE72846C7/0/valoflearnnwmodvalca.pdf

Anderson's article explores how HRD practitioners can measure and demonstrate the value of learning for their organization.

http://www.ilo.org/Search3/search.do?searchWhat=ev aluation+of+HRD+programmes&searchLanguage=en
A repository of HRD resources, including evaluation programmes, can be accessed from the website of the International Labour Organization, an agency that promotes rights at work, enhances social protection, and strengthens dialogue on work-related issues.

http://www.kirkpatrickpartners.com/
The official site of the Kirkpatrick four-level evaluation model incorporating tools and techniques that equip people to create significant value for their stakeholders and demonstrate impact to the bottom line.

http://www.roiinstitute.net/
A research, benchmarking and consulting organization providing workshops, publications and consulting services promoting the use of the Phillips' ROI evaluation methodology.

BIBLIOGRAPHY

Alliger, G. S., Tannenbaum, S. I., Bennett, W., Traver, H. and Shotland, A. (1997) A Meta-Analysis of the Relationship among Training Outcomes, *Personnel Psychology*, 50(2), 341–358.

Anderson, V. (2007) *The Change Agenda. The Value of Learning: A New Model of Value and Evaluation*, London: CIPD.

Armstrong, M. (2014) *Handbook of Human Resource Management Practice* (13th ed.), London: Kogan Page.

Baldwin, T. T. and Ford, J. K. (1988) Transfer Training: A Review and Directions for Future Research. *Personal Psychology*, 41(1), 63–105.

BBC (2013) *Sir Alex Ferguson: Final Farewell Was a Party 26 Years in the Making*. Available at http://www.bbc.co.uk/sport/0/football/22505640. Accessed 24 April 2014.

BBC (2013) *Man Utd: Ryan Giggs & Phil Neville Join Coaching Staff*. Available at http://www.bbc.co.uk/sport/0/football/23177876. Accessed 24 April 2014.

BBC (2014) *Manchester United: Manager Hunt Starts but Ryan Giggs Not In the Race*. Available at http://www.bbc.com/sport/0/football/27114788. Accessed 24 April 2014.

Beets, K. and Goodman, S. (2012) Evaluating a Training Programme for Executive Coaches, *SA Journal of Human Resource Management*, 10(23), 1–10.

Blanchard, P. N. and Thacker, J. W. (2013) *Effective Training: Systems, Strategies, and Practices*, Harlow: Pearson Education Limited.

Bramley, P. (2003) *Evaluating Training* (2nd ed.), London: CIPD.

Brinkerhoff, R. O. (1987) *Achieving Results through Training: How to Evaluate HRD to Strengthen Programs and Increase Impact*, San Francisco, CA: Jossey-Bass.

CIPD (2013) *Learning and Talent Development Annual Survey Report 2013*, London: CIPD.

Colquitt, J. A., LePine, J. A. and Noe, R. A. (2000) Towards an Integrative Theory of Training Motivation: A Meta-Analytical Path Analysis of 20 Years of Research, *Journal of Applied Psychology*, 85(5), 678–707.

De Alwis, A. C. and Rajaratne, W. D. H. M. (2011) A Study on Measuring Return on Investment of a Key Account Management Training Orogram, *Jorunal of Scientific Papers of the University of Pardubice* [series d Special Edition], 2011, vol. xiv, no. 21, ISSN :1211–555X.

Devins, D. and Smith, J. (2013) Evaluation of HRD, In J. Gold, R. Holden, P. Iles, J. Stewart and J. Beardwell (Eds) *Human Resource Development: Theory and Practice* (2nd ed.), Basingstoke: Palgrave Macmillan (75–204).

Easterby-Smith, M. (1986) *Evaluation of Management, Training and Development*, Aldershot: Gower.

Easterby-Smith, M. (1994) *Evaluating Management Development, Training and Education* (2nd ed.), Aldershot: Gower.

Enkuzena, S. and Kliedere, E. (2011) Management Training Evaluation: A Case Study of a Retail Store Chain, *Journal of Business Management*, 4, 221–232.

Fuchs (2013) *Annual Report: Growing Together*, Frankfurt: Fuchs.

Garavan, T., Hogan, C. and Cahir-O'Donnell, A. (2003) *Making Training and Development Work*, Dublin: Oak Tree Press.

Gibb, S. (2002) *Learning and Development: Processes, Practices and Perspectives at Work*, Basingstoke: Palgrave Macmillan.

Gunnigle, P., Heraty, N. and Morley, M. (2011) *Human Resource Management in Ireland* (4th ed.), Dublin: Gill and Macmillan.

Hamblin, A. C. (1974) *Evaluation and Control of Training*, Maidenhead: McGraw-Hill.

Harrison, R. (2009) *Learning and Development* (5th ed.), London: CIPD.

Hutchins, H. M., Burke, L. A. and Berthelsen, A. M. (2010) A Missing Link in the Transfer Problem? Examining How Trainers Learn about Training Transfer, *Human Resource Management*, 49(4), 599–618.

Kirkpatrick, D. L. (1959) Techniques for Evaluating Training Programs, *Journal of the American Society of Training Directors*, 13, 3–26.

Kirkpatrick, D. L. (1979) Techniques for Evaluating Training Programs, *Training and Development Journal*, 33(6), 78–92.

Kirkpatrick, D. L. (2007) *The Four Levels of Evaluation: Tips, Tools, and Intelligence for Trainers*, Virginia: ASTD.

Kirkpatrick, D. L. and Kirkpatrick, J. D. (2006) *Evaluating Training Programs* (3rd ed.), San Francisco, CA: Berrett-Koehler.

Kong, Y. J. and Jacobs, R. L. (2012) A Comparison of the Practices Used by Human Resource Development Professionals to Evaluate Web-Based and Classroom-Based Training Programmes within Seven Korean Companies, *Human Resource Development International*, 15(1), 79–98.

Laker, D. R. and Powell, J. L. (2011) The Differences between Hard and Soft Skills and Their Relative Impact on Training Transfer, *Human Resource Development Quarterly*, 22(1), 111–122.

Liebermann, S. and Hoffmann, S. (2008) The Impact of Practical Relevance on Training Transfer: Evidence from a Service Quality Training Program for German Bank Clerks, *International Journal of Training and Development*, 12(2), 74–86.

Marchington, M. and Wilkinson, A. (2012) *Human Resource Management at Work* (5th ed.), London: CIPD.

Martin, M., Whiting, F. and Jackson, T. (2010) *Human Resource Practice* (5th ed.), London: CIPD.

McGuire, D. and Mølbjerg Jørgensen, K. (2011) *Human Resource Development: A Critical Text*, London: Sage.

Nickols, F. W. (2005) Why a Stakeholder Approach to Evaluating Training, *Advances in Developing Human Resources*, 7(1), 121–134.

Northcroft, J. (2013) I've Given Them the Hairdryer, *Sunday Times Sport Supplement*, 14 July: 11.

Phillips, J. J. (1991) *Handbook of Training Evaluation and Measurement Methods*, Houston: Gulf Publishing Company.

Phillips, J. J. (1997) *Handbook of Training Evaluation and Measurement Methods* (2nd ed.), London: Kogan Page.

Phillips, J. J. (2011) *Handbook of Training Evaluation and Measurement Methods* (3rd ed.), Oxon: Routledge.

Phillips, J. M. and Gully, S. M. (2014) *Human Resource Management*, Mason, OH: Cengage Learning.

Pilbeam, S. and Corbridge, M. (2010) *People Resourcing and Talent Planning: Human Resource Management in Practice* (4th ed.), Essex: Pearson Education.

Saks, A. M. and Burke, L. A. (2012) An Investigation into the Relationship between Training Evaluation and the Transfer of Training, *International Journal of Training and Development*, 16(2), 118–127.

Simmonds, D. (2003) *Designing and Delivering Training*, London: CIPD.

Swart, J., Mann C., Brown, S. and Price, A. (2005) *Human Resource Development: Strategy and Tactics*, Oxford: Elsevier Butterworth-Heinemann.

Tomé, E. (2009) The Evaluation of HRD: A Critical Study with Applications, *Journal of European Industrial Training*, 33(6), 513–538.

Warr, P. B., Bird, M. W. and Rackham, N. (1970) *Evaluation of Management Training*, Aldershot: Gower.

Werner, J. M. and DeSimone, R. L. (2012) *Human Resource Development* (6th ed.), Mason, OH: Cengage Learning.

Wikipedia (2014) *Manchester United F.C.* Available at http://en.wikipedia.org/wiki/Manchester_United_F.C. Accessed 24 April 2014.

PART

III

CONTEMPORARY CHALLENGES

Human Resource Development:
A Concise Introduction

Fundamentals of HRD
2. Strategic HRD
3. Managing the HRD function
4. Individual-level learning
5. Organizational learning
6. Organization development

Contemporary challenges
11. Managing talented employees
12. Leadership development
13. Graduate employability
14. Ethics, corporate social responsibility, sustainability and HRD

Process of HRD
7. Identifying learning needs
8. Designing HRD programmes
9. Delivering HRD programmes
10. Evaluating HRD programmes

The final part of the book, Contemporary Challenges, comprises four chapters that reflect on topics that are particularly relevant to HRD in a contemporary climate.

Chapter 11 considers how talented employees can be managed and looks at the role HRD plays in identifying and managing talented employees. Talent management is a commitment to implementing a strategic approach to the management of employees. This is based on the belief that human resources are an organization's main starting point for competitive advantage. Talented employees are an essential asset that is becoming increasingly short in supply. It is important to consider the role that HRD plays in managing these talented individuals.

Chapter 12 looks at how leaders can be developed. It is important to understand the significance that many organizations give to leadership and management development and how it differs from other types of HRD activities. The terms 'leadership development' and 'management development' are often used interchangeably, but there are differences between the two, which are clarified here. If organizations want a coherent strategic approach to HRD that encompasses talent management, it is important that leadership development is also part of this.

Chapter 13 looks at graduate employability and the role HRD plays in facilitating graduate employability. Graduates are currently entering into one of the most challenging recruitment markets for almost two decades. They are not only competing for jobs with one other; they are also competing with graduates from other countries and continents. It is important to understand the role that HRD plays in developing the skills of new graduates and facilitating graduate employability.

Chapter 14, the final chapter, considers how ethics, corporate social responsibility and sustainability are related to HRD. Having outlined the importance of HRD in previous chapters, it is difficult to argue that HRD practices, policies and procedures can be separated from ethics and socially responsible business practices when the development of people and the organization is a core goal for HRD.

11 MANAGING TALENTED EMPLOYEES

Clare Rigg

By the end of this chapter you will be able to:

LEARNING OUTCOMES

- Explain what is mean by the terms 'talent' and 'talented employees' and how they can be identified

- Explain how a strategic approach to managing and developing talented employees can contribute to the success of an organization

- Discuss the key components of a talent management strategy and system, including the measurement and evaluation of outcomes

- Identify the difference in approaches between SMEs and large organizations

- Identify specific HRD options for developing talent with little or no budget

Nurturing talented employees

This chapter discusses ...

INTRODUCTION

This chapter focuses on managing talented employees and the role of HRD in designing and implementing a talent management strategy and systems that can motivate, develop and retain employees who are particularly crucial to the organization's success. Most organizations will claim that people are their greatest asset and many recognize that the biggest influence on their success, whether it be in customer relations, rates of innovation, service provision or other measures, is the extent to which they are able to attract, develop and keep 'good' people. Collins (2001) terms this 'getting the right people on the bus'. For many organizations, large and small, the biggest constraint on their ability to grow, innovate or sustain a good reputation with customers is their difficulty in holding on to their best and brightest employees or their failure to adequately invest in developing their employees' capabilities.

As organizations have increasingly recognized the idea of people as a source of competitive advantage, alongside acknowledging the significance of their own employer branding for attracting and retaining the best employees, HR has taken a more strategic role in the whole cycle of recruitment, induction, retention and development ▶ Chapter 2. A full talent management strategy encompasses this range of HRM-related activities; however, the focus of this chapter is on the particular role and contribution of HRD to talent management. We begin by looking at who talented employees are and how they can be identified.

talent refers to those employees who make a particularly strong contribution to organization performance either currently or in terms of their high potential for the longer term

talent management a systematic, holistic and integrated approach taken within an organization to the identification, attraction, development, engagement, retention and deployment of those talented employees who are seen to be of particular value to the organization

capability requirements the combined scope of knowledge, skills and abilities of an individual or a whole organization

exclusive approach an approach to talent management and development that targets only certain, exceptional employees, who either are seen to have 'high potential' as the future managers and leaders of the company or have commercially essential skills and knowledge which the organization wants to keep and extend

inclusive approach an approach to talent management that focuses on bringing out the full capability of all organization members

WHO ARE TALENTED EMPLOYEES?

The terms **talent** and **talent management** came into use after the American consultancy firm McKinsey in 1997 described the 'war for talent', referring to recruitment of an organization's most valuable employees, as a main driver for corporate performance.

A central role for HRD professionals, working in partnership with line managers and senior managers, is not only to identify immediate skill needs of an organization that are essential to carry out the day-to-day tasks, but also to think and plan for the longer term **capability requirements** that will be necessary for the organization to meet its strategic goals.

Broadly speaking, there are two main ways in which talented employees are identified, based on whether an organization takes an **exclusive approach** or an **inclusive approach** to defining talent. In this context, a high-potential employee describes an employee who, compared with others, is seen as having strong capacity to develop their skills and capabilities and is predicted to go far in the organization.

Some see talent management as the nurturing, development and career advancement of those identified as having unique and special skills, while in other organizations talent management is looked on from an organization-wide perspective, to ensure succession planning. In the latter case all employees are defined as either talent or potential talent, in which case HRD encompasses everyone. Other organizations have talent management and development programmes that are restricted, but which all employees have equal opportunity to access through a competitive application and selection process. Many talent development programmes are targeted at future managers and use an exclusive approach to identifying talent, with entry restricted to specific individuals. For example, a graduate recruitment and training programme is commonly used to identify and develop future managers, using a structured selection process at the point of recruitment. This is an exclusive approach because it is not an opportunity open to existing employees.

CIPD (2013) identified that three fifths of organizations take an exclusive approach, defining talented employees as the high-potential employees and senior managers, on whom they focus their talent management activities. The remaining two fifths of organizations take an inclusive approach whereby talent management activities involve all or most employees.

WHY IS IT IMPORTANT FOR AN ORGANIZATION'S PERFORMANCE AND SUCCESS TO FOCUS ON TALENTED EMPLOYEES?

Whichever approach to defining talent is taken, exclusive or inclusive, there is now a wide recognition of the business case for taking a strategic approach to talent management: in other words, looking ahead beyond immediate skill shortages, to consider the longer-term requirements for employee skills and capabilities. This is particularly the case in knowledge-intensive industries, where organizations rely on scarce intellectual or technical skills, for which they are in competition with other employers. The evidence is that those organizations that do invest in talent management and development see financial benefits, with a 90 per cent increased shareholder value compared with companies that do not (Watson Wyatt, 2002). Those that align their talent management strategy with business strategy have a 20 per cent higher rate of profit earned. In addition, those that have an internally integrated talent management system as well as aligning it with business strategy show 38 per cent higher financial results compared with companies that do not (Ernst and Young, 2010).

CIPD (2013) confirms that growing future senior managers and leaders and developing high-potential employees remain the key objectives of talent management activities. However, there are a number of other reasons why organizations focus on developing talent in employees, including:

- Being prepared for future essential skill requirements
- Retaining key staff by continuing to invest in their growth and development
- A major growth initiative or other significant change in the organizational structure
- Responding to changes in the business environment
- Developing a high-performance workforce
- Encouraging a culture of learning and innovation
- Contributing to employer branding to assist the organization to be an employer of choice
- Diversity management, ensuring a diverse pool for succession planning
- Limited external supply of essential skills
- Significant external regulatory changes, e.g. minimum levels of qualification required in the industry; essential training legally required to be completed by employees

Retention of key staff is more commonly reported to be an objective of talent management strategy in the private sector (40 per cent) than in the public (26 per cent) or non-profit sectors (28 per cent). Non-profit organizations are more than twice as likely as those from other sectors to report that their talent management activities are to support changes in the organizational structure or business environment (CIPD, 2013). In addition, another

BUILDING YOUR SKILLS

You are the HRD lead in a medium-sized local authority employing 350 people. Significant budget cuts have had a severe impact on recruitment and development activities. An early retirement process has resulted in the loss, over a short period of time, of many of the more experienced staff. The organization is in a constant state of change and everyone is being asked to 'do more with less'. The HR department have held a series of discussions with the senior management team to identify which roles are essential to maintain core services to the public. You are in the process of using 360-degree feedback and performance management information to identify potential successors to these roles and creating a talent pool. In this context of limited budget and high pressure, how would you go about developing this talent pool in the coming year?

benefit of focusing on talent is that the very creation and existence of a customized, organization-wide talent management strategy places the subject of investment in human capital high on the corporate agenda and provides a focus for integrating other HRD and HRM strategies ▶Chapter 1.

PREPARING A TALENT MANAGEMENT STRATEGY

The starting point for developing a talent management strategy is the recognition of how this contributes to achieving business strategy and identification of the expectations key stakeholders have. Linking talent development to business strategy is described as *strategic alignment*, which should happen both vertically and horizontally. Vertical alignment of talent management with overall business strategy means that employees' skills and capabilities are developed so as to position the organization with the competencies, behaviours and capabilities required for ongoing success. For example, if a company intends to expand internationally, it may identify that it needs both to upskill sales staff in particular language skills and also to increase understanding and awareness of working cross-culturally across many staff over the next two to three years.

Horizontal alignment refers to the internal consistency of talent management with other HR interventions. There is little point in investing in specific HRD initiatives, such as a graduate training programme or leadership development programme ▶Chapters 12 and 13, if their benefits are undermined by other contradictory practices, such as weak employee engagement or absence of opportunities for challenging work assignments, which fail to reinforce the employees' development or result in ambitious, talented individuals leaving. The objective is an integrated and interlocking system of attracting, developing, managing and evaluating talented employees. With horizontal alignment, an organization's talent management processes are tied together so that they complement one other. Information from workforce analytics can be used to identify high-performing employees and key areas of essential skills. This information is then used to develop the appropriate training, development and succession management systems.

talent management strategy the overall business rationale, plan and range of talent development activities integrated with other HR processes for recruitment, reward, performance management and succession planning

CONSIDER THIS...

GE is an international company that describes itself as providing innovative technological solutions for the finance, medical, energy and aviation industries. To support a renewed focus on technological leadership and innovation, GE began targeting technological skills as a key development requirement during its annual organizational and individual review process, which GE calls Session C. In all business segments, a full block of time was allocated to a review of the business's engineering pipeline, the organizational structure of its engineering function and an evaluation of the potential of engineering talent.

In response to the chief executive's concern that technology-oriented managers were under-represented in the company's senior management ranks, the Session C reviews moved more engineers into GE's senior executive band. Talent management practices also helped to drive and implement GE's other strategic priorities, for example, establishing a more diverse and internationally experienced management cadre.

METHODS FOR IDENTIFYING TALENTED EMPLOYEES

Identification of talent is conducted at three levels – the whole organization; the job or occupation level; and the individual level. Where the objective is to be prepared for future changes in market, product or organization arrangements, a useful starting point is to conduct a SWOT analysis of the external and internal environment of the organization and an internal audit of skills and knowledge, with a view to highlighting gaps.

If the objective for talent development is succession planning, identification will focus on the position itself. Through analysis of labour turnover, age profiles and other business activity forecasts, projected requirements for replacements in senior and middle-level positions can be made. The result will express the organizational-level need. There will also need to be some specification of the

Table 11.1 Sample organization competence framework – core themes

• Leadership
• Managing Performance • Sets clear and challenging objectives with teams   and individuals • Encourages high performance • Recognizes achievements
• Managing Resources
• Managing Yourself and Your Development
• Managing Change and Quality

Source: http://www.northamptoncollege.ac.uk/docs/doc2_20130422172028.pdf Accessed 17 November 2013

managerial and leadership qualities, skills and abilities needed by those who occupy the senior and middle manager positions. A common method for doing this is through some form of competence or competency analysis leading to a competence framework (Gold et al., 2013). Such a framework can be used to inform the design of a management/leadership development programme intended to develop the required competencies or skills of the role of manager/leader.

A typical competence framework has a small number of core themes and a series of subthemes (see Table 11.1 for core themes).

For an example of an organization's competency framework applied to different levels of management and leadership, look up the following link:

http://www.northamptoncollege.ac.uk/docs/doc2_20130422172028.pdf

Cannon and McGee (2007) suggest that organizations use a framework to assess a high-potential employee that includes the following elements:

- Has the respect and trust of peers, supervisors and subordinates
- Maintains a high level of competence in their role/job
- Has a bias for action and is a proactive catalyst for change
- Thinks and solves problems creatively and from a position of inquiry (versus advocacy)
- Is open to constructive criticism and feedback
- Uses critical judgement
- Has a broad understanding of the organization's business and their role in achieving its goals
- Has high capacity to learn
- Consistently produces measurable results above expectations
- Self-manages in a manner that fosters learning and high performance

- Ensures that team goals are achieved within ethical and cultural guidelines
- Manages and leads teams that demonstrate a sense of loyalty and community
- Strives to deliver and exceed customers' needs
- Arranges and leverages resources within an organization
- Has high resilience

BUILDING YOUR SKILLS

You work for a small, family-owned business that buys and distributes olive oil from southern Europe. Around 50 employees work for the company. Staff turnover is low, particularly at senior levels. You are the only person in the HR department, and the company is just starting to think about how it is going to survive the impending retirement of the founder in two years' time. He is the one who has built and maintained most client relationships and has most knowledge of the buying process, for which he still does most of the travelling. You have already developed a competency framework, so that recruitment to sales and administrative roles is carried out in line with this. The challenge is now to develop a succession plan for the top three roles. How would you go about drawing up role profiles for these three jobs? What would you do to identify and develop an internal talent pool over the next 18 months?

Once a competence framework is agreed, individuals will be assessed against the different elements. Common methods of establishing individual strengths and needs within an organization include some form of performance management system and/or associated appraisal scheme, often including 360° feedback. The use of 360° feedback involves individuals receiving information and data about themselves from a range of sources, usually including line managers, colleagues, their own staff and, perhaps, customers. Some form of rating scale and self-assessment using the same instrument are additional features of 360° feedback. Externally, the most commonly used method for doing this is an assessment centre or development centre, traditionally including a suite of exercises designed to simulate the work environment so as to draw up a psychometric profile of participants. Typically lasting from half a day to three or more days, a combination of team exercises, role-plays and other assessment methods such as psychometric testing and interviews are used to assess particular competencies of individuals, against a job competency profile. The assumption is that the best way to predict future job performance is to have an individual carry out a set of tasks that mirror those required in the job and observe and measure their actual behaviours. Common behaviours include relating to people; resistance to stress; planning and organizing; motivation; adaptability and flexibility; problem solving; leadership; communication; decision making and initiative. Key features include independent assessors, observation and multi-rater feedback.

PREPARING A TALENT MANAGEMENT STRATEGY

Preparing a talent management strategy (TMS) involves a series of stages of data collection, analysis, stakeholder engagement and planning. The framework below highlights some of the important areas associated with talent management and suggests a means of diagnosing the following stages:

1 Desired position of the organization
2 Current readiness of the organization
3 Stakeholder engagement
4 Gap between the current position and where you want to be
5 Implementation plan and evaluation measures

Stage 1: Desired Position of the Organization
Let us assume that the organization has prepared a strategic plan, or at least a vision statement, for the next three to five years. The starting point is, therefore, the strategic objectives expressed in this plan:
 – Identify main objectives.
 – Decide on definition and focus of talent.
 – Also identify strengths which might offer strategically unique capabilities.

Stage 2: Current Readiness of the Organization
 – Analyse the talent environment.
 – Audit current skills and HR processes.
 – Check alignment with other HR processes (recruitment, reward, performance management etc.).

To assess the current readiness of the organization, we need to collect data on the following kinds of questions:
● Who are the best people in the organization?
● What is done to keep these individuals?

● What is done to help these individuals to keep expanding their skills and experience?
● What are the organization's key positions and what are their skill requirements?
● When are these key positions likely to need replacing?
● Who is envisaged to fill these key positions?
● To what extent do they have the skills and experience required?
● Does the company have a competency framework?
● If so, how is this used to plan and track employees' development?
● How does the performance management system align with the strategic aims and plans of the organization?
● How often do people get feedback within the organization, and what is the quality of the feedback they get?
● How do people get promoted? Are there consistent, fair and transparent processes in place to support movement within and upwards in the organization?
● Does the company have a diversity management policy, and, if so, how does this align with the development policy?

Stage 3: Stakeholder Engagement
A critical factor in the success of a talent management strategy is ensuring that all stakeholders are engaged. This means that they know the rationale and aims of the TMS; they have been consulted where relevant; they know how they are expected to contribute; and they have also had the opportunity to communicate their own expectation of the organization's TMS.

Who are the stakeholders? A classic definition of a stakeholder is anyone who cares about, controls or otherwise has an interest in something. For an organization's TMS, the stakeholders will therefore include at least the following:
 – The chief executive
 – The board
 – Senior managers
 – HR, HRD and talent management specialists
 – Line managers
 – Employees

Other stakeholders who may also be included are customers/clients, suppliers and partners.

Stage 4: Conduct a Gap Analysis
 – Decide on which employees are to be included.
 – Based on data from Stages 1 and 2, prepare a SWOT to identify gaps in skills, knowledge and experience.

Stage 5: Implementation plan and evaluation measures

Having completed the stages of preparing a talent management strategy outlined above, namely, identifying the organization's strategic direction and core objectives, analysing the strategic environment, and auditing the organization's readiness in terms of current skills and HR processes, the outcome should be identification of the skill/knowledge gaps at organization, job/occupation and individual level. The next stage is to agree a plan to address such gaps, through a comprehensive talent management system:

- Decide on key HRD interventions to use to develop talent.
- Decide on evaluation measures.
- Brief/train those responsible.
- Launch.
- Evaluate and review.
- Plan next steps.

What needs to happen next?
What resources will be required?
Who should do what, by when?

 CONSIDER THIS ...

Over the past decade, Brazil's economy has evolved from one with a primarily agricultural base to one powered by manufacturing, construction, mining, oil and gas. Combined with demographic changes, this shift in the country's economic base has presented Brazil with some formidable challenges. One of them has to do with Brazil's younger-than-average workforce. Its members are looking for exciting careers, sparking a talent war among companies there. Many have responded by creating two-year trainee programmes aimed at attracting and retaining Generation Y employees. These programmes rotate new hires throughout different business units and assign a senior executive to serve as a mentor or counsellor. Some companies incorporate an international assignment into these programmes – a powerful tool for attracting and keeping talent. The young employees view international assignments as a stepping stone to their career development. Many organizations also use international assignments to develop the careers of fast-track, high-potential employees.

DEVELOPING TALENT: WHAT ARE THE OPTIONS?

A talent management system could encompass a range of activities, from formal structured post-graduate programmes delivered by an external university to informal work-based learning such as networking events and client exposure. As the list below indicates, there is a wide range of HRD activities that could be used. The choice for any particular organization will partly depend on the gaps identified, but particularly on the resources available to them. As we shall see, organization size plays a part here, but just the fact that an organization is small does not mean there are not still a wide variety of options available for investing in talent development.

- Coaching by external practitioners
- Instructor-led training delivered off the job
- Action learning sets
- Collaborative and social learning
- Internal knowledge-sharing events
- Formal education courses
- External conferences, workshops and events
- E-learning methods
- Video-based learning
- In-house development programmes
- Internal 'stretch' opportunities
- Coaching by line managers
- On-the-job training
- Job rotation
- Secondment
- Shadowing
- Mentoring
- Apprenticeships

According to the CIPD (2013), the most common learning and talent development methods currently used in organizations are instructor-led training delivered off the job, on-the-job training, in-house development programmes and coaching by line managers.

MOTIVATING TALENTED EMPLOYEES

Talent management and motivation have been linked in two contrasting ways: as a transactional exchange, and as one of engagement. Looked at as a transaction, the argument is that talented employees are motivated to give their effort in exchange for the organization's investment in their development. This implies that, for as long as the organization continues to offer an individual the opportunity to grow and develop, they will work hard and show commitment to the company.

The contrasting argument (Kumar and Raghavendran, 2013) is that talent management brings out the best from talented employees because, as highly skilled professionals, they value autonomy and meaningful engagement. In other words, people give their best because they gain fulfilment from their work and feel able to influence the organization.

> **talent pipeline** the available supply of talented employees coming into the organization and their continuous development and career progression within it

CHOOSING A COMMON OR DIFFERENTIATED APPROACH TO TALENT MANAGEMENT

Is there one best system for talent management? This question of whether a standard approach to talent management is more or less effective compared with a differentiated approach depends on the rationale and purpose for the organization developing a talent management strategy, as well as features of the organization such as size and industrial sector.

We have seen that the practices or interventions designed to develop talent will vary across organizations. When 'talent' is used to refer to the exceptional few, interventions tend to focus on the attraction, retention and development of the best employees through such HRD practices as leadership development, but also aligning the TMS with other policies such as work–life balance, employer branding and corporate social responsibility. In larger organizations, talent management is particularly likely to be targeted at future leaders and high-potential employees.

Where an organization takes the more inclusive view that talent management is about maximizing all employees' potential, developing capabilities and competency more extensively, interventions include a broader range of learning and development interventions at all levels, from training to management and leadership programmes to international assignments, coaching and mentoring. However, they are also open to existing employees at many levels, not only to specific recruits.

Different approaches are also more popular with different sectors. For example, public sector organizations and manufacturing and production companies, particularly those with more than 250 employees, are particularly likely to employ apprentices as a means of building a **talent pipeline** and obtaining required skills over the longer term (CIPD, 2013)

Talent management in SMEs

Organization size also affects talent management strategies. In part this is to do with resources available, as larger organizations will have more resources than smaller ones. In small organizations every employee is important, and the consequences of poor recruitment decisions, loss of key individuals or failing to motivate and develop employees to fulfil their potential are expensive. In this regard, it is arguably even more important for SMEs to think and plan how to manage and develop their talented employees. Traditionally it was thought that SMEs paid little attention to the talent development of their employees (Rigg and Trehan, 2004); however, it is now clear that SMEs do engage in a variety of formal HR policies (Sheehan, 2013). In respect of talent management, informal and work-based learning methods are particularly valued and widely used by SMEs. Getting involved in projects, having a mentor and shadowing someone in another role are all development methods readily available to SMEs.

SMEs have been found to be twice as likely to take an inclusive approach to talent management, focusing on drawing out the potential of all employees. In contrast, an exclusive approach is more common in larger organizations, with talent management activities targeted at particular employee groups, particularly high-potential employees, graduates and senior managers, while smaller organizations are twice as likely to include all employees – 58 per cent of organizations with fewer than 50 employees include all employees in their talent management compared with just 27 per cent of organizations with more than 1,000 employees (CIPD, 2013). It has been found that, irrespective of organization size, commercial companies are most likely to invest in talent management activities, while those in the non-profit sector, which would tend to be small, are half as likely to do so (CIPD, 2013).

MANAGING TALENT IN A RECESSIONARY ENVIRONMENT

In uncertain economic times, most organizations see talent as even more important to their survival. Training budgets continue to exist but are more sharply prioritized for succession planning and leadership development. Many organizations, particularly in the private sector, recognize that talent and skills are the essence of their survival and recovery from recession, because it will be their employee capabilities that will lead efficiencies, innovation and competitive differentiation.

Interestingly, in the current recession, one of the ways organizations are addressing their talent supply is by broadening their usual recruitment sources so they can benefit from the cuts and redundancies that have afflicted other organizations and left many highly talented people job-hunting. For example, one small cafe chain in rural Ireland now benefits from an administrator who used to be the personal assistant in a major US corporate bank. While expensive investments in off-the-job training might be less attractive in a recession, organizations still have a range of talent development options at a lower budget. On-the-job learning has found favour again, including reliance on informal methods such as work-based and experiential learning, as well as more formal methods of in-house coaching and organization development ▶ Chapter 6. MacCartney (2009) reports increased use of internal 'stretch' assignments, such as special projects and temporary roles and the creation of leadership exchange groups across businesses. Technology-enabled or e-learning, facilitating bite-sized learning and independent learning that does not take employees away from their jobs, is also an option for talent development when the budget is low.

However, the quality and effectiveness of e-learning, instructional design and facilitation are dependent on high investment of resources, so the large upfront investment may only pay off for larger organizations or where the resource is shared across a network of several organizations, as, for example, across a number of health and social care organizations in a region.

'Piggybacking on richer partners' is another variety of shared development, whereby companies across the supply chain share talent development activity. In one example of this nature, Coghlan and Coughlan (2011) describe facilitating action learning designed to bring about improvements in a supply chain network comprising a central company (termed the system integrator) and a series of suppliers:

> For several years, one low-cost high volume component part had caused problems. Despite many attempts, the supplier had not been able to resolve this puzzle ... despite quality inspections and a high resulting internal scrap rate. In the context of the action learning project, the system integrator and the supplier agreed to initiate a collaborative improvement initiative. The system integrator and the supplier expanded the group, to include both senior purchasing managers and engineers, who attempted to build on their strategic relationship ... The ultimate technical solution to the issue was embedded in the resolution of an inter-organizational problem: through developing a richer collaborative relationship between the system integrator and the supplier, together they found a solution to the puzzle. More strategically, they demonstrated the value of such a new relationship and understood the potential for learning with and from each other in commercial safety. (Coghlan and Coughlan, 2011: 2)

Husain Makes History on Radio 4 Flagship

It was announced in July 2013 that, for the first time in five years, there will be more than one woman presenter on the BBC's flagship *Today* programme after the BBC's rising star Mishal Husain joined the BBC Radio 4 breakfast programme. Husain, who presents BBC1's *Weekend News* and has also presented BBC2's *Newsnight*, will also become the first minority ethnic – and first Muslim – presenter in the programme's 56-year history.

Husain's appointment follows widespread criticism of the lack of female presenters across the BBC's news output. The BBC Director General, Tony Hall, said: 'improving the gender balance on programming has been a priority for me ... I am keen to see more women in key presenting and back stage roles.' Tony Hall announced his decision to readdress the gender balance in a statement, saying: 'It is such great news that Mishal will be joining the Today programme. She is a first-rate journalist who will be an excellent addition to what is already a very strong team. I am also particularly pleased that her appointment means there will be another female voice on the programme, which I believe is extremely important.' When Hall took up his new position as the head of the BBC in April 2013, he said: 'Improving the gender balance in our programming has been a priority for me since I returned to the BBC. I'm keen to see more women in key presenting and backstage roles as we move forward.'

The *Today* show has long been criticized for its lack of female newsreaders. Husain, a Cambridge-educated mother of three, has long been identified as one to watch by BBC management. She was included in a list of the corporation's 'top talent' four years ago, when she was bracketed with others as 'on the way up' and 'worth investment'. A rising star who currently fronts BBC1's *Weekend News*, Husain is one of

the faces of the BBC's coverage of the London Olympics, presenting a morning show which led critics to identify her as 'one to watch'.

Recruiting and developing talented presenters at the BBC starts with the creation of a production talent pool, acting like a temp agency. Being part of this pool gives access to short-term, paid entry-level work on a wide range of BBC programmes and productions. From this, pool members can apply to the BBC's Production Trainee Scheme, an intensive 12-month paid traineeship. Thereafter, development is primarily through experiential and work-based learning, gaining access to opportunities to extend experience and expertise.

Born in England, Mishal Husain was brought up in Abu Dhabi and Saudi Arabia before completing her secondary schooling in England. She joined BBC World News as a junior reporter after a stint in the US. 'My first break came when I stood in for a business report at 4am in the morning. It was from

there that I went on to become the BBC's first Washington news anchor', she recalled.

Sources

BBC – Leadership Talent Management Strategy http://www.lfhe.ac.uk/en/research-resources/resources/case-studies.cfm/theBBC

The Guardian, http://www.theguardian.com/media/2013/jul/16/mishal-husain-bbc-radio-4-today

Questions

1 What does this case study illustrate are the benefits, both direct and indirect, to an organization of nurturing and promoting high-profile talented individuals?
2 In this case study, how is diversity management strategically linked to talent management and development?
3 Look at the BBC Production Talent Review 2008 and share your findings in class http://www.bbc.co.uk/bbctrust/assets/files/pdf/review_report_research/talent_costs/report.pdf

HOW DO WE KNOW WHETHER TALENT MANAGEMENT HAS SUCCEEDED?

What does successful talent management look like and how would we know? This, of course, depends on what the original purpose for talent management is in a particular organization, the intended outcomes, and the expectations held by the various stakeholders. For example, if a key aim of talent management in your organization was to reduce the proportion of management jobs filled by external recruitment, you would expect to see the proportion filled by internal candidates rise. Stakeholders need to agree on what success looks like. For example, if the proportion of vacancies currently filled by external recruitment is 50 per cent, you might agree that successful talent

management will result in at least 25 per cent being externally filled and 75 per cent internally filled within two years. If this was achieved you might set another higher target, or it might be agreed that this was a suitable balance. If this was not achieved, HRD, working with other stakeholders, would need to look at the possible reasons why not, and adjust the TMS.

Outcomes of talent management can be measured by the traditional ROI (return on investment) or the newer ROE (return on expectation) ▶ Chapter 10. ROI seeks to convert metrics into a business cost. Common HR metrics used in organizations are rates of absence, sickness, retention, engagement and performance. Effectiveness of leadership development programmes might also use employee opinion surveys or comparative 360-degree feedback tools. Repeat skills gaps analyses can be used to compare individual or team skill audits before and after a talent management programme. Other business metrics are also commonly used at individual, group and organization levels, for example improved performance against objectives or KPIs, customer complaints and client feedback. Metrics for success will tend to be expressed as a target number within a target time period.

Return on stakeholder expectations

Research by Anderson (2007) has found that the interpretation of success from talent management activities can have quite diverse meanings for different stakeholders, because they have different priorities. For a chief executive officer with a long-term view of where the organization is headed, her expectation might be that TM produces a transformational change in the organization culture over the longer term (say three to five years). She might judge success by the extent to which she sees new behaviours in employees demonstrated. Senior managers might hope that a TM programme improves the extent to which their employees show 'strategic readiness', or can deliver performance improvements, or improvements in the size of the talent pool and the successful management of succession. These are less tangible outcomes and not easily evaluated by quantitative measures. For other managers, their expectation might be that they see an improvement in capability in the short term (six months to one year) as measured in bottom-line results, such as service quality, productivity, management succession and employee retention. For example, participants in a team leader development programme might particularly value the qualification they receive at the end and might hope to see advancement in their careers soon afterwards. Their line managers might expect to see them expand in capability and confidence and hope to be able to delegate to them more. Senior management might expect the training to result in an increased talent pool, ready to be moved to new roles wherever required.

Anderson (2007) found that, while ROI is popular with HRD professionals, it carries little weight with senior managers, who place more value on ROE (return on expectation), which is determined by the results they anticipate from a TMS at the outset. ROE is the idea that evaluation of TM depends on the wider expectations that different stakeholders have of what success might look like, or, in other words, of the value of the TM activity to them. This makes it important that, when objectives for a TMS are set, the process encompasses the expectations of not only top managers, the learners themselves and HRD professionals, but also the line managers and possibly other stakeholders, as mentioned earlier in the chapter. This implies that objective setting needs to be a collaborative process. A further implication is that the measures of success and evaluation methods are best considered at the design and planning stage of a TMS, so that they can generate feedback on what is of real value to the different stakeholders.

SPOTLIGHT ON SKILLS

To retain talented employees, HRD professionals need to think about their retention, engagement and continued development at different stages:

- Identification and recruitment of talented employees
- While they are formally involved in talent management activities
- After they have completed these activities

Think about the specific initiatives you would seek to implement as an HRD professional for an organization to ensure that those employees identified as talented continue to develop their skills and capabilities and do not leave the organization. For each initiative, identify what success would look like and identify at least one HR or business metric to measure success.

To help you answer the questions above, visit www.macmillanihe.com/companion/carbery-hrd and watch the video of Jackie Murphy talking about talent management.

WHAT IS THE ROLE FOR HRD?

HRD professionals, or the HRD function in an organization, have an essential and strategic role to play in managing talented employees. They are people who work across various internal organizational boundaries who link up different strands and priorities, connecting:

- The business strategy and senior manager priorities
- Different parts of the HRM and HRD cycle
- Line manager expectations and readiness to play their role
- Identification of talented employees
- Alignment of talent management with other HR and development activities

The HRD function is the lead architect in the design of a talent management strategy and system. It must foster relationships with other stakeholders, e.g. line managers, senior managers and participants, both during and after participation. The HRD function is the commissioner and client of talent management activities, as well as coordinator and often partner in the implementation of the talent management system. They will set up coaching, mentoring and networking opportunities for TMS participants so they meet and learn from senior people in the organization. As the above examples of measuring

success show, a further important role for HRD is informatics for record keeping, monitoring and tracking.

The HRD function must make the business case for talent management, to justify expenditure and persuade other organization members to engage. The HRD function is often also charged with the responsibility of evaluating talent management.

Making the business case

For alignment of any specific talent management activity or programme, it has to be clear how the intervention is intended to contribute to achievement of corporate strategic objectives, typically articulated in the organization's strategic plan, or the individual employee's objectives, which typically would be identified through performance review. To secure resources for a training course, a coaching programme or any other activity, the first step for HRD is to spell out the purpose in strategic terms. In other words, HRD has to make the business case and communicate how

O'Brien's Homeware

O'Brien's is a family-owned homeware retail company in Ireland, with ten stores across the country. There are 350 regular employees, most of them department sales assistants working in the retail shops. There are also buyers, store hands and drivers, as well as those based in head office. Each store has a manager and assistant manager, as well as at least one and sometimes two training managers. Strategic leadership is provided by a small board of directors, comprising five people: the founder and chairman, one other family member and three non-family members.

Making Learning and Talent Development Strategic

In 2001 O'Brien's brought in an Operations & HR Director to the board, who saw Excellence through People (Ireland's national standard

for human resource management) as a positive way of structuring HR systems and practices, and of linking learning and development within the overall business strategy to achieve an inclusive talent development strategy. The result of implementing this by the mid-2000s was a very structured approach to training, driven now by the business strategy. A corporate training plan is prepared annually, costed and evaluated through metrics such as sales and profitability. A modified balanced scorecard (Kaplan and Norton, 1996) provides a framework for the strategy, including a segment in the scorecard termed 'talent management'.

From Management Strategy to Learning Needs Analysis

Each year a training plan is prepared for each store. Considerable time is spent

identifying employees' training needs, using the appraisal system to provide an opportunity to identify training needed and based on a needs analysis for their job. The company uses a competence-based framework, with much emphasis put on behavioural competences applicable to all jobs, such as customer service, working as a team and 'subtle selling'. Since these are seen as such essential capabilities for the company's strategic success, training in these skills is provided in each store two or three times a year.

Training Providers – External and Internal

O'Brien's uses an external provider for specialist retail training, for example, in sales, marketing, IT, finance and logistical expertise. For some generic skills, such as customer service or team building, great emphasis has been placed on developing internal training expertise. Each store has at least one and often two trained trainers.

The HR person from each store is one of the trainers, while the second is typically one of the checkout supervisors. They receive training themselves twice a year in, for, example, evaluation, transfer to work, or making training relevant.

Evaluation

At a corporate level the ROI measures used for evaluation are sales and profit figures. For example, comparison is made of sales and margins before and two months after a particular course. Generally there is an uplift in sales figures following training, and this data is used to justify further HRD investment to retail managers and the board.

Managers' Expectations

Initially the operations and HR director had to work hard to persuade the middle managers (store managers) of the value of training, because releasing an employee for eight hours' training means that not only do store managers have to pay the person for these hours despite their being away from the shop floor, but they also have to buy in a replacement to cover the shift. However, the managers also had other performance measures, such as mystery shoppers, and they could see that if they did not put investment into the training they were not getting the same recognition for customer service.

Persuading board members of the value of investing in talent development was not so difficult, because the operations and HR director was a member of the board and was explicitly hired into the company with this brief. Nevertheless, it was important to highlight deliverables and to continuously provide evidence to link HRD to profitability or sales, for example, demonstrating improvements that followed training or providing evidence of the improved pool for succession planning.

Talent Management and Employer Branding

The emphasis on identifying high-potential employees and investing in their future capabilities is driven by a clear strategic plan and recognition of the strategic importance of talented employees to the company's operations. In previous years of relatively full employment there had been a real difficulty in recruiting talent. For the retail sector as a whole this is a challenge, because a career in the sector is not seen as offering great potential. The sector does not pay high wages and the work is tough, including regular evening and weekend working, as well as dealing with customers.

Having found it difficult to attract supervisors and good trainee managers, the company made the decision to home grow their own. The O'Brien's definition of 'talent' is people 'having capacity to be more than they currently are'. They recognize that talent in the sector is very much related to personality and whether a person can relate to the customers or has people management skills, regardless of the qualifications they have on paper. Managers had regularly to identify an employee, part time or full time, who had the potential to progress. Talent development consisted of an 18-month trainee manager structured fast-track development. Trainee managers can also be recruited directly to the programme, which involves on-the-job training to learn all aspects of the job as well as external training. During the 18 months they have bi-monthly reviews to agree training objectives and monitor monthly milestones. Their line manager is accountable for making sure they progress and are adding value to the store. Each 'talent' is assigned a mentor, one of the board members, whom they meet for regular review meetings.

For O'Brien's, the development opportunities offered to employees are distinctive in the sector and contribute to their employer branding. Being known to treat employees well and train well has meant the company has recruited some excellent employees.

Current Challenges

Overall, the company has no doubt that investment in employees' talent development produces results to the bottom line, or that strategically managing HRD is essential to get the best out of people. But what of the future challenges in the face of the current economic downturn? It is tougher to keep the focus on investing and the risk is that training will be reduced, not only because of the cost of training, but also due to the operational impacts of covering people taken out for training. In the short term the company board believe that, because staff turnover is low, there is some cushioning from past investment in talent development, and they can reduce investment in the coming year.

Questions

1 What are the advantages and disadvantages of having a specific talent strategy?
2 To what extent do you think it is an advantage to have the lead HR person on the company board?
3 The case study illustrates at least one significant tension within the O'Brien's HRD approach. What is this?
4 Now that the company is operating in recessionary times, how would you advise it to adjust its talent development activities?

the particular activity contributes to achievement of the individual, team and/or strategic objectives.

As discussed earlier in the chapter, alignment of talent management in practice involves identifying and meeting different stakeholder expectations, and these are not always consistent. HRD practitioners have to become skilled in arguing the business case and articulating the value proposition of the proposed talent management activity.

SUMMARY

Talent management is an approach to thinking strategically about the skills, competences and capabilities of an organization focused on the long-term success of the organization, facilitating strategic success and meeting future skill requirements, rather than on more immediate development issues such as current skill shortages or the redeployment of staff to other roles. Although there is variation in the definition of who counts as talent in an organization, and whether an exclusive or inclusive approach is adopted, there are commonalities both in the recognition that talented employees are essential to organization performance and in the steps to be taken when an organization develops a talent management strategy, so that, led by the business strategy, the TMS aligns with other HR practices internally to help deliver business objectives. Talent management practices span a wide range of activities, from formal, off-the job management development qualification programmes to experiential, work-based learning such as stretch assignments and shadowing. As a result all organizations, both small or large, and even in recessionary times, have a choice of talent management practices they can still call on. In fact, the evidence shows that organizations cannot afford not to invest in TM, in that the financial returns of those that do engage in TM outperform those that do not.

 CHAPTER REVIEW QUESTIONS

1 Who are talented employees and how can they be identified?

2 Why is it important for an organization's performance and success to focus on talented employees?

3 What are the key elements of a talent management strategy?

4 How can talent development activities contribute to organizational performance?

5 Is a common or a differentiated approach to talent management more effective?

6 What is the role for the HRD function in talent management?

7 What are the options available for measuring the success of talent management?

8 How might talent management systems and practices have to be adapted depending on the size and budget of an organization?

FURTHER READING

Anderson, V. (2007) *The Value of Learning: A New Model of Value and Evaluation*, London: CIPD.

Caplan, J. (2011) *The Value of Talent: Promoting Talent Management across the Organization*, London: Kogan Page.

CIPD (2013) *Learning and Talent Development: Annual Survey Report*, London: CIPD.

Fernandez-Araoz, C., Groysberg, B. and Nohria, N. (2011) How to Hang on to Your High Potentials, *Harvard Business Review*, 89(10), October, 76, 78–83.

Stewart, J. and Rigg, C. (2011) *Learning and Talent Development*, London: CIPD.

Tansley, C., Turner, P. A., Foster, C., Harris, L. M., Stewart, J., Sempik, A. and Williams, H. (2007) *Talent; Strategy, Management and Measurement*, London: CIPD.

USEFUL WEBSITES

UK Civil Service
http://www.civilservice.gov.uk/wp-content/uploads/2011/09/Talent-Strategies-Practitioner-Guide_tcm6-35853.pdf, accessed 13/1/2014.
This link provides a useful example of a guide to preparing a talent management strategy.

CIPD podcast 24: 'Strategies for Attracting and Retaining Talent'
http://www.cipd.co.uk/podcasts/_articles/_strategiesforattractingandretainingtalent.htm?link=title.
Philippa Lamb discusses the issues with Emily Lawson, partner in the London office of McKinsey & Company and the global leader of McKinsey's talent management and HR service line.

World Human Asset summit 2011, DAVE ULRICH
http://www.youtube.com/watch?v=-hmpbVLYjoI

Interview with Professor Dave Ulrich on HR value creation, recruitment, talent management and creation of high-performing teams (eight minutes).

Towers Watson *Global Talent 2021 Study*
http://www.towerswatson.com/en/Insights/Knowledge-Central
Reports from this US-based international consultancy company.

BIBLIOGRAPHY

Anderson, V. (2007) *The Value of Learning – A New Model of Value and Evaluation,* London: CIPD.

Cannon, J.A. and McGee, R. (2007) *Talent Management and Succession Planning,* London: CIPD.

Chami-Malaeb, R. and Garavan, T. (2013) Talent and Leadership Development Practices as Drivers of Intention to Stay in Lebanese Organisations: The Mediating Role of Affective Commitment, *International Journal of Human Resource Management,* 24(21), 4046–4062.

CIPD (2013) *Learning and Talent Development – Annual Survey Report 2013,* London: CIPD.

Coghlan, D. and Coughlan, P. (2011) Transforming Networks through Action Learning, *OD Practitioner,* 43(2), 1–6.

Collins, J. (2001) *Good to Great: Why Some Companies Make the Leap ... And Others Don't,* New York: HarperCollins.

Collings, David G. Mellahi, Kamel. (2013) Commentary on: Talent – Innate or Acquired? Theoretical Considerations and Their Implications for Talent Management, *Human Resource Management Review,* 23(4), 322–325.

Ernst and Young (2010) Managing Today's Global Workforce: Elevating Talent Management to Improve Business, available at https://www2.eycom.ch/publications/items/humanressources/2010_todays_global_workforce/2010_EY_Managing_todays_global_workforce.pdf accessed 15/9/2014

Gold, J., Holden, R., Iles, P., Stewart, J. and Beardwell, J. (2013) *Human Resource Development: Theory and Practice,* Basingstoke: Palgrave Macmillan.

Kaplan, R. S. and Norton, D. P. (1996) *The Balanced Scorecard: Translating Strategy into Action,* Boston: Harvard University Press.

Kumar, H. and Raghavendran, S. (2013) Not by Money Alone: the Emotional Wallet and Talent Management, *Journal of Business Strategy,* 34(3), 16–23.

MacCartney, C. (2009) *Fighting Back through Talent Innovation – Talent Management under Threat in Uncertain Times,* London: CIPD.

Rigg, C. and Trehan, K. (2004) Now You See It, Now You Don't: A Discourse Perspective on Researching HRD in SMEs, In J. Stewart and G. Beaver (Eds), *HRD in Small Organisations,* London: Routledge, 48–73.

Sheehan, M. (2013) Human Resource Management and Performance: Evidence from Small and Medium-Sized Firms, *International Small Business Journal,* onlinefirst January, 1–26.

Tansley, C., Kirk, S. and Tietze, S. (2013) The Currency of Talent Management – A Reply to Talent Management and the Relevance of Context: Towards a Pluralistic Approach, *Human Resource Management Review,* 23(4), 337–340.

Thunnissen, M., Boselie, P. and Fruytier, B. (2013). Talent Management and the Relevance of Context: Towards a Pluralistic Approach, *Human Resource Management Review,* December 2013, 23(4), 326–336.

Watson Wyatt (2002) *European Human Capital Index Study,* New York: Towers Watson.

12 LEADERSHIP DEVELOPMENT

Thomas N. Garavan

By the end of this chapter you will be able to:

LEARNING OUTCOMES

- Explain the concepts of management, leader and leadership development
- Understand why leadership development is an important dimension of HRD
- Describe the competencies required to effectively lead and manage in contemporary organizations
- Understand the contribution that leadership development makes to the performance of organizations

- Explain the importance of adopting a strategic approach to the development of leaders
- Outline the contemporary challenges that leadership development must now address in organizations
- Evaluate the effectiveness of selected leadership development interventions

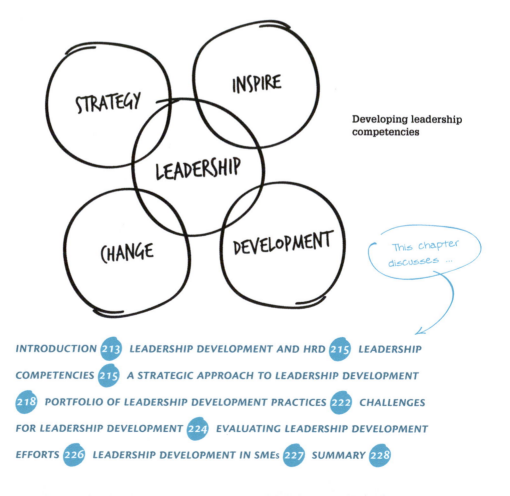

Developing leadership competencies

This chapter discusses ...

INTRODUCTION

Leadership development is an important organizational activity that is critical to organizational success. However, historically, when budgets have been tightened during periods of economic downturn, investment in leadership development was one of the first activities to have its funding reduced. However, organizations increasingly understand the implications of failing to develop individuals who have responsibility for formulating an organization's strategy, growing and developing an organization's talent, and managing the day-to-day operational issues. Organizations that invest in human capital development, which inevitably includes leadership development, will achieve significant advantages in terms of business performance. Leadership development is a multi-billion euro business worldwide and the costs of leadership development continue to increase. However, many organizations have moved past the 'worth of the investment' question to the question of which approach brings the best results and is most effective in impacting the bottom line. It is estimated that leadership development can have significant pay-off for organizations in terms of creating a sustained competitive advantage (Day *et al.*, 2009). As an example, it is estimated that the market value of General Electric (GE) is at a minimum $30 billion higher than its breakup value, and most of this additional value can be attributed to the quality and depth of its leadership human capital. However, the key lesson to be learned from the GE experience is that leadership development should have a strong fit with the organization's business strategy and its resource capabilities.

It is against this backdrop that we discuss how best to position leadership development in organizations to enhance its contribution to organizational success. In doing so, we consider how leader and leadership development differ, the key elements of leadership development in organizations, the differences between leading and managing competencies, and the challenges in evaluating the contribution of leadership development to organizational effectiveness. Our view of how best to develop leaders has changed over the past 20 years. For example, the 70:20:10 model suggests that approximately 70 per cent of the learning and development for individuals who eventually take on senior leadership roles stems from experience, 20 per cent from coaching and mentoring

leadership development activities and practices that enhance the quality of leaders to work as part of a team to develop relationships with organizational stakeholders

management development a process by which managers develop their knowledge and skills to be effective in their role and contribute to organizational performance

leader development the development of a person's capacity to be effective in a leadership role, including enhanced self-awareness and a strong leader identity

experiences, and 10 per cent from formal classroom education and training interventions. In Hewlett Packard, for example, they make use of all three ways of developing leaders but adopt a more balanced approach. This example suggests that it is important to contextualize leadership development to the contingencies of the organization.

What is leader and leadership development?

There is much debate as to whether the development of leaders is different from the development of leadership capabilities. There is also discussion about whether leader and leadership development differs from management development. 'Management development' is the term most frequently used in the UK and Ireland, whereas in the US the preferred term is 'leadership development'. Traditional definitions of management development focused on formal, planned and deliberate activities undertaken by organizations to develop management skills (Mumford, 1993). Storey (1989) suggested that management development focused on the development of management capabilities for the future. Garavan *et al.* (2009) have suggested that management development is task-specific and organization-specific and the focus is on enhancing performance in a managerial role. The typical competencies that are the concern of management development include problem solving, decision making, and time and task management.

Day (2000) in a seminal contribution highlighted the distinction between management, leader and leadership development; however, the element that has received the greatest attention by scholars and practitioners in the interim is the distinction between leader and leadership development. Day (2000) emphasized that leader development focuses on the individual, whereas leadership development focuses on relationships and the social context of leadership. Leader development emphasizes individual change and how the leader thinks of himself or herself as a leader. London (2001) suggested that there are three critical psychological processes that are key to becoming an effective leader: self-insight, self-regulation and self-identity. This approach emphasizes that the challenge in leader development is to help leaders find their own individual way of being effective through understanding their strengths and weaknesses, understanding of the context, and understanding other people and their needs in the situation. Therefore, leader development has as its primary purpose the systematic development of those psychological processes with a strong emphasis on feedback interventions.

Leadership development in contrast focuses on the development of relationship-building skills; on skills to build effective teams, social awareness, including political understanding; and the social skills to manage conflict, implement change and deliver on commitments. A variety of definitions emphasize these dimensions. The Society of Human Resource Management (SHRM, 2010:66) defined leadership development as 'Formal and informal training and professional development programmes designed for all management and executive-level employees to assist them in developing leadership skills and styles required to deal with a variety of situations'. McCauley *et al.* (2008) emphasize the role of leadership development in expanding the collective capacity of individuals to engage effectively in leadership roles and processes.

> **horizontal development** the adding of more skills, knowledge and competencies. It focuses on what a leader already knows
>
> **Collective leadership development** focuses on development activities that occur within a social network consisting a set of individuals and the relationships that bind them

Definitions of leader and leadership development do, however, make a number of important assumptions that may be considered to represent biases in the literature concerning how organizations function and the role of the individual leader. Specifically:

- They espouse a unitary view of organizations. Organizations are considered to have clear goals and objectives that are understood and accepted by all employees. This may not necessarily be a realistic assumption.
- They assume that a large organization model can offer the level of sophistication required to deliver formal management and leadership development activities.
- They do not fully acknowledge the contribution of wider life experience and 'situated' learning and development and they often underestimate the complex and uncertain nature of leadership.
- They view organizations as objective independent entities rather than being constructed of shared experiences and language which is used to make sense of experience.
- Too much emphasis is placed on formal development processes, and they ignore the many informal development activities in which leaders engage in organizations that can result in significant development (Table 12.1).

Table 12.1 Future trends in leadership development

Trend 1: Increased Ownership of Development by the Individual Leader
There is an increased focus on placing responsibility for leadership development on the individual leader. This shift in responsibility to the leader is consistent with the expectation that employees can be more proactive and self-managed. Therefore the individual leader decides what development needs to focus on and the leadership development process is customized to the needs of the leader. Development is no longer a programme to be undertaken, or content to be covered; it is a process, rather than an event, which is driven by the leader.
Trend 2: Increased Emphasis on Vertical Development of Leaders
There is a shift away from horizontal development processes which focus on competencies and a move towards vertical development processes that emphasize stages of development that leaders progress through as they grow. Vertical development processes involve the leader taking on more complex problem solving and new learnings. These vertical development stages move from self-awareness to self-authoring to self-transforming. In the self-awareness stage, the leader becomes aware that it is possible to understand the world in different ways and that it is possible to do things differently. As the leader progresses through the self-authoring stage of vertical development process, old assumptions are challenged and new assumptions are tested through a process of experiential learning. Transformation occurs when the leader does things differently and demonstrates a new confidence and behaviour set as a leader.
Trend 3: A Focus on Collective Leadership Development
Collective leadership development views development as a shared process rather than an individual skill set. In this scenario, leadership is enacted through networks, flexible hierarchies, distributed decision making and more open flows of information. This suggests that leadership development practices will focus on developing team capabilities, networking skills and organizational learning capabilities. This will require leadership development to occur in different ways and with a focus on teams of leaders. It highlights the need to move away from a model of leadership development that emphasizes taking the leader out of the work context and the use of formal leadership development activities.

Sources: SHRM (2010); Peters *et al.* (2011); Virakul and McLean (2012)

BUILDING YOUR

LEADERSHIP DEVELOPMENT AND HRD

The question therefore arises: what place or role does leadership development have in the context of human resource development? This question can be answered in a number of ways. First, both human resource development and leadership development share a common goal, which is the development of human capital. Human resource development focuses on the development of the total human capital pool of the organization (Garavan, 2007), whereas leadership development focuses on the development of a particular group of employees – leaders (Bailey and Clarke, 2008).

Second, from a structural perspective, leadership development is one of a cluster of practices that fall within the subject matter of HRD and the organizational practice of HRD. A number of HRD models emphasize activities such as workforce development, which is primarily concerned with the development of technical and job skills of core employees; career development, which focuses on the use of development practices to enhance the careers of employees; organization development, which focuses on the use of development practices to enhance the overall effectiveness of the organization; and leadership development, which focuses on the development of leadership capabilities (Egan *et al.*, 2004; Fisher, 2005; Werner and DeSimone, 2006).

Both leadership development and human resource development contain competing and potentially conflicting notions concerning the focus of both activities: is it the development of the resource component and/or the development of humans?

However, the concept of development is itself contested. Is there an end point when it comes to development, and does development focus on the individual acting alone or are others involved in creating and constructing leadership identity? These are important questions that are shared by both HRD and leadership development. Lee (2003) suggests that it may be more appropriate to think about different aspects of development which help us to understand development processes in a multi-dimensional way. She suggests that development can be undertaken as shown in Table 12.2.

- **Maturation:** This notion suggests that the endpoint of leadership development is known and that there are known and predetermined stages. The leader is the key driver of the development process.
- **Shaping:** This notion suggests that the end point of development is known but it is co-regulated and the learner makes choices that fundamentally influence the process of development.
- **Voyage:** This notion suggests that leader development is a journey into the self and it is not possible to specify the endpoint.
- **Emergent:** This notion suggests that leadership development is achieved through interaction with others. It suggests that leaders dynamically alter their actions to cope with the actions of others.

LEADERSHIP COMPETENCIES

Given the competencies of the global business environment, organizations are challenged to determine whether leaders have the capabilities needed to contribute to competitive advantage. Increasingly, they are using competency models to help them identify the knowledge, skills and personal characteristics needed to achieve successful organizational performance (Noe, 2010). Competency models are considered an effective way of ensuring that leadership development practices make a contribution to the bottom line (Kapp and O'Driscoll, 2010).

Numerous definitions exist concerning what is meant by the term 'competencies'. SHRM (2010) defined competencies as 'the knowledge, skills and abilities required to perform a specific task or function' (p. 18). Competencies are a core integrating element of leadership development across the organization. Alkin (1987) suggested that managerial

Table 12.2 The spectrum of development activities that comprise HRD

	Management/leadership development	Workforce development	Organization development	Career development
Purpose/ focus	• Development of individuals in ways compatible with the organization • Focuses on meeting individual's management leadership and career development needs	• Development of the skills of front-line and operational employees • Focuses on job-related skills and knowledge necessary to enhance performance	• Focuses on the development of organizational structures, culture and systems • Strong focus on the enablement of organizational change	• Can focus on either individual or organization or both • The development, implementation and monitoring of career goals and strategies
Processes/ strategies	• Utilizes both formal and informal activities and processes • Needs are rooted in organizational context and current/ future role parameters • Strong focus on the development of competencies that are portable to different contexts • Strong focus in recent years on customization	• Utilizes job-based instruction and on-the-job training processes and short training programmes	• Action-based methodology • Strong emphasis on use of surveys and feedback processes • Team and organization-wide interactions with experimentation and trial and error • Use of a change agent internal or external to the organization	• Strong emphasis on the use of career instruments and psychometric assessment • Balancing of individual and organizational needs • Preparation of plans of varying lengths
Prerequisite conditions	• A strong culture of learning and positive attitudes to learning by manager and leaders • A willingness to develop and self-efficacy for learning • Strong support and resources from the organization • Capability on the part of the developers	• Needs for development are determined by the task and technical requirements of the job	• Knowledge of corporate objectives and culture • Creation of a sense of purpose and willingness to change • Commitment to a long-term process of development	• Career clarity and strong self-awareness • Motivation to plan and identify future career options

competence consists of (a) interpersonal skills, (b) communication skills, (c) analytical skills, (d) job knowledge, (e) knowledge of the organization and professional norms, and (f) self-confidence. The term *leadership competencies* is now increasingly used. Swiercz and Lydon (2002) classified leadership competencies into two sets: (a) functional competencies and (b) self-competencies. However, Quinn *et al.* (2003) identified leadership competencies in terms of the roles leaders were expected to perform. GlaxoSmithKline, for example, have six core values and 21 leadership competencies. They emphasize competencies such as think strategically, change champion, lead courageously, manage execution, and foster enthusiasm and teamwork. Competencies are used to develop a consistent, reliable and standardized leadership development process (Table 12.3).

Many of the debates on competencies suggest that there are important distinctions between management and leadership competencies. Some of these distinctions are summarized in Table 12.3. These suggest that the tasks of managing and leading are distinctly different and require the development of different competencies. Competency models have a number of advantages and disadvantages; however, there are a number of important best practice principles that organizations should consider when using leadership competencies for development purposes. These best practice principles include:

● Competencies should not be viewed as static concepts but should be regularly reviewed to identify their fit with the strategy and goals of the organization.
● Organizations should define competencies required for future rather than past success.

Table 12.3 Leading vs. managing competencies

Leading competencies	Managing competencies
Visualizing greatness • Thinks strategically • Appropriate risk taking and innovation • Sees, in his/her mind's eye, what could be • Emotes enthusiasm and inspiration *Creating and empowering the 'we'* • Builds teams • Develops others • Appropriately involves others in decision making • Creates ownership/commitment in others • Delegates responsibility *Communicating for meaning* • Communication is principle and value-based • Communicates in facts, values and symbols • Makes communicating for meaning a priority • Takes required time to explain why something is important *Managing one's self* • Maintains an even temperament • Keeps personal energy high • Is self-confident • Maintains focus, persistence and constancy of purpose *Care and recognition* • Publicizes people's effort and successes • Focuses on the positive and recognizes positive progress • Cares about others • Recognizes and rewards people frequently and appropriately	*Planning and organizing* • Determining long-term objectives and strategies • Deciding how to use personnel and other resources *Informing* • Disseminating information about decisions, plans, etc. • Answering requests for information *Representing* • Telling others about the organizational unit and its accomplishments • Providing a fair accounting of subordinates' ideas and proposals *Problem solving* • Identifying and analysing work-related problems to identify causes and solutions • Acting decisively to implement solutions and resolve problems or crises *Conflict managing* • Encouraging and facilitating the resolution of conflict • Encouraging cooperation and teamwork *Monitoring* • Gathering information about work activities and progress towards goals • Evaluating the performance of individuals and the work unit
Networking • Developing contacts with people who are a source of information and support • Maintaining contacts through periodic interaction, visits, calls etc.	*Consulting and delegation* • Encouraging suggestions, inviting participation in decision making • Allowing others to have substantial responsibility and discretion in decisions *Clarifying* • Assigning tasks, providing direction, etc. • Communicating job responsibilities, task objectives, deadlines and expectations

Sources: Yukl *et al.* (1990); Kent *et al.* (2001); Day *et al.* (2009)

- Organizations should avoid the pitfalls, including ill-defined characteristics in competency descriptions which have no measurable or demonstrable impact on leader and organizational performance.
- Organizations should be aware of what other organizations are doing. Approaches to competency development should be informed by this, but should not be simple copies of what happens in other organizations.

CONSIDER THIS ...

Think about an individual in the public eye who, you believe, recently demonstrated effective leadership in handling a difficult or challenging situation. What particular leadership competencies did you see demonstrated? What was interesting about that leader's emotional competencies? Did the gender of the leader make a difference in your assessment?

Organizations need to ask a number of questions before they consider the use of leadership development competencies. These questions are:

● Is it appropriate to adopt a single set of competencies to describe all effective leaders in an organization?
● What evidence is available to organizations that having all the competencies specified by an organization makes a person a more effective leader?
● Is it possible for organizations to accurately predict the leadership competencies that are required for the future?
● Does the organization have the leadership and HR systems that support the use of leadership competencies?

SPOTLIGHT ON SKILLS

Consider working for a consulting firm that has been tasked with helping major international clients to develop programmes for managers who are making the transition from first line to middle management. At the beginning of the programme each group of participants discusses the characteristics of an effective manager and what defines leadership. These questions are threaded throughout the programme and encourage participants to think about the differences between management and leadership. Throughout the programme, participants explore management models and compare them with their own personal ideas. What are the personal and organizational factors that influence how participants will respond to the question of the differences between leading and managing?

To help you answer the questions above, visit www.macmillanihe.com/companion/carbery-hrd and watch the video of Marie Connelly talking about leadership.

A STRATEGIC APPROACH TO LEADERSHIP DEVELOPMENT

It is surprising how many organizations fail to understand the need to adopt a strategic approach to leadership development ▶ Chapter 2. Day (2007) suggests a number of important deficiencies in how organizations approach leadership development.

○ **No Clear Strategy for Leadership Development:** The organization lacks a clear statement of its philosophy of leadership and development. It is important to present and define what principles drive leadership development in an organization.
○ **Event-Based Leadership Development:** Leadership development is considered an ongoing process; however, many organizations consider it to be perhaps a once-off event or series of events. Development is therefore isolated from day-to-day organizational activities.
○ **Leadership Development is the Responsibility of HR:** Organizations frequently make the mistake of believing that leadership development should be driven by the HR or leadership development function. As a consequence, there is little effort to engage line managers in the design and delivery of leadership development activities.
○ **Poor Strategic Fit:** Organizations make the mistake of believing that development is important for development's sake. This may work as a short-term strategy but is not sustainable in the long term. To be successful, leadership development must speak to the strategic goals of the business and contribute to their achievement.
○ **Poor Fit with Organizational Culture:** It is important that leadership development activities are clearly embedded in the organization's culture. Some cultures are more supportive of informal development processes and approaches that emphasize development from experience. Other cultures are more aligned with the use of formal approaches.
○ **Limited Resources and Support:** Leadership development activities will fail where there is inadequate provision of resources and support. Support involves helping leaders to implement changes in thinking and behaving post development activities and providing feedback and psychological support when required.

strategic approach to leadership development
an approach to leadership development that links leadership development with the strategic needs of an organization and ensures that it has the leadership human capital to grow

○ **Lack of Personal Ownership and Accountability:** We highlighted earlier the need for individuals to be proactive and self-managed when it comes to development. The ultimate responsibility for development rests with the individual leader. Personal accountability involves activities such as development planning, socializing, feedback and implementing behavioural changes.

○ **Lack of Organizational Champion:** Leadership development activities are often initiated by the HR function with only limited engagement by the senior team. The existence of a champion at the top level in an organization is an important contribution to success. Ultimately, the initiative should not become too closely associated with one key individual.

We argue that leadership development is at its most powerful where it is strategic in focus and contributes to the performance and competitiveness of an organization. Table 12.4 presents a number of key elements of this strategic approach.

Strategic Alignment the process and the result of linking an organization's leadership development approach with the strategy of the organization

architecture An organization's leadership development architecture focuses on the programmes, processes and roles that are put in place to align leadership development with organization strategy

We will discuss a number of these issues here.

Leadership and Organizational Accountability for Development and Business Results: It is necessary to hold leaders accountable for both development initiatives and the results they produce for the business in order to justify investment. Cisco Systems, for example, places a strong emphasis on creating strategically relevant collective learning opportunities and evaluating the contribution of leaders to development activities when evaluating performance. PepsiCo historically allocates one third of incentive rewards to developing people and the remainder to business results; however, in 2009 it moved to an equal allocation of rewards for both people development and results. It utilizes the results from its six-months climate survey and multi-source feedback as part of its evaluation process ▶ Chapter 10.

Strategic Alignment: The business strategy should shape the leadership development activities of the organization. It is important to design a leadership development framework or **architecture** that

Table 12.4 Key elements of development in organizations

Senior management accountability	• Senior leadership views the development of leaders as a top priority. • Senior leadership drives leadership development activities. • Personal support and championing of leadership development by the CEO. • Each top executive takes responsibility for the development of a specific leadership competency.
Strategic alignment	• Leadership development is integrated with business strategy and HR practices. • Leadership development activities contribute to key business objectives. • Leadership development processes are sufficiently dynamic to cope with changing business strategies. • Development and implementation of relevant competency frameworks.
A leadership development roadmap	• Differentiate leadership development programmes by each level of leadership. • Customize leadership development strategies to each level of leadership. • Focus on the use of blended solutions for each level of leadership.
An effective architecture to deliver leadership development	• HR takes responsibility for developing and delivering leadership development. • Leadership development is undertaken using internal and external capabilities. • The delivery structure is sufficiency flexible to cope with the needs of the business. • Coaching is strongly emphasized as a key task of leaders in the organization. • HRD function acts directly to facilitate/organize/monitor the organization's leadership development activities.
Portfolio of leadership development practices	• Strong emphasis on a flexible portfolio that can be customized and individualized. • Strong emphasis on coaching and mentoring activities. • Strong emphasis on individual and collective development processes.
Metrics and measurement of leadership development	• Systematic outcome measurement processes to understand contribution of leadership development. • Development of tag and lead metrics. • Communication of the outcomes of leadership development to stakeholders.

is both integrated and linked to strategy and the needs of the business. Questions that organizations should ask in this context include:

- Does the organization have a strategic plan?
- Does the strategic plan contain sections on leadership development?
- Does the organization designate a specific percentage of revenue to leadership development?
- Does the organization use the strategic plan to assess future leadership needs?
- Does the organization have an annual leadership effectiveness evaluation process?
- Is there a focus on both the performance and the potential of leaders?

A Clear Leadership Development Roadmap: Best practice approaches suggest that it is important for organizations to differentiate leadership programmes for different levels of leader. The Centre for Creative Leadership (2013) proposes a model that emphasizes a suite of development resources that is targeted to five levels of leadership. These levels are as follows:

- **Leading Self:** This level focuses on emerging leaders, individual contributors and professional employees. Development practices at this level can focus on building a common leadership language within an organization and enhancing the competencies of individuals who are being prepared for leadership roles.
- **Leading Others:** This level focuses on developing leaders who will have responsibility for developing individual contributors. The emphasis of leadership development activities is on helping individuals transition from being an individual performer to leading a team, and helping new leaders build effective work relationships and deal effectively with conflict. Particular emphasis is placed on coaching and development skills and achieving team goals.
- **Leading Managers:** This level focuses on leaders who have responsibility for managing leaders or senior professional employees. This level of development focuses on helping leaders handle complexity, manage politics, engage in upward influence and integrate cross-functional perspectives and contributions.
- **Leading the Function:** This level focuses on developing leaders to manage functions and divisions. Particular emphasis is placed on developing strategic vision, aligning the function to ensure implementation and think both short- and long-term.
- **Leading the Organization:** This level focuses on the strategic leadership of organizations. Particular emphasis is placed on developing strategic capabilities, aligning organizational units and building strategic visioning skills, and enhancing organizational performance.

Make a Persuasive Case for Investment in Leadership Development: Leadership development is carried out in organizations to meet a multiplicity of objectives and agendas. These reasons are summarized in Table 12.4. However, these development agendas change over time and there is a need to review these purposes on a regular basis. Making an effective case requires that organizations consider the following:

- Analyse and review the business: This step involves forming a view of the main challenges facing the business. It is important to understand how senior managers view the key business challenges. To develop this understanding it is important to talk to key organizational stakeholders.
- Establish the performance benefits required: It is important to focus on developing a compelling story for investment in management and leadership development. The specialist will need to achieve a clear understanding concerning the most important and/or urgent performance issues. It also involves consideration of the best opportunities for a management development intervention.
- Analyse the organization and people capability outcomes that are preconditions for success: This requires consideration of the capabilities required at organizational, group and individual level. This will involve the generation of a shared view concerning the gaps between short-term/long-term performance expectations and current performance. There is sufficient evidence to indicate that many organizations tend to focus externally on strategic terms and overlook the role of building internal capability. CIPD recommends that the specialist should engage senior managers in a business organization and management review process. This review process helps managers to think about the relationships between business and performance imperatives.
- Agree priorities and develop a master plan: The management development specialist should reach a shared view with senior management concerning the management development priorities. Once priorities have been established, it is then necessary to define a detailed plan for tackling the priorities for action for management development and to specify the resource requirements. A strong case will consider who has responsibility to achieve the goals and priorities specified; however, it is important that key stakeholders are continuously involved. There may be a tendency for the management development specialist to take over the project management of the plan.

Designing the Most Effective Leadership Development Architecture: The architecture for leadership development should be mindful of where the business is strategically, the role of stakeholders and the capabilities of the leadership team. Organizations have a number of options when they consider how best to structure management development activities. These include a consultancy function, a business partner model, a line-manager function, an outsourcing model and a shared-services model. We will briefly evaluate the nature and merits of each option.

A Consultancy Function: Under this arrangement leadership development will operate as an internal consultancy. This consultancy function can be centralized or decentralized. In large organizations it is possible that a central team of professionals may exist who provide services to business units; alternatively, a specialist may be permanently located in the business unit with a small, more strategically oriented core located centrally in the organization.

An internal consulting function will achieve its credibility through a history of interactions with the business. The consultant is expected to have a detailed and deep understanding of the business, including its culture, language and strategies, and to have a strong focus on the corporate agenda. However, this approach is not without its problems.

The internal consultant may be faced with the challenge of how best to balance central with localized needs. It may also lead to fragmentation of the management development effort, simply because each business unit may begin to pursue its own agenda regardless of the corporate-wide approach to management development. It is possible that the consultant in a decentralized model may suffer from a lack of understanding of the role within the business unit. There is also evidence to indicate that trust issues may arise and the consultant at a local level may lack the power to action projects and proposals. A centralized approach may be more valuable in terms of gaining senior management support.

A Business Partner Model: Holbeche (1999) defines a business partner as a specialist who works alongside senior managers and provides the link between business and organizational strategies. The specialist provides support and challenge to the senior team while at the same time developing credible leadership development initiatives. It is envisaged that the business partner will have a seat at the executive table and will be viewed as an equal partner in making strategic decisions about the business. The specialist will likely have responsibility for a wider brief than leadership development: it may also include elements of organizational design, strategy development and planned organizational change. The business partner model operates at a more strategic level and demands a broad and deep skill set.

A business partner model is very challenging for a leadership development specialist. It is likely to operate more successfully in large organizations. CIPD (2003) found that a large number of HR professionals are increasingly engaged in strategy issues. They are required to have credibility as business partners; however, many feel poorly skilled for their roles. Other research has highlighted that some HR professionals have less effective people skills. They do not possess the assertiveness, self-confidence and openness to others required to be successful in the role.

Leadership Development as a Line Management Function: This model advocates that line managers should have the primary responsibility for managing management and leadership development. Leadership development specialists consider this option to be risky and potentially doomed to failure due to a lack of commitment by line managers to put leadership development sufficiently high up on their agenda. Under this arrangement, line managers will perform the operational and tactical aspects of leadership development, with the more strategic aspects dealt with by a small core of leadership development specialists at the corporate centre.

An Outsourcing Model: Outsourcing is a long-term arrangement to provide leadership development services, whereas contracting out may be viewed as more of a once-off arrangement with a leadership development consultant provider, largely on the basis of need. Organizations will utilize outsourcing or contracting out because it offers cost effectiveness, increased flexibility, added value and greater control. It also offers an extension of a partnership approach, in this case with external partners.

This model may be used in conjunction with some of the models described earlier. This model enables organizations to build a small expert core of leadership development specialists who work in an internal consultant

---

internal consultant A leadership development specialist as an internal consultant operates within the organization and provides professional expertise in leadership development issues. The role requires engagement with multiple and changing clients

business partner Business partnering represents a process through which the individual responsible for leadership development participates in strategic planning to help the business meet present and future goals

role. The organization can then buy in the leadership development services that it requires. It provides specialists with the flexibility to respond to unusual needs and provide a customized/specialized service to the business.

CONSIDER THIS ...

Who, in your view, has responsibility for leadership development? To what extent is it solely the responsibility of organizations? Should individual leaders take responsibility for their own development? How realistic do you think is this notion of individual leaders taking responsibility for development?

PORTFOLIO OF LEADERSHIP DEVELOPMENT PRACTICES

Organizations have a large number of choices when it comes to selecting the optimal leadership development mix. These include job assignments, formal coaching and mentoring, action learning, peer networks, job shadowing and technology-enabled practices. The Centre for Creative Leadership proposes a 70:20:10 development mix (see Figure 12.1), where it considers

the 70 per cent component to have the greatest impact and to be easier to implement. It is beyond the scope of this chapter to detail all the practices that can be used by organizations. We therefore focus on a small number of practices in this section.

○ **360-Degree Feedback:** This is a very popular development practice. It involves the systematic measurement of the perceptions of an individual's leadership performance from an entire circle of relevant viewpoints, including self, subordinates, peers, supervisors and even external stakeholders such as customers and suppliers (McCarthy and Garavan, 2006). A comprehensive assessment from various role perspectives can provide an accurate picture of the impact of a leader's behaviour on others. The gap between self-ratings and others' ratings can be used to estimate individual self-awareness, which has been shown to be positively related to managerial performance. A weakness of this practice is that the resulting ratings can lead to confusion if there is major disparity across rating sources.

○ **Coaching:** Coaching is useful in helping leaders make sense of assessment data, put together actionable development plans, implement the plan, and provide support and follow-up assessment of behavioural change (Ellinger and Kim, 2014). An important factor to consider with coaching is the training and experience of the particular coach. Coaching is a very tailored and personalized intervention and has many applications in a leadership development context. It can be used for both individual

Figure 12.1 Optimal leadership development matrix

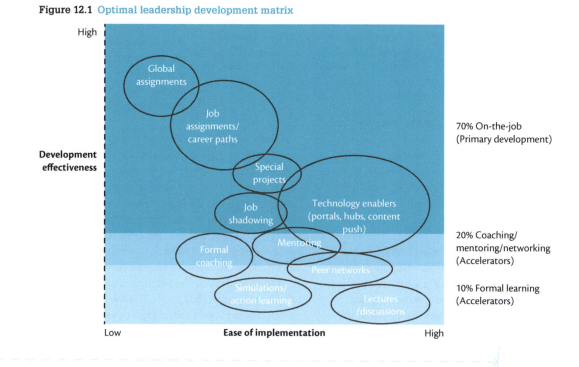

leaders and teams of leaders; however, it is important that its role is clearly articulated within the leadership development process. Coaching should be viewed as a developmental rather than a remedial process.

○ **Mentoring:** Mentoring can be a formal or informal process in which a more senior person takes a vested interest in the personal and professional development of a more junior person, usually a professional colleague. Informal mentoring programmes tend to be more effective and receive more favourable responses than formal programmes (Megginson, 2006). Mentoring is very time-intensive for both parties and there may be insufficient numbers of qualified mentors. Mentoring may, therefore, only be used in targeted situations involving high-potential managers and senior-level executives. It may be more realistic to set up mentoring networks, in which employees are assisted in identifying existing helpful relationships and then trained in how to better use these relationships for their development.

○ **Job Assignments:** Considered a very effective leadership development practice, especially those assignments that 'stretch' the thinking or other capabilities of the target leader

(Ohlott, 2004). Leaders view their most potent development activities to be experientially based, especially on-the-job experiences. Putting development leaders into stretch job assignments is a valuable development tool; however, two fundamental questions need to be answered: (a) how prepared should someone be for a stretch assignment? and (b) what is the right assignment for a particular leader at this time? It requires a detailed knowledge of the career goals, career paths and development readiness of a leader.

○ **Action-Learning Projects:** An approach that is based on the assumption from adult learning theory that people learn most effectively when working on organizational problems in real time (Leonard and Lang, 2010). Action learning typically takes place in project teams composed of people from diverse functions and locations working together for six to 12 months on an issue considered to be strategically important to the organization. What makes or breaks action learning in terms of development is the degree to which ongoing learning is valued as much as performing well. External coaches are often used to help facilitate team self-reflections and to enhance learning and development.

Fosco Data Handling: The Leadership Challenges

Fosco is a major US-based data handling firm that has a number of sites throughout the UK and mainland Europe. It employs 4,000 people and its core business involves transactional services related to the processing of data received from its key customers. The data is delivered to Fosco in either electronic or hard-copy form and consists of market survey questionnaires and customer opinion data. Fosco adds value to this data by transferring it to data files, coding data analyses and generating a variety of report formats. These reports may be delivered electronically to customers or printed as bound reports. The data that Fosco handles is highly sensitive and confidential. Its customers include government departments, the National Health Service and commercial organizations. Work

is carried out to very precise specifications and tight deadlines.

Fosco implements a flexible employment resource model. It has a large pool of agency staff (15 per cent of employees) that consists of data entry clerks, data processors and data printers. It also has a large number of employees from two subcontractor firms (BTech and TeCno). They consist of technical staff who provide computer troubleshooting services and a variety of technical support services. BTech managers work on Fosco premises and manage BTech staff. TeCno manages work on a remote basis and is rarely on Fosco premises. Fosco implements this employment model to ensure flexibility, quick turnaround and lower costs.

Fosco has encountered a number of challenges in

implementing its resourcing model. First, contractor staff have created problems due to their inability to prioritize the work that needs to be completed. They are frequently reluctant to drop a low-priority troubleshooting task to deal with a problem that is holding up the completion of a high-priority batch of data analyses. Fosco managers are experiencing difficulties in engaging with BTech employees, and on occasions they have had to engage with BTech managers if they required a problem to be addressed quickly. Frequently, BTech managers are not available, with the result that Fosco has had to pay overtime in order to get tasks completed. This has given rise to major conflicts, a lack of clear lines of communication and poor accountability.

Second, a number of problems have arisen in relationships between agency and subcontractor staff, although relationships have generally been good.

These problems have centred on how best to prioritize work and a lack of observance of health and safety and breaches of confidentiality. Some agency and contractor staff are not aware of health and safety procedures and do not comply with regulatory requirements. Agency employees on occasions do not fully appreciate the sensitivity of data. Contractor staff have on two occasions taken highly confidential electronic records belonging to a government department from the Fosco premises to work on them at home.

Fosco has come to the conclusion that there is a lack of leadership and management skills. In particular, managers are not sufficiently proactive and they get bogged down in unnecessary detail. Recent engagement survey data suggests that employee morale is low. There is an absence of strategic awareness and forward planning. Problems are frequently left unsolved and conflict issues are not addressed. Recent customer surveys have highlighted significant dissatisfaction with service levels. Customer relationship management was highlighted as a particular deficiency. Employees complain that they receive little feedback from managers and the work they perform is very boring.

As a result, Fosco has called in an external consultant to analyse the management skill situation and provide solutions.

Questions

1 What leadership development challenges are illustrated in this case study?
2 What particular leadership competencies would you see as priority to enable managers to be effective in this context?
3 What suggestions do you have in terms of the design and delivery of leadership development interventions to address the issues highlighted in the case study?

CHALLENGES FOR LEADERSHIP DEVELOPMENT

Leadership development is increasingly viewed in a global context where issues of diversity and cross-cultural values become particularly salient. Similarly, leadership development is expected to make a contribution to sustainability, creativity and innovation in organizations. These issues have a number of important implications for leadership development.

Cross-Cultural Leadership Development:
Increasingly, leadership development activities have to focus on enhancing the cross-cultural competence of leaders to operate in a multicultural context. An important consequence of globalization is the requirement to manage the increasingly diverse environment in which organizations now operate. In recognition of this, many organizations are developing leadership programmes to develop leaders in intercultural competence and global management skills. These leadership development activities focus on the development of cultural intelligence (Chin and Gaynier, 2006) and global leadership competencies (Javidan and House, 2001). The The 'Global Leadership and Organizational Behavior Effectiveness' Research Program (GLOBE) findings highlight the importance of style versatility, whereby a leader can recognize universal leadership characteristics across cultural contexts and be able to deploy styles that are culturally specific.

Sustainability and Sustainable Development:
There is an increased focus on sustainability issues in organizations and the role of sustainable leadership. Hargreaves and Fink (2004) argue that sustainable leadership focuses on sustaining rather than depleting human resources. They suggest seven principles of sustainable leadership:

- It focuses on creating and preserving sustaining learning.
- It ensures success over time.
- It sustains the leadership of others.
- It addresses issues of social justice.
- It develops rather than depletes human and natural resources.
- It undertakes activist engagement with the environment.

Therefore, leadership development activities must enhance leader sustainability. This is a difficult challenge for leadership development and will focus on providing leaders with a cycle of ongoing leadership. Development helps individual leaders to understand the complexities of sustainability and how they can transform organizations and the environments in which they operate.

Diversity Issues and Leadership Development:
Leadership development activities in organizations increasingly engage with issues of diversity. Despite many efforts to diversify organizations, women and people of colour remain significantly under-represented in leadership positions. Eagly and Carli (2007) argued that there exists a gender bias to the effect that men are associated with being leaders because they demonstrate masculine traits, such as dominance, that people associate with leadership. Similarly, people of colour experience various forms of discrimination that impact promotions, access to mentoring and coaching, and leadership development opportunities. A study by DeGroot *et al.* (2013) found that some organizations view diversity as a compliance issue and, as a result, do not invest in diversity-focused leadership development activities. Organizations that are committed to diversity among their leadership populations implement a variety of initiatives such as mentoring programmes, affinity groups, top talent development initiatives and tailored programmes to help talented women and minorities move into leadership positions.

Creativity and Innovation: Creativity and innovation have become key priorities for organizations. In order for organizations to grow, leaders are required to work to ensure effective adaptation and transformation. Horth and Buchner (2009) have suggested that innovative leadership requires a skill set that focuses on: (1) perceiving more deeply beyond first impressions; (2) tapping into personal experiences; (3) bringing information to life; (4) generating insights through exploration and experimentation; (5) facilitating dialogue; and (6) facilitating syntheses. Through this skill set, leaders will develop an organization that is conducive for creativity and innovation to flourish. Leadership development programmes, therefore, should focus on helping leaders to be skilled in constructing opportunities for dialogue, discussion and debate and to remove barriers that prevent people from learning more effectively from each other. Harris (2009) has suggested that creative leadership is a form of servant leadership, in which the primary leadership task is to connect different people, ideas and ways of thinking about issues. She describes creative leadership as 'leadership without ego'.

Fashion Factories: Time for HRD Education to Take a Stance

In June 2013, a clothing factory collapse in Bangladesh highlighted the fact that many workers are subject to labour exploitation and have few development and career opportunities. There is evidence of widespread exploitation at various stages in the supply chain that brings clothes to the high street. Children are frequently forced into bonded labour to work in cotton fields. Schools are frequently closed for periods of a few months at a time to harvest the annual cotton crops. Children are frequently required to work long hours and suffer from exhaustion, hunger and heatstroke. Children also work in factories where cotton is processed without any attention being given to their safety, health and welfare. They frequently inhale white cotton dust. Garment workers within the clothing industry in developing countries are frequently exploited. They are required to work at some of the lowest pay rates in the world in dangerous buildings and are forced to work overtime – mostly unpaid. Efforts to form trade unions have been frustrated and employees have little knowledge of their rights.

Managers and leaders of retailers and major fashion houses have been slow to show enthusiasm to implement initiatives to protect employees. Their business practices have had a particularly harmful effect on employee rights. Fast fashion focuses on giving high street shoppers the latest styles, just a few weeks after they first appear on the catwalk and at prices that allow shoppers to wear an outfit just once or twice before replacing it. This trend puts pressure on employees, who have to produce more garments in less time, but without any increase in pay or improvement in working conditions. Managers in many factories use the unreasonable targets set by high street retailers as a justification to exploit workers, who have few other employment opportunities available to them.

As a result, many people are asking questions as to why so much high street fashion is made in developing countries, and they are also asking questions about the ethics of how these clothes are made. HRD education is not immune to considering these questions. There is a duty on the providers of management and leadership development to help HRD students to explore the issues related to companies that have their clothes made in developing countries and to explore how management and leadership development can make an impact on helping those workers.

Sources

Forum for the Future (2010) *Fashion Futures 2025: Global Scenarios for a Sustainable Fashion Industry*. London: Forum for the Future.

Oxfam (2009) *Frequently Asked Questions: Labour Rights and Ethical Manufacturing in the Footwear and Garment Sector*. Sydney, Australia: Oxfam.

War on Want (2008) *Fashion Victims II: How UK Clothing Retailers Are Keeping Workers in Poverty*. London: War on Want.

Questions

1 What words, emotions and images do you associate with this issue?
2 What do you think should be done to protect workers' rights in developing countries?
3 What can leadership development practices in fashion organizations be doing to ensure that they act ethically and are socially responsible?

EVALUATING LEADERSHIP DEVELOPMENT EFFORTS

The evaluation of leadership development is considered something of a holy grail simply because the demonstration of the impact and added-value to the organization of leadership development is difficult to achieve. The focus on ROI is perhaps a folly because of the complexities involved. Attempts to demonstrate a direct link between investments in leadership development and organizational performance are likely to result in failure because of the many other factors that can impact outcomes. There are also difficulties in using experiments in organizations, so many attempts at evaluation are not particularly rigorous and are therefore more subjective. This is unfortunate, because organizations frequently emphasize a functional performance rationale for investment in leadership development. This rationale posits that there is a direct relationship between leadership development and individual and organizational performance. Organizations typically measure the impact of management development by simply recording the average number of development days per annum. This is both an imprecise and a possibly misleading measure. It tells us little about the effectiveness of leadership development practices and the quality of the development undertaken. We highlight the following challenges:

- The majority of evaluation models are better applied to a training rather than a development context. Leadership development activities can take different forms, from formal to informal, and many of the evaluation models are geared towards the evaluation of formal development interventions.

- Managerial work is contextual. This usually means that, even where a manager develops new skills, he/she may be unable to implement what has been decided due to barriers of an organizational or individual nature.
- The learning preferences of managers have an impact on the value they derive from management development.
- The outcomes of leadership development are likely to accrue long-term. Many organizations want a quick fix and evaluate management development interventions too quickly.
- It is sometimes difficult to get managers to participate in scientifically designed evaluation processes. They often find it burdensome to complete questionnaires and participate in interviews. It can prove difficult to get a pre-measure of managerial performance, which is necessary in order to show changes in both skill and performance.
- ROI studies are costly to undertake. They are best used for a high-profile leadership development initiative. They are time-consuming to undertake and require the application of a rigorous methodology ▶ Chapter 10.

These difficulties provide justification as to why many organizations prefer to focus on the evaluation criteria of reactions to transfer. Dell Computers, for example, focuses on the demonstration of value added to the bottom line. It concentrates on issues such as alignment of development with business needs rather than trying to estimate the direct effects of development through the use of ROI. It accepts that there is value in leadership development and it does not require justification through the use of ROI. The dominant concern is alignment of leadership development with business goals (Table 12.5).

Table 12.5 Criteria for evaluating leadership development

Criteria	Definition	Measurement approaches (examples)
Reactions	How participants liked or felt about the experience (affect); or participants' perception of the usefulness of the experience to subsequent performance (utility judgements)	• Post-experience questionnaire of emotional affect ('smile sheet') • Post-experience questionnaire of perceived practical value
Learning	The level of knowledge compared with before the experience; how much knowledge is retained over time; behavioural changes as a result of leadership development	• Knowledge tests • Mental models (e.g. understanding of a domain) • Skill demonstration
Transfer	The extent to which what was learned through leadership development is applied in the workplace. The level of support for the transfer of learning. The facilitators and barriers to effective transfer	• Ratings of behaviour (e.g. 360-degree ratings) • Self-report
Results	How did leadership development impact human resource, organizational performance and financial outcomes? What factors impacted these results?	• Productivity gains • Customer satisfaction • Employee morale • Profitability

BUILDING YOUR SKILLS

The HRD function in a large pharmaceutical multinational is seeking to enhance the effectiveness of its leadership development processes. Traditionally it relied on managers and leaders to emerge naturally; however, they frequently lacked the skills to manage effectively. Senior management began to recognize this problem and implemented a number of initiatives, including:

a   Training of leaders to coach more effectively

b   Introduction of a mentoring programme for high potentials

c   The promotion of informal leadership development activities

d   Enhanced evaluation of leadership development initiatives

A number of these initiatives were not successful. Based on what you have read in this chapter, could you suggest reasons why this may have been the case?

LEADERSHIP DEVELOPMENT IN SMEs

There is a general recognition of the importance of leadership in SMEs, particularly in terms of enhancing the strategic focus of the firm and its capacity to cope with major change (Carter *et al.*, 2000; Kempster and Cope, 2010). However, there is limited understanding and commitment of owner-managers to investment in formal leadership development. The majority of small firms are started by entrepreneurs who will continue to exert a key influence on the firm's strategies and activities. Therefore, they represent a key locus of decision making when it comes to investment in formal leadership development. There are also a number of other significant impediments to investment in formal leadership development. These include a lack of human resource expertise to advise owner-managers on the importance of leadership development; a lack of financial resources to invest in leadership development; too much of a focus on short-term operational priorities; unwillingness to make use of external advice and resources; and a lack of critical mass in terms of the number of managers to develop customized leadership development solutions.

However, SMEs also make significant use of informal leadership development strategies such as informal mentoring and coaching processes; observation; learning through conversations and problem solving; and team-working activities (Garavan *et al.*, 2009). These informal leadership development activities may represent a better fit with the SME context, given the more organic structures that exist and the emergent approach to the development of SME strategy. This informal approach aligns with the well-known fact that SME managers are 'home grown', with considerable company-based knowledge but limited formal experience of broader management competencies. Formal leadership development activities may be more effective in developing these competencies.

SUMMARY

The overarching goal of leadership development in organizations is the capacity for individuals to be effective in leadership roles. For leadership development to be effective, it must be closely aligned with and designed for the organizational context, including its strategy, its culture and the needs of individual leaders. Leadership development competencies are frequently used by organizations to ensure that their leadership development practices are effectively aligned. Effectively aligned leadership development practices require organizations to consider how best to ensure strong senior manager engagement, clear alignment with goals and culture, an effective structure to deliver leadership development, an integrated portfolio of leadership development practices, and customized metrics and measurement of leadership development activities. The evaluation of leadership development activities is something of a holy grail and efforts to demonstrate ROI are likely to fail. Many organizations accept that leadership development is a sound investment for organizations to make in their future; therefore the focus should be on enhancing the alignment or fit of leadership development with organizational goals.

 ### CHAPTER REVIEW QUESTIONS

1 What arguments would you make to support investment by organizations in leadership development?
2 Which is more difficult to achieve – leader or leadership development? Justify your answer.

3 Explain four limitations of a competency approach to leadership development.
4 Explain four characteristics of a strategic approach to leadership development.
5 Does management differ from leadership? What are the implications of your answer for leadership development?
6 What skills are required of leadership development specialists to be effective internal consultants?
7 Why might organizations outsource leadership development? What disadvantages do you see with such an arrangement?
8 What challenges are leaders likely to encounter when transferring the outcomes of leadership development to their work behaviour?

 ### FURTHER READING

Bilsberry, J. (2009) *Discovering Leadership*, Basingstoke: Palgrave Macmillan.

Charmichel, J., Collins, C., Emsell, P. and Hayden, J. (2011) *Leadership and Management Development*, Oxford University Press.

Day, D. V., Harrison, M. M. and Halpin, S. M. (2009) *An Integrative Approach to Leader Development*, New York: Routledge Taylor & Francis Group.

Garavan, T. N., Hogan, C. and Cahir-O'Donnell, A. (2009) *Developing Managers and Leaders*, Dublin: Gill and Macmillan.

USEFUL WEBSITES

www.ccl.org
Center for Creative Leadership: A very useful website that provides useful articles, white papers and blogs on contemporary leadership development issues.
www.executiveboard.com
CEB Corporate Leadership Council: A valuable website that includes a variety of resources on hot-button leadership development topics.
www.I-L-M.com
Institute of Leadership and Management: Provides resources including education and publications on leadership topics.
www.leadership.opm.gov
Center for Leadership Development: An official website of the US Government, it contains many examples of leadership development programmes for different levels of leadership.

BIBLIOGRAPHY

Alkin, M. C. (1987) Evaluation: Who Needs It? Who Cares?, In R. Murphy and H. Torrance (Eds) *Evaluating Education: Issues and Methods*, London: Harper and Row/Open University, 314–329.

Bailey, C. and Clarke, M. (2008) Aligning Business Leadership Development with Business Needs: The Value of Discrimination, *Journal of Management Development*, 27(9), 912–934.

Carter, S., Ennis, S., Lowe, A., Tagg, S., Tzokas, N., Webb, J. and Andriopoulus, C. (2000) Barriers to Survival and Growth in UK Small Firms, London: Federation of Small Businesses.

Centre for Creative Leadership (2013) *Leadership Development Roadmap: Build the Skills Critical for Success at Each Level*.

Chin, C. O. and Gaynier, L. P. (2006) Global Leadership Competence: A Cultural Intelligence Perspective, 2006 Midwest Business Administration Association conference.

CIPD HR Survey Report (2003) *Where We Are, Where We're Heading*. Available at http://www.cipd.co.uk/subjects/hrpract/hrtrends/hrsurvey.htm?IsSrchRes=1, accessed 11/1/2014.

Day, D. V. (2000) Leadership Development: A Review in Context, *The Leadership Quarterly*, 11(4), 581–613.

Day, D. V. (2007) Structuring the Organization for Leadership Development, *Monographs in Leadership and Management*, 4, 13–30.

Day, D. V., Harrison, M. M. and Halpin, S. M. (2009) *An Integrative Approach to Leader Development*, New York: Routledge.

DeGroot, C., Mohapatra, A. and Lippman, J. (2013) Examining the Cracks in the Ceiling: A Survey of Corporate Diversity Practices in the S&D 100. Calvert Investments Maryland, available at http://www.earthday.org/filesfolder/BR10063.pdf accessed 13/9/2014.

Eagly, H. H. and Carli, L. L. (2007) *Through the Labyrinth: The Truth about how Women become Leaders*, Boston: MA, Harvard Business School Press.

Egan, T. M., Yang, B., and Bartlett, K. R. (2004) The Effects of Organizational Learning Culture and Job Satisfaction on Motivation to Transfer Learning and Turnover Intention, *Human Resource Development Quarterly*, 15(3), 279–301.

Ellinger, A. D. and Kim, S. (2014) Coaching and Human Resource Development: Examining Relevant Theories, Coaching Genres and Scales to Advance Research and Practice. *Advances in Developing Human Resources*, 16(2) 127–138.

Fisher, E. A. (2005) Facing the Challenges of Outcomes Measurement: The Role of Transformational Leadership, *Administration in Social Work*, 29(4), 35–49.

Garavan, T. N. (2007) A Strategic Perspective on Human Resource Development, *Advances in Developing Human Resources*, 9(1), 11–30.

Garavan, T. N., Hogan, C. and Cahir-O'Donnell, A. (2009) *Developing Managers and Leaders*, Dublin: Gill and Macmillan.

Hargreaves, A. and Fink, D. (2004) The Seven Principles of Sustainable Leadership, *Educational Leadership*, 61(7) 8–13.

Harris, A. (2009) Creative Leadership. Developing Future Leaders, *Managing Education*, 23, 9–11.

Holbeche, L. (1999) *Aligning Human Resources and Business Strategy*, Oxford: Butterworth-Heinemann.

Horth, D. and Buchner, D. (2009) *Innovation Leadership*. Greensboro: Center for Creative Leadership Press.

Javidan, M. and House, R. J. (2001) Cultural Acumen for the Global Manager: Lessons from Project GLOBE, *Organisational Dynamics*, 29(4), 289–305.

Kapp, K. M. and O'Driscoll, T. (2010) *Learning in 3D: Adding a New Dimension to Enterprise Learning and Collaboration*. San Francisco, CA: Pfeiffer.

Kempster, S. and Cope, J. (2010) Learning to Lead in the Entrepreneurial Context, *International Journal of Entrepreneurial Behaviour and Research*, 16(1), 5–34.

Kent, T. W., Crotts, J. C. and Aziz, A. (2001) Four Factors of Transformational Leadership Behavior, *Leadership & Organization Development Journal*, 22(5/6), 221–229.

Lee, G. (2003) *Leadership Coaching: From Personal Insight to Organisational Performance*. London: CIPD Publishing.

Leonard, H. S. and Lang, F. (2010) Leadership Development via Action Learning, *Advances in Developing Human Resources*, 12, 225–240.

London, M. (2001) *Leadership Development: Paths to Self-insight and Professional Growth*, New Jersey: Psychology Press.

McCarthy, A. and Garavan, T. (2006) Post-Feedback Development Perceptions: Applying the Theory of Planned Behaviour, *Human Resource Development Quarterly*, 17(3), 245–267.

McCauley, C. D., Moxley, R. S., & Van Velsor, E. (1998) *The Handbook for Leadership Development*. San Francisco: Jossey-Bass.

Megginson, D. (2006) *Mentoring in Action: A Practical Guide*, London: Kogan Page.

Mumford, A. (1993) *How Managers Can Develop Managers*, Hampshire: Gower Publishing, Ltd.

Noe, A. R. (2010) *Employee Training and Development* (5th ed.), New York, NY: McGraw-Hill.

Ohlott, P. J. (2004) Answering the Call: Job Assignments That Grow Leaders, *Leadership in Action*, 23(5), 19–21.

Peters, L., Baum, J. and Stephens, G. (2011) Creating ROI in Leadership Development, *Organizational Dynamics*, 40(2), 104–110.

Quinn, R.E., Faerman, S.R., Thompson, M.P., & McGrath, M.R. (2003). *Becoming a Master Manager: A Competency Framework* (3rd edn.). New York: John Wiley.

Society for Human Resource Management (2010) *Workplace Diversity Practices: How has Diversity and Inclusion Changed over Time?* Alexandria, VA: SHRM. Retrieved from http://www.thehrgroupinc.net/assets/galleries/Events/Diversity-Leadership-Conf-2010/PowerPoint-presentations/Workplace-Diversity-Practices-Change-Over-Time.pdf

Storey, J. (1989) Management Development: A Literature Review and Implications for Future Research – Part I: Conceptualisations and Practices, *Personnel Review*, 18(6), 3–19.

Swiercz, P. M. and Lydon, S. R. (2002) Entrepreneurial Leadership in High-tech Firms: A Field Study, *Leadership & Organization Development Journal*, 23(7), 380–389.

Virakul, B. and McLean, G. N. (2012) Leadership Development in Selected Leading Thai Companies, *Journal of Leadership Studies*, 6(1), 6–22.

Werner, J. and DeSimone, R. (2006) *Human Resource Development* (4th ed.), Melbourne: Thomson South-Western.

Yukl, G., Wall, S. and Lepsinger, R. (1990) Preliminary Report on Validation of the Managerial Practices Survey, In K. E. Clark and M. B. Clark (Eds) *Measures of Leadership*, West Orange, NJ: Leadership Library of America (223–238).

13 GRADUATE EMPLOYABILITY

T. J. McCabe

By the end of this chapter you should be able to:

LEARNING OUTCOMES

- Explain the changing context of graduate employment and the current challenges facing both graduate employers and new graduates

- Identify the skills, attributes and qualities required by new graduates entering a challenging and competitive labour market

- Discuss the concept of graduate employability

- Explain how the transferable, soft and hard skills of new graduates can best be developed

- Recognize the role of HRD practitioners in developing the skills of new graduates in developing graduate employability

- Discuss the role of the state, employers, universities and colleges in developing the skills, work experience and overall employability of new graduates

- Identify recent trends and developments in graduate recruitment and selection

- Describe future growth areas in graduate employment, with associated core skill requirements

The world awaits!

This chapter discusses ...

INTRODUCTION

The Graduate Salary & Graduate Recruitment Trends Survey (2012) suggests that students are entering into one of the most challenging graduate recruitment markets for almost two decades. Graduates are not only competing for jobs with each other; they are also competing with graduates from other countries and continents. Having a degree no longer guarantees a graduate an employment position in a desired organization (Branine, 2008). An increasing proportion of new graduates are finding it difficult to find traditional kinds of graduate employment, and have had to apply for jobs previously held by school-leavers. This is particularly the case in the UK and the US, where many graduates with expensive liberal arts degrees are currently struggling to get 'decent' jobs (*The Economist*, 2013). This is partly a result of the high level of competition for graduate jobs and can also be attributed to the fact that many graduates face serious financial difficulties after graduation as they have large student loans.

The reality is that, when graduates leave their university and college life, they often do so without being sufficiently equipped with the skills required for employment. Additional reasons why graduates struggle to gain employment include poor English, mathematics and communication skills. Many graduate employers believe that new graduates have not pursued studies relevant to the needs of the marketplace in terms of academic content, competencies and skills. What often matters is not just the number of years and time spent in education, but, rather, the content of the courses graduates study while they are in education. Many graduates themselves also believe that the knowledge they have acquired in higher education degrees is secondary to the range of other transferable skills they have acquired from work-related learning and team-based activities during college (Lowden *et al.*, 2011). Because many larger employers are willing to provide extensive training on organizational and role-specific knowledge and skills required by graduates, this often means that the graduate's degree subject is of less importance than the other qualities and skills they can demonstrate.

This chapter discusses graduate employment and examines the expectations of both employers and new graduates. We look at the skills, attributes and qualities required by new graduates entering a competitive labour market, examining how the transferable, soft and hard skills of new graduates can best be developed. We appraise the HRD challenges involved, and discuss the role of HRD practitioners in developing the skills of new graduates and in developing graduate employability. We then examine the role of government, employers' representatives, universities, colleges and graduates themselves in developing the skills and the experience necessary to gain and remain in employment. Finally, the chapter ends by examining recent trends in graduate employment and looks at developments in graduate recruitment and selection and future growth areas. We begin by examining the wider developments affecting and shaping graduate employment.

NEW FORMS OF ORGANIZATION, LABOUR MARKETS AND TECHNOLOGY

As a result of the global financial crisis, many businesses and corporations were forced to become more efficient in order to remain in

SPOTLIGHT ON SKILLS

Certain skills are considered best developed through graduate internships and work experience assignments. Consider a role or occupation in a particular industry or sector of the economy, such as the information communications technology (ICT), finance, pharmaceuticals, health care or energy sectors. Identify the skills best developed in a workplace context for this particular role or occupation. Consider how you would devise a workplace graduate internship or work experience assignment to develop these skills.

To help you answer the questions above, visit www.macmillanihe.com/companion/carbery-hrd and watch the video of Linda Edgeworth talking about graduate skills.

business ▶ Chapter 1. They used the technologies available to achieve greater efficiencies and as a result made many employees redundant. This trend hit middle-class workers lacking special skills the hardest. Ninety-five per cent of the net job losses during the recession were in middle-skill occupations, such as office workers, bank tellers and machine operators (Cascio, 2013). While governments have been making their own attempts to address the mismatch between education provision and the labour market, policy makers are finding it difficult to adapt their labour market institutions fast enough to these new developments (*The Economist*, 2013). A major public policy issue and HRD challenge now involves reskilling and up-skilling those who have lost their jobs during the recent global downturn, as well as new graduates now entering the labour market. While this presents a

challenge for those involved, it also offers a significant opportunity for HRD specialists to demonstrate their ability to contribute to the betterment of 'human welfare' (Cascio, 2014a). Cascio (2013) also suggests that, while HRD expenditures may dip during economic recessions, the competitive pressures to deploy a well-trained workforce with the ability to constantly innovate will not go away. He suggests that the new 21st-century organization consists of a form that is flat, 'intricately-woven' and designed to link the various management structures, employees, partners, external contractors, suppliers and customers in a variety of collaborations. In this respect the new 21st-century organization looks like a spider's web, in which the participants involved are required to become increasingly interdependent.

An increasing number of workers in these organizations are contract-based, mobile and working 'flexible' hours. As a result, organizations are in a continuous process of redesigning work – many are separating routine tasks that can be automated, or contracted out, from skilled jobs. In addition to this, they are in a constant process of redesigning themselves through 'upsizing', 'downsizing' and 'contracting out'. There has been a much greater use of labour market intermediaries, outsourcing agents and contracting out services and functions that had previously been done 'in-house' (*The Economist*, 2013). Another labour market development relates to the increasing diversity of workers. Higher value has been placed on workers with a 'local knowledge' of emerging markets who also possess a 'global outlook' and have an 'intuitive sense' of the 'corporate culture' of the organization in which they work. The ability to work across cultures in building relationships with different constituents will be of much greater importance in the workplace of the future (Lublin, 2011).

While a highly competitive labour market gives employers more choices about whom they hire and how much they pay, there is a danger that their focus and priorities can become short-term. Many HRM and HRD practitioners warn against taking a short-term view of graduates and trainees. Companies are cautioned against using graduate recruitment like a tap that can be 'turned off' and 'on' at will, with minimal negative consequences for their future operations and output expectations (Philips, 2009). For many firms that are under pressure for immediate results, there is a temptation not to invest in the careers of new graduates. Immediate commercial pressures can often curtail the necessary investment in training and developing new employees. Employers need to keep a strong focus on investing in their 'talent pool' if they are to retain key experienced workers (Philips, 2009).

GRADUATE IDENTITY AND GRADUATE EMPLOYABILITY

Universities and colleges are finding it necessary to reconcile traditional notions of graduate identity with graduate employability. Graduate identity is a term which assists with our understanding of graduate employability. Graduate identity (Holmes, 2001; 2006) can be seen as a transitional identity by which the student moves from being a student to being an employee. Student identity is formed by the subject discipline and the range of experiences the graduate undergoes while at their university or college. Graduate employers also play a significant role in shaping graduate identity, in their role as the employer with its associated expectations of what a graduate will contribute to the organization. Hinchchliffe and Jolly (2011) conceptualize graduate identity under four different types of graduate experience – 'values', 'intellect', 'performance' and 'engagement':

- Extent to which the graduate has engaged with **values**: This reflects an employers' concern with diversity and personal ethics.
- Employers value the role of **intellect**: This is seen as delivered through discipline-related study.
- The role of **performance**: This involves both the effectiveness and credibility of the graduates role and their ability to deliver results.
- The role of **engagement**: This involves evidence of engagement with others across a variety of contexts and ability to develop and sustain networks.

The current economic climate has resulted in a heightened awareness of the 'employability agenda'. The concept of Graduate employability. In the context of a challenging business environment it is not sufficient that graduates demonstrate possession of

a particular set of skills, they must also demonstrate an ability to transfer them in the performance of their role (Wickramasinghe and Perera, 2010). Employability skills encompass those skills that are required to progress within an enterprise, enabling the achievement of the graduate's full potential and enhancing their ability to successfully contribute to enterprise strategic decision making (Hamzah, *et al.*, 2012). In possessing employability skills graduates are more likely to choose an occupation where they are satisfied and can successfully benefit the wider economy (Knight and Yorke, 2004; Dacre Pool and Sewell, 2007). A related concept is the idea of a 'graduate mind set'. According to many universities and colleges the 'graduate mind set' should emphasize the four E's (Lowden et al, 2011):

(i) Enterprising, showing initiative and entrepreneurship

(ii) Ethical, demonstrating good ethics and values in dealing with others

(iii) Engaged, demonstrating engagement and involvement in learning and in university/college life and activities

(iv) Enquiring, showing curiosity and skills related to academic research, scholarship and exploration

---

Graduate identity is a changing construct that is influenced and shaped by a number of social and economic pressures

Graduate employability refers to the level of work readiness, which involves the knowledge, skills, attitudes and the commercial understanding of new graduates. These enable new graduates to make a productive contribution towards organizational objectives soon after they gain employment

Employability skills are those basic skills needed by new graduates for getting, keeping and doing well in their chosen job, career and occupation

---

Educational institutions have come under intense pressure to equip their students with more than just academic skills. Within the UK many universities and colleges in the third level sector have a central careers service, whose role is to review the employability skills of future graduates, develop skills planning, skills sourcing and signpost new work and employment opportunities (Hinchliffe and Jolly, 2011; Lowden *et al.*, 2011). Many universities and colleges are now giving employability greater priority at central or strategic level and are increasing their efforts to promote the employability of their graduates. This can be enhanced through the creation of employability programmes and awards, with allocated personnel championing and coordinating employability initiatives (Lowden et al, 2011). Employability has been defined as a set of skills, knowledge and personal attributes that make an individual more likely to secure and be successful in their chosen occupation to the benefit of themselves, the workforce, the community and the economy (Moreland, 2006). Knight and Yorke (2004: 38) suggest using a model of employability that draws upon the deeper learning and broader student experience that goes beyond the narrow skills agenda. They suggest that employability encompasses the combination of four aspects of higher education:

1 'Understanding of subject matter' – propositional knowledge in the form of mastery of the subject matter of the degree

2 'Skilful practices' – characterized as procedural knowledge

3 'Efficacy beliefs' – belief that one generally can make some impact on situations and events

4 'Metacognition' – awareness of what one knows and can do, and of how one learns more

In terms of the perceptions of universities and colleges, the attributes, characteristics and skills that promote graduates' employability include those areas identified in Table 13.1. This 'list approach' has been adopted by a number of universities and colleges (University

Table 13.1 Attributes, characteristics and skills that promote graduates' employability

• Strong communicators – both written and oral
• Ability to work under own initiative
• Able to work independently
• An ability to take responsibility
• Creativity and ability to solve problems
• Time management
• Presentation skills
• Ability to work as part of a team
• Ability to lead when and where appropriate
• Ability to network, ability to form relationships and get to know people
• Commercial and industry awareness
• Willingness to learn and take on responsibility for personal development
• Self-reflection and awareness about what they wanted from the job
• Motivation and enthusiasm
• Self-confidence: in line with the graduate's own personal aspirations
• Work-readiness and awareness of appropriate work behaviour

Source: Lowden et al. (2011)

of Sydney, 2010). It identifies a number of graduate attributes that include scholarship, lifelong learning and global citizenship (Lowden *et al.*, 2011). Scholarship involves good study skills and lifelong learning involves a commitment to ongoing learning and development. Global citizenship involves adopting an international outlook and perspective. A problem with the list approach, however, is that some elements either are not required or are missing. Graduate identity cannot be simplified to a list, as there are many factors involved in employability. The 'list mix' or 'combination' should depend on student experience and on the role, occupation or career they wish to pursue. Also, little attempt has been made to rank employability skills or to assess their relative importance from the graduate employers' perspective. The result is essentially no more than an 'employer wish list'. The list approach has also been criticized on the basis that it does not sufficiently address the need for skills relating to 'critical thinking' and 'judgement' among new graduates.

The main trend in graduate recruitment and selection is that it has become more 'person-orientated' than 'job-orientated'. There has been a noticeable shift away from 'the job' and 'the role' and a move more towards the individual (Branine, 2008). Many graduate employers are now more interested in the attitudes, personality and transferable skills of graduate applicants, rather than just the type or level of qualifications they hold. Employers require graduates who are versatile and flexible, who have good commercial awareness and are sensitive to the needs of customers. This applies to graduates seeking employment in the public as well as the private sector.

Being flexible, versatile and adaptable enables graduates to remain competitive in a tough job market. In the context of an unpredictable labour market, employee 'flexibility' is considered a 'key criterion' among new graduates and, indeed, for all employees (Hansen, 2007). Where once graduate jobs and positions had clearly marked specific job boundaries, there is now a much greater emphasis on multi-tasking and multiple roles and responsibilities. In addition to evidence of good academic achievements, it is important that successful new graduates demonstrate an ability to adapt well to rapid change in the industry and business in which they work. This requires that they remain up to date in terms of the knowledge and skills they have related to their choice of career and the challenges in their sector, the industry, the organization and their role (Hamzah *et al.*, 2012).

Consider the nature of graduate identity, employability and employability skills. What are the main differences between these concepts? In pursuing graduate employability and employability skills, is there a danger that universities and colleges are compromising traditional notions of graduate identity? What can universities and colleges do to ensure greater employment opportunities and prospects for their students upon graduating?

- A positive work environment where they can reach their full potential.
- Rewards appropriate to the job. Rewards need to be appropriate in terms of production goals and the alignment with the attitudes and behaviours sought by the employer – typically resulting in high performance and positive organizational outcomes.
- Real 'engagement': many graduates are looking for a sense that they are valued, that their role contributes to the firm's goals and strategy and that their opinions will be listened to and respected.

GRADUATE SKILLS: TRANSFERABLE, SOFT AND HARD SKILLS

While employers generally tend to look for certain skills, behaviours and attitudes in potential employees (Hamzah, et al, 2012), they particularly value **transferable skills** (Branine, 2008). Transferable skills have been identified as enabling graduate career progression, facilitating organizational success and ultimately helping graduates contribute towards the economy and the wider society. In developing skills that can be used across departments, businesses, industries and sectors, graduates can significantly increase their employment prospects. Graduates are required to have skills that cut horizontally across all industrial sectors of the economy, and move vertically across all jobs, from entry-level roles and positions to strategic-level positions (Branine, 2008). For example, problem-solving, literacy and numeracy skills are generally useful in all departments, and are used for managing departmental finances and assimilating company documents and reports. In terms of IT, basic IT skills such as Microsoft Word, Excel and PowerPoint can be used across various positions in finance, human resource, IT and marketing departments. Employers, universities and colleges have identified combinations of transferable skills which they consider particularly relevant. According to Lowden *et al.* (2011), these key transferable or generic skills identified when recruiting newly qualified graduates include:

- Problem solving
- Self-management
- Knowledge of the business

Graduate employability: What graduates want

New graduates are increasingly looking for degrees to improve their likelihood of securing employment in a context where competition for vacancies is intensifying. Close and systematic links with employers are likely to be present in situations where the institution concerned has either a strong vocational remit, or objectives that regard employability as a compatible component of the wider academic and educational capacities and attributes. While the current economic climate is generally characterized by high unemployment, those industries that are doing well are currently experiencing a 'talent shortage'. These include industries such as ICT, niche manufacturing and insurance, which are currently experiencing a competency and skills shortage (Tibergien, 2013). As a result, hiring leverage has shifted to talented individuals who possess the competencies, skills, work ethic and drive to succeed in these industries. In order to fill these vacancies, employers need to have an understanding of what motivates graduates to apply for these positions and remain within their organization. Many graduates tend to look for businesses and industries with a viable future and outlook and seek out the following (Tibergien, 2013):

- Businesses and industries with positive growth and outlook.
- Jobs and roles with opportunities for growth at a personal as well as a professional level.

transferable skills Transferable skills are those skills that can be applied across a number of areas, functions and roles within an organization. These include literacy, communication and IT proficiency. They also include 'soft skills' such as team-working and negotiation skills.

- Literacy and numeracy relevant to the post
- ICT knowledge
- Good interpersonal and communication skills
- The ability to use own initiative but also to follow instructions
- Leadership skills (where necessary)
- Teamwork

Soft skills and hard skills

When it comes to 'soft' and 'hard' skills among new graduates, soft skills were ranked in the top half of the critical management skills list. Velasco (2012) highlights the salience of soft skills among graduate employers and suggests that many graduate employers are no longer hiring candidates based solely on experience, grades or hard skills. Many employers desire soft skills among recent graduates, such as communication, teamwork and leadership (Velasco 2012: 514). Soft skills are often the area where employers feel that graduates are lacking (Branine, 2008). Graduate employers consider internship and/ or work placement as the most effective method to develop these much-sought-after 'soft skills'. During their university and college years students have many non-lecture-based opportunities to develop their soft skills: for example, being involved in team-based activities and taking on leadership roles in sports or in clubs and societies. The development of these soft skills can contribute to an impressive graduate CV and thus enhance their employability. Table 13.2 identifies the top seven soft skills desired by prospective employers (in order of importance) as described by Shuayto (2013).

> soft skills essentially involve personal attributes and character. They relate to emotional intelligence, an individual's ability to manage their own emotions and to relate to other people
>
> hard skills are specific trainable and teachable abilities and skills sets that can be easily quantified.

While hard skills were considered important by graduate employers, they were ranked lower than the 'soft skills' set (Shuayto, 2013). When it came to specific knowledge areas, many employers felt that the greatest lack of knowledge among new graduates within the 'hard skills set' included basic skills in IT and technology. IT skills, including social media, were viewed as critical for all graduates across all sectors of the economy (Lowden et al., 2011). Potential employers highlighted mathematics as one area where new graduates were perceived as weak. One positive trend noted by the Graduate Salary & Graduate Recruitment Trends Survey (2012) concerned an increase in business and management skills among new graduates. This was considered as a positive indicator, given the large proportion of graduate jobs in both this and associated sectors. Graduates' writing skills remained a source of concern for many graduate employers. In addition to the above, there is an increasing demand for 'language skills' across all sectors of the 'global' economy. This is reflected by the shortage of skills in foreign languages among many new graduates. Graduates with skills combinations are also popular with graduate employers. Specific combinations often include a second language, for example sales or business combined with a foreign language, or science with a second language. This should be a key area and focus for future new graduates (Gradireland, 2012).

Table 13.2 Soft skills and hard skills

Soft skills	Hard skills
Responsibility and accountability	Written communication
Interpersonal skills	Time management
Oral communication	Project management
Teamwork	Presentation skills
Ethical values	Ability to assimilate new technologies
Decision-making and analytical skills	Computer skills
Creativity/critical thinking	Global/international business skills

Source: Adapted from Shuayto (2013)

BUILDING YOUR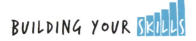

Using the list above, assess and appraise your own 'soft' and 'hard' skills. How would you go about best developing your own 'soft' and 'hard' skills further? Ideally, what would this involve? Take into consideration your own preferred learning styles and preferred method/s of learning.

CONSIDER THIS...

Think about a graduate position within a specific industry or sector of the economy, such as the ICT, finance, pharmaceuticals, health care or energy sector. Reflect on how the various soft and hard skills discussed above apply to the graduate role.

GLOBAL HRD AND GRADUATE EMPLOYABILITY

The challenge for most graduates is to successfully gain employment after graduating in a labour market that emphasizes both technical and social skills (Prokou, 2008). Graduates' chances for employment are to a greater extent determined by the link between higher education and the world of work, and the 'level of skills' links between higher education and work. The emphasis on skills development has produced changes in the role of the university. Universities throughout Europe have been called upon to make students more 'employable'. This has facilitated the emergence of a more 'market-oriented' university with much greater emphasis upon the link between higher education and the labour market across Europe (Prokou, 2008). Third-level institutions are required to further develop partnerships and cooperation with employers in the ongoing process of curriculum innovation based on learning outcomes. In April 2009 the ministers responsible for higher education in the 46 signatory states met to set the priorities over the forthcoming decade. The top three priorities were:

1 The social dimension – national targets for widening participation
2 Making lifelong learning (LLL) an integral part of higher education systems
3 Fostering employability – to encourage work placements to be embedded in study programmes (Edvardsson Stiwne and Gaio Alves, 2010).

The role of the state in many countries is to provide the links and incentives between educational establishments and industry that are essential to the development of graduate skills ▶ **Chapter 1**. Employers have been urging universities and colleges to focus their efforts on developing skills needed in many types of employment. Many universities and colleges are currently under pressure to develop graduate employability and improve the stock and quality of the generic skills among new graduates (Hinchliffe and Jolly, 2011; Ashe, 2012). Across many countries there is a perceived mismatch between the needs of the economy and the focus and structure of many of the degrees currently on offer. There is also growing pressure on higher education systems to develop strong policies and frameworks that offer graduates the opportunity to develop 'employability' skills. This is evidenced across the EU, the US, Australia, Ireland and the UK (Lowden *et al.*, 2011; Gradireland, 2012; IBEC, 2013; Shuayto, 2013). Many experts argue that graduates' skills should be better aligned with the requirements of future employers (Hinchchliffe and Jolly 2011; Ashe, 2012; Shuayto, 2013). A main criticism by employers in the US of both business schools and graduates concerns an inability to transfer and apply knowledge content to 'real life situations' in a fast-changing and dynamic global business environment (Shuayto, 2013). An awareness of current labour market conditions is also very important for universities, colleges and graduates, particularly in relation to those sectors with future growth potential (*The Economist*, 2013).

In their study on global HRD, Oh *et al.* (2013) looked at HRD across 34 Organisation for Economic Co-operation and Development (OECD) countries. They use four criteria in measuring global HRD. These include supply, demand, supporting systems and the environment. These are discussed as follows:

1 'Supply' involves the acquisition and development of human resources in terms of volume and quality of human resources. This includes the workforce and education levels.
2 'Demand condition' refers to the use of human resources in the market and the attractiveness of the labour market. This also relates to how many human resources are utilized in the labour market, such as employment rates and the structure and attractiveness of the labour market, with roles such as the number of creative professionals, technicians and associate professionals.
3 The 'supporting system' involves those activities relating to the acquisition, development and utilization of human resources. It also refers to a country's investment and policy-related infrastructure related to national human resource development.
4 External factors that affect human resource development are measured and identified as the 'environment'. This includes technology infrastructure, social capital, globalization and industrial sophistication.

Table 13.3 Country groups by global HRD competitiveness scores

Grouping countries	
Strong group	Switzerland, Sweden, the US, the Netherlands, Finland, Denmark, Norway, Canada, Iceland, the UK and Australia
Intermediate group	New Zealand, Germany, France, Belgium, Luxemburg, Austria, Ireland, Israel, Slovenia, Estonia, Japan and Korea
Weak group	Spain, Czech Republic, Poland, Portugal, Italy, Hungary, Slovak Republic, Greece, Chile, Mexico and Turkey

Table 13.3 highlights global HRD and competiveness by country. Switzerland was considered as having the most competitive advantage in national human resource development systems among the 34 OECD member countries within this study (Oh *et al.*, 2013). The results of this study are highlighted in Table 13.3.

Increasingly, employers are working in partnership and collaborating with universities and colleges in designing their HRD programmes ▶ Chapter 8. Companies such as IBM, Rolls-Royce, McDonalds and Premier Inn have been revamping their graduate training programmes. Some firms are taking a more active interest in the education, training and development of their own employees. For example, IBM has sponsored a school in New York. McDonalds has also set out a new ambitious graduate training scheme; it is currently one of the UK's biggest trainers, with a McDonalds University in East Finchley, London. The training in McDonalds University focuses on practicalities such as conflict management and dealing with difficult customers. Self-esteem and self-management are also on the syllabus, and it comprises a year-long apprenticeship programme emphasizing English and maths (*The Economist*, 2013). In India the IT firm Infosys has plans to train 45,000 new employees a year, including 14,000 at a time at its main campus in Mysore, while American Group, a regional food and restaurant company whose HQ is located in Kuwait, allows trainees to spend up to half their time at work and the rest at college (*The Economist*, 2013).

In designing a more valuable and responsive higher education to meet the needs of employers, graduates and the wider labour market, universities and colleges require imagination, initiative and flexibility (Lowden *et al.*, 2011). This also requires good relationships with

key people in industry and education in responding to the needs of employers and the wider economy. Careers services across universities and colleges are usually the main drivers in their institution concerning efforts to liaise with employers, and in providing links that promote periodic input from employers and graduate recruiters. This is particularly the case in relation to providing careers information and advice on campus and at careers events. Often these can take the form of university and college careers services holding annual conferences with employers to encourage greater liaison and communication. It is important that employer, university and college partnerships move away from situations where they are 'people-dependent' and become more 'system-dependent' (Lowden, 2011). This involves ongoing systematic practice to promote employability as well as evidence of good practice at course, faculty and departmental level. In exploring approaches to improve employability, employers need to work in partnership with universities and colleges. An example of where employers, universities and colleges can collaborate concerns the area of curriculum development. The evidence in the US, the UK and Ireland strongly highlights the necessity for universities and colleges to work more closely in curriculum redesign and in incorporating the training and skills viewed as most important by business and industry leaders (Lowden et al, 2011; Gradireland, 2012; Shuayto, 2013).

The current priority for many governments, universities and colleges is to expand the study of science and technology and bridge the gap between the world of education and the world of work (*The Economist*, 2013). This responsibility should ideally be shared between the state, industry and graduates themselves. This can be achieved by upgrading vocational and technical education and by creating closer relationships between companies, universities and colleges. Germany's long-established system of vocational schooling and apprenticeships is widely considered a model of good practice in this regard (Beardwell and Claydon, 2010). Germany has a vocational education and training system that encourages a broad base of training for defined occupations, ensuring that German employees are competent in a wide range of tasks.

Germany's 'dual system' vocational educational training, which is over 100 years old, has remained one of the most frequently copied training systems in the world (Deissinger, 2000: 605). Similarly to France, Germany uses a 'process'-orientated approach to education and training, where educational paths are largely anchored in institutional (or academic) communities. This is in contrast to many English-speaking countries that adopt an 'outcomes'-orientated approach, which forms the basis of an essential element of their vocational education and training (Deissinger, 2000). Under the German system of training, practical and skill requirements are led by and defined around the workplace (Beardwell and Claydon, 2010). On- and off-the-job instruction is carefully coordinated. The German vocational education and training system is essentially based on learning on the job (Hippach-Schneider *et al.* 2007), delivered through a centralized, highly structured system reliant on a dualism of learning venues that assigns funding, legal responsibilities and the overall development of programmes to a number of stakeholders (Dybowski, 2005). The cost of the system is shared between employers and the state. Employers also have an influence on the content and organization of training. Over three years of the process, participants typically spend 30 per cent of their time in vocational school and 70 per cent in the workplace. This helps produce a vocational course that provides development of three areas of skills:

1 Occupational competence – this involves systems and equipment.
2 Methodological competence – this involves reasoning and problem solving.
3 Personal and social competence – this involves team working and creativity (Dybowski, 2005: 16).

Despite its success, however, the German model has been challenged by the pressures across Europe brought about by globalization and the 2008 global financial crisis (see Moraal *et al.*, 2009). Despite this, other countries, such as South Korea, Singapore and Britain, are now trying to follow suit (*The Economist*, 2013).

Some common themes have emerged across all the international surveys reviewed by the National Survey of Employers' views of Irish Higher Education Outcomes (IBEC, 2013) (see Table 13.4). In addition to Ireland and the UK, this survey includes findings from studies carried out across the EU, the US and Australia. The various studies all looked at three main points. First, they identify the skills employers require from new graduates. Second, they explore the extent to which new graduates possess these skills. They do so by examining levels of employer satisfaction with the standard of graduates available. Third, the studies look at how they can best inform education policy and strategies and help to develop better links between education and enterprise in developing the required graduate skills. The findings addressed issues surrounding supply and demand, skills, education, skills developed, drop-out rates, work experience and engagement.

We now move the focus of our discussion towards the importance of placements, internships and work-based learning opportunities in providing university students and graduates with relevant employment skills, knowledge and awareness of employer culture.

Table 13.4 National survey of employers' views of Irish higher education outcomes (2013)

• **Supply and demand** involved skills demanded by employers, and the degree to which these skills were readily available among graduates in the labour market. This can be broken down further into skills requirements by sector and industry. This focuses on the readiness of graduates entering the labour market, emphasizing the link between education and labour market needs.
• **Skills** relate to those skills that are measured. They include basic numeracy, literacy and employability skills. They also include problem solving, teamwork and creativity. Foreign language skills were also considered very important by employers, both now and in the future.
• **Education** was a top concern for most, if not all, countries, currently required by the labour market now and into the future.
• **Skills developed** involved measuring those skills developed by higher education institutions. This involves reporting and measuring both basic skills and employability skills at secondary level, and can highlight remedial and basic skills training as necessary.
• **Drop-out rates:** High 'incompletion' and high 'drop-out' rates are viewed as an indication that the education system (high school as well as university and college education) is lacking relevance to the labour market and is not equipping students with the skills they require on entering the workforce.
• **Work experience** measures and looks at the importance of employer views on work experience and studying abroad among graduates.
• **Engagement** concerns levels of involvement, cooperation and the relationships between educators and business leaders.

€300 Million Investment in Seven World-Class Research Centres

The Irish government is taking a more active role in scientific research which is closely aligned to industry and enterprise needs, job opportunities and societal goals, and has announced a 300 million euro investment in seven world-class research centres. This is the largest ever state/industry co-funded research investment in Ireland and has been undertaken to support key growth areas targeted for jobs growth. The research is being targeted at major social challenges, including health and energy, and is being used to directly support 800 top-class researcher positions. These scientists will develop cutting-edge research and new technologies, attract dynamic partnerships with industry and ultimately help to create the jobs. One hundred and fifty-six industry partners are connected to the centres, both multinationals and SMEs, including Cisco, Hewlett Packard, Microsoft, GlaxoSmithKline, Pfizer, Kerry Group, *The Irish Times*, Intel and IBM and many more. The research activities funded include:

1 Big Data – the development of breakthrough data analytics technologies to make Ireland a global leader in this rapidly expanding area.

2 Marine renewable energy – this centre will look to generate energy technologies for industry from wave, tidal and floating wind devices.

3 Nanotechnology/engineered materials – will deliver world-leading research across a number of key enterprise sectors, most notably ICT, industrial technology, and medical devices and delivery systems. Ireland is currently ranked sixth globally in nanotechnology and eighth in materials science.

4 Food for health/functional foods – the centre will address important issues such as disease prevention, healthy ageing and improved population health in general. Ireland is currently ranked second in the world in probiotics research.

5 Photonics – the generation, manipulation and utilization of light – is an important enabling technology that underpins many areas such as future networks, communications systems and medical devices.

6 Perinatal translational research – which will focus on fast-tracking discoveries relating to most complications of pregnancy and newborn babies and service a huge societal and economic need globally.

7 Drug synthesis/crystallization – develop new mechanisms and better control processes to produce new and improved drug formulations and safe medicines.

Countries need to develop models to enable centres to add new industry and academic partners in 'spokes' or linked research streams to ensure that funding is used in a collaborative and consolidated way. This 'hub and spoke' model will allow every centre to maximize the potential of the platform research to provide flexibility and scalability by allowing new and existing multinational companies, SMEs and academic groups to partner in research projects and potentially create new research breakthroughs. The seven centres involve a collaborative partnership across research institutions in Ireland, with participation from University College Cork, University College Dublin, Tyndall National Institute (UCC), Trinity College Dublin, University of Limerick, NUI Galway, Dublin City University, Cork Institute of Technology, Teagasc, the Marine Institute, Geological Survey Ireland, Royal College of Surgeons and CSO Cork, among others.

Source:

RTE News 25 February 2013
http://www.rte.ie/blogs/digital/2013/02/25/e300million-investment-in-seven-world-class-research-centres-minister-bruton-minister-sherlock/

€300 million investment in Irish research announced
http://www.science.ie/science-news/landmark-research-investment.html, Accessed 5th September 2013

Questions

1 Discuss the role of the government in developing graduate employment opportunities in your country.
2 What skills and competencies do graduates require to avail themselves of the job opportunities discussed in this report?

GRADUATE WORK EXPERIENCE, PLACEMENTS, INTERNSHIPS AND EXTRA-CURRICULAR ACTIVITIES

Academic qualifications are only one of the criteria considered by an employer. Given the importance of developing 'employability' skills among new graduates, the strategic role played by 'work-based' learning has never been greater (Branine, 2008). Workplace programmes and internships help students develop the skills needed to succeed in their academic studies and their future career (Lowden *et al.*, 2011). Work placements and internships also help new graduates market themselves to potential employers. They provide students with an opportunity to reflect on their university experiences and consider how their experiences have contributed to their personal and professional development. Work experience, placements, internships and extra-curricular activities while at university are particularly useful in helping graduates develop transferable skills (Lowden *et al.*, 2011).

Many graduates tend to value extra-curricular experiences at university and work experience more highly than the content of their degrees. These can add considerable value to candidates' CVs and help them secure employment. Placements and internships are increasingly being used by universities and colleges to provide students with valuable experience and skills. Internships can be very popular with students, but are most likely to be found on management and business courses, particularly in degrees accredited by professional bodies, such as finance and accounting degrees. Work placements and internships are particularly useful in situations where the practical skills and experience of a business are viewed as key to achieving the required competences for enhancing employment opportunities. Some internships are, however, not always available for those interested in working for charities, or those seeking employment in the public sector (Lowden *et al.*, 2011). Many employers also believe that there are more opportunities for the academic component of the degrees to provide generic skills (Lowden *et al.*, 2011). This is particularly

> **personal development planning** involves the adoption of a 'self-managed' approach towards learning, where individuals take ownership over their own learning and development, with the aim of helping them build their self-confidence and relate their own learning to a wider context

the case in situations where coursework involves work-related learning, such as presentations and team-based projects. Also, some employers are now stressing the importance of graduates developing 'critical' and 'evaluative' skills.

From a university and college perspective, internships and work-based placements enhance the employability of their graduates. They help build student self-confidence, improve their skills and ensure that they are better able to apply the technical skills and abilities they acquired from their degree programmes (Lowden *et al.*, 2011; Gradireland, 2012; Shuayto, 2013). Some universities and colleges encourage **personal development planning**. Graduate work experiences and work placements should ideally involve combining the following key skill areas:

- **Academic skills:** These include skills such as research skills, academic writing, time management, exam preparation and academic skills development.
- **Extra-curricular activities:** These include clubs and societies, involvement in volunteering, hobbies and interests, and acting as a student representative on various councils and bodies while at university or college.
- **Work-related and work-based learning:** These include work placements, meeting employers, reflecting on part-time work, and receiving support to start own company.
- **Jobs and careers:** These include meeting employers, building CVs, interviews, career planning and developing the skills required to find a job at the end of the degree.

The above four elements are considered to be representative of the broad range of activities and skills development opportunities which universities and colleges can offer students. By engaging with all four elements, students promote their chances of succeeding at university and college, developing personally and professionally, and increasing their attractiveness to future employers (Lowden *et al.*, 2011).

Ideally, employers, universities and colleges should play complementary roles in developing graduate employability (Lowden et al., 2011; Gradireland, 2012; Shuayto, 2013). Where universities and colleges provide high-quality careers services and advice, employers can offer opportunities for relevant work placements and valuable experience for graduates to pick up additional skills and awareness of different types of work. Where placements, internships and work experience are offered and gained, it is important that the work experience is 'authentic', with appropriate support to ensure the students benefit and maximize the value from the work experience. While the cost of providing placements and internships can be considerable, particularly when it involves supervision by senior staff, providing these opportunities can result in benefits for both employers and students. According to Gradireland (2012), many employers use work experience to 'source talent' at an early stage. 'Work experience' has, therefore, become strategically very important within the graduate recruitment market. A key factor determining the usefulness of work experience and placements involves the duration of the work experience concerned. In order for students and employers to acquire the full benefits of this type of experience, employers stress that it has to last for at least six months. Year-long sandwich placements and vacation work are particularly valued by employers, and can play an important role in helping graduates gain employment (Lowden *et al.*, 2011; Gradireland, 2012).

BUILDING YOUR SKILLS

Consider the role played by governments in ensuring that third-level institutions provide the skills required by graduate employers both now and in the future. How would you go about advising national governments in successfully creating strong links between third-level institutions and industry and promoting graduate employment? What factors would you consider?

GRADUATE RECRUITMENT AND SELECTION

The process of graduate recruitment and selection currently involves a variety of methods that have developed and changed in type and use over time. Socioeconomic and political changes, as well as developments in information technology, have all led to the introduction of new and more sophisticated methods of graduate recruitment and selection (Branine, 2008). Graduate recruiters have to respond faster and more efficiently, not only to an increasing number of applicants, but also to beat increasing competition from other graduate employers. There has been a general shift globally in human resource management theory and practice. Previously, applicants were put through a mechanistic administrative process of 'job-oriented', 'measurable' methods in selecting employees for future job performance. Changes in labour market conditions have necessitated the use of more technology and 'cost-driven' methods of recruitment and selection (Lievens *et al.*, 2002; Anderson and Witvliet, 2008; Sackett and Lievens, 2008). There is also much greater use of social networking sites as part of the recruitment and selection process in graduate recruitment, including the use of LinkedIn, Twitter and Facebook.

Graduate recruiters now have access to a greater variety of more effective recruitment and selection methods to ensure that the most suitable and appropriate graduates apply and are selected (Lievens *et al.*, 2002; Sackett and Lievens, 2008; Chartered Institute of Personnel and Development, 2010). The use of different selection methods used to select graduates varies from one employer to another and generally depends on the nature of the role and the vacancy being offered. While some of the usual methods, such as interviewing, remain popular, there is a greater variety of methods used by which graduates are attracted to and selected for their first jobs.

Chartered Institute of Personnel and Development (2010) found that the most common selection method was still the interview. Despite an awareness of the dangers of subjectivity and unreliability, interviews still remain the most popular method of selection (Anderson and Witvliet, 2008; Sackett and Lievens, 2008). It seems that face-to-face contact with the applicant and the possibility of assessing the candidate's social and communication skills are the main advantages of the interview, and are the main reason why they are still used. To avoid the danger of subjectivity and low reliability, many companies use panels of two interviewers, or further sequential interviews with different people. A study of selection methods in five European countries (Shackleton and Newell, 1994) found that the use of tests was increasing, while application forms, references and interviews remained the most popular.

While it has been common practice for many employers to select graduates through face-to-face interviews and tests, an increasing number of employers are also using other methods such as telephone interviews, psychometric testing, assessment centres and online testing (Straus *et al.*, 2001; Lievens *et al.*, 2002). More organizations, as a result of technological developments, are now using computerized testing and multimedia tests for selecting applicants (McBride, 1998; Salgado and Lado, 2000).

Psychometric testing

Psychometric testing is a general reference to all forms of psychological assessment that relate to personality and ability (Bratton and Gold, 2012). As the number of multinational companies from the US has increased, more and more large companies are making use of psychological tests. These include a variety of tests ranging from ability to aptitude, from personality to intelligence. This is particularly the case for those companies that receive large numbers of applications and those that require highly skilled employees (Roberts, 2005; Chartered Institute of Personnel and Development, 2007a). Psychometric tests that can be systematically scored and administered are used to measure individual differences such as personality, aptitude, ability, attainment or intelligence (Bratton and Gold, 2012). There are five broad categories:

1 Attainment – this examines current levels of knowledge or skill, such as word processing or examinations.
2 General intelligence – this measures overall intellectual capacity for thinking and reasoning.
3 Specific cognitive ability – this looks at verbal reasoning, numerical reasoning or spatial ability.
4 Trainability – this looks at responsiveness to instruction or training and seeks to assess learning potential and rate of response in relation to specific tasks or activities.
5 Personality questionnaires – these aim to infer enduring individual characteristics and traits as a basis for predicting behaviour. (Pilbeam and Corbridge, 2010).

Psychometric tests have a good record for reliability and validity (Bratton and Gold, 2012). Testing offers organizations a cost-effective process in searching for the right people to match the company's personality, which can include the candidates' achievement orientation (Dawson, 2005). A Chartered Institute of Personnel and Development survey (2010) showed that 44 per cent of organizations used personality/attitude/psychometric questionnaires, 43 per cent used literacy and numeracy tests, and 27 per cent used general ability tests.

Assessment centres

Assessment centres are a popular tool for selecting candidates, identifying their potential and assessing their training and development needs (Lievens and Conway, 2001; Chartered Institute of Personnel and Development, 2007b). The Chartered Institute of Personnel and Development (2010) has found that 42 per cent of organizations have used assessment centres during selection. In addition to recruitment and selection, assessment centres can be used to select participants for training programmes, especially for leadership and management development (Thornton and Gibbons, 2009). By using a combination of techniques, assessment centres provide a fuller picture of an applicant's strengths and weaknesses. General methods used involve group discussions, simulations, role plays, interviews and tests (Spychalski *et al.*, 1997). Woodruffe (2000) makes four generalizations about assessment centres:

1 Candidates are observed by professionals trained in measurement dimensions such as competencies.
2 The assessments used consist of a combination of methods and include simulations of key elements of work.
3 The information is brought together from all the methods, usually under competency headings.
4 Candidates can be assessed in groups.

For most organizations, while the trio of application form, interview and references is still popular, there have been further developments incorporating the use of assessment centres (Lievens *et al.*, 2002; Sackett and Lievens, 2008). Assessment centres are considered useful in penetrating and uncovering graduate attitudes and behaviours relating to 'interpersonal relationships, leadership, influencing ability, sociability, competitiveness, self-motivation, tolerance, persuasiveness, and decisiveness' (Pilbeam and Corbridge, 2010: 206). They attempt to improve validity and reliability through multiple techniques. There is a wide range of techniques, including: group discussions and activities, presentations, in-tray exercises and analytical activities, role-plays, work simulations, interviews – individual and/or group, personality questionnaires and other forms of psychometric assessment (Pilbeam and Corbridge, 2010).

Enterprise Rent-a-Car Graduate Training and Development Programme

Enterprise Rent-A-Car is a $15 billion car rental company with more than 7,700 offices worldwide. The success of the company can be largely attributed to the success in training and promoting the best talent to become leaders within the organization. Enterprise Rent-A-Car's fundamental belief is that hard work and high performance should be rewarded. Promotion from within is a core business principle in developing and educating employees from the ground up to become future leaders. Trainees are given the opportunity to run their own business and are given independence at the early stages of their career. Enterprise has been recognized for its commitment to training, and has been named in *BusinessWeek*'s Annual '50 Best Places to Launch a Career' for the last five years. In terms of programme design, planning and execution, assistant and branch managers are responsible for the performance of their branch and the development of their employees. Branch performance is measured by four core areas called 'the balance areas'. These comprise customer service, employee development, fleet growth and profitability. These core areas are measured monthly. All members of the management team are ranked on a performance matrix. In order to be eligible for promotion to the next role or level, employees must be performing at the 'corporate average'. Training consists of a blend of practical and classroom-based learning. This project-based training is specifically designed to help employees engage in the

ACTIVE CASE STUDY

business quickly and gain a full understanding of how they can also impact change and increase performance. The projects must fall within the scope of four core areas of the business: customer retention, growth, revenue generation and cost reduction.

The objectives of Enterprise Rent-a-Car graduate training and development programme

Enterprise Rent-a-Car's 'business model' is reliant on a successful graduate training programme, promoting solely from within. It is imperative that a talent pipeline is created within the business, starting with the management training programme. All directors, 19 in Ireland and the UK, have progressed through the company, beginning on the management training programme. The senior management composition is a testament to the success of the graduate programme. The graduate programme helps trainees to both understand the fundamentals of the business and stay true to the core values of Enterprise Rent-a-Car. A good indication of the value placed on the company's career management initiatives is reflected in the overall positive business performance and employee retention at Enterprise Rent-a-Car.

The main objectives of the graduate programme are to:

1 Create structured learning opportunities for graduates by fully exposing them to every aspect of the business operations

2 Provide an environment that effectively integrates academic and project-based learning for maximum performance and productivity

3 Foster a culture that recognizes and celebrates the autonomy, creativity, diversity and innovation of new graduates

4 Ensure that Enterprise Rent-a-Car continues to recognize and reward individual success through career progression and further career opportunities

Trainees have an initial week of classroom training. This is followed by working in a rental branch in an 'on-the-job'-style training approach. The entrepreneurial graduates who start the training programme initially learn the basics of business management. They are exposed to every aspect of operating a business, from fleet management and marketing to profit and loss, analysis and sales techniques. Employees meet regularly with their management team to set realistic, measurable targets for their individual performance and for the performance of the team as a whole. As part of the learning and development process, the employees then receive specific coaching and training through structured training classes as well as individually tailored daily, weekly and monthly performance development meetings (PDMs) with their management teams. They are then held accountable for their performance towards those targets as their progress is tracked and monitored. Most importantly, they are rewarded for their success through pay and promotional opportunities. Ongoing development ranges from formal classroom-based training to teaching a new employee about an area of the business or managing a partnership with a key customer account. All employees set personal goals in their performance reviews, helping them to demonstrate their ability for future promotion opportunities.

Tailored to the graduate

Enterprise believes that it is important that employees are given responsibility and empowered to make decisions. On completion of the training programme, employees have the opportunity to diversify into other core areas such as finance, human resources, marketing, vehicle acquisition, business support divisions, or opening up a new pathway of promotional opportunity. There is a formal mentoring programme in which all new hires select their own mentor. Mentors are all mid to upper-level managers within the organization and come from a cross-section of departments and career paths. The mentors meet with the employees once a month to provide feedback, coaching and training. The mentors' performance and effectiveness for their mentees is monitored and managed. Reports on completion percentages are then delivered on a monthly basis to the managing director, who frequently provides top-down feedback and support for the programme. The employees exit the formal mentoring programme upon receiving their first promotion into management, at which point they are then invited to join the programme as career mentors themselves.

The effectiveness of the Enterprise Rent-A-Car graduate training and development programme can be identified in the loyalty employees demonstrate to the company. It is not unusual to have employees remain and work in Enterprise Rent-A-Car for 5, 10, 15 or even 20 years. Enterprise Rent-A-Car continues to support employee development as they progress through different stages in their lives and careers.

Questions

1 How does the current graduate training and development programme meet the business needs of Enterprise Rent-A-Car?

2 Discuss the link between the graduate training and development programme and performance management at Enterprise Rent-A-Car.

3 Explain how the mentoring programme is managed and its link to organizational performance at Enterprise Rent-A-Car.

GRADUATE EMPLOYMENT IN SMALL AND MEDIUM ENTERPRISES (SMEs)

Universities and colleges generally tend to have stronger links with large employers that have sufficient manpower and resources to sustain links with universities and provide placements for students. Many companies within the small and medium enterprise (SME) sector often lack the necessary time and resources to do so. While large organizations still dominate the graduate recruitment market, an increasing number of small and medium-sized organizations also now employ graduates.

One of the main changes in the relationship between higher education and employability is that higher education caters for more than one type of employer size or employment sector. There is also evidence to suggest that the gap between large and small to medium enterprises has been closing in terms of attracting and employing graduates (Branine, 2008). According to the Gradireland (2012), the number of companies within Ireland's SME sector predicting that they will take on one or two graduates in 2012 rose from 13.9 per cent in 2011 to 19.7 per cent in 2012. Graduates are no longer prepared for doing just medical, legal, financial, engineering and managerial jobs; they are now preparing to serve all the different sectors of the economy. These include those jobs that were traditionally considered for non-graduates.

SUMMARY

In this chapter we have highlighted the changing context of graduate employment and the current challenges facing graduate employers and new graduates. An understanding of what graduate employers want, and the skills, attributes and qualities required by new graduates entering this challenging and competitive labour market, is important for both students and the third-level education sector. Graduate employability involves all stakeholders understanding the importance of transferable skills for new graduates. There are numerous challenges involved for HRD practitioners in both developing the skills of new graduates and enhancing their future employability. Recent trends and developments in graduate recruitment and selection, as well as future growth areas in graduate employment with associated core skills, suggest that future areas for jobs growth with associated skills include IT and technology, finance, science and health care, sales, marketing and languages.

CHAPTER REVIEW QUESTIONS

1 Discuss the main challenges facing graduate employers and new graduates in the current economic context.
2 Identify the skills, attributes and qualities required from new graduates on entering the labour market.
3 What is meant by graduate employability?
4 Discuss the ways in which the transferable, soft and hard skills of new graduates can best be developed.
5 What are the HRD challenges and the role of HRD practitioners in developing graduate skills and employability?
6 Discuss the respective roles of the state, employers, universities and colleges in developing the skills, work experience and overall employability of new graduates.
7 Identify and discuss recent trends and developments in graduate recruitment and selection.
8 What are the future growth areas in graduate employment?

 FURTHER READING

Cascio, W. F. (2010) The Changing World of Work, In P. A. Linley, S. Harrington and N. Garcea (Eds), *Oxford Handbook of Positive Psychology and Work*, Oxford, UK: Oxford University Press (13–24).

Hinchliffe, G. W. and Jolly, A. (2011) Graduate Identity and Employability, *British Educational Research Journal*, 37(4), 563–584.

Shuayto, N. (2013) Management Skills Desired by Business School Deans and Employers: An Empirical Investigation, *Business Education & Accreditation*, 5(2), 93–105.

Velasco, M. S. (2012) More Than Just Good Grades: Candidates' Perceptions about the Skills and Attributes Employers Seek in New Graduates, *Journal of Business Economics and Management*, 13(3), 499–517.

 USEFUL WEBSITES

http://www.agcas.org.uk/communities/5
The Careers Advice and Guidance community is for anyone interested in careers advice and guidance in a higher education context. It is intended as a forum for sharing and discussing theory and good practice, as well as a signpost to resources and events of interest.
http://www.agcas.org.uk/agcas_resources/365-Employers-perceptions-of-the-employability-skills-of-new-graduates

This report provides the findings of a study of employers' perceptions of the employability skills of new graduates conducted by the SCRE Centre (University of Glasgow). The research was funded by the Edge Foundation.
http://www.agcas.org.uk/agcas_resources/596
This paper estimates the sorting (signalling or screening) effects of university degree class on labour market outcomes. It compares labour market outcomes by degree class, six months after completing a course.
http://www.hea.ie/files/files/National%20Employer's%20Survey%20(Pilot)%20Report.pdf
Higher Education Authority and IBEC Survey. The Higher Education Authority is the statutory planning and policy development body for higher education and research in Ireland.
http://www.agcas.org.uk/agcas_resources/549
This report analyses the results of Cedefop's (European Centre for the Development of Vocational Training, 2012) latest skill supply and demand forecasts up to 2020. The forecasts aim to provide evidence on future labour market developments to help to make informed decisions. They identify major economic and socio-demographic trends and examine their implications for labour market sectors, occupations and qualifications.
http://www.cedefop.europa.eu/EN/Files/5526_en.pdf
European Centre for the Development of Vocational Training (Cedefop), 2012, Research Paper Number 26, Future Skills Supply and Demand in Europe.

BIBLIOGRAPHY

Anderson, N. and Witvliet, C. (2008) Fairness Reactions to Personnel Selection Methods: An International Comparison between The Netherlands, the United States, France, Spain, Portugal, and Singapore, *International Journal of Selection and Assessment*, 16(1), 1–13.

Ashe, F. (2012) Harnessing Political Theory to Facilitate Students' Engagement with Graduate 'Employability': A Critical Pyramid Approach, *Politics*, 32, 129–137.

Beardwell, J. and Claydon, T. (2010) *Human Resource Management, A Contemporary Approach*, Chapter 15 (6th ed.), Harlow, FT Prentice Hall.

Branine, M. (2008) Graduate Recruitment and Selection in the UK, A Study of the Recent Changes in Methods and Expectations, *Career Development International*, 13(6), 497–513.

Bratton, J. and Gold, J. (2012) *Human Resource Management: Theory and Practice* (5th ed.), Basingstoke: Palgrave Macmillan.

Cascio, W. F. (2013) *Managing Human Resources: Productivity, Quality of Work Life, Profits* (9th ed.), New York, NY: McGraw-Hill.

Cascio, W. F. (2014a) Investing in HRD in Uncertain Times Now and In the Future, *Advances in Developing Human Resources*, 16(1), 108–122.

Cascio, W. F. (2014b) Looking Back, Looking Forward: Technology In the Workplace, In M. Coovert and L. F. Thompson (Eds) *The Psychology of Workplace Technology*, San Francisco, CA: Jossey-Bass (307–313).

Chartered Institute of Personnel and Development (2007a) Psychological Testing, available at: www.cipd.co.uk/subjects/recruitmen/tests/psytest.htm (accessed 12 May 2013).

Chartered Institute of Personnel and Development (2007b) Assessment Centres for Recruitment and Selection, available at: www.cipd.co.uk/subjects/recruitmen/assmntcent/asscentre.htm?IsSrchRes=1 (accessed 12 May 2013).

Chartered Institute of Personnel and Development (2010) *Resourcing and Talent Planning*, London: CIPD.

Dawson, M. (2005) Costa's 'Filter' gets the Right Employees, *Human Resource Management International Digest*, 13(4), 21–22.

Deissinger, T. (2000) The German 'Philosophy' of Linking Academic and Work-Based Learning in Higher Education: The Case of Vocational Academies, *Journal of Vocational Education and Training*, 52(4), 605–626.

Dybowski, D. G. (2005) The Dual Vocational Education and Training System in Germany. Keynote Speech on Dual Vocational Training International Conference, Taiwan. *The Economist*, 27 April 2013, *Generation Jobless*, 9, 49–52.

Edvardsson Stiwne, E. and Gaio Alves, M. (2010) Higher Education and Employability of Graduates: Will Bologna Make a Difference?, *European Educational Research Journal*, 9(1), 32–44.

Enterprise Rent-a-Car Case Study (2013), Dublin: Enterprise Rent-a-Car.

Gradireland (2012), Graduate Salary & Graduate Recruitment Trends Survey 2012, The Official Survey of Graduate Starting Salaries in Ireland and Northern Ireland, Association of Higher Education Career Services, Dublin.

Hamzah, M. S., Hapidah, B. M. and Abdullah, S. K. (2012), The Scenario From an Employer Perspective: Employability Profiles of Graduates, *US-China Education Review*, B7, 675–681.

Hansen, U. (2007) Building Employability Skills into the Higher Education Curriculum, *Role of Lecturers Educational and Training*, 42(2), 75–83.

Hinchliffe, G. W. and Jolly, A. (2011) Graduate Identity and Employability, *British Educational Research Journal*, 37(4), August 2011, 563–584.

Hippach-Schneider, U., Martina, K. and Woll, C. (2007) *Vocational Education and Training in Germany*, Luxembourg: Office for Official Publications of the European Communities.

Holmes, L. (2001) Reconsidering Graduate Employability: the 'graduate identity' approach, *Quality in Higher Education*, 7 (2), 111–119.

Holmes, L. (2006) Reconsidering Graduate Employability: Beyond Possessive-Individualism, *Presented to Seventh International Conference on HRD Research and Practice across Europe*, University of Tilburg, 22–24 May 2006.

Irish Independent, 25 August 2009 'The six top growth industries in Ireland today', Dave Kilmartin, Head of Careers, Dublin Institute of Technology.

Knight, P. and Yorke, M. (2004) *Learning, Curriculum and Employability in Higher Education*, London: Routledge.

Lievens, F. and Conway, J. M. (2001) Dimension and Exercise Variance in Assessment Center Scores: A Large-Scale Evaluation of Multitrait-Multimethod Studies, *Journal of Applied Psychology*, 86, 1202–1222.

Lievens, F., van Dam, K. and Anderson, N. (2002) Recent Trends and Challenges in Personnel Selection, *Personnel Review*, 31(5), 580–601.

Lowden, L., Hall, S., Elliot, D. and Lewin J. (2011) *Employers' Perceptions of the Employability Skills of New Graduates*, Research commissioned by the Edge Foundations, University of Glasgow SCRE Centre and Edge Foundation 2011.

Lublin, J. S. (11 April 2011) Hunt is on for Fresh Executive Talent: Cultural Flexibility in Demand. *The Wall Street Journal*, pp. B1, B9.

McBride, J. R. (1998) Innovations in Computer-Based Ability Testing: Promise, Problems and Perils, In M. D. Hakel (Ed.) *Beyond Multiple Choice*, Mahwah, NJ: Lawrence Erlbaum Associates (113–129).

Branine, M. (2008) Graduate Recruitment and Selection in the UK: A Study of the Recent Changes in Methods and Expectations, *Career Development International*, 13(6), 497–513.

Moraal, D., Lorig, B., Schreiber, D. and Azeez, U. (2009) *Bibb Report: A Look behind the Scenes of Continuing Vocational Training in Germany*, BIBB (Federal Institute for Vocational Education and Training).

Moreland, N. (2006) *Entrepreneurship in Higher Education: An Employability Perspective*, York: The Higher Education Academy.

National Survey of Employers' Views of Irish Higher Education Outcomes National Outcomes (2013), Dublin, Ireland: IBEC.

Oh, H., Choi, Y. and Choi, M. (2013) Comparative Analysis of OECD Member Countries' Competitive Advantage in

National Human Resource Development System, *Asia Pacific Education Review* 14, 189–208.

Philips, L. (2009) 'Slash Graduate Recruitment at Your Peril': Firms Advised to Plan for the Future. *People Management*, 15(8): 8–9.

Pilbeam, S. and Corbridge, M. (2010) *People Resourcing and Talent Planning: HRM in Practice* (4th ed.), Harlow: Pearson Education Limited.

Prokou, E. (2008) The Emphasis on Employability and the Changing Role of the University in Europe, *Higher Education in Europe*, 33(4), 387–394.

Roberts, G. (2005) *Recruitment and Selection* (2nd ed.), London: Chartered Institute of Professional Development.

RTE News (25 February 2013) €300 Million Investment in Seven World-Class Research Centres – Minister Bruton, Minister Sherlock.

Sackett, P. R. and Lievens, F. (2008) Personnel Selection, *Annual Review of Psychology*, 59, 419–450.

Salgado, J. F. and Lado, M. (2000) Validity Generalization of Video Tests for Predicting Job Performance Ratings, Paper Presented at the Annual Conference of the Society for Industrial and Organizational Psychology, New Orleans, LA, April.

Shackleton, V. and Newell, S. (1994) European Management Selection Methods: A Comparison of Five Countries, *International Journal of Selection and Assessment*, 2, 91–102.

Shuayto, N. (2013) Management Skills Desired by Business School Deans and Employers: An Empirical Investigation, *Business Education & Accreditation*, 5(2), 93–105.

Spychalski, A. C., Quinones, M. A., Gaugler, B. B. and Pohley, K. (1997) A Survey of Assessment Center Practices in the United States, *Personnel Psychology*, 50, 71–90.

Straus, S. G., Miles, J. A. and Levesque, L. L. (2001) The Effects of Videoconference, Telephone, and Face-to-Face Media on Interviewer and Applicant Judgments in Employment Interviews, *Journal of Management*, 27, 363–381.

Thornton, G. and Gibbons, A. (2009) Validity of Assessment Centres for Personnel Selection, *Human Resource Review*, 19(3), 69–187.

Tibergien, M. (2013), The Human Capital Dilemma, Recruiting talented people and enticing them to stay challenges today's business leaders, Investment Advisor, Feb2013, Vol. 33 Issue 2, 37–38.

Velasco, M. S. (2012) More Than Just Good Grades: Candidates' Perceptions about the Skills and Attributes Employers Seek in New Graduates, *Journal of Business Economics and Management*, (3), 499–517.

Wickramasinghe, V. and Perera, L. (2010) Graduates', University Lecturers' and Employers' Perceptions towards Employability Skills, *Education + Training*, 52(3), 226–244.

Woodruffe, C. (2000) *Development and Assessment Centres* (3rd ed.), London: Chartered Institute of Personnel and Development.

14 ETHICS, CORPORATE SOCIAL RESPONSIBILITY, SUSTAINABILITY AND HRD

Clíodhna MacKenzie

LEARNING OUTCOMES

By the end of this chapter you should be able to:

- Explain what is meant by the triple bottom-line philosophy

- Discuss the challenges faced by HRD practitioners in implementing ethics, sustainability and social responsibility policies in an organizational setting

- Understand what is meant by an 'ethical culture' and know how to 'manage' it

- Understand the challenges and limitations faced by HRD practitioners who have to justify spending money to be 'seen' as 'green'

- Explain what is meant by the 'HR value chain' and why it is a vital component of HRD's ethics, sustainability and social responsibility strategy

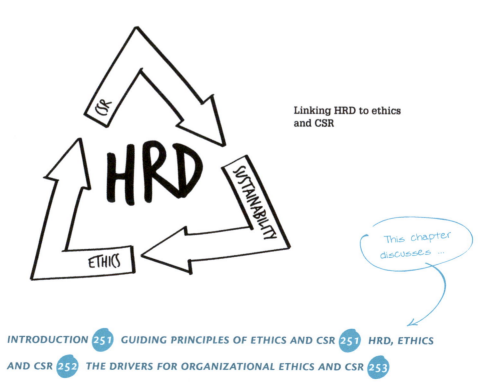

Linking HRD to ethics and CSR

This chapter discusses ...

INTRODUCTION

This chapter focuses on the role HRD plays in ensuring ethics and corporate social responsibility (CSR) function as core aspects of organizational life. HRD practitioners are considered human capital developers (Ulrich and Brockbank, 2005), business partners (Peterson, 2008; Wright, 2008) and critical to the development of ethical senior management role models (Ardichvili and Jondle, 2009). HRD practitioners therefore play a central role in incorporating ethical behaviour into the organization's culture and climate (Foote and Ruona, 2008). The successful development and implementation of these HRD interventions is critically important, not just to organizational development ▶Chapter 6 but to organizational viability. Traditionally, HRD has been associated with delivering learning, training and development programmes in an effort to develop human expertise in pursuit of long-term organizational success (Garavan, 1991; Swanson, 2001; O'Donnell et al., 2006; Garavan, 2007; Bierema, 2009; Stewart and Sambrook, 2012). This goal of sustaining competitive advantage, however, does need to be considered beyond the short-term results-driven performance objectives (Legge, 2005) that HR professionals are often required to achieve.

The negative economic and societal impact resulting directly from the recent global financial crisis would suggest that, when the *human* dimension of HRD fails, the consequences can be far-reaching and disastrous. The various public inquiries convened in the UK and the US to establish the root causes of the financial crises found that banks had 'lied to' and 'deceived' their regulators (US Senate Report, 2010: 245), indicating organizational cultures that were ignoring good ethical standards to achieve unrealistic financial objectives, a point also indicated by the Financial Crisis Inquiry Commission, which stated that there was an 'erosion of standards of responsibility and ethics that exacerbated the financial crisis' (FCIC Report, 2011: xxii). The UK banking inquiry also highlighted the erosion in ethical standards and argued that the culture of 'responsibility, integrity, honesty' had been

replaced by 'irresponsibility, greed, obfuscation, denial and unprofessionalism' (Treasury Select Committee, 2009, ev 47). Indeed, every official report and public inquiry exploring the causes of the various banking crises in Ireland, the UK and the US has cited the failure of senior management to uphold ethical practices as being responsible for the financial crisis.

If HRD is to be considered a strategic business partner ▶Chapter 2, then it is difficult to argue that HRD practices, policies and procedures can be separated from ethics and socially responsible business practices when the development of people and the organization is a core goal for HRD.

The concept of CSR reflects the discretionary responsibility of businesses (Surroca *et al.*, 2010: 464), which means that organizations may or may not adhere to socially and environmentally sound business practices or behave in socially conscious ways. Unlike most other textbooks focused on exploring ethics and CSR from a theoretical perspective, this chapter departs from a purely theoretical discussion and looks at the role HRD practitioners and the HRD function play in developing organizational structures that support ethical behaviour and socially responsible business practices. We illustrate the links between HRD functions and the delivery of organizational policies aimed at achieving an ethical and socially responsible business practices and, in doing so, will equip you with the necessary skills to make informed decisions about doing the right thing rather than merely doing things right. In the next section we will explore the key drivers for ethical behaviour and the adoption of CSR in today's organization. We draw on examples of organizational successes and failures over the last two decades to illuminate the importance of organizational ethics and CSR.

ethics the study of morality with respect to what is good, bad, right or wrong and reflects an explicit philosophical debate on moral beliefs and practices

GUIDING PRINCIPLES OF ETHICS AND CSR

In contemporary organizations, ethics and CSR have become important measures of how well organizations fulfil their wider societal responsibilities.

The development and delivery of CSR policies are often representative of how the organization views the financial bottom line (McWilliams and Siegel, 2001; Ardichvili et al., 2009). So, while organizations that are concerned with the **triple bottom-line philosophy** of the social, economic and environmental impact of their business practices provide a clear 'sustainability' message internally (to their employees) and externally (to their stakeholder community), organizations that are solely focused on economic viability may be more ambiguous in the delivery of their message. The triple bottom-line philosophy is also known as the three P's: *people, planet* and *profits*. The wider social community also plays an influential role in how the organization develops its CSR policies (which include diversity policies and ethical treatment of employees) through lobby groups and public awareness campaigns such as, for example, multicoloured cancer wristbands, the Irish Cancer Society website promoting cancer awareness, and the FTSE4good Index (FTSE, 2010), which was designed to 'objectively measure the performance of companies that meet globally recognized corporate responsibility standards'.

Ethics and CSR reflect a reciprocal relationship between the organization and its multi-stakeholder community including employees, customers, suppliers, shareholders, focus groups and society at large. Ethics and CSR policies focus on producing a change in behaviour; therefore, there is a strong people and HR dimension to their implementation. The practice of HRD is central to the development, delivery and management of these policies and, therefore, HRD practitioners are critical in ensuring that organizations behave in an ethically, socially and environmentally responsible way.

The ethical and socially responsible orientation of an organization has the capacity to influence the share price, its financial viability and whether or not potential future employees are attracted to the organization (Logsdon and Wood, 2002; FTSE, 2010). In his book *Screw Business as Usual*, Richard Branson (2013: 17) epitomizes the approach that many organizations advocate with respect to how they approach ethics and CSR, noting:

> As Virgin expanded, so did our ideas for treating the people who worked for us well, and for considering the environment. We've always had at our core a

triple bottom-line philosophy focuses on the need to reduce the negative impact and increase the positive impact of the organization on society. Examples of the positive impact organizations can have on society include The AIB Better Ireland Program; Cisco Systems Community Knowledge Centres; and Pfizer's Global Healthcare Programs

boundary spanning refers to policies, practices or procedures that can 'span' beyond the organization

focus on our people and making sure that they are empowered to make decisions and feel part of the company that stands for something beyond money.

In these words Richard Branson captures the essence of why organizations engage in ethical and socially responsible business practices – in doing so, the organization is seen as being known for more than maximizing shareholder wealth (Friedman, 1970) and is considered a paragon among its peers. More importantly, as Branson argues, the organization views the responsibility in CSR as being part of the DNA of all the organization's employees. To ensure this happens, HRD practices such as management and leadership development programmes ▶ Chapter 12, ethical awareness programmes, and organizational development practices ▶ Chapter 5 will play both a crucial and an active role in its delivery. Virgin Unite, the non-profit foundation of the Virgin Group (Virgin Unite, 2013), promotes new approaches to leadership such as 'The Elders, Carbon War Room and The B Team' in pursuit of an agenda that seeks to 'reinvent how we live and work to help make people's lives better'. Virgin's laudable approach to embedding ethics and CSR as a core dimension of its own organization has laid the foundation for the **boundary spanning** possibilities of its ethics and CSR practices. The Virgin 'Elders' initiative works both 'publicly and privately' to engage with 'global leaders and civil society to help resolve conflict and address its root causes, to challenge injustice, to promote good governance and to inspire ethical leadership'. Virgin's approach is very much aimed at helping to create a more just and tolerant society – when an organization such as Virgin embraces ethics and social responsibility as a core function and approach to its business practices, we can begin to see the significant impact HRD policies, practices and procedures can have on achieving the triple bottom-line philosophy.

HRD, ETHICS AND CSR

Ethics and CSR, while appearing to be somewhat abstract concepts, have a significant impact on HRD policies such as diversity programmes, ethics awareness programmes and culture development. HRD practitioners will have

BUILDING YOUR SKILLS

Ethics, sustainability and social responsibility have become synonymous with organizations 'doing business' following the impact of the global financial crisis. As the newly appointed HRD manager for a local, and very busy, call centre, you must balance the needs of the organization engaging in what might be considered 'sharp sales practices', ethics awareness, programme development and organizational sales targets that are clearly causing high levels of stress, anxiety and depression among your staff. How do you propose to prioritize *and* balance the needs of all your 'stakeholders' in achieving a harmonious environment, happy customers and organizational objectives?

CONSIDER THIS …

How would you describe as an ethical organization? What would it look like? Would an ethical organization be a paragon of virtue in its community? Discuss some of the characteristics that differentiate ethical CSR-oriented contemporary organizations from less ethical ones. Are these examples confined to one particular industry? Are these examples a reflection of ethical/positive CSR organizations or just charismatic leaders?

the potential to influence how the organization utilizes these policies to attract, retain and reward individuals considered important to the organization's long-term sustainability. Over the past decade, organizational failures due to unethical and socially irresponsible behaviour have received significant press and academic coverage, warranting a more thorough understanding of how organizations approach their ethical and social responsibilities (Roubini and Mihm, 2011; Stein, 2011; Stein and Pinto, 2011; MacKenzie et al., 2012). Organizations such as Enron, Worldcom and Parmalat and, more recently, many banking institutions such as Lehman Brothers, Goldman Sachs and IBRC (formerly Anglo Irish Bank) have been accused of immoral and unethical business practices, which has demonstrated that the ethical orientation and social responsibility of organizations can sometimes be more symbolic than substantive.

While many organizations embrace the idea of ethics and CSR, the application and delivery of these concepts can prove difficult, given contextual factors such as organizational culture, organizational goals and objectives, the environment in which the organization operates, and the size of the organization relative to its peers (Lange and Washburn, 2012). The difficulty for some organizations (for example, in the banking and financial sector) may reflect **ideological dispositions** that focus on a primary stakeholder such as shareholders or stockholders. This ideological orientation may see 'profit' or wealth

ideological dispositions refers to a manner or the content of thinking characteristic of an individual, group, profession or culture

maximization as the only measure of organizational success. The relationship between organizational ethics, CSR and employee/organizational development is complex but vitally important to understand, given the key role HRD practitioners play in developing individuals and their organizations. In contemporary organizations, the need to ensure that business practices are ethical, socially responsible and sustainable is now more than ever before the difference between organizational success and failure.

HRD practitioners are tasked with developing the ethical culture of the organization (Foote and Ruona, 2008; Ardichvili and Jondle, 2009) and identifying, recruiting, developing and retaining talented employees (Fambrough and Hart, 2008; MacKenzie et al., 2011b; Stolz, 2012). They are also responsible for the learning and development (L&D) functions that contribute to sustained competitive advantage (Garavan and McGuire, 2010; McGuire and Garavan, 2011), and, following the impact of the financial crisis, they may be required to assume a more strategic role in organizational governance and compliance (see MacKenzie et al., 2011b). This places HRD in an important and very central role in how the organization approaches the ethics and CSR debate.

THE DRIVERS FOR ORGANIZATIONAL ETHICS AND CSR

In this section we examine the reasons why organizations aspire to being ethical and socially responsible. We consider the some of the key drivers that influence, coerce and at times force organizations to behave in an ethically and socially responsible way. We provide insight from organizations that are considered to exemplify what it means to be ethical and operate in socially responsible ways, and we explore those organizations that fall short. If the social responsibility of business is to increase profits, as Milton Friedman (1970) once argued, then organizations need only be concerned about a small number of stakeholders – *shareholders* and institutional investors. This argument is premised on the notion that, in order for organizations to remain viable, financial and economic returns are the only measures of success. While Friedman argued somewhat convincingly that organizations that are profitable provide ancillary jobs (local service industry, logistics companies and healthcare providers) for the communities in which they are located, the reverse is also true when organizations are unprofitable. CSR represents the organization's efforts to ensure effective corporate governance resulting in organizational sustainability through ethical business practices that promote accountability, transparency and societal philanthropy (McWilliams and Siegel, 2001; McWilliams *et al.*, 2006; Cai *et al.*, 2012).

Although organizations have the ability to act ethically and demonstrate a very positive external CSR image, they are constantly under pressure to respond to myriad change forces, such as economic, social, environmental, technological and strategic demands. It is in responding to these change forces that organizations act in a less ethically and socially responsible way. An example might be the working conditions in Foxconn Technologies, the manufacturing partner of Apple Computers and manufacturer of the iPhone 5. Working conditions in the Foxconn Technologies factory in China were referred to as a 'sweat shop', prompting Apple Computers to hire a non-profit Fair Labor Association to audit working conditions at its manufacturing partner's facility. It is following organizational crises, disasters (Shrivastava *et al.*, 1988) or large-scale redundancies that a positive organizational image may become damaged, resulting in lost trust, employee disengagement, societal backlash and – in extreme cases – organizational failure. This prompts a number of important questions: why do some organizations behave in an ethically, socially and environmentally responsible way and others do not? Why do some organizations treat people, cultures,

> institutional investors includes banks, finance companies, insurance companies, pension funds, mutual funds, union funds and are an important source of funding by way of share purchase for large corporations. Institutional investors therefore play an influential role in how organizations conduct business

environments and society with respect while other appear almost contemptuous of their stakeholders? Perhaps one of the most perplexing questions is whether an organization can be ethical while being socially irresponsible, and vice versa.

Following the negative human impact of the financial crisis (e.g. high unemployment levels, increased home repossessions, and high levels of skilled

SPOTLIGHT ON SKILLS

You are the HRD manager of a well-known banking organization and have just attended one of the quarterly management meetings, where the senior manager of the bank has indicated that the 'new' focus of the bank will be on sales targets with performance and incentives linked to very aggressive growth figures.

1 As the HRD manager, you are concerned with the very aggressive growth rates she has indicated and worry that these incentives may influence staff to engage in 'unethical' behaviour.

2 How might you suggest to the senior managers that performance-linked incentives may not be the most appropriate way to promote an ethical culture?

3 In particular, how might the company implement a 'sustainable' and 'ethical' growth strategy without compromising the financial viability of the organization?

To help you answer the questions above, visit www.macmillanihe.com/companion/carbery-hrd and watch the video of Philip Ducie talking about ethics.

graduate emigration), the ethical behaviour of banking institutions at the centre of the financial crisis, as well as the leaders who ran those institutions, is now a matter of public record. Were these banking institutions engaged in unethical behaviour, or were they responding to external stakeholder pressures to continue growing their organizations at a rate that was unsustainable over the long term? It is argued by many commentators that the decision-making process of banking and financial institutions was flawed and that the strategic decisions made by these organizations reflected a lack of ethical awareness and diminished social responsibility. This lack of awareness may have damaged not just the integrity of the organizations in question but also the banking, finance and economics professions, financial markets and corporate governance systems developed to circumvent this type of behaviour. Although banking and financial institutions are recent examples of organizations that engaged in ethically questionable business practices in pursuit of competitive advantage, there is a long history of organizations in disparate industries engaging in similar behaviours.

The answer to the question of what drives the adoption of ethics and CSR in contemporary organizations has been answered following instances of historical organizational failures. Sims and Brinkmann (2003), for example, provided a possible answer to this question

following the failure of Enron on 2 December 2001. They argued that Enron was the 'ultimate contradiction between words and deeds, between a deceiving glossy façade and a rotten structure behind' (p. 243). In this trenchant observation, Sims and Brinkman highlight the disconnect between what the organization espouses publicly and organizational reality. Now, as in the past, the societal pressure to restore an ethical consciousness to organizations and institutions is driven by the fact that, when organizations behave in an unethical or socially irresponsible way, the impact can be disastrous. This prompts the question: What role do HRD practitioners play in addressing societal concerns about organizational ethics and CSR? Research on organizational ethics and organizational leadership suggests that ethical and unethical behaviour is heavily influenced by both individual dispositions and contextual variables (Ardichvili and Jondle, 2009) such as culture, organizational socialization and group/professional membership (Ashforth et al., 2008), thus putting HRD practitioners in a central position to influence the organization's ethical and CSR orientation. In the next section we discuss the theoretical development of CSR over the last five decades and provide examples of how organizations might approach CSR. We categorize CSR under four distinct social realities in which organizations exist and operate.

The BP disaster in the Gulf of Mexico in 2010 has highlighted the social, economic and environmental impact of failing to live up to the triple bottom-line philosophy. In what can be described as the worst environmental disaster in US history, the BP Gulf of Mexico disaster figures are almost unbelievable, especially when compared with what had been considered the worst environmental disaster in US history up to that point – the Exxon Valdez oil spill in 1989. The Exxon Valdez disaster was caused by human error that resulted in an oil tanker running aground in Prince William Sound and spilling

10.8 million gallons of crude oil. Contrasting the Exxon Valdez oil spill with the BP disaster and the estimated 172 million gallons of crude oil that spilled into the Gulf of Mexico, the environmental, economic and social impacts of BP's CSR failures will be felt, perhaps, for decades.

While accidents do happen, BP has engaged in tactics that have frustrated the legal proceedings, ranging from telling 'outright lies' and trying to hide the amount of oil that was spilling into the Gulf of Mexico following the Deepwater Horizon oil rig disaster to allegations of 'obstruction of justice' by deleting mobile phone

records. The US prosecution of BP and the environmental disaster it has been responsible for is less worrisome than the attempts of BP to lie about the flow rate of oil into the Gulf of Mexico and the tactics it has engaged in to circumvent the discovery of facts relating to the disaster. BP attorney Mike Brock said that second-guessing the company's efforts to cap the well is 'Monday morning quarterbacking at its worst'. He said that BP's spill response was 'extraordinary' and that the company 'did not misrepresent flow rate in a way that caused a delay in the shut-in of the well'. The claims that BP's actions were akin to 'gross negligence' highlights the knock-on effects of CSR failures.

HRD – IN THE NEWS

The ongoing (as of December 2013) criminal trial of an ex-BP engineer accused of having a 'corrupt intent and a clear motive' to delete text messages about the flow rate of the blown drilling platform demonstrates a willingness to hide the facts from the government, US Federal prosecutors have claimed in court papers.

The Department of Justice claims that 4.2 million barrels poured from Deepwater Horizon after the fatal fire and explosion that claimed 11 lives, and, although BP estimates of the figure were significantly lower that those estimated by the US government, it is nonetheless considerable. While the economic costs to BP and those who carve out a living in the Gulf of Mexico are evident and can be calculated, the environmental costs, like those of the Exxon Valdez disaster in 1989, may take decades to determine. In an effort to raise awareness of the environmental impact of BP's CSR failure, environmental

groups had protested outside the New Orleans courthouse ahead of the trial. Bethany Kraft, director of Ocean Conservancy's Gulf restoration programme, said:

Despite BP's best efforts to deflect attention from their role in the worst environmental disaster in US history, I'm confident that every phase of the trial will show that this on-going tragedy happened because of their careless actions and those of other responsible parties. It's time to dispense with the grandstanding and dig into the work of restoring the Gulf and the livelihoods of the people who depend on it.

In a time of increasing awareness of organizations' responsibilities beyond those of shareholder values, it is perhaps important to consider why social and environmental concerns are as important as, if not more important than, economic concerns. The triple bottom-line philosophy is grounded in an almost symbiotic relationship between the

economic, environmental and social, in which none of the three can exist without the others.

Sources

http://www.nwf.org/What-We-Do/Protect-Habitat/Gulf-Restoration/Oil-Spill/Effects-on-Wildlife/Compare-Exxon-Valdez-and-BP-Oil-Spills.aspx, accessed 15/1/2014.

http://www.businessweek.com/articles/2013-12-02/first-criminal-trial-from-gulf-oil-spill-puts-bp-in-grim-spotlight

http://www.bloomberg.com/news/2013-12-02/ex-bp-engineer-begins-first-criminal-trial-from-oil-spill.html

Questions

1 How might you describe BP's respect for the stakeholders impacted by the oil spill in the Gulf?
2 How might employees interpret this combative stance with US Federal prosecutors?
3 Could HRD ethics and CSR policies have minimized the potential for wilfully 'negligent' behaviour?

SMEs, ETHICS AND CORPORATE SOCIAL RESPONSIBILITY

While much of the literature exploring the concepts of ethics and CSR is generally associated with large organizations, the development of ethics and CSR initiatives within the small to medium enterprise (SME) market is no less important. These enterprises can be considered a significant source of entrepreneurial activity, skills, innovation and employment (Jenkins, 2006; Perrini et al., 2007; Lawless et al., 2012). Indeed, the importance of the SME market should not be underestimated. In 2012 the SME market in Europe accounted for approximately 86.8 million people in employment, representing 66.5 per cent of all European jobs. Moreover, the financial contribution of these enterprises to the European economy was calculated at 57.6 per cent, or 3.395 billion euros, compared with a 42.2 per cent, or

2.495 billion, contribution of larger organizations such as multinational corporations (Gagliardi et al., 2013). One of the primary reasons for needing to differentiate SMEs from larger organizations is succinctly articulated by Brenkert (2002) (cited in Sen and Cowley, 2013: 414), who argued that 'business ethicists have treated the ethics of entrepreneurship with benign neglect' due in part to their failure to recognize that SMEs and larger organizations differ in fundamental ways: accordingly, ethics and CSR interventions are likely to differ in similarly critical ways. In large organizations that are resource-rich, a dedicated CSR manager is the corporate face of the person who engages with the triple bottom line on behalf of the organization. In the case of SMEs, the 'corporate person' *is* the SME (Fuller and Tian, 2006: 294).

Earlier SME-focused CSR research such as Rutherford *et al.* (1997) (cited in Spence, 1999: 164) criticized SMEs for being 'highly disconnected, internally fragmented … and alienated from local and social and political life', focused primarily on revenue generation and market growth. However, this position has been called into question by Sen and Cowley (2013: 422), whose research on Australian SMEs found that the disconnection from community was due primarily to 'resource poorness' rather than being strategically myopic. Arend (2013), however, found mixed results in his research on US SMEs when he explored the concept of ethics-focused dynamic capabilities (skills and resources a SME needs to balance ethics and performance over time). Arend established that, while ethics-focused dynamic capability had the potential to improve ethical performance, it was considered a 'luxury item', given that the cost of improving ethical performance was larger than the benefit derived (in the short term) from doing so (p. 16). That said, he also found that highly entrepreneurial firms can benefit when they recognize the longer-term benefits of employing ethics-focused dynamic capabilities. This has implications for HRD.

HRD practitioners play many roles in formulating and implementing ethics and CSR initiatives such as policy design, development and delivery (Garavan and McGuire, 2010; Garavan et al., 2010; Gond et al., 2011), ethical culture and climate development and institutionalization (Foote and Ruona, 2008; Ardichvili and Jondle, 2009; Ardichvili, 2013), designing sustainability policies that attract future employees (Jenkins, 2006; Arend, 2013), and employee engagement and retention interventions (Fuller and Tian, 2006; Udayasankar, 2008; Preuss et al., 2009) and as such they have a vital contribution to make to SMEs. For example, HRD through the CIPD can develop synergistic relationships with professional associations such as Enterprise Ireland, the Irish Small and Medium Enterprise Association (ISME), the British Chamber of Commerce, and Scottish Enterprise to aid SMEs in growing their strategies and policies around ethics and CSR. These synergistic relationships can leverage the expertise of CIPD and HRD professionals with trade and enterprise associations and translate it into a powerful tool to allow SMEs to balance the sometimes conflicting needs of their stakeholder groups.

THE ROLE OF CSR AND ETHICS TRAINING PROGRAMMES

In light of the failure of so many financial institutions as a result of the global financial crisis, and perhaps more recently other high-profile organizational 'ethics and sustainability failures' such as the BP Gulf of Mexico disaster (see HRD in the News), ethics, CSR and sustainability strategies may be viewed by the public as little more than 'smokescreens that obscure the grim realities' (Banerjee, 2011: 725) of organizational behaviour. Indeed, it is these high-profile organizational failures that raise the question of whether ethical awareness programmes are meant for anything other than a box-ticking exercise (Ashforth et al., 2008). The question of how HRD practitioners can implement permanent changes in behaviour that achieve more than superficial CSR intentions (Matten and Moon, 2008) has been asked more frequently in light of these organizational failures and serves to highlight the many challenges faced by HRD practitioners as they grapple with ensuring the organizations' members act in an ethically, socially and environmentally responsible way.

Over the past decade the role of HRD has become strategically important in developing organizations' human capital and achieving and sustaining competitive advantage (Garavan, 2007; Peterson, 2008; Stewart et al., 2010). Competitive advantage, however, comes at a price, and, as the failure of corporate giants in the early 2000s and, more recently, financial institutions has demonstrated, CSR may need to come with its own health warning. The delivery of ethical training programmes and the creation of ethical business cultures that facilitate sustainability and other 'CSR-related objectives' (Ardichvili, 2013: 6) are now considered some of the most critical functions of HRD in ensuring business practices remain ethical and become socialized and normalized within the organization's culture. Indeed, according to Ardichvili (2011: 373), HRD's focus should consider more than just the delivery of ethics training programmes; the profession should also include improving organizational members' ability to make ethical and responsible choices, thereby moving beyond training interventions and into modifying behavioural dispositions and attitudes and embedding sustainability (Garavan and McGuire, 2010) into every aspect of the organization's operations.

To ensure that ethics and sustainability become part of the organization's values, they must be embedded within the culture (Ardichvili and Jondle, 2009; Greenwood, 2013a). According to Ardichvili and Jondle (2009), clear communications and codes of practice play a crucial role in the development of an ethical culture. These communications send out a clear message that all behaviour and decision making should be linked to societal and environmental goals as well as economic ones (MacKenzie et al., 2011a).

BUILDING YOUR SKILLS

Identifying Drivers for Organizational Ethics and CSR

In this exercise, consider a positive/negative economic impact for each of the concepts in the diagram below. The X-axis represents the social/environmental impact of CSR and the Y-axis represents the economic impact of CSR. The concepts in green represent positive CSR efforts that have a direct/indirect HRD input/intervention. The concepts in red represent negative CSR outcomes where HRD interventions have been either ineffective or influential. This task should take no more than 10 minutes. When you have assigned an economic, social and environmental impact, consider how you arrived at these conclusions, how they are linked to real-life issues such as the BP Gulf of Mexico disaster and how your answers might relate to HRD interventions.

THE ROLE OF HRD IN SHAPING ORGANIZATIONAL ETHICS AND CORPORATE SOCIAL RESPONSIBILITY

In what can be described as a departure from the more traditional concept of HRD, that is, purveyors of training and development interventions, Garavan and McGuire (2010: 489) argue that HRD now plays a role in helping organizations achieve societal, environmental and economic goals through 'raising awareness of employees and developing positive attitudes towards sustainability, environmentalism, and green work practices'. More importantly, Garavan and McGuire argue that HRD practitioners are well placed to develop an organizational culture capable of supporting sustainability, ethics and CSR.

While there is little doubt that HRD practitioners can help shape the ethics and CSR orientation of the organization in a number of key areas, such as organizational culture development, leadership development, development of ethics awareness

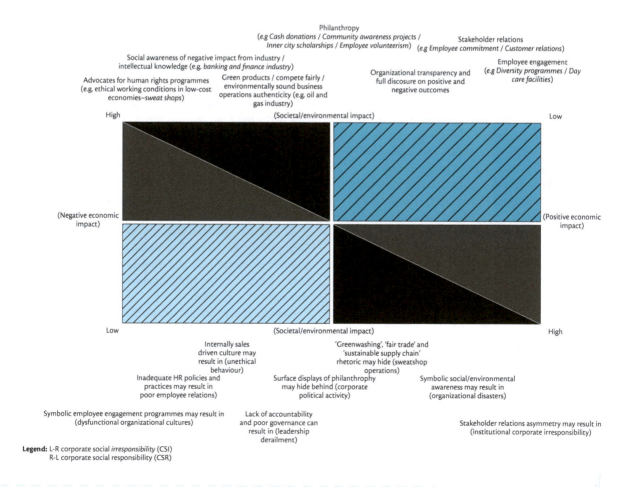

Philanthropy
(e.g Cash donations / Community awareness projects / Inner city scholarships / Employee volunteerism)

Stakeholder relations
(e.g Employee commitment / Customer relations)

Social awareness of negative impact from industry / intellectual knowledge (e.g. banking and finance industry)

Employee engagement
(e.g Diversity programmes / Day care facilities)

Advocates for human rights programmes (e.g. ethical working conditions in low-cost economies–sweat shops)

Green products / compete fairly / environmentally sound business operations authenticity (e.g. oil and gas industry)

Organizational transparency and full discosure on positive and negative outcomes

High　　　　　　　(Societal/environmental impact)　　　　　　　Low

(Negative economic impact)　　　　　　　　　　　　　　　　　　　(Positive economic impact)

Low　　　　　　　(Societal/environmental impact)　　　　　　　High

Internally sales driven culture may result in (unethical behaviour)

'Greenwashing', 'fair trade' and 'sustainable supply chain' rhetoric may hide (sweatshop operations)

Inadequate HR policies and practices may result in poor employee relations)

Surface displays of philanthrophy may hide behind (corporate political activity)

Symbolic social/environmental awareness may result in (organizational disasters)

Symbolic employee engagement programmes may result in (dysfunctional organizational cultures)

Lack of accountability and poor governance can result in (leadership derailment)

Stakeholder relations asymmetry may result in (institutional corporate irresponsibility)

Legend: L-R corporate social *irresponsibility* (CSI)
R-L corporate social responsibility (CSR)

programmes and strategic engagement with senior leadership, the primary role that HRD practitioners play in the organization is to convert human intellectual capital into economic output (O'Donnell *et al.*, 2006; Fenwick and Bierema, 2008). Nevertheless, HRD practitioners may be the management group best placed to ensure that organizations act ethically and operate socially responsible business practices. There are three key areas in which HRD practitioners can make a valuable contribution to the creation of ethical CSR practices: (1) development of an organizational culture that promotes ethical behaviour; (2) development of organizational leadership that recognizes the importance of the triple bottom-line philosophy; (3) embedding of CSR practices and policies that provide a tangible and measurable contribution to the organization's CSR objectives.

Organizational culture development

The question is often asked: 'Why do honest people engage in dishonest behaviour'? The answer generally falls into one of three categories: good people making poor decisions (out of ignorance or confusion), good people being persuaded to do bad things (peer pressure, social construction) or bad people doing bad things (it's just who they are). When asking why honest people engage in dishonest behaviour, the question invariably sidesteps the context in which it happens – from an organizational perspective, especially within the confines of the organization, actions and behaviours often reflect cultural dimensions (Meyers, 2004). Unethical behaviour in an organizational context reflects both an individual predisposition and contextual factors (Ardichvili *et al.*, 2009) – the most influential of these contextual factors being organizational culture. Organizational culture represents a complex combination of both formal and informal systems process and interactions (Schein, 2004), with formal culture comprising leadership dimensions (Brown and Trevino, 2006) and policies, rewards systems and socialization mechanisms (Ardichvili *et al.*, 2009; Werbal and Balkin, 2010). The informal dimensions include the rules, norms, beliefs, values, stories and anecdotes that unite organizational members into a 'shared vision' of how the world works (Trevino *et al.*, 1998, 2008; Schein, 2009; MacKenzie *et al.*, 2011).

With all these variables to consider, HRD practitioners will face many challenges in developing an organizational culture resistant to influences that have been shown to result in organizational failure and social impact

(Ashforth and Anand, 2003; Beenen and Pinto, 2009). Although organizational culture is a complex concept, Ardichvili *et al.* (2009: 449) have argued that five mission and values clusters of characters are essential in the development of an ethical organizational culture: Stakeholder Balance (a multi-fiduciary orientation that seeks to balance the needs of all the organization's stakeholders), Leadership Effectiveness (focused on survivability and long-term viability of the organization), Long-term Perspective (considers organizational objectives beyond short-term quarterly objectives), Process Integrity (focused on key functions of the business such as recruiting, hiring, firing, promotion, compensation and communications), and Mission and Vision Drivers (these refer to the organization's core mission, such as Google's 'we can make money without doing evil').

Together, these characteristics represent a core function of HRD activity and are of strategic importance in developing an organizational culture focus on ethics and sustainability with, at the same time, resistance to the influence of unethical, corrupt and immoral behaviour.

Embedding organizational ethics

Foote and Ruona (2008:301) argue that infrastructure, leadership and involved stakeholders represent the most important factors in developing an organizational culture that fosters ethical behaviour. Organizational infrastructure represents the systems and structures that support the day-to-day running of the organization. Ethical work practices, vision and mission statements, codes of ethics and environmental awareness programmes are part of the organization's infrastructure and inform ethical decision making and socially responsible business practices (Trevino *et al.*, 1998; Greenwood, 2013a). The role of HR is fundamentally an ethical one, given that HRD practitioners work with developing human capital with a view to achieving sustained competitive advantage. As such, HR policies relating to recruitment and selection, learning and development, career development and succession management planning all need to be ethically oriented.

The integration of ethical behaviour into the organization's culture is a critical building block of any HRD ethics/CSR programme. As a first step, HRD practitioners will need to create educational programmes that embrace the ideals of an organization that is equally committed to its wider social and environmental partners as it is to its own employees, and to communicate to their stakeholders the benefits of participation. Doing so will ensure that all stakeholders in the supply chain (employees, vendors, partners and potential employees) understand the values and beliefs that underscore the organization's commitment to ethics and CSR. The necessity for an ethical supply chain has been illustrated in the *Forbes* article 'Building Sustainable and Ethical Supply Chains' (Guthrie, 2012) in the Useful Websites at the end of the chapter.

CONSIDER THIS ...

Contemporary organizations operate in an always-on, global economy that spans far beyond the organization's front door. This can pose problems for organizations as they attempt to 'manage' their 'supply chain partners', who may be located in different parts of the word and whose ethical policies and practices may be far removed from corporate policies. Organizations may utilize 'manufacturing partners' in an effort to reduce costs and maintain competitiveness; however, failure to recognize the potential 'human costs' associated with 'cost management' and 'flexible ethics' can have dire consequences, as Apple Computers found out when its partner Fonconn Technologies was brought to the attention of global media following a number of suicides over working conditions at its plant in Shenzhen and Chengdu, China. Access the *Forbes* article in the Additional Links section and consider the following questions:

1 What types of HRD policies can Apple use to ensure partners in its supply chain ensure sustainability and ethics are consistently carried out?

2 Are there challenges in adapting US HRD policies in a foreign country such as China?

3 What are the benefits for Apple of its commitment to a sustainable and ethical supply chain?

4 Do the costs of implementing a sustainable and ethical supply chain sometimes outweigh the benefits?

The organization's culture reflects the ethical consciousness of the employees and is recognized in the well-defined policies and practices that ensure only ethical business practices and achievements are rewarded.

Policy and practice development

As evidenced in the failure of many organizations purported to embrace ethics and CSR, the challenge for HRD practitioners is to circumvent unethical organizational behaviour before it become normalized. To do this, HRD practitioners will need to ensure that HR policies and practices can contribute to the development of an ethically aware and socially responsible organizational culture. The challenge, however, is to ensure that policies that reward short-term performance goals do not come with long-term implications (Bierema, 2009; Werbel and Balkin, 2010). Sherron Watkins, a former Enron executive, argued that stated values at Enron differed entirely from the real values, noting that Enron's stated value of 'honesty and integrity is how we deal with all of our customers' (Beenen and Pinto, 2009: 279) was a smokescreen for dishonesty and lack of integrity. Moreover, the integrity issues in Enron were a function of the culture and became a socialized way of doing business (Sims and Brinkmann, 2003; Anand *et al.*, 2005). In recent years, the failure of many banking institutions as a result of similar business practices and behaviours highlights an organizational reality – once unethical business practices become part of the culture it is difficult to change that orientation.

By aligning HRD interventions, such as generic CSR policies and practices and ethical awareness and compliance programmes, with the balanced scorecard (Kaplan and Norton, 2007) as a measurable delivery tool, HRD interventions have the potential to positively impact how organizational members perceive or understand CSR practices by demonstrating their social and environmental impact. Communication and accountability can also positively influence the way in which employees develop an ethically oriented organizational identity (Beu and Buckley, 2004). As illustrated previously, Virgin employees embrace the values of the organization, which views the wider society as being as important as achieving profit. Systems that allow whistle-blowing without fear of retribution in the event of ethical violation (SHRM, 2008) can also serve as a measurable outcome in that they can be linked into the organization's balanced scorecard (Kaplan and Norton, 2007).

Ardichvili *et al.* (2009: 446) make a compelling argument that the 'socialization process of an organization with an ethical culture reinforces the practice of the values in a mission statement on a daily basis'. This will be critically important for HRD practitioners for two reasons. One, the socialization process can push back on downward pressure to align with organizational objectives that are too focused on the financial bottom line if sufficient numbers of organizational members believe HRD's ethical culture message is credible. Two, HRD practitioners will be recognized for challenging short-term objectives that contravene socially responsible behaviour and have the potential to damage the organization and its people in the long term. The socialization of the ethics and sustainability message thus becomes not just part of the culture but part of the organizational identity.

Organizations can take steps to minimize risk associated with recruiting the wrong types of employees. HRD practitioners can utilize an array of instruments designed to test for integrity, ethics and moral development (see Trevino *et al.*, 1998; Trevino and Youngblood, 1990; Ashkanasy *et al.*, 2006) in all potential recruits where integrity, ethics or moral dilemmas present. Moreover, senior leadership support for using these instruments will send out a very clear message to industry that the organization and HRD practitioners are taking a stand over their commitment to socially responsible rather than irresponsible behaviour by not picking the fruit from the barrel but, instead, going directly to the orchard. HRD practitioners could also deploy training courses to increase cognitive moral development and lower the potential for dispositions such as the 'dark triad' (Furnham, 2010; Campbell *et al.*, 2011; O'Boyle *et al.*, 2012) in an effort to embed an ethical culture that may minimize the risk of unethical behaviour. Through infusing ethical policy and principles in *every* employee, HRD practitioners lay the 'bedrock' for CSR initiatives and ethical business practices (Cornelius *et al.*, 2008: 365).

HRD practitioners face the reality of ensuring not just that ethics and CSR practices are embraced by all organizational members but also that they make a tangible contribution aimed at supporting the organization's goals (Garavan *et al.*, 2004; Brickson, 2005; Gond *et al.*, 2011). Ardichvili and Jondle (2009), Becker *et al* (2010) and Garavan and McGuire (2010) all note the importance of infrastructural interventions, such as performing a governance role within the organization, engaging in the socialization process, relationship building with multiple stakeholders, and development of a functional organizational culture in pursuit of CSR. The role of HRD practitioners will be to manage how CSR initiatives are communicated. HRD practitioners will play an important role in ensuring transparency around CSR practices and achievements, and, by doing so, will ensure that deception aimed at glossing over unethical practices is minimized or removed completely. Sims

and Brinkmann (2003: 249) highlighted this point when they noted that Enron's value statements and codes of ethics, included in their annual reports, maintained communications about commitments to 'respect, integrity and excellence', yet, following the collapse of Enron, there was 'little evidence that management modelled those behaviors'. HRD practitioners can develop ethical awareness programmes that translate at all levels within the organization and can facilitate positive CSR outcomes when the language used by leadership helps to 'create an interpretive framework' that conveys the message that ethics is as important as the financial bottom line (Beu and Buckley, 2004: 77). The social impact of the financial crisis may provide a momentum for this new organizational reality.

Communication on CSR commitments and performance must be more than surface level; it will need 'sincere commitment from leadership at all levels' (Trevino *et al.*, 1999: 149), which includes HRD practitioners. Basu and Palazzo (2008) also highlight this concern and argue that the way organizations justify their actions signals their stakeholder orientation. HRD practitioners can aid senior management and leadership by driving a 'balanced approach' (Basu and Palazzo, 2008: 128) to CSR measurement that not only reflects positively in terms of external monitoring (e.g. FTSE, 2010) but can also help develop and sustain an ethical culture and organizational identity. Doing so can signal to the organization and its stakeholder community that an ethical standard will not be compromised – by anyone. Over time it will become embedded in a recursive cycle of internal and external reflection that solidifies a deeper commitment to CSR practices but also has the capacity to influence the ethical orientation of the organizational leadership. If HRD interventions can ensure strategic consistency in terms of the organization's CSR message and practices that are measured through a balanced scorecard methodology, they will reflect measurable CSR impact. This, in turn, will positively impact internal stakeholders in terms of morale and commitment, but equally has the capacity to positively impact the external stakeholders, who can measure CSR performance by referring to external CSR rating agencies (Scalet and Kelly, 2010).

Communicating about CSR commitments extends beyond surface-level media such as financial and sustainability reports to now include the power of the internet, stock market indices (e.g. FTSE4Good, the Dow Jones Sustainability Index), and tech-savvy employees and external stakeholders (Haugh and Talwar, 2010). Through these channels, HRD practitioners can utilize

IT infrastructure and social media such as blogs, both to provide a safe and secure means to flag concerns about the organization's substantive commitment to CSR initiatives and, at the same time, to provide a quantifiable indication to organizational leadership about internal stakeholder engagement and external stakeholder buy-in to CSR initiatives.

Many HRD policies and practices, such as remuneration, incentive structures and short-term performance-based objectives, were unduly influenced by downward pressures from the organizational leadership and external competition for key human capital (Garavan and McGuire, 2010; Donaldson, 2012; Greenwood, 2013b). These pressures were evident during the lead-up to the global financial crisis as banking institutions engaged in business practices that were predatory and based on unethical business models (Select Committee, 2008; Honohan, 2010). The challenge for HRD practitioners in dealing with ethical behaviour and CSR practices at the institutional level is twofold. First, HR scholars and practitioners will need to be cognizant of what types of institutional pressures exist so that appropriate interventions can be put in place to ensure these pressures do not result in unethical or irresponsible organizational behaviour (Fahlenbrach and Stulz, 2011). Second, much of the widespread corporate irresponsibility at the centre of the financial crisis was the result of a number of intellectual and knowledge imbalances (Honohan, 2010: 8). Bridging any intellectual or knowledge gaps must be a priority for HRD practitioners, who must move back from their value creation roles and back to their 'stewards of the social contract' roles (Kochan cited in Wright, 2008: 1068).

Donaldson (2012) argued that the socialization of bad practices was predicated on pressures for survival rather than overt acceptance of profit-seeking greed. Nevertheless, HRD practitioners, like regulators, have a responsibility to the organization to ensure policies and practices are congruent with the long-term goals of the organization and do not just service the short-term performance horizons. Barth *et al.* (2012) and MacKenzie *et al.* (2011b) have cited similar approaches to moderating the potential for socially impactful organizational behaviour. According to Barth *et al.* (2012: 204–205), the root causes of the financial crisis were not directly the result of lax regulation, insufficient regulatory power or financial innovation, but were, in fact, more likely the result of 'defective regulatory and political systems' that were unable to adequately respond to the crisis. They propose the creation of an institution whose purpose is to act on behalf of the public and provide informed, expert, independent and timely information on financial regulation.

MacKenzie *et al.* (2011:367) proposed a similar role, but for the HRD profession. They argued that a governance role for HRD business partners might maximize the potential to offset unethical behaviour. This role is referred to as the organizational governance and agency mediation (OGAM) role, and is aimed at filtering out pressure that can unduly influence extreme forms of unethical behaviour, such as we have seen in banking institutions, and also acting to prevent these behaviours from becoming embedded within the organization. This role requires a degree of independence from organizational management structures in order to succeed in its mandate. The OGAM role is more advanced than the independent ethics group proposed by the Society for Human Resource Management (SHRM) (2008: 18–19) insofar as it encompasses both CSR initiatives and also a governance mandate.

The Ethical HR Value Chain

Roarke Systems, a hi-tech darling of Silicon Valley with a market capitalization of over $300 billion, has recruited you as its European HR head of ethics, sustainability and social responsibility. This, for you, is a dream job. You have admired this company for many years, and, with only 5 per cent of its applicants successfully joining the organization, you feel you have finally made it to the big leagues. The interview process at Roarke Systems is gruelling: on average, eight interviews are conducted during the interview process to ensure the successful applicant is a good 'fit' for the organizational culture. Roarke Systems (or Roarke, as it is known in Silicon Valley) is considered one of the most innovate, creative and culturally diverse companies in the hi-tech community and its brand one of the most valuable brands in the world after Apple, Microsoft and Google. Rather than flood the market with cheap 'me too' products, Roarke has created a product range that instils incredible customer loyalty, respect and admiration, which

ACTIVE CASE STUDY

is, perhaps, why the company maintains very high profit margins due to the relative 'high cost' of its products. People are willing to pay almost anything for the company's products.

During your first few weeks at the organization, you get to grips with the organization's strategy and how it delivers on its core principles, which are proudly displayed on coffee cups, in the main reception in the building, in the staff restaurant and even in the break-out and recreation areas:

Our most valuable asset is our people

Given that this is an organization comprised of thousands of 'knowledge workers' it is hardly surprising that this would be a core principle

We stress creativity, innovation in everything we do

While recognizing what has worked in the past may be the best way to do it in the future, it doesn't stop us from 'creating' our future through innovation and abstract thinking

Everything we do benefits both our company and the communities we impact

The development of our products cannot cause harm or damage the environment in any way

We live by our code of honesty and integrity in everything we do

We expect our people to maintain the highest ethical standards in everything they do, both within and outside the organization – our respect is measured by how our community sees us not by how we see each other

Like almost all its employees, you feel a sense of belonging and pride in your new company. The values you hold dear are a good fit for the organization to which you now belong. Roarke is intent on progressing technology and, at the same time, the company is focused on ensuring everything it does is

to the highest ethical, moral and sustainable standards. Unethical behaviour in the organization is just not tolerated.

As the new European head of ethics, sustainability and social responsibility (ESSR as it's known in the company), you are required to attend a number of meetings in Silicon Valley just south of San Francisco every fiscal quarter. You arrive at the company's HQ after a gruelling 12-hour flight. Even in business class, a long flight is tiring. You are picked up at the airport by one of the company's many 'hybrid' cars and deposited at their HQ an hour later. The outside of the company HQ is imposing, with the Roarke Systems emblem displayed proudly on the 100 ft glass front of the main building. As you view this sight, you think to yourself: 'This is just the greatest company in the world – how lucky am I?'

Within an hour of arriving, you attend one of the many important strategy meetings on product innovation, growth forecasts and the 'management of the supply chain' partners. Roarke does not manufacture any of its own products; like many other hi-tech companies in Silicon Valley, it outsources or utilizes 'manufacturing partners' to build its products. To you, this makes complete sense, given that the company is focused on the 'intellectual' side of product development and, as an HRD professional, your focus is on getting the most out of 'your people'. At one of the meetings you are casually looking through the documentation and notice that two of the best-selling products are manufactured in South America in manufacturing facilities that are known to have very questionable 'labour practices' and have been cited a number of times in the past for their

mistreatment of child workers and women. You raise this concern at the meeting, only to be told that the focus of the company is on delivering the 'most innovative' products customers are willing to pay for at a 'cost' that will keep our products 'exclusive' – if that means using the cheapest place to manufacture, then what's the problem? You voice your concerns that the use of known 'labour violators' could potentially impact on the brand, the recruitment strategies and the reputation of being an ethical and socially responsible company if it emerges that the company knowingly utilizes manufacturing partners that have been prosecuted for violations of international labour law and ethical standards. It troubles you that you might be the only one who has spotted this potential 'ethical issue', and you wonder whether the gloss of the core principles masks a 'look the other way culture' – how might you ensure that the culture matches the core principles espoused by the company? You are now concerned that there may be an ethical culture issue at your company and are concerned at how far it might go.

Questions

1 How would you go about improving the ethics awareness programme so as to 'improve' the ethical culture of the organization?

2 You need to come up with a critical examination of where the company might be exposed in terms of its overall ethics, sustainability and social responsibility strategy and present your findings to the senior management team – what would you look for?

3 Are there risks associated with trying to change the culture of the organization?

SUMMARY

This chapter has sought to explore the role HRD plays in ensuring that ethics and CSR become embedded within the organization's culture and identity. We have seen that, while many organizations that have failed and had disastrous societal impact conveyed a public image that their business practices were both ethical and socially responsible, the reality was quite different. We have demonstrated that HRD plays a crucial role in the development and socialization of ethical and sustainable business practices that can become a central part of the organization's function. HRD practices also have the capacity to influence how organizational members identify with their organization in a virtuous way. Given the social impact of the global financial and economic crisis, ethics and sustainable business practices will form a core dimension of every organization's strategic goals and will most assuredly rely on the skill and expertise of HRD practitioners to ensure that organizations engage in substantive and sustainable ethical business practices.

 CHAPTER REVIEW QUESTIONS

1   What is meant by the triple bottom-line philosophy and why is it important from an HRD perspective?
2   The widespread use of financial incentives proved disastrous in many banking institutions that failed following the global financial disaster. Outline some of the ways in which incentives can be linked to socially responsible business practices.
3   If the economic goals of the organization are to remain profitable, how might HRD practitioners, in their ethics and CSR role, ensure that the organization adopts internal policies that embed ethics and CSR in everything organizational members do?
4   What is the 'HR value chain' and how important is it?
5   How can HRD practitioners 'manage' the ethical culture of the organization?
6   What are the challenges faced by HRD in implementing ethical and sustainability policies and practices that are seen as not 'cost effective'?
7   How might ethics, sustainability and social responsibility policies be influenced by 'local' conditions in the case of multinational corporations?
8   Can HRD ethics, sustainability and social responsibility policies truly deliver on their goals?

FURTHER READING

Ardichvili, A. and Jondle, D. (2009) Integrative Literature Review: Ethical Business Cultures: A Literature Review and Implications for HRD, *Human Resource Development Review*, 8(2), 223–244.

Ashforth, B. E., Gioia, D. A., Robinson, S. L. and Trevino, L. K. (2008) Re-viewing Organizational Corruption, *Academy of Management Review*, 33(3), 670–684.

Foote, M. F. and Ruona, W. E. A. (2008) Institutionalizing Ethics: A Synthesis of Frameworks and the Implications for HRD, *Human Resource Development Review*, 7(3), 292–308.

Garriga, E. and Melé, D. (2004) Corporate Social Responsibility Theories: Mapping the Territory, *Journal of Business Ethics*, 53(1), 51–71.

Trevino, L. K., Butterfield, K. D. and McCabe, D. L. (1998) The Ethical Context in Organizations: Influences on Employee Attitudes and Behaviors, *Business Ethics Quarterly*, 8(3), 447–476.

Ulrich, D. and Beatty, D. (2001) From Partners to Players: Extending the HR Playing Field, *Human Resource Management*, 40(4), 293–307.

USEFUL WEBSITES

http://www.ftse.com/Indices/FTSE4Good_Index_Series/index.jsp

The FTSE4Good Index was developed to objectively measure performance of companies that meet or exceed globally recognized corporate responsibility standards. This is an excellent resource for students interested in understanding how organizations achieve the triple bottom-line philosophy in a substantive and tangible way. Guaranteed to open your eyes.

http://www.virgin.com/unite

The Virgin Unite website is aimed at uniting great people and entrepreneurial ideas, reinventing how we live and work to help make people's lives better. They believe business can and must be a force for good in the world – and that this is also good for business.

http://ethisphere.com/worlds-most-ethical/wme-honorees/

The Ethisphere website provides a comprehensive current and historical listing of the world's most ethical organizations by industry. This is a very useful website for anyone interested in how organizations engage in substantive ethical practices. The scoring and methodology section is of particular importance for those interested in how the ratings and weightings are assigned that make up the Ethics Quotient (EQ) framework.

http://www.forbes.com/sites/dougguthrie/2012/03/09/building-sustainable-and-ethical-supply-chains/

Forbes article on 'Building Sustainable and Ethical Supply Chains'.

http://www.ilo.org/global/lang--en/index.htm

The International Labor Organization (ILO) is focused on promoting workers' rights, encouraging humane working conditions and enhancing social protection for those without a voice. This resource is of particular importance to HRD students and practitioners in that it provides a very real social and environmental context for the important role HRD plays in the development of CSR policies that are ethical, socially aware and environmentally sound.

http://www.theguardian.com/environment/2013/sep/30/bp-gulf-oil-spill-negligence-fines

BP oil spill article from *The Guardian*.

BIBLIOGRAPHY

Anand, V., Ashforth, B. E. and Joshi, M. (2005) Business as Usual: The Acceptance and Perpetuation of Corruption in Organizations. *Academy of Management Executive*, 19, 9–23.

Ardichvili, A. (2011) Sustainability of Nations, Communities, Organizations and Individuals: The Role of HRD. *Human Resource Development International*, 14, 371–374.

Ashforth, B. E. and Anand, V. (2003) The Normalization of Corruption in Organizations. *Research in Organizational Behavior*, 25, 1–52.

Ashkanasy, N. M., Windsor, C. A. and Treviño, L. K. (2006) Bad Apples in Bad Barrells Revisited: Cognitive Moral Development, Just World Beliefs, Rewards, and Ethical Decision Making. *Business Ethics Quarterly*, 16, 449–473.

Banerjee, S. B. (2011) Embedding Sustainability Across the Organization: A Critical Perspective. *Academy of Management Learning & Education*, 10, 719–731.

Barth, J. R., Caprio Jr., G. and Levine, R. (2012) *Guardians of Finance*. Cambridge, MA: MIT Press.

Basu, K. and Palazzo, G. (2008) Corporate Social Responsibility: A Process Model of Sensemaking. *Academy of Management Review*, 33, 122–136.

Becker, W. S., Carbo, J. A. and Langella, I. M. (2010) Beyond Self-Interest: Integrating Social Responsibility and Supply Chain Management With Human Resource Development. *Human Resource Development Review*, 9, 144–168.

Beenen, G. and Pinto, J. (2009) *Resisting Organizational Level Corruption: An Interview with Sherron Watkins*. Academy of Management.

Beu, D. S. and Buckley, M. R. (2004) Using Accountability to Create a More Ethical Climate. *Human Resource Management Review*, 14, 67–83.

Branson, R. (2013) *Screw Business as Usual*. London: Random House.

Brickson, S. L. (2005) Organizational Identity Orientation: Forging a Link between Organizational Identity and Organizations' Relations with Stakeholders. *Administrative Science Quarterly*, 50, 576–609.

Brown, M. E. and Treviño, L. K. (2006) Ethical Leadership: A Review and Future Directions [theoretical]. *The Leadership Quarterly*, 17, 595–616.

Cai, Y., Jo, H. and Pan, C. (2012) Doing Well While Doing Bad? CSR in Controversial Industry Sectors. *Journal of Business Ethics*, 108, 467–480.

Campbell, W. K., Hoffman, B. J., Campbell, S. M. and Marchisio, G. (2011) Narcissism in Organizational Contexts. *Human Resource Management Review*, 21, 268–284.

Cornelius, N., Todres, M., Janjuha-Jivraj, S., Woods, A. and Wallace, J. (2008) Corporate Social Responsibility and the Social Enterprise. *Journal of Business Ethics*, 81, 355–370.

Donaldson, T. (2012) Three Ethical Roots of the Economic Crisis. *Journal of Business Ethics*, 106, 5–8.

Fambrough, M. J. and Hart, R. K. (2008) Emotions in Leadership Development: A Critique of Emotional Intelligence. *Advances in Developing Human Resources*, 10, 18.

Fenwick, T. and Bierema, L. (2008) Corporate Social Responsibility: Issues for Human Resource Development Professionals. *International Journal of Training & Development*, 12, 24–35.

Friedman, M. (1970) The Social Responsibility of Business is to Increase its Profits. *The New York Times Magazine*.

FTSE. (2010) FTSE4GOOD Index [Online]. Available: http://www.ftse.com/Indices/FTSE4Good_Index_Series/index.jsp.

Furnham, A. (2010) *The Elephant in the Boardroom*, New York: Palgrave Macmillan.

Gagliardi, D., Muller, P., Glossop, E., Caliandro, C., Fritsch, M., Brtkova, G., Bohn, N. U., Klitou, D., Avigdor, G., Marzocchi, C. and Ramlogan, R. (2013) A Recovery on the Horizon? In: Commission, E. (ed.). Brussels: European Commission.

Garavan, T. N., Mcguire, D. and O'Donnell, D. (2004) Exploring Human Resource Development: A Levels of Analysis Approach. *Human Resource Development Review*, 3, 417–441.

Greenwood, M. (2013) Ethical Analyses of HRM: A Review and Research Agenda. *Journal of Business Ethics*, 114, 355–366.

Guthrie, D. (2012) Building Sustainable and Ethical Supply Chains [Online]. *Forbes*. Available: http://www.forbes.com/sites/dougguthrie/2012/03/09/building-sustainable-and-ethical-supply-chains/ [Accessed January 14th 2014].

Haugh, H. M. and Talwar, A. (2010) How Do Corporations Embed Sustainability Across the Organization? *Academy of Management Learning & Education*, 9, 384–396.

Honohan, P. (2010) The Irish Banking Crisis Regulatory and Financial Stability Policy 2003-2008: A Report to the Minister for Finance by the Governor of the Central Bank [Online]. Central Bank and Financial Services Authority of Ireland. Available: http://www.bankinginquiry.gov.ie/The Irish Banking Crisis Regulatory and Financial Stability Policy 2003-2008.pdf [accessed June 2010].

Kaplan, R. S. and Norton, D. P. (2007) Using the Balanced Scorecard as a Strategic Management System. *Harvard Business Review*, 85, 150–161.

Lange, D. and Washburn, N. T. (2012) Understanding Attributions of Corporate Social Irresponsibility. *Academy of Management Review*, 37, 300–326.

Logsdon, J. M. and Wood, D. J. (2002) Business Citizenship: From Domestic to Global Level of Analysis. *Business Ethics Quarterly*, 12, 155–187.

Mackenzie, C., Garavan, T. N. and Carbery, R. (2011a) Corporate Social Responsibility: HRD as a Mediator of Organizational Ethical Behavior. *12th International Conference on Human Resource Development Research and Practice across Europe University of Gloucestershire*, UK, 2011.

Mackenzie, C., Garavan, T. N. and Carbery, R. (2011b) Understanding and Preventing Dysfunctional Behavior in Organizations. *Human Resource Development Review*, 10, 346–380.

Mackenzie, C. A., Garavan, T. N. and Carbery, R. (2012) Through the Looking Glass: Challenges for Human Resource Development (HRD) Post the Global Financial Crisis – Business as Usual? *Human Resource Development International*, 15, 353–364.

Matten, D. and Moon, J. (2008) 'Implicit' and 'Explicit' CSR: A Conceptual Framework For A Comparative Understanding Of Corporate Social Responsibility. *Academy of Management Review*, 33, 404–424.

Mcguire, D. and Garavan, T. (2011) Critical Human Resource Development: A Levels of Analysis Approach. 12th International Conference on Human Resource Development Research and Practice across Europe, Gloucester, UK 24th–26th May 2011.

Mcwilliams, A. and Siegel, D. (2001) Corporate Social Responsibility: A Theory of the Firm Perspective. *Academy of Management Review*, 26, 117–127.

Mcwilliams, A., Siegel, D. S. and Wright, P. M. (2006) Corporate Social Responsibility: Strategic Implications. *Journal of Management Studies*, 43, 1–18.

O'boyle, E. H., Jr., Forsyth, D. R., Banks, G. C. and Mcdaniel, M. A. (2012) A Meta-analysis of the Dark Triad and Work Behavior: A Social Exchange Perspective. *Journal of Applied Psychology*, 97, 557–579.

Peterson, S. L. (2008) Creating and Sustaining a Strategic Partnership: A Model for Human Resource Development. *Journal of Leadership Studies*, 2, 83–97.

Roubini, N. and Mihm, S. (2011) *Crisis Economics: A Crash Course in the Future of Finance.* London: Penguin Group.

Scalet, S. and Kelly, T. (2010) CSR Rating Agencies: What is Their Global Impact? *Journal of Business Ethics*, 94, 69–88.

Schein, E. H. (2004) *Organizational Culture and Leadership,* San Francsisco: Jossey-Bass.

Schein, E. H. (2009) *The Corporate Culture Survival Guide,* San Francisco: Jossey-Bass.

Shrivastava, P. (1988) Industrial Crisis Management: Learning from Organizational Failures. *Journal of Management Studies*, 25, 283–284.

Shrm (2008). The Ethics Landscape in American Business. *Society for Human Resource Mangement.*

Sims, R. R. and Brinkmann, J. (2003) Enron Ethics (Or: Culture Matters More than Codes). *Journal of Business Ethics*, 45, 243–256.

Stein, M. (2011) A Culture of Mania: A Psychoanalytic View of the Incubation of the 2008 Credit Crisis. *Organization*, 18, 173–186.

Stein, M. and Pinto, J. (2011) The Dark Side of Groups: A 'Gang at Work' in Enron. *Group & Organization Management*, 36, 692–721.

Stolz, I. (2012) In Order to Stay Relevant: OD and HRD for Corporate Citizenship. *Advances in Developing Human Resources*, 14, 291–304.

Surroca, J., Tribó, J. A. and Waddock, S. (2010) Corporate Responsibility and Financial Performance: The Role of Intangible Resources. *Strategic Management Journal*, 31, 463–490.

Treasury Select Committee. (2009) Banking Crisis: Dealing with the Failure of the UK Banks [Online]. London: House of Commons. Available: http://www.publications.parliament.uk/pa/cm200809/cmselect/cmtreasy/416/416.pdf [accessed March, 2010].

Treviño, L. K., Weaver, G. R. and Brown, M. E. 2008. It's Lovely at the Top: Hierarchical Levels, Identities, and Perceptions of Organizational Ethics. *Business Ethics Quarterly*, 18, 233–252.

Trevino, L. K., Weaver, G. R., Gibson, D. G. and Toffler, B. L. (1999) Managing Ethics and Legal Compliance: What Works and What Hurts. *California Management Review*, 41, 131–151.

Trevino, L. K. and Youngblood, S. A. (1990) Bad Apples in Bad Barrels: A Causal Analysis of Ethical Decision-Making Behavior. *Journal of Applied Psychology*, 75, 378–385.

Ulrich, D. and Brockbank, W. (2005) *The HR Value Proposition*, Boston: Harvard Business School Press.

Virgin. (2014) Virgin Unite [Online]. Virgin. Available: http://www.virgin.com/unite.

Werbel, J. and Balkin, D. B. (2010) Are Human Resource Practices Linked to Employee Misconduct? A Rational Choice Perspective. *Human Resource Management Review*, 20, 317–326.

Wright, C. (2008) Reinventing Human Resource Management: Business Partners, Internal Consultants and the Limits to Professionalization. *Human Relations*, 61, 1063–1086.

INDEX

Note: Locators followed by '*t*' and '*f*' refers to *tables* and *figures* respectively.

9 781137 360090